ENGINEERING EUROPEAN UNITY

ENGINEERING EUROPEAN UNITY

The Quest for the Right Solution Across Centuries

Éva Bóka

Central European University Press
Budapest–Vienna–New York

©2022 Éva Bóka

Published in 2022 by
Central European University Press

Nádor utca 9, H-1051 Budapest, Hungary
Tel: +36-1-327-3138 or 327-3000
E-mail: ceupress@press.ceu.edu
Website: www.ceupress.com

All rights reserved. No part of this publication may be reproduced, stored in a retrieval system, or transmitted, in any form or by any means, without the permission of the Publisher.

ISBN 978-963-386-598-9 (hardback)
ISBN 978-963-386-601-6 (PDF)
ISBN 978-963-386-629-0 (ePUB)

Library of Congress Cataloging-in-Publication Data

Names: Bóka, Éva, author.
Title: Engineering European unity : the historical quest for the institutional solution / Éva Bóka.
Description: Budapest ; New York : CEU Press | Central European University Press, 2023. | Includes bibliographical references and index.
Identifiers: LCCN 2022044123 (print) | LCCN 2022044124 (ebook) | ISBN 9789633865989 (Hardback) | ISBN 9789633866016 (pdf)
Subjects: LCSH: European Union. | European Economic Community. | BISAC: HISTORY / Modern / 20th Century / General | POLITICAL SCIENCE / International Relations / General
Classification: LCC JN30 .B6434 2023 (print) | LCC JN30 (ebook) | DDC 341.242/2--dc23/eng/20221108
LC record available at https://lccn.loc.gov/2022044123
LC ebook record available at https://lccn.loc.gov/2022044124

Contents

Preface — viii

Introduction: The Idea of European Unity, the Western System of Liberties, and the Dichotomy of Federalism versus Intergovernmentalism — 1

1 The Most Important Achievements of the Idea of European Unity in the Field of State and International Organization before the Declaration of the Rights of Man and of the Citizen (1789) — 7

    1.1 Defense Unions and the Theoretical Differentiation between the Alliances of States — 8
    1.2 European Universalism — 14
    1.3 The Idea of Liberty and the Principles of a Civil State and Union of States — 15

2 A New Democratic Constitutional Federal State in Opposition to Feudalism and Colonization: The Constitution of the United States of America (1787) and Its Influence in Europe — 21

    2.1 The Constitution of a Democratic Federal Republic under a President (1787) — 21
    2.2 The "Hamilton Method" — 25
    2.3 The Dichotomy of a Fictive versus Real Economy — 28
    2.4 The Main Phases of Democratization of the Idea of European Unity — 29

3 The Dilemma of Democratization of the Idea of European Unity (1789–1815) — 30

    3.1 The French Revolution and the Attempt to Establish Democracy and Popular Sovereignty in a Unitary Nation State — 30

    3.2 Kant in Search of a Democratic International Policy
        (Foedus Pacificum)   42
    3.3 The Conservative Breakthrough   44

4 The European Phenomenon of Nation State and National Empire, and the Chances of a European Federation (1815–1919)   47

    4.1 Romantic Nationalism   48
    4.2 The German and Italian Unification   50
    4.3 The Swiss Confederation (1848)   55
    4.4 Plans for the Reconstruction of the Habsburg Monarchy   55
    4.5 The Federalist Opposition to the Liberal Democratic Unitary Nation-State   58
    4.6 Colonialism of European Great Powers and the Forgotten Idea of European Unity   61
    4.7 The Forgotten Europe: The Treaty of Versailles, and the League of Nations   65

5 The Crisis of Realization of the Western System of Liberties and the Idea of European Unity between the Two World Wars   68

    5.1 In the Shadow of Dictatorships   68
    5.2 The Idea of Pan-Europa   74
    5.3 Plans for a European Economic Union   77
        5.3.1 The Dichotomy of Liberal versus Statist Economic Theory   78
        5.3.2 Planning European Economic Unity   79
    5.4 The Great Depression and the New Deal of Roosevelt   84
    5.5 The Great Depression and Hitler's Europe   86

6 Fight for a Democratic Europe   90

    6.1 Coudenhove-Kalergi and the Pan-European Movement   90
    6.2 L'Ordre Nouveau and Personalist or Integral Federalism   94
    6.3 The Resistance Movement—Launching the Policy of a European Democratic Federation Based on the Idea of Liberty   96

7 In Search of a New Europe: Three Alternatives   98

    7.1 Atlantic Cooperation   100
    7.2 Confronting the Legacy of Colonization—"Eurafrica" in a Decolonization Perspective   101
    7.3 To Become a Great Power from Europe's Own Democratic Forces: The Federalist Reform   106

Contents

8 Realizing the Idea of European Unity in the Framework of the Council of Europe   113

    8.1 *The Hague Congress (1948): Intergovernmentalist, Federalist, and Functionalist Bases of a European Union*   113
    8.2 *Intergovernmentalist Majority and the Council of Europe*   119

9 Shaping the Supranational European Union   124

    9.1 *Functionalist Sectoral Integration: The "Monnet-Method"*   124
        9.1.1 *Criticism of the "Monnet-Method" by Contemporaries*   126
    9.2 *Supranationalism toward Federalism (1952–1954)*   128
    9.3 *The Rome Treaties and the European Economic Community (1957)*   131
    9.4 *De Gaulle's Intergovernmentalist "European Concert"*   134
    9.5 *Spinelli: Relaunching Integration, Reviving Federalism*   137
    9.6 *The Delors's Reform: Federation of Nation States and of People*   141
    9.7 *European Union (1992): A New Type of Federalist Functionalist and Intergovernmentalist Functionalist Union of States Based on Subsidiarity and Multilevelism*   143

10 Outlook: Future Paths and Perspectives   145

11 The World and Europe (EU): Some Responses to the Challenge of European Modernity   149

    11.1 *Responses from India (Gandhi and Nehru)*   150
    11.2 *Some African Answers (Nkrumah, Senghor, Nyerere)*   156
    11.3 *Responses and Challenges from Confucian East Asia (Japan, China)*   170
        11.3.1 *The Japanese Answer (Yukichi Fukuzawa)*   172
        11.3.2 *The Chinese Responses and Challenge (K'ang Yu-wei, Sun Yat-sen, Mao Zedong, Deng Xiaoping)*   182
    11.4 *The Vision of Peaceful International Organization*   198

12 Concluding Thoughts   203

Bibliography   208
About the Author   236
Index   237

Preface

This historical essay investigates those state and international organization ideas and plans of the past which contributed to the development of the union among the European states. It concentrates on the interconnectedness of the idea of European unity with the development of the Western system of liberties and with the dichotomy of federalism versus intergovernmentalism characterizing the cooperation among European states. The essay presents the path of the idea of European unity from the early modern plans and the balance of power policy of the 'European concert' to the supranational and intergovernmental union of states based on subsidiarity, multilevelism, and European law established by the Treaty of Maastricht in 1992.

On the pages of the book the author recalls the plans supporting the European union, among them the plans of Sully, Abbé de Saint-Pierre, Penn, Kant or Briand; the political essays of political thinkers discussing the democratization of the states and international organization, among them Aristotle, Althusius, Vattel, Locke, Montesquieu, Tocqueville, Proudhon, Eötvös, Keynes, Coudenhove-Kalergi, Spinelli, Rougemont, Brugmans, Monnet, De Gaulle, Delors, or Fischer; the treaties or constitutions of defense unions against conquest and colonization (the Treaty of Utrecht (1579), the American Declaration of Independence (1776) and the Constitution of the United States of America (1787)); the most important documents of the development of the Western system of liberties and the international law, among them the French Declaration of the Rights of Man and of the Citizen (1789), the Swiss Constitution (1848), the Covenant of the League of Nations (1918), the Charter of the United Nations Organization (1945), the Universal Declaration of Human Rights (1948), and the basic treaties of European integration. The book also addresses the responses of some important non-European political, economic and social modernizers to the challenge of European colonization and modernizing expansion (Gandhi, Nehru, Nkrumah, Senghor, Nyerere, Yukichi Fukuzawa, K'ang You-wei, Sun Yat-sen, Mao Zedong, Deng Xiao-ping) aiming to find the meeting points towards a peaceful world.

In the midst of conflicts, fight for power and wars between European national monarchies and national empires, the proponents of the idea of European unity were seen by the realists as idealist thinkers writing Utopias for a peaceful future. But history developed so that these utopian ideas, opposing the power policy and wars, became the gradual shapers of the international legal principles of a peaceful and democratic European union and international organization. So, the ideas of the idealists of the past, mutually influencing each other as an opposition to power politics and wars, worked in the direction of a raising peace (peaceful future) in troubled European history. In fact, the European Union was able to develop from this opposition struggle, and the author brings this struggle to life on the pages of the book.

What the authors of the above mentioned sources had in common was, on the one side, the struggle for humanization of power. On the other side, the purpose to build up a society (states and international relations) which was based on liberty and the real interests of people which was peace, well-being and prosperity. On the basis of these common goals they thought out those values and legal principles of a democratic state and international organization which constituted the basic principles and values of the European Union. The most important stages of this development were the followings:

Ancient Greeks organized the first court of arbitration; Aristotle was for bottom-up federalism in democratic polis organization; English barons achieved rights from the absolute king in the Magna Carta; the old Swiss cantons organized a confederalist defense union against the conquering policy of the Habsburg ruler; George Podiebrad suggested to establish a federalist defense union against the Ottoman Empire directed by a European council dealing with the common military matters and conflict solution, and leaving the member states autonomous in all other things; Erasmus rejected the wars and started peace policy with his *Complaint of Peace*; the Dutch provinces organized the first aristocratic federation in the Treaty of Utrecht (1579) as a defense union against the Spanish Habsburg conquest; Althusius discovered popular sovereignty, democracy and federalism, and distinguished between confederalism and federalism; John Locke elaborated the principles of a constitutional parliamentary representative monarchy (civil state); the English Glorious Revolution abolished the absolute rule of the king; William Penn suggested to adopt Locke's ideas on a representative parliamentary system in the international law and to establish a European Council, Parliament and Court of Justice; Abbé de Saint-Pierre was for a federal type union of states directed by a European council dealing with the common matters; Montesquieu elaborated the idea of a federal republic directing the shared common matters of the member states by common institutions; the Founding Fathers of the United States of America established a federal republic under a president as the first democratic state representing popular sovereignty, democracy and federalism; the French revolutionaries declared the civil and human rights of man in the Declaration of the Rights of Man and of the Citizen (1789) and established a one and indivisible nation state; Kant suggested to make an eternal peace treaty (foedus pacificum) based on international law and legal harmonization; the Swiss cantons organized a federal republic under a federal government; Tocqueville believed that the history of European civilization represented a progressive democratization process; Victor Hugo used the watchword of the European United States at first; Proudhon was for a Europe composed of small political entities which were created as bottom-up free associations of people (persons) concentrating on their security and livelihood; József Eötvös thought out the personalist federal multinational state; Keynes suggested to end laissez-faire liberal capitalism and start functional sectoral cooperation; the League of Nations established the first intergovernmental international organization; the Pan-European Movement, led by Coudenhove-Kalergi, was for a European parliamentary federation following the Swiss example; Denis de Rougemont was for personal or integral federalism based on bottom-up associations of persons and their communities; the Resistance Movement and the *Ventotene Manifesto* favored a European Federation following the American or the Swiss example; the United Nations Organization was established as an intergovernmental world organization with independent coordinating agencies; the Universal Declaration of Human Rights (1948) condemned nationalism, racism and slavery, and declared human rights; the Hague Congress (1948) outlined the values and principles of a new democratic Europe; the Council of Europe was established as the first European intergovernmental council accepting coordinating agencies; the Schuman Declaration (1950) started the federalist functionalist sectoral integration in Europe; the Rome Treaties (1957) established the supranational European Common Market and the functional federalist European Atomic Energy Community; the Treaty of Maastricht created the European Union, in 1992, which was a supranational and intergovernmental union of states based on multilevelism and subsidiarity. All these historical achievements contributed to the struggle for the humanization of power and the creation of union and peace among the European states. Their spirituality showed continuity and ways for the future. The driving force was the democratization of the system of liberties, and the federalist versus confederalist dichotomy in correlation. The book undertakes to enlighten this history.

The author aims to avoid the classical Eurocentric approach of the idea of European unity by involving the ideas of non-European political thinkers about European social development and modernity. That is why the book also deals with the responses of renowned Indian, African, Japanese and Chinese social modernizers to the challenge of European colonization, modernization and creation of union. This also belongs to the history of the European idea.

The author used the historical research method based on historical sources (including Internet sources) and chronological order to investigate those historical achievements, state and international organization theories and legal practices that contributed to the emergence of the European Union in 1992. The book is not intended to deal with current political and sociological theories and debates on Europe because it would go beyond the scope of it. Rather, it focuses on the historical debate between contemporaries on the modernization and democratization of the state and international organization.

Preface

The main profile of the book is the history of state and international organization ideas, law and constitutions concentrating on the Western system of liberties and the dichotomy of intergovernmentalism versus federalism. Its aim is twofold: on the one hand, to show how a peace union could develop in European history which was full of power struggles and wars. On the other hand, to rethink the ideas of those – Europeans and non-Europeans – whom we can thank for the creation of the European Union.

The author thanks Rose Berl for her help in writing correct English.

Introduction: The Idea of European Unity, the Western System of Liberties, and the Dichotomy of Federalism versus Intergovernmentalism

The idea of European unity has a long history. The famous anthology of Denis de Rougemont, Swiss personal or integral federalist political thinker, refers to about 28 centuries (since Hesiod, 8th century BC) of Europe which were rich with projects on European unity.[1] It has ancient Greek mythological foundations represented by Europa, the Phoenician princess. According to the founding legend, European civilization was the product of the love of Europa and Zeus, who kidnapped her. This mythological story became the symbol of European unity, and the favorite theme for artists, painters, sculptors, writers, and thinkers. Europa appeared as a queen on the 16th century's maps and, later, as a symbol of liberty in the period of Europe's revolutions.

The idea of European unity is a pluralistic idea, with different political interpretations on how to cooperate among people and states. It is characterized by the dichotomy of federalism versus intergovernmentalism.

In European international practice the organization of the world and Europe was strongly connected due to European expansion worldwide.[2] The European principles were considered as universal.

European civilization has a double-faced cultural heritage, one which thrives for power and is expansive and violent, but also lawful and peaceful. The antagonism of these two opposing facets contributed to the complex nature of European social history.

Perhaps Denis de Rougemont's definition is most characteristic of Europe:

> Defining Europe, then, by its social forms, we see that it is pluralist in principle, not unitary as were the great traditional, static civilizations of Asia, and of pre-Columbian America, and as the totalitarian regimes of our time wish to be. It is a civilization based on antagonisms, on ceaselessly renewed conflicts; a civilization of discussion and debate, whose overmastering passion seems to be constantly to re-examine the

---

1 Rougemont, *Vingt-huit siècles d'Europe*.
2 Zorgbibe, *Histoire de l'Union Européenne*, 9.

natural universe and human relationships, destiny and the meaning of life.

It is this remarkable concentration of pluralist institutions in tension, and this perpetual and overt struggle between tradition and innovation, which have rendered Europe capable of assimilating technical advance rather better than some other parts of the world.[3]

Supporters of a European union were usually part of the tradition of a law-abiding and peaceful confederal or federal state organization. The idea of European unity strongly connected to the peace policy, humanization of power, and the fight for liberty. However, power policy also used it for protecting authoritarian and domineering purposes.

The history of the idea of European unity reflected the development of the Western (European) system of liberties as a fight of people for liberty and participation in state and international organization. The struggle for liberty resulted in the development of the Western system of liberties which was the most important achievement of European civilization. All these were made possible by the fact that Europe was characterized by diversity (different state forms, different cultures, different languages), pluralism, discussions, differences in meaning, and the fight for liberty.[4]

The most important internal and external principles of the Western system of liberties are: representative parliament created by general elections, elected by the people for a specific length of time; the separation of powers; an executive branch that is either responsible to the legislative parliament or subject to popular recall; judiciary power independent of the executive branch; free press; freedom of conscience, freedom of assembly, and other civic rights; extensive local autonomy.[5]

This is how István Bibó, the esteemed democratic Hungarian political thinker, formulated the Western system of liberties in his well-known essay entitled *Reflections on the Social Development of Europe (1971–1972)*. In his words:

> The separation of powers; a broadly representative parliament created by general elections; an executive branch that is either responsible to the parliament, elected by the people for a specific length of time or subject to popular recall; a judiciary which is independent of the executive branch (indeed with jurisdiction in one form or another over the executive itself); a free press making possible the public supervision of all these institutions; freedom of conscience, assembly and other civic rights; and extensive local autonomy.[6]

---

3 Rougemont, *The Meaning of Europe*, 48, 55.
4 Fukuzawa, "The Origins of the Western Civilization," 161.
5 Bibó, "Social Development of Europe," 467.
6 Bibó, "Social Development of Europe," 467.

Introduction

These principles were also applied to unions of states. Consequently a modern democratic federal union of states had a representative bicameral parliament, a federal government, and a separated three power system: legislative, executive, and judiciary. In the interpretation of the American and the Swiss democratic reformers federalism, popular sovereignty and democracy formed an organic unit.

Historically federalism meant a bottom-up association policy of persons and the creation of different local and larger communities and states in all things of life which needed common management. It demanded the transfer of common things toward larger, provincial states and supranational units, directed by the principles of subsidiarity and multilevelism. The federalist association policy ended in a world federal union or peaceful world federation. It could be imagined as shown in Fig. 0.1.

In the center there were the persons (families). The family had a natural protective and social security role for them. Persons created different associations in all those things of life which they could not manage alone, by transferring them to larger units: local community, province, state, and federation of states. So, around the persons different circles, representing different levels of cooperation, could develop. The state was the first level which was self-supporting and sovereign. States (as associations of persons) could also continue this association policy by transferring to the supra-state (supranational) level common (exclusive) fields based on subsidiarity and solving the direction of the common fields through a bicameral parliamentary federal union of states with a federal government (like the United States and Switzerland) or with open multilevel governance (like the European Union). Federal unions could continue to associate and create a peaceful world federation.

The essential principles of federalism were personalism (personal associations), subsidiarity, multilevelism, the sharing of sovereignty in common fields, and human rights. Personalism was advocated for because it expressed the interests of persons as members of their social groups (local community, state, federation) through a free association policy. Its opposition was individualism, which advocated that the interests of the individual should achieve precedence over the social group. Subsidiarity represented the autonomy and liberty of the persons as members of their social groups: local community, state, and federal union. Multilevelism stated that the organization of the different matters of life demanded different levels of common cooperation. Sharing of sovereignty was necessary because the common things needed common institutions and governance in a representative parliamentary system. Human rights were promoted because basic moral principles and norms were necessary.

The opposition to federalism was confederalism (anti-federalism). The most important difference between the two was the question of divisibility and joint institutional exercise of state sovereignty regarding common matters. Confederalism sought to preserve the sovereignty of the states by cooperating through the mediation of a coordinating council or specialized agencies. It did not consider the constitutional bicameral parliamentary system above the states necessary.

Because of the domination of centralization and expansive power policy of feudal, aristocratic and business elites in European history, and of the belief in the dogma of the indivisibility of the sovereignty of the state, the issue of liberty, democracy, popular sovereignty and federalism proved to be a difficult problem for Europeans. History showed that classical centralized, authoritarian and sovereign nation states and national empires, characterizing European state history, could not federate by sharing sovereignty. They could only pursue confederal policy by establishing a council and cooperate through negotiations, bargaining, and agreements.

The historical sources show that the terms federalism and confederalism were used inconsistently.[7] This is why the debate about the separation and definition of confederalism and federalism became one of the main topics of the history of the idea of European unity. All this was expressed in the federalist versus intergovernmentalist dichotomy characterizing European international policy. Count Richard Coudenhove-Kalergi (1894–1972), the founder of the Paneuropean Union and of the European Parliamentary Union, in a Le Monde article, on January 20, 1953, tried to explain the difference. He emphasized that federations were formed by the citizens, confederations by the nation states. A confederation maintained the sovereignty of the nation state intact, whereas a federation made it necessary to relinquish some sovereignty to a common authority.[8]

In what follows, I will use the principles of federalism, confederalism, and the system of liberties in the sense explained above.

The development of the European system of liberties, federalism and international law had an impressive period in the 18th century, and in the first half of the 19th century when a liberal capitalist economic and social system gradually emerged. The old feudal authoritarian forces were losing power and the new forces of liberal capitalism gradually gained participation in power.[9] In this period, the idea of European unity, influenced by the American federal republic under a president, represented the fight between classical authoritarian monarchical confederalism and the new federal forces of popular sovereignty.

The development of the Western system of liberties slowed down in the second half of the 19th century when laissez-faire free market capitalism and colonial imperialism dominated. After the First World War a deep crisis started. In this period the idea of European unity was almost forgotten, the fight for colonies, nationalism, and chauvinism dominated. The totalitarian ideologies of fascism and National Socialism rejected the system of liberties. But the democratic

---

7 The Constitution of the Swiss Confederation (1848), which is the classical example of a European federal union under a federal government, was named a confederation by its creators.
8 Coudenhove-Kalergi, "Confédération ou fédération?," 2.
9 Tocqueville, *Democracy in America*, 6.

opposition continued the fight for the system of liberties, democracy, universal suffrage, and the realization of the idea of European unity as a European federation. The members of the Resistance Movement wanted to renew the European social organization in the name of democracy, popular sovereignty, and federalism, and this creative force could launch the European integration.

The Western system of liberties was restored, and continued to be democratized after the Second World War in the framework of the European integration process. The placing of Europe, as the civilization of modernity, in the context of world history, has also begun in recent decades in the framework of a dialogue with the other civilizations.

Introduction

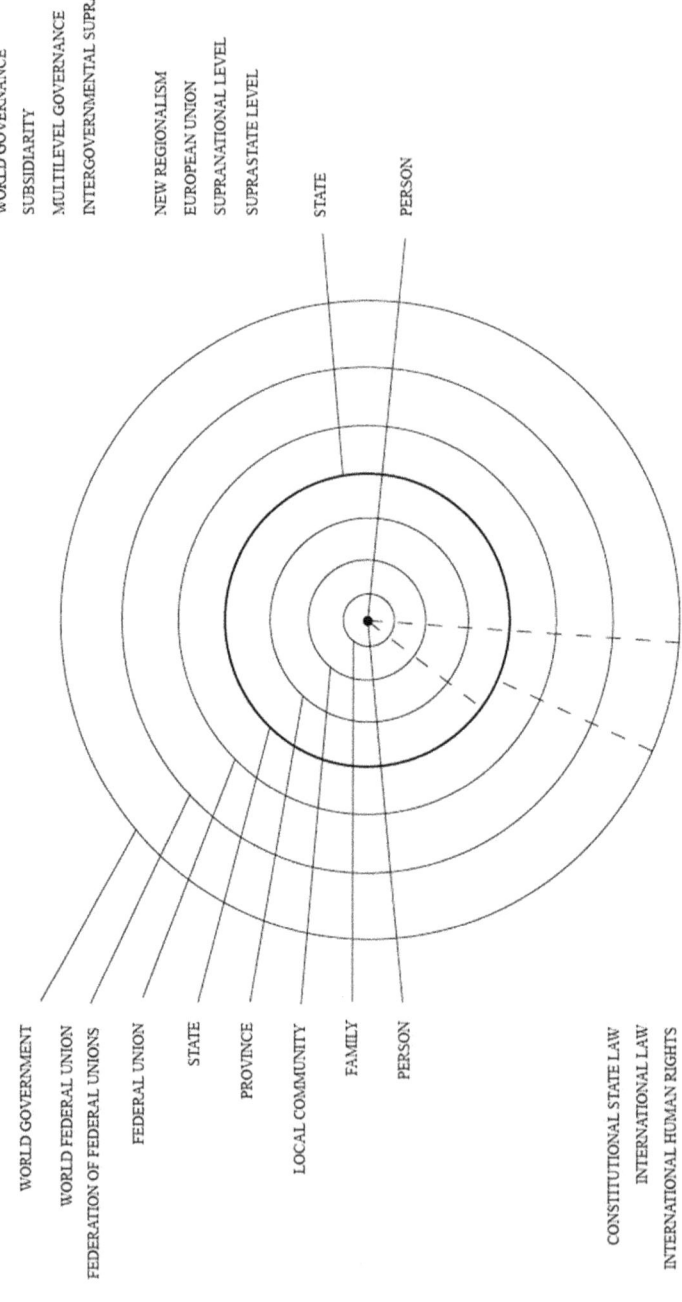

Figure 0.1 Illustration of the idea of a peaceful world federation

1

THE MOST IMPORTANT ACHIEVEMENTS OF THE IDEA OF EUROPEAN UNITY IN THE FIELD OF STATE AND INTERNATIONAL ORGANIZATION BEFORE THE DECLARATION OF THE RIGHTS OF MAN AND OF THE CITIZEN (1789)

The most important achievements of the idea of European unity in the field of state and international organization, before 1789, were the theoretical differentiation between the alliances of states, and the development of the idea of a civil state. The differentiation between the alliances of states developed in the framework of defense plans against the Ottoman Empire and in defense unions against conquest (the old Swiss Confederation (1291), the Union of Utrecht (1579), the American Constitution (1787)). The principles of a civil state developed as the result of the fight for liberty against absolute rule and conquest (Magna Carta, English Glorious Revolution, American Revolution). The ideas about the cooperation among states developed in peace projects starting with Erasmus' *Querela Pacis* (1517) [The Complaint of Peace] opposing unlimited power, the bellicose power policy and wars of the princes, and religious and national hostility aiming at the humanization of power.[1] Hugo Grotius continued the work of Erasmus and summarized the ideas of his age on war and peace in his *De jure belli ac pacis* (1625) [The Rights of War and Peace]. He was the first to elaborate on a legal framework for making wars impossible. He believed that states should be organized based on common legal principles, and he also proposed to do the same for the community of states. In the *De jure belli ac pacis* he developed his ideas on a "jus gentium," or law of nation, and laid the foundations of international law. He did not prohibit war because he accepted the right to self-defense. But he legally limited the usage of war as a means of solving problems, and emphasized that wars should be carried on only within the bounds of law and good faith.[2] His book was highly debated, and it was also suggested that he might have been irresponsible.

The idea of European unity and pacifism were a constant duo. Defense unions and peace projects motivated the development of legal principles of peaceful

---

[1] Erasmus, *The Complaint of Peace*.
[2] Grotius, *Le droit de la guerre et de la paix*, Discours préliminaire, paragraphes XVIII, XIX, XXIV, XXVI, 12–13, 15–16, 17.

cooperation among states.³ All this was in a strong relationship with the development of the system of liberties and the dichotomy of confederalism versus federalism. It represented the struggle for emancipation (the liberation of a person from the authority and control of another person) and the fight for freedom and liberty against oppressive tendencies.⁴

1.1 Defense Unions and the Theoretical Differentiation between the Alliances of States

The oldest conflict resolution institution between states we know was the Amphictyony (about the 7th century BC). It was the assembly of the confederated Greek states (polis) functioning as a court of arbitration above the states.

The ancient Greek polis, in the presentation of Aristotle, was sovereign and represented personalism. It was governed by a popular assembly in which the free native adult male citizens of the city-state aimed to handle state affairs in the form of direct democracy. Slaves and women were excluded from this democratic form. The famous Greek philosopher Aristotle (384–322 BC), who is regarded as the father of European political culture, was for a personalist association policy in the polis organization. In his view social organization started from below with the persons and families. As a result of their association policy, larger and larger communities (local community, village, province) could be created. On top of these associations the state (polis) was self-sufficient and sovereign.⁵ He believed that states should remain sovereign even if they allied. This idea of Aristotle had a great influence on posterity, on confederalist defense unions, and on Althusius who further developed it in the direction of federalism.

The old Swiss Confederation [Eidgenossenschaft] was established in 1291 by the Bundesbrief [Letter of Alliance]. It was the association of three cantons (Unterwalden, Schwyz, and Uri) with the goal of safeguarding independence against the Habsburg House through a treaty of military alliance, of arbitration, and of judiciary assistance. Then other cantons, Lucerne in 1332, and Zurich in 1351, joined. Later the modern Switzerland, composed of 26 cantons, was established through the Constitution of 1848, which will be analyzed below.⁶ The success of Switzerland was based on the bottom-up organization of the cantons and their alliances.

The union of the Dutch provinces, the Treaty of the Union of Utrecht (1579), can be regarded as the first aristocratic federal type defense union in European

---

3 Bitsch, *Histoire de la construction européenne*, 16.
4 Croisat, *Le fédéralisme en Europe*, 11.
5 Aristotle, *Politics*, book 1, 7.
6 Croisat, *Le Federalism en Europe*, 13.

history.[7] In its framework, seven northern provinces of the Netherlands united against the conquering of the Spanish Habsburgs. The Union of Utrecht was based on the concept of unifying the provinces in one by safeguarding the autonomy of the parts. This meant respecting the autonomy, laws, and structures of the member provinces. Based on these principles, the Union of Utrecht, in the framework of a defense union, created a permanent union of the cooperating provinces and, at the same time, safeguarded the autonomy of the parts. The provinces shared a part of their sovereignty because they realized that they could defend independence in this way. Under the given historical circumstances, achieving unity was possible only through a union having an effective central power.

The Union of Utrecht made steps in the direction of the unification of the economic policy: the provinces had a common financial policy, they had to agree on the exchange rate of the currency and could not levy tax arbitrarily. So, the Union of Utrecht was not only a defense union, it was also an economic union representing the concept of a custom and financial union.

The union had a federal assembly, as a central institution in The Hague, with a legislative function. It was composed of the representatives of the participating provinces and headed by a stadtholder [in Dutch: stadhouder], who had an executive function. The stadtholder of the union came from the wealthiest and most important noble family. He was the commander-in-chief of the army and the fleet. The assembly dealt with foreign policy and defense, and the finances relating to defense. It sent the draft laws to the provincial assemblies to ratify. The provinces delegated unequal numbers of representatives in the assembly but each province had one vote. The decisions had to be unanimous on the most important questions, otherwise the majority vote was used. The provinces had their own provincial assembly where citizens, merchants, bankers, the delegates of the cities, and religious communities assembled. It was led by the provincial stadtholder.

The fathers of the Union of Utrecht used the words union, confederation, and alliance. This shows that they were uncertain how to name the union. The institutional structure of the Dutch aristocratic union started discussions about the question of a close or loose union. In European international legal practice until the American revolution, in most cases, the word confederation was used for all types of alliances (defense union, league, association, union, aristocratic federation among the rulers). However, legal thinkers realized the inexactness of this and began to clarify the differences of international cooperation among states. So it could happen that the dichotomy of confederation versus federation was realized.

Influenced by the Swiss and Dutch unions Johannes Althusius (1557–1638), German jurist and Calvinist political thinker, described the difference between

---

7 "Treaty of the Union, Eternal Alliance and Confederation Made in the Town of Utrecht" (1579), 165–173.

the "partial confederation" of autocratic centralized sovereign states and the "complete confederation" of bottom-up decentralized states sharing sovereignty. He discovered the theory of a modern democratic federal union in his essay *Politica* (1614), where he discussed the Bodinian unitary monarchical sovereign state conception.[8] Later, Emer de Vattel continued to elaborate on this problem.

Althusius rejected the theory of Jean Bodin (1530–1569), French jurist and political philosopher, who described sovereignty as the embodiment of centralization policy in his successful and very influential political essay, *Les six livres de la République*, published in 1576. His work became the classic rationalization of the unitary monarchical state, claiming that the authority of the state should be absolute, centralized, and indivisible. In his view the supreme sovereign power should reside in a monarch, serving the people, answerable only to God, and limited by natural law.[9] Bodin called for the establishment of centralized states in which all power was embodied by a divinely ordained king at the top of the power pyramid of a sovereign state.

Althusius contested the Bodinian concept of a sovereign monarchical nation-state that predominated in Europe because it was authoritarian, centralizing, and represented the idea of supreme and indivisible power of the sovereign. He was against regarding the right of sovereignty as the supreme and perpetual power limited neither by law nor by time, as Bodin proposed it. He opposed states imposed by a ruler or an elite from above.[10] Influenced by the ideas of Aristotle, he was for a bottom-up association policy among persons, families, and clans as the basic units of social organization. He was also influenced by the Union of Utrecht (1579).

The political essay of Althusius, *Politica* (1614), was the first book representing a comprehensive theory of a federal republic (complete confederation) based on a covenantal view of human society dividing ecclesiastic and secular state organization. He advocated an associative theory of state organization of the citizens through their primary and broader associations on the basis of consent and constitutional plan. In his view sovereignty belonged to the people and popular sovereignty was the precondition of a good polity, a res publica or commonwealth in a constitutional form. Popular sovereignty and the decentralized association policy made possible a universitas composed of collegia, since people could delegate the exercise of sovereign power to different bodies following their interest and will.[11] It also made possible the sharing of sovereignty among states in all those fields where cooperation was necessary. Taking all this into consideration he shaped the idea of a federal republic and of world federation.

---

8 Althusius, *Politica*, 3–208.
9 Bodin, *Les six livres de la République,* livre premier, chapitre 8, 187, chapitre 10, 306–340, 329; livre second, chapitre 3, 44–47.
10 Elazar, "Althusius' Grand Design," Foreword, xxxv.
11 Elazar, "Althusius' Grand Design," Foreword, xxxv, xlii.

In the Althusian view a political association developed out of the smallest self-governing cells from bottom to top and culminated in the universal commonwealth. He differentiated natural and civil associations, and regarded association as a natural right. The family was a natural association based on two covenantal relationships: conjugal and kinship. The first civil and spontaneous association was the collegium (civil association) which meant communication among colleagues. It had a civil and an ecclesiastical form and both forms were covenantal.[12]

From the association policy among collegia mixed and public covenantal associations developed, which could be particular and minor or universal and major. The most important particular and minor organizations were the cities which, as covenantal republics, formed a union of collegia. The most important universal and major covenantal unions were the provinces which developed from the rural and urban unions of cities. The union of provinces, as a universal and major association, constituted the commonwealth (state). The state had an ecclesiastical and a secular part. The ecclesiastical part dealt with the establishment and conservation of religion, the opening of schools, and the public exercise of divine worship. The secular part of the state managed the execution of general constitutional law and dealt with the special fields of state organization: commerce, money, language, defense, care of the public goods, and commonplace and extraordinary duties. The universal administration of the ecclesiastical part of the commonwealth (state) happened through the ephors. The secular part of the state was administered by the supreme magistrate. It had a constitutional part and an administrative part. The constitutional part dealt with the constitution, the bills, the election, and the inauguration. The administrative part arranged and managed the requisites of administration. The administration had two parts: the public and the private administration. To public administration belonged the ecclesiastical and public matters, to private administration the personal matters.[13]

Althusius believed that such an association policy could continue among states too because trade made cooperation in the form of a confederation necessary. Such a confederation with foreign people or another body, was either complete or partial depending on what happened with the sovereignty. The contracting states could share the sovereignty or regard it as indivisible.

In the case of a complete confederation, the contracting states shared the sovereignty. In his words:

> A complete confederation is one in which a foreign realm, province, or any other universal association, together with its inhabitants, are fully and integrally coopted and admitted into the right and communion of the realm by a communicating of its fundamental laws and right of

---

12 Elazar, "Althusius' Grand Design," Foreword, xli.
13 Althusius, "Politica. A Schema by Althusius," lviii–lix.

sovereignty. To the extent that they coalesce and are united into one and the same body they become members of that one and same body.[14]

In the case of a partial confederation the contracting states did not share their sovereignty. In his words:

> A partial confederation is one in which various realms or provinces, while reserving their rights of sovereignty, solemnly obligate themselves one to the other by a treaty or covenant made preferably for a fixed period of time. Such a partial confederation is for the purpose of conducting mutual defense against enemies, for extending trust and cultivating peace and friendship among themselves, and for holding common friends and enemies, with a sharing of expenses.[15]

By this thought process Althusius arrived at the idea of popular sovereignty, democracy, modern federalism, and the model of the peaceful world federation enriching, by all these, the Western system of liberties. The essence of his idea was to differentiate between the state imposed by the ruler or an elite and the state which was the creation of the citizens through their association policy from the bottom-up. So he made clear that the idea of a federalist state and international organization was in opposition to the idea of a centralized sovereign state characterized by the indivisibility of sovereignty.

Althusius' merit was that he elaborated the ideas of Aristotle on the sovereignty of the state (polis) in the direction of modern federal political philosophy based on the sharing of sovereignty. He called for the creation of decentralized federal states and a federal international policy built up from below, starting with the persons. According to his conception, political organization started with the persons and ranged from private associations composed of small groups, families, and voluntary corporations, to public associations and territorial units such as the local community, the province, the canton, the state, and the federation of cantons and states. In this structure of society every union (association) was a real and original community with a distinct common life and legal sphere, and gave up to the higher union only so much of its sovereign rights as was necessary to attain its specific purpose.[16]

Besides Althusius, it was Emer de Vattel (1714–1767), Swiss philosopher, diplomat, and legal expert who, more than one century later, succeeded in differentiating between federalism and confederalism in his *Le droit des gens* [*The Law of Nations*] (1758). In his world view the international or interstate system was composed of single states. The single state constituted one political body which was sovereign. The sovereign states could create either federations [république

---

14 Althusius, *Politica*, 89–90.
15 Althusius, *Politica*, 90.
16 Burgess, *Federation and European Union*, 7.

fédérative] or they could remain autocratic states. In the case of a federal republic, the sovereign states united into a permanent confederation. They agreed on common competences and obligations but they safeguarded their autonomy. As examples Vattel mentioned the unions among the Grecian states, the union of the provinces of the Netherlands, and the union of the Swiss cantons. The opposite of the federation [république fédérative] was the autocratic centralized sate. The international relations of these states were characterized by expansion and subjection. As an example he mentioned the Roman Empire where the autonomous parts were directed from a center. He was convinced that the autocratic sovereign states did not accept any law of nations that dealt with the regulation of the rights and duties of the sovereign states in their international relations. They safeguarded their sovereignty in international policy and did not want to subordinate it to the law of nations.[17] Vattel emphasized that sovereign centralized states were not able to create peaceful international cooperation based on international law. Only the federal type states with a bottom-up personalist organization could do that because they represented both the sharing of sovereignty and, at the same time, the safeguarding of the sovereignty of the states. He was the first thinker in the history of international law who, without mentioning the term of subsidiarity, contributed to the formulation of the essence of the principle of subsidiarity.[18]

The theory of federalism was further developed by Montesquieu (1689–1755), a French political thinker who thought out the idea of a federal republic. He did not regard as satisfactory the traditional, confederal type unions of states represented by the monarchical diplomacy. In his *De l'esprit des lois* [*The Spirit of the Laws*] (1748) he proposed changing classical confederation into a federal republic [république fédérative]. For him a federal republic was a society of societies [société de sociétés] based on a convention through which many political bodies could become members of a larger state, if they wanted, and which could be enlarged by new associates. In his words:

> Cette forme de gouvernement est une convention, par laquelle plusieurs corps politiques consentent à devenir citoyens d'un État plus grand qu'ils veulent former. C'est une société de sociétés, qui en font une nouvelle, qui peut s'agrandir par de nouveaux associés qui se sont unis.[19]

> This form of government is a convention, by which several petty states agree to become members of a larger one, which they intend to establish. It is a kind of assemblage of societies, that constitute a new one, capable of increasing by means of farther association, till they arrive to

---

17 Vattel, *Le droit des gens*, tome 1, Preliminaires, 1–16; livre 1, chapitre 1, 20–21.
18 Bóka, *The Idea of Subsidiarity*, 9.
19 Montesquieu, *De l'esprit des lois*, vol. 1, livre 9, chapitre 1, 265.

such a degree of power, as to be able to provide for the security of the whole body.[20]

In modern judicial terms, the model of federal republic presented by Montesquieu can be explained as a voluntary association of sovereign states that, through the treaty among themselves, renounced their sovereignty in certain fields for the benefit of common institutions. However, in a classical confederation the participating states were sovereign.[21]

1.2 European Universalism

European expansion had a particular aspect, and that was the phenomenon of universalism. It appeared when European expansion strengthened worldwide, from the 17th century and did not disappear until the end of the First World War. Universalism meant that European thinkers assimilated the world with Europe, and were more concerned with the organization of the world than Europe. The European universal projects expressed the desire for the establishment of an international organization responsible for collective security and represented the ideal of a world society of nations.[22]

Among the 17th century authors, Emeric Crucé (1590–1648), French political writer and contemporary of Louis XIII, represented the best of this universal thinking. In his *The New Cyneas* [*Le Nouveau Cynée*], published in 1623, he proposed an international organization of peace embracing the whole world through arbitration. According to his plan, a permanent assembly would be established in Venice with the participation of the delegates of the rulers dealing with peace keeping and the development of economic exchange. The decisions of the assembly would be binding. Sanctions would be used against the violators of the agreements. The organization would include the countries in Asia, Africa, and Europe (including the Ottoman Empire). Crucé was for religious toleration as a necessary principle of world peace. He protected the status quo, and called on all rulers to contribute to establishing the universal republic of world peace which could ensure the freedom of commerce, transport, and services, and could help the development of economic relations. He proposed abolishing custom duties and standardizing weights and measures.[23]

Crucé's merit was that he suggested establishing a worldwide economic, commercial, and political union that would be capable of ensuring peaceful cooperation among the rulers and transcending the classical means of fighting for power, including wars. He can be considered the predecessor of the international organization serving peace.

---

20 [In English] Montesquieu, "The Spirit of Laws," vol, 1, book 9, chapter 1.
21 Croisat, *Le fédéralisme en Europe*, 13.
22 Zorgbibe, *Histoire de l'Union Européenne*, 9.
23 Crucé, *The New Cyneas*, 40–48, 84–86, 97, 101–118, 121–122, 136, 302, 342–346.

European universalism, as will be seen below, was strengthened by the advancement of capitalism, successful bourgeois revolutions, and European expansion and colonization worldwide. The French revolutionaries regarded the principles of the Declaration of the Rights of Man and of the Citizen (1789) as valid throughout the world. In the spirit of European universalism, a global world was emerging. Non-European civilizations had to choose from the examples of the different state and international organization ideas and practices of the pluralistic Europe, and adopt them in their state organization practices in the 19th and 20th centuries if they wanted to avoid colonization.

1.3 The Idea of Liberty and the Principles of a Civil State and Union of States

The fight for liberties started with the Magna Carta (1215), in which the rebellious English barons achieved rights from King John of England (including, among others, freedom of the English Church's elections, protection for the barons from illegal imprisonment, access to swift justice, and limitations on feudal payments to the crown) in the framework of the first English Parliament. The royal charter of rights limited the arbitrary power of the king and launched the way toward the Westminster system of the rule of law: a bicameral representative parliamentary governmental system (indirect democracy) which gradually developed, and served as an example for the modernizing world. The struggle against the absolute rule of the king continued in the framework of the English Parliament and resulted in a constitutional monarchy (with an uncodified constitution). The Parliament was divided into two houses, the House of Lords encompassing the noblemen, and the House of Commons made up of the local representatives.

The principles of a constitutional representative monarchy, in opposition to the absolute rule of the king, were elaborated by John Locke (1632–1704), English philosopher. His concept of civil government involved the citizens in the shaping of the state. In his essay on civil government, published in 1689, he emphasized that absolute monarchy was inconsistent with civil society and could be no form of civil government. In his view men were by nature all free, equal, and independent. Through a bottom-up association policy they created a civil society. Civil society needed a civil government, in which the legislature was placed in collective bodies of men, called senate or parliament, and was divided from the executive power. No man was exempted from the laws of it.[24] Locke favored government by the consent of the people. He represented the direction of the rights of man and the representative parliamentary system. He raised the problem of establishing federal unions among civil governments but did not elaborate on

---

24 Locke, *Two Treatises of Government*, book 2, chapter 7, paragraph 90, 326, paragraph 94, 329–330; chapter 8, paragraphs 95, 96, 330–332.

modern federalism.²⁵ The English Glorious Revolution, in 1688, abolished the absolute rule of the king and established the bicameral constitutional monarchy following the ideas of Locke.

Locke's ideas on a representative parliamentary system were elaborated in the direction of international law by William Penn (1644–1718), English nobleman, writer, Quaker, and the founder of Pennsylvania. He proposed, in his *An Essay Towards the Present and Future Peace of Europe* (1693), a European parliamentary solution for European international organization. As the advocate of the civil government and parliamentary representative system described by Locke, he suggested to follow the principles of the civil government in organizing international (interstate) relations. In European practice this meant that the European sovereign rulers met in an important city and negotiated until the European alliance of states and its institutions and laws, the General Diet, Estates, or Parliament, and the European Court would be established. The Parliament met at certain intervals and discussed controversial issues. The resolutions of the Parliament would be binding on everyone. Violators would be subject to arbitration and sanctions. He suggested that the numbers of the representatives in the Parliament should be determined in proportion to the size and richness of the member countries (German Empire 12, France 10, Spain 10, Italy 8, England 6, Portugal 3, Sweden 4, Denmark 3, Poland 4, Venice 3, the Seven Provinces 4; if the Turks and Muscovites were taken in, which would be fit and just, they would make 10). However, each state would receive only one vote. He defined tolerance as the basic principle of the alliance. Any country which accepted the rules of the alliance could join. So the alliance was open to all countries which accepted state organization based on civil liberties and tolerance.²⁶ He believed that a European parliamentary solution would be able to humanize power and establish peace.

Penn rejected conquering as a way of gaining territory because no sovereign ruler had the right to subordinate or conquer another sovereign state. He suggested reducing the army and concluding mutually binding agreements on it.

Penn's conclusion was that establishing legal order among states could lead to peaceful relations. He had a great influence on the Founding Fathers of the United States of America and on Coudenhove-Kalergi, the leader of the Pan-European Movement who tried to act with the aim of creating a European parliamentary federation. Because of this Penn is regarded as one of the Founding Fathers of the European Union.

The projects on European unity of Sully and Abbé de Saint-Pierre safeguarded the classical framework of the fight against the Ottoman Empire and proposed different and oppositional ideas on international organization.²⁷ In the name

---

25 Burgess, *Federation and European Union*, 3.
26 Penn, *Essay Towards the Present and Future Peace of Europe*, 16–19, 26–35.
27 Bóka, *Európa és az Oszmán Birodalom*; Bóka, "From Holy War to a Balance of Power," 333–341.

of the idea of European unity Sully represented a modern expansionist power policy and Abbé de Saint-Pierre a modern peace policy.

Maximilien de Béthune, Duke of Sully (1559–1641), minister of Henry IV, expressed his own ideas, in the name of the king, in his Great Design of Henri IV (1610). After the shocking experience of religious wars and the St. Bartholomew's Day massacre (1572), Henry IV promulgated the Edict of Nantes (1598), which guaranteed religious liberties to Protestants, thereby effectively ending the Wars of Religion. Following in the footsteps of the king of peace, Sully sought the path of a European peace system based on a balance of power under French hegemony.

He suggested a Europe reorganized in 15 states and directed by a common council under French leadership. The 15 states would be the German Empire, the Papal State, France, Spain, England, Hungary, Bohemia, Poland, Denmark, Sweden, Lombardy, Venice, and the states of the Italian peninsula, the Netherlands, and Switzerland. This showed that Sully was not for the status quo. He represented French hegemonic aims and wanted the partition of the Habsburg Empire. His plan inspired the nation-state type of development based on the consideration of cultural and linguistic specialties and the balance of power policy. [28]

Sully's most important idea was that the European states should establish a European council and use the means of negotiations and compromises to solve problems in its framework. The council of Europe [Conseil Général de l'Europe], "a prototype for the European Parliament" of the European confederation would be organized following the example of the Greek Amphictyonic Council (court of arbitration), but with amendments. The permanent council of Europe would be composed of the commissaries, ministers, or plenipotentiaries of the governments of the member states. Its role would be to direct the common internal and external affairs of the confederation. The political and religious disputes and conflicts of interest would be solved through mediation. France would be the arbitrator (magistrate) of peace. Sully also proposed establishing six independent and autonomous regional councils [conseil particuliers] in the framework of the council of Europe and subordinated to it, which represented the member states. So, he was for the regionally based representation of the European states in the council, instead of the state based representation.[29]

The world policy of Sully's European confederation continued the mentality of the crusades and missionary thinking. The primary purpose of the confederation would be to fight against the common enemy (the Ottoman Empire). When there would be no more common enemy the European rulers would extend their confederal system in Asia, on the bordering coast of Africa, and everywhere in the neighborhood of the European states. The newly conquered states would be united with the European confederation.

---

28 Sully, "Le projet politique," 87.
29 Sully, "Le projet politique," 88–90; Seth and Kulessa, *Idea of Europe*, 35–36.

The plan could not be realized because absolutism was strengthened in France, and Sully himself was a believer in a strong central government. The fight for power between the Habsburg House and the French Kingdom led finally to the Spanish War of Succession.

Under the influence of the War of the Spanish Succession, at the beginning of the 18th century, influenced by Sully, Charles-Irénée Castel de Saint-Pierre, better known as the Abbé de Saint-Pierre (1658–1743), a French abbot, proposed ideas on an international organization to maintain peace in his *Projet de paix perpétuelle pour l'Europe* [*Project for Perpetual Peace in Europe*] (1713). He suggested establishing a European Senate [Sénat], with legislative and judiciary competences. His project was different from Sully's plan because he wanted to create a European union based on the status quo. While Abbé de Saint-Pierre was a pacifist, this could not be said of Sully. The abbot suggested disarmament, the limitation of military force, and making the number of soldiers equal in all countries. He wanted to reform the monarchic political principle through international law. Sully, on the contrary, used the monarchic political principle and the balance of powers policy against the Habsburg Monarchy. He was for the leading role of France in the European confederation.

But what did Abbé de Saint-Pierre propose regarding the reform of the monarchical diplomacy and the balance of power policy in his eternal peace project?

Saint-Pierre's goal was to make peace-making the main goal of international relations through international law. He believed that the monarchical diplomatic organizing principles that used commercial agreements and leagues to manage the balance of power were not suitable for establishing peaceful international relations. Only the federal type constructions proved to be stable and peaceful, as the example of the Swiss cantons and the Dutch provinces showed. Therefore it would be necessary to establish a European grand alliance and to develop it into a secure federal system. The first step would be to convene a congress where the participants would conclude a basic treaty (a constitution) on the European alliance and formulate the operating principles of the federation. This basic treaty should consist of fundamental articles [12 articles fondamentaux] and important articles [8 articles importants]. The fundamental articles should be adopted unanimously, the important articles should have a 75 percent majority.

Following the fundamental articles there should be a permanent eternal peace contract between the allies, based on the status quo, and an offensive and defensive alliance with the Ottoman Empire serving the interest of peace and commerce. The federation should be directed by a European council [Sénat d'Europe] in which the rulers were represented by their permanent representatives. The federal council should deal with things within its competences and the member states should remain sovereign in all other things. Sanctions would be used against the violators of the agreement. Arbitrary conquest was prohibited and the monarchs could not continue to use their former land acquisition methods (territorial claims, exchanges, and gifts; territorial integration through inheritance and marriage policy). In territorial disputes the federation had to arbitrate. It was prohibited to arbitrarily initiate war. In the important articles, Saint-Pierre took the position of limiting the army, and of protecting the idea of general disarmament.[30]

Abbé de Saint-Pierre also suggested ideas for the organization of an economic union. He protected free trade, but considered the necessity of regulating trade in the whole territory of the federation by establishing chambers of commerce. In his view the commercial rules should be the same for all peoples. He believed that in this way the European union could become a political and economic union.[31]

Saint-Pierre's ideas on European unity went far beyond the possibilities of his own age. The Peace of Utrecht (1713–1715), which ended the War of the Spanish Succession, ensured that France and Spain should not merge. In this way it preserved the balance of power in Europe, but it could not establish durable peace between the European great powers: the rivalry between the French, the English, and the Habsburg dynasties continued. His ideas on the basic principles of a federal type league of nations later influenced the Founding Fathers of the American federal republic under a president and the Founding Fathers of the European Union.

Jean Jacques Rousseau (1712–1778), Genevan philosopher, highly appreciated Saint-Pierre's eternal peace project because it motivated powers to reform and democratize the monarchical diplomacy, following the example of the Swiss confederation. But he emphasized that the project was not realizable in the 18th century because the European monarchical system was not able to establish a universal peace system. For this popular sovereignty, democracy and a social contract would be necessary. In Europe a centralized authoritarian monarchical governmental system dominated, there was no external threat, and the European great powers pursued colonization policies worldwide, so they were not really motivated to cooperate.

Rousseau was of the opinion that in Europe there was an endless power game between two or three great powers and the smaller powers in the framework of the balance of power policy. In these circumstances he could not imagine that the German-Roman emperor, the Russian tsar, the French, Spanish, English, Danish, Swedish, and Portuguese kings, the Prussian ruler, Poland, the Netherlands, the Papal State, the princes of Bavaria and Palatinate, the Republic of Venice, the Swiss Confederation, and the sovereign states of the Kingdom of Naples and Sardinia would be able to create a confederal system of peaceful cooperation. He was of the opinion that it would be utopian to think that the monarchical diplomatic principle and power policy could be replaced by a more democratic one because only wars and conflicts could arise from the foreign

---

30 Saint-Pierre, "Projet de paix perpétuelle pour l'Europe," tome 1, quatrième discours, 206–232; [In English] Schlochauer, Die idee des Ewigen Friedens, 86–99.
31 Saint-Pierre, "Projet de paix perpétuelle pour l'Europe," tome 1, quatrième discours, 215–216.

policy of the European nation-states and national empires being in expansion all over the world.[32]

With regard to the political reality of the age of the Enlightenment, Rousseau raised the question of liberty in *The Social Contract*, saying that

Man was born free, and he is everywhere in chains.[33]

Why has history developed in this way and what to do?

His answer was that the states were not well organized during history because the simplest way of direct democracy, when peasants under an oak tree agreed in a social contract on the organization of their state, had not followed in history. The reality was that people lived according to the will of their rulers, and they could not change that. In his view, the state had to serve the interests of the people, who were the sovereign and who had the right to legislate. So the challenge for a rational state organization was the creation of a bottom-up state, by reversing the direction, and organizing the state not from above but from below, as a direct democracy based on the social contract of the people, in order to avoid authoritarian rule. But his ideas on direct democracy, in the framework of sovereign nation-states representing the indivisibility of national sovereignty, were controversial and demanded profound social change.

The message from the 17th and 18th centuries' thinkers of the Enlightenment to the future generations was clear: the feudal organization of the state must be transcended in the direction of humanization of power and lasting peace. For this, bottom-up organized federal states, direct democracy or representative parliamentary democracy, popular sovereignty, sharing the sovereignty of the states in common fields, federal institutions, and governance, were necessary. One can say that the ideas for a democratic transformation of European society were there, but reality and social conditions were not. Democratic reform aimed to transcend feudal society, starting with the establishment of the first federal republic, the United States of America, on the basis of the above-mentioned European ideas. And the American Revolution motivated Europeans to start to modernize and democratize the state and international relations according to the needs of the emerging civil society.

---

32 Rousseau, "Projet de paix perpétuelle & Jugement," 115–158.
33 Rousseau, *The Social Contract*, book 1, chapter 1, 49.

2

A NEW DEMOCRATIC CONSTITUTIONAL FEDERAL STATE IN OPPOSITION TO FEUDALISM AND COLONIZATION: THE CONSTITUTION OF THE UNITED STATES OF AMERICA (1787) AND ITS INFLUENCE IN EUROPE

2.1 The Constitution of a Democratic Federal Republic under a President (1787)

The political history of modern democratic constitutional federalism started with the American Revolution and the establishment of a democratic political regime breaking with feudalism, the centralizing (unitary) tradition, and the colonization policy of the English constitutional monarchy in the name of liberty. The Declaration of Independence (1776) declared the right to liberty:

> That all men are created equal; that they are endowed by their Creator with certain unalienable rights; that among these are life, liberty, and the pursuit of happiness.[1]

With this started a new period in the history of the state and international organization of society based on the idea of liberty. The French revolutionaries fighting against the absolute rule of the king, two years later, demonstrated that they accepted freedom as a leading idea of the Western system of liberties. The first article of the Declaration of the Rights of Man and of the Citizen (1789) declared:

> Men are born and remain free and equal in rights.[2]

The goal of the American Protestant Founding Fathers was to establish a defense union that was stable enough to defend freedom and independence against British colonial rule. To realize this aim, they studied the most important ideas and achievements of the former state and international organizations and discussed them in *The Federalist (The Federalist Papers)* which was a collection of essays written by Alexander Hamilton, James Madison, and John Jay in favor

---

1 "Declaration of Independence, 1776," 10–11.
2 "Declaration of the Rights of Man and of the Citizen 1789," 78.

of the new constitution as agreed upon by the Federal Convention, September 17, 1787.[3] They took their thoughts from the teachings and ideas of the abovementioned Aristotle, Locke, Montesquieu, Penn, Abbé de Saint-Pierre, and Vattel. The Union of Utrecht also served as an example for them. The Founding Fathers of the United States of America rediscovered all that Althusius had earlier, namely that a federal republic should be based on popular sovereignty and democracy in a bottom-up state.

The Founding Fathers of the United States successfully framed the Constitution of the first modern federal republic under a president at the Philadelphia Convention (Federal Convention), from May 25 to September 17, 1787, by reforming the Westminster system. The Constitution of the United States of America (1787) described the federal government and delineated how the legislative, the executive, and the judiciary power function. It represented popular sovereignty, and rejected feudalism, monarchism, and the dogma of indivisibility of sovereignty. It modernized the English two chamber parliamentary system: Congress was composed of the House of Representatives and of the House of States or Senate (the English House of Peers was replaced with the House of States). The principles of the federal republic laid down in the Constitution were the following: self-determination, popular sovereignty, bicameral parliamentary federation, checks and balances, separation of powers, sharing of sovereignty, transfer of competences to the federal institutions, and saving the autonomy of the participating states in all those fields which belonged to the state competences (subsidiarity). By separation of powers, the federal government was divided into three branches: the legislative, consisting of the bicameral Congress composed of the Senate and the House of Representatives; the executive, consisting of the President and the subordinate officers; and the judicial power, consisting of the Supreme Court and other federal courts.

All legislative power was vested in the Congress of the United States. The House of Representatives was composed of members chosen by the people of several states, in proportion to the population. The suffrage was determined by property. The Senate was composed of two Senators of each state chosen by the legislature for six years, and each Senator had one vote. The two houses of the Congress made the laws in cooperation with the President under the co-decision procedure set out in the Constitution.

The executive power was vested in the President of the United States elected by electors as described in the Constitution, and for a limited period of time. The President had a strong power: he was the commander-in-chief of the army and navy, and he appointed the ministers, the judges of the Supreme Court, and all officers of the United States, but with the advice and consent of the Senate. He informed the Congress on the State of the Union and recommended measures. In extraordinary situations he convened the Congress. But he was removable from office on impeachment. Every bill which passed the House of Representatives

3 Hamilton et al., *The Federalist Papers*.

and the Senate, before it became law, had to be presented to the President. If he approved, and signed, it became law. If not, he returned the bill with objections to the house where it originated, where it would be reconsidered and voted on by both houses. If Congress by adjournment prevented its return, it would not be law. The co-decision procedure between the two houses of the Congress and the President acted as checks and balances and secured the balance of powers.

The independent judiciary interpreted constitutional law and preserved its enforcement.

The Constitution defined the powers of the Congress, the most important of which were defense, trade, finances, and welfare: Congress had power to lay and collect taxes, pay debts, and ensure the common defense and general welfare of the United States; to borrow money on the credit of the United States; to regulate commerce with foreign nations; to coin money, fix the standard of weights and measures; to establish post offices and post-roads; to promote the progress of science; to declare war; to raise and support armies, maintain the navy, make rules for the government and regulation of the land and naval forces; and to organize the militia. The affairs of the federation were handled by a federal government according to the constitutional law. The Constitution was amendable, whenever two-thirds of both houses proposed amendments.[4]

The Constitution, based on these principles, founded American society and represented the basic rules for it. It was a Constitution thought out by the Founding Fathers, discussed in *The Federalist Papers*, and accepted by the representatives of the constitutional convention. The Federal Convention was the most significant event in the history of the United States. It represented a double-level community organization (state and federal), unity in diversity, and a search for equilibrium between the member states and the federation. Democracy and human rights belonged to the basic principles and values. The power of the sovereign people was divided between two governmental spheres (state and federation), and the legislative, executive, and judicial powers were separated. This separation of powers represented for the people's rights a double security because the different governments were mutually controlled.[5]

The US Constitution of 1787 was an original model of territorial state organization based on the unity of the new state respecting the political autonomy of the 13 member states. It marked the passage from confederation to federation. It created, at the same time, a confederation and a perpetual union, a union, or society of the citizens. The subjects of the United States, as a federal republic, were not the sovereign states, but the citizens. The key to federal modernization was popular sovereignty, as Madison explained.[6] In a United States type federal republic, people were citizens of two communities: of their own states and of the federal state. The federal state was a constitutional federal republic with a

---

4 "The Constitution of the United States, 1787," 20–36.
5 Croisat, *Le fédéralisme en Europe*, 14–15.
6 Brinkley, *The Unfinished Nation*, 145.

federal government. So people could become sovereign in a parliamentary representative federal state.[7] The tenth article of the Bill of Rights amending the Constitution (1791) guaranteed the rights of the states under the Constitution:

> The powers not delegated to the United States by the Constitution, nor prohibited by it to the states, are reserved to the states respectively, or to the people.[8]

The federal government could be regarded as an incomplete national government that was neither completely national nor federal. The central power acted directly upon the governed but in a more limited circle.[9]

The Constitution of 1787 was enlarged in 1791 by the Bill of Rights comprising the first ten amendments to the Constitution. These were specific guaranties of personal freedoms and rights, of judicial proceedings, and of personal rights and the rights of the states. Congress, for example, could not make law abridging the freedom of speech, or of the press; or the rights of people peaceably to assemble, and to petition the Government for a redress of grievances. A well-regulated militia had to guarantee the security of a free state, and the right of people to keep and bear arms could not be infringed; the right of people to be secure in their persons, houses, papers, and effects against unreasonable searches and seizures could not be violated; the right to legal defense must be ensured. And Article 10 of the Bill of Rights (1791)—as it was mentioned above—confirmed the rights of the states, saying that the powers not delegated to the United States by the Constitution were reserved to the states or the persons.[10] Democracy in the United States of America has developed in the future through constitutional amendments.

Regarding the theory and the institutional solution, the Constitution of the United States (1787) was an impressive legal construction. It served as a reference for all those countries which wanted to associate their geographically and historically separated territories in a federal alliance. Modern federalism served the market economy well. The federalist method was suitable to reconciling authority (sovereignty) and liberty. For all this it became a method of peace making. But one cannot forget that the Constitution of 1787 accepted that freedom was limited, suffrage was based on wealth, and it could not solve the problem of racial slavery. Popular sovereignty represented the rule of free people possessing the right to vote. But free people at that time were, in most states, only white men with real estate (land) and sufficient wealth for taxation. White men without property, women, African American slaves, and Native Americans (Indians) were denied the franchise. All these contradicted to the idea of liberty and the

---

7 Croisat, *Le fédéralisme en Europe*, 14.
8 "The Constitution of the United States," Amendments, 1791, 36.
9 Tocqueville, *Democracy in America*, 158–159.
10 "The Constitution of the United States," Amendments, 1791, 34–36.

Bill of Rights amending the Constitution. Furthermore, it should not be forgotten that the Hamiltonian economic policy established a new wealthy ruling elite, and later the United States joined the free market expansion model of colonization using unequal treaties. In 1853–1854 the Commodore Perry expedition opened the Japanese ports to American trade by using might.

These facts, contradictory to the idea of liberty, challenged the Americans to amend the Constitution toward democracy and popular sovereignty.

2.2 The "Hamilton Method"

When the American Founding Fathers created the Constitution of the United States of America (1787), enlarged by the Bill of Rights, which laid down the principles of a modern democratic federal union of states under a president and a federal government, they were faced with having to invent an appropriate economic system. There were two alternatives for the citizens with property-based suffrage, which excluded the Native Americans, the African Americans, and women: agrarianism or industrialism. Agrarianism meant the continuation of the farmer life based on agriculture and a moderate modernization concerning the natural needs of livelihood. Industrialism meant to follow the British way of industrial, commercial, and business expansion, and at the same time defend the independence of the country against British colonization.

In the shaping of the economic and financial policy Alexander Hamilton (1755/1757–1804), one of the Founding Fathers of the United States, played the leading role. He was for an aristocratic democracy, and protected industrialism and business capitalism. He was opposed by Thomas Jefferson (1743–1826), another Founding Father of the United States, who was for an agrarian democracy protecting the livelihood of the people, in harmony with the equality and liberty principle of the Declaration of Independence (1776), the original draft of which was composed by him.[11]

Hamilton, as the representative of a capitalist entrepreneurial industrial society, made the emphasis on liberal capitalism and opposed slavery. Jefferson was a wealthy Virginian plantation and slave owner who economically depended on slavery. He made the emphasis on the livelihood, well-being, and prosperity of the farmers. His views on the institution of slavery and on African slaves were very complex, and it is discussed whether Jefferson truly opposed slavery or not. In his *Notes on Virginia*, published in 1787, he wrote against the abolition of slavery. He expressed his belief that the African Americans "are inferior to the whites in the endowments both of body and mind," and "this unfortunate difference of color, and perhaps of faculty, is a powerful obstacle to the emancipation of these people."[12] It can be said that the historical situation was complicated and the ideas were controversial from the point of view of the realization of the idea

---

11 Bóka, *Modernizáció és értékrend*, 80–105.
12 Jefferson, *Notes on Virginia*, 243.

of freedom and equality in the social and economic organization as a guiding principle.

Hamilton formulated his political economic policy on the basis of British political economic principles with the aim to defend the freedom and independence of the country. His political philosophy was aristocratic. He protected an elite ruling class because he believed that the government and the economy needed the support of the wealthy and powerful. His economic plan was based on a credit and debt system realized through bonds. The wealthy class lent money to government to finance expenditure and investments, and for his money protected the government. The federal state (the central government), as a borrower (debtor), issued bonds in which it undertook to repay the borrowed amount with interest to the creditor (bondholder). He wanted to create a permanent national debt, with new bonds being issued as old ones were paid off. This is how he wanted to make the United States a wealthy nation, with an enlightened ruling class, independent economy, and a thriving manufacturing sector.[13]

In his "Report on Public Credit," Hamilton explained why was it necessary to introduce the public credit and state debt system: the new American state had public debt, had only little moneyed capital, and had to face the danger of a foreign war to defend independence. Therefore the state needed credit based on contracts. By investing money it was possible, for example, to extend trade, and promote agriculture and manufacturing.

In his report, Hamilton outlined the legal principles of the credit contracts between creditors and debtors in the case of state debt. He believed that "the proper funding of the present debt will render it a national blessing . . . that public debts were public benefits."[14] He ardently wished to see his thought incorporated, as a fundamental maxim, in the system of public credit of the United States. At the same time he emphasized that the creation of debt should always be accompanied with the means of extinguishment.[15]

Hamilton proposed also to create a national bank with the aim of providing loans and currency to business, giving the government a safe place for the deposit of federal funds, and providing a stable center for the banking system of the United States. The bank would be chartered by the federal government, but much of its capital would come from private investors.

His economic policy showed that he favored an effective central government and a strong national power. As a mercantilist he was the representative of economic nationalism, and opposed the liberal trade theory of Adam Smith. He favored economic protectionism and state control over international trade and developed a dynamic theory of economic development based on the import-substitution strategy.

---

13 Brinkley, *The Unfinished Nation*, 151–152.
14 Hamilton, "Report on Public Credit," 569.
15 Hamilton, "Report on Public Credit," 570.

2.2.1 Contemporary Debates about the "Hamilton Method"

Hamilton's role in the creation of a federal state economy was much discussed by his contemporaries because he successfully could establish a so-called aristocratic capitalism. The wealthy aristocracy lent money to the state and became stockholder in state investments. In this way the aristocracy could safeguard its influence and power above the state. The state debt system of Hamilton made the state an instrument serving the interests of a new business aristocracy and speculators because the state became the debtor of the aristocracy. By creating the controversial state debt system he contributed to the emergence of a fictive economy of laissez-faire in opposition to a real economy serving the livelihood and prosperity of the people.

The agrarian James Jackson, Georgia state politician, for example, rejected Hamilton's plan on state debt and speculation. He emphasized that such an economic system would result in permanent troubles, crises, and in a speculative state and world economy breaking with the reality and real needs of the people. Such a world economy would serve the interests of speculators.[16]

Jefferson also opposed Hamilton's concept of public credit and state debt. He emphasized that one generation had no right to incur debts for another.[17] He emphasized the advantages of agricultural economy over commercial and business economy. In his view commercial economy, based on liberal public credit and state debt, would result in a troubled state and world economy, and devastating crises. It would lead to misery and decay. He was of the opinion that only agricultural democracy could be a true and realist idea, while commercial democracy was a false and fictive one. He favored and idealized the agricultural society composed of farms, loved husbandry, and had fear of the influence of manufactures and large cities. In his view agriculturals represented virtue and industrials corruption (the degradation of virtue).[18] He believed that industrial capitalist society was fictive and troubled, in which people became dependent marionettes, and, as a consequence, they could lose virtue. He was against following the example of European manufacturing and urban development.

In opposition to Jefferson, Hamilton was for encouraging manufacturing which could improve the agriculture and could contribute to the prosperity of the country.[19]

No doubt it was a cognitive dissonance between the federal republican Constitution of the sovereign people, enlarged by the Bill of Rights, and the laissez-faire debt-loan economic system of aristocratic capitalism, as Henry David Thoreau (1817–1862) pointed out later, in the 50s of the 19th century. He was an American essayist, poet, philosopher, abolitionist, naturalist, tax resister, and development critic, and the author of "Civil Disobedience." He criticized also

---

16 Taylor, *Hamilton and the National Debt*, 20–21.
17 Padover, *Jefferson on Democracy*, 71–73.
18 Jefferson, "Notes on Virginia," 259.
19 Hamilton, "Report on the Subject of Manufactures," 175–176.

the majority system of aristocratic democracy from the point of view of democratic rights of the minority and of the possibility of improving democracy.[20]

Wealth-based suffrage ensured the victory of the Hamilton method. His program could win the support of the manufacturers, creditors, and other segments of the business civilization. Small farmers complained because of the high taxes. They argued that the Federalist program served the interests of the wealthy elites and not of the people. But the Hamilton method was applied, and let to good economic results. The growth of the United States from a small agrarian federal republic on the periphery of European civilization to a world power can be regarded as the result of the realization of Hamilton's economic vision. Or, perhaps the opposite was the truth: Hamilton laid the foundation for the permanent troubles and crises.

2.3 The Dichotomy of a Fictive versus Real Economy

The ideology of a loan-based big business enterprise system—as was mentioned above—was essentially Hamiltonian. It was based on government aid for economic expansion using loans, on the leadership of the elite, on legal contracts, and on the belief of the wealthy elite's leading role in the organization of a money-based society. But business capitalism did not work according to the ideas and moral principles of the Constitution and of the Bill of Rights. As an artificial man-made creation, directed by government policies, by laws for the protection of property rights, and by financial mechanisms tending to increase the wealth of creditor groups, it became a laissez-faire fictive economy with its consequences.[21] The drive of individual will toward wealth and power did not know limits in an expansive, money-based business society with property and wealth-based voting rights.

History showed that Hamilton's economic vision justified both alternatives. Business capitalism built and destroyed. It was characterized by the dichotomy of a fictive versus real economy as oppositional economic organization methods. The fictive capitalist economy dealt with financial transactions and assets and resulted in laissez-faire economic expansion, colonization, a center-periphery world system of rich and poor countries, power struggles, world wars, and economic crises. The real capitalist economy made the emphasis on the activities that allowed human beings to satisfy their needs and desires, and served their prosperity without any speculative considerations. It focused on how to use capitalism for promoting people's livelihood, prosperity, liberty, and human rights. As such it represented the opposition to the fictive capitalist economy.

Because it was no more possible to return to the rationalism of the agrarian societies, and because a rationally organized industrial and financial capitalism based on free entrepreneurship and loan-based system had become an attractive

20 Thoreau, "Civil Disobedience," 97, 110.
21 Parkes, *The American Experience*, 230–231.

and widely accepted idea, the question arose of how to avoid the crises of fictive economy and how to use capitalism in the service of a real economy.[22] The struggle for bottom-up decentralized states, democratic representative parliamentary institutions, universal suffrage, pluralism, human and social rights, well-being, the welfare state, and international economic law and institutions showed the way toward a democratic liberal capitalist economic future.

2.4 The Main Phases of Democratization of the Idea of European Unity

The dilemma of fictive versus real economy, and the dichotomy of federalism versus anti-federalism that characterized the politics of the American constitutional federal republic was present in the theory and practice of European international relations, too. However, in European political practice, classical feudal monarchical centralization policy, and the fight for power and colonies of centralized and authoritarian states dominated. Under the influence of the Constitution of the United States (1787) the democratization of European states and international relations started with the Declaration of the Rights of Man and of the Citizen in 1789. But in Europe, due to the lack of a bottom-up association policy, democracy, popular sovereignty, and federalism, the idea of European unity served as a framework for the modernization of the theory and practice of cooperation among the states. It had five important historical periods after 1789 until the Treaty of Maastricht (1992) which were the following:

1. From the Declaration of the Rights of Man and of the Citizen (1789) until 1815.
2. From 1815 to the end of the First World War.
3. Between the two world wars (1919–1945).
4. After the Second World War to the establishment of the Council of Europe (1949).
5. From the Schuman Declaration (1950) until the Treaty of Maastricht (1992).

---

22 Polanyi, *La grande transformation*, 117–127.

3

THE DILEMMA OF DEMOCRATIZATION OF THE IDEA OF EUROPEAN UNITY (1789–1815)

3.1 The French Revolution and the Attempt to Establish Democracy and Popular Sovereignty in a Unitary Nation State

The fight for freedom of the American colonies and the establishment of the first modern democratic state, in the form of a constitutional federal republic under a president, had a great influence in France. A revolution broke out against the absolute power of the king with the aim of abolishing feudalism and establishing popular sovereignty and democracy. The revolution between 1789 and 1794 aimed to liberate people from the rule of the church, from the absolute rule of the king, and from the conquering, colonizing, and racist economic policy, in the name of the natural rights of the people.[1]

The Declaration of the Rights of Man and of the Citizen (1789) declared the universal principles of a new democratic civil society providing an ambitious universal vision.

> Article 1. Men are born and remain free and equal in rights. Social distinctions may be based only on common utility.
>
> Article 2. The purpose of all political association is the preservation of the natural and imprescriptible rights of man. These rights are liberty, property, security, and resistance to oppression.[2]

The third article of the Declaration of the Rights of Man and of the Citizen (1789) declared that the nation was the sovereign:

> Le principe de toute souveraineté réside essentiellement dans la nation. Nul corps, nul individu ne peut exercer d'autorité qui n'en émane expressément.[3]

---

1 Gauthier, *Triomphe et mort de la révolution des droit de l'homme et du citoyen*, 363–364.
2 "Declaration of the Rights of Man and of the Citizen 1789," 78.
3 Godechot, *Les Constitutions de la France*, 33–34; Rials, *Déclaration*, 22.

The principle of all sovereignty rests essentially in the nation. No body and no individual may exercise authority which does not emanate expressly proceed from the nation.[4]

The declaration had a distinctly abstract character, and the rights of individuals were stated in general formulas. It was not the Constitution, but the preamble to it, setting the goal to reach in a universal perspective. It represented a new set of values and principles for peoples on the path to freedom.[5] These principles were rooted in the Enlightenment movement of the 18th century and were in synchrony with the principles of the Constitution of the United States of 1786, with the exception of the principle of federalism. The principle of popular sovereignty was extended to the wider male population through universal suffrage. The declaration proclaimed as new principles and values of state organization: self-determination, popular sovereignty, equality of the political rights of persons, parliamentary representation, right to vote, right to property, right to legal defense, right to safety, right to resistance to oppression, right to free communication of ideas and opinions, right to speak, write, and print freely, but without abusing this freedom. It was attached as a preamble to the French Constitution of 1791, which was viewed as a starting point of social reconstruction in the direction of a royal democracy.[6]

On July 14, 1790, one year after the siege of the Bastille, at the Fête de la Fédération, the delegations coming from the whole territory of France and representing the different peoples living there, declared the will of the departments to belong to the French nation as their free will.[7] So, the French people, representing the nation, became the sovereign through fusion in a plebiscite, and not through a federal type constituent assembly and institutional system. This is how the phenomenon of a unitary nation-state, which became dominant in the European state organization, was created. The liberal theory interpreted the nation-state as the collective of the citizens, with the right to vote, whose collective sovereignty constituted the state and expressed the political will of the citizens.[8] All this signaled two things from the point of view of the idea of liberty: the first was that the fight for the right to vote was crucial in the fight for democracy. The second was that the usage of the concept of a unitary and indivisible nation state signaled the birth of nationalism opposing federalism and pluralism. The Constitution of 1791 referred to "one and indivisible kingdom" ("Le Royaume est un et indivisible"), and the Constitution of the First Republic of 1793 referred to "one and indivisible republic" ("La République française est

---

4 "Declaration of the Rights of Man and of the Citizen 1789," 78.
5 Zorgbibe, *Histoire politique et constitutionnelle de la France*, 30–31.
6 Godechot, *Les Constitutions de la France*, 33–35.
7 Duroselle, *L'idée d'Europe*, 137.
8 Réau, *L'idée d'Europe au XXe siècle*, 44.

une et indivisible").[9] Both maintained the former policy of centralization and could not replace it with decentralization.

The royal Constitution of 1791 formulated a constitutional monarchy and abolished the feudal privileges. Under nation the French people were understood, therefore national sovereignty meant popular sovereignty in a "royal democracy."[10] The Constitution divided the territory of the indivisible kingdom into 83 departments, each department into districts, and each district into cantons. It declared sovereignty as indivisible, inalienable, and imprescriptible belonging to the nation. It meant that no section of the people, nor any individual, could assume the exercise of sovereignty. The nation was represented by the Legislative Assembly, which constituted the legislative power together with the king. It was composed of one chamber (single house) representing the one and indivisible nation because there was a fear that, in a bicameral parliament, the Senate would become an aristocratic chamber, and the forces of the old regime would be able to survive and regain power.

Royal power remained strong and centralized, and the person of the king was inviolable and sacred. But he was no longer the supreme authority of the state: above him the Constitution affirmed the authority of the law.[11] The supreme executive power resided exclusively in the hand of the king. He was also involved in the legislation: the bills and decrees of the legislative body were presented to the king, who could refuse their consent; the king had to sanction the laws, and had the right to veto. But his right of veto was only suspensive as the referendum—the popular vote of the sovereign people—decided. The king was the supreme head of the general administration of the kingdom, and he ensured the maintenance of order and public tranquility. He was the supreme leader of the army and the navy, and the head of external policy.[12]

The judicial power was presented as independent; more precisely, Chapter V presented the judicial power as one of the three main powers, but judges had in the revolutionary conception only a subordinate power of application of the laws. In reality, there were not three separated powers, but only two. From the beginning of the revolution, the idea prevailed that jurisdiction was an operation of execution of the laws, and therefore an activity of an executive nature.[13]

The constitutional monarchy was only short-lived. An internal political struggle broke out between the supporters of the old regime and the revolutionaries dominated by the Jacobins. Parallel to all this the revolutionary wars started because the conservative European monarchies viewed the French Revolution as a threat. In the midst of these circumstances, Louis XVI, by using his right of veto, hindered the defense of France. He sought foreign help, and

---

9 Godechot, *Les Constitutions de la France*, 37, 83.
10 Zorgbibe, *Histoire politique et constitutionnelle de la France*, 7.
11 Zorgbibe, *Histoire politique et constitutionnelle de la France*, 41.
12 Godechot, *Les Constitutions de la France*, 39, 44–46, 50–57.
13 Zorgbibe, *Histoire politique et constitutionnelle de la France*, 39–40.

The Dilemma of Democratization 33

was not convinced of the utility and adequacy of a constitution of royal democracy. His conservatism and hesitation gave the appearance of supporting the counter-revolutionaries and conspiring with the royalists against the revolution. On August 10, 1792, the crowd invaded the Tuileries Palace, where the royal family resided. The Jacobins proclaimed the first republic in September 1792. King Louis XVI was sentenced to death for conspiracy by the assembly and was executed not long after, on January 21, 1793. The monarchy disappeared and with it the Constitution of 1791, too. Thus the establishment of a constitutional monarchy failed in France. But did the Republic have a chance to make people free and sovereign by law?

The first French Republic lasted until the declaration of the first empire by Napoleon Bonaparte in 1804. But the form of government changed several times which was accompanied by constitutional changes. In its history a significant event was the establishment of the National Convention which functioned as the first French republican government (1792–1795) elected by a direct universal male suffrage. The Constitution of the First Republic (June 24, 1793), the first democratic republican Constitution, did not regard as an example to follow either the bicameral Westminster system or the bicameral federal Congress of the United States of America (1787) because these were not based on universal suffrage (suffrage was determined by property, race, and sex), and they represented a compromise between the old and new elites.[14] The French First Republic was based on the ideas of the ancient Greek direct democracy, the direct democracy of Rousseau, the semi-direct democracy of Robespierre, and the utopia of integral democracy of Saint-Just.[15]

Maximilien de Robespierre (1758–1794), one of the most influential and controversial figures of the Jacobin period of the French Revolution, for example, was in search of a democratic Constitution of the sovereign people representing the general will. He also searched for the guarantees of the rights of the people in a very complicated historical situation. The representatives of the old order did not support the revolutionary change and rejected popular sovereignty. They wanted to preserve their privileged situation and did not want to let the people into power. Robespierre bitterly stated that people were everywhere slaves and miserable even though they were born for happiness and freedom by nature.

> L'homme est né pour le bonheur et pour la liberté, et partout il est esclave et malheureux.[16]

> Man was born for happiness and for freedom, and everywhere he is a slave and unhappy.[17]

---

14 Godechot, *Les Constitutions de la France*, 79–95.
15 Zorgbibe, *Histoire politique et constitutionnelle de la France*, 58–61.
16 Robespierre, "Discours sur la Constitution, 1793," tome 9, 495.
17 English translation by Éva Bóka.

Like Rousseau, he also imagined popular sovereignty as a direct democracy based on universal male suffrage, representing the will of the people in a unitary French nation-state. He accepted all anathemas raised by Rousseau against the representative system. At the same time he recognized that people could not always be mobilized to participate in legislation. So the legislature needed representatives and measures to prevent them from becoming tyrants and placing themselves above the law. Robespierre proposed strict measures, among them a revocable mandate of the representatives, and the right of the people's tribunal to prosecute them if it was necessary. He emphasized that the legislature had to solve the double problem of giving the government the necessary power to secure the rights of the citizens and to prevent it from abusing power and violating the rights. To defend public liberty against the government, he recommended to the Convention, among other things, the following: to combat against the corruption of the deputies and the representative system through popular control; to limit the power of the magistrates (the duration of their power must be short; no one can exercise several functions); to carefully separate the legislation and execution; to distinguish as much as possible the various branches of the execution; to avoid power concentration by making the executive power weak; to protect public treasures from public servants through independent supervisors; to defend the formation of opinion from the influence of financiers; to avoid the governors to manipulate public opinion; to put public officers in the service of the people; and to regard as the goal of the government promoting the freedom, prosperity, and happiness of the people.[18]

Robespierre was understandably worried about how to preserve the republic after the revolutionary overthrow of the kingdom. But his concern for the centralizing aspirations and abuses of power by those in power was in stark contrast to his belief in a bottom-up state organization that, in his view, could solve this problem automatically. He was for a federalist bottom-up state organization of individuals, families, and their communities that entrusted the state to manage only those areas that they could not, and so let people be free.

> Fuyez la manie ancienne des gouvernements de vouloir trop gouverner; laissez aux individus, laissez aux familles le droit de faire ce qui ne nuit point à autrui; laissez aux communes le pouvoir de régler elles-mêmes leurs propres affaires, en tout ce qui ne tient point essentiellement à l'administration générale de la république. En un mot, rendez à la liberté individuelle tout ce qui n'appartient pas naturellement à l'autorité publique, et vous aurez laissé d'autant moins de prise à l'arbitraire.[19]

> Flee the old mania of governments to want to govern too much; leave to individuals, leave to families the right to do what does not harm others;

---

18 Robespierre, "Discours sur la Constitution, 1793," tome 9, 495–510.
19 Robespierre, "Discours sur la Constitution, 1793," tome 9, 501–502.

leave to the communes the power to regulate themselves their own affairs in all that is not essential to manage with the general administration of the republic; in short, give back to individual liberty in all that does not naturally belong to public authority, and you will have left even less scope for ambition and arbitration.[20]

However, the bottom-up structure he envisioned could only prevail on the level of the Primary Assemblies of cantons, as evidenced by the Constitution of 1793, because the uni-cameral structure of the Legislative Assembly protecting popular power and the general will at the higher levels of government made pluralism impossible, and paved the way for a one-party ideological system which was reinforced by a unifying nation-state. His concern for the preservation of sovereignty of the people, which also manifested itself at the level of the institutions, reflected a complex psychology of fear of losing power during the revolutionary fight for freedom. This could have been mitigated by a pluralistic approach and a concept of a state that accepted diversity as the will of the people. But the unifying nation-state concept that represented the united will of the people ruled out the possibility of democratic federalism, and all this was already known, at the level of theories, in Robespierre's time. Thus, the question arises whether it was possible to establish a democratic republic on the basis of the Jacobin Constitution, as Robespierre envisioned.

The Constitution of 1793 (Constitution of the Year I or Montagnard Constitution), which was designed by Robespierre and Louis Saint-Just, aimed to realize popular sovereignty in the form of a semi-direct democracy using plebiscite in the framework of a single and indivisible French nation-state. The Constitution was based on the universal right to vote of all adult male citizens regardless of income, property, tax-paying, religion, race, or any other qualification. Even foreigners domiciled in France for a year had the right to vote, but women were excluded. At the local level, the Constitution represented the personalist federalist association policy, as explained below. At the higher levels, however, it was centralized, the federalist principle could not prevail. The principle of the separation of powers, represented by Montesquieu, was rejected, and the representative principle was eroded. The deputy did not represent the sovereignty of the people, he was a simple representative in the legislative domain: he proposed the law which had to be sanctioned by the people.[21] The citizens became sovereign through direct legislation using referendum (plebiscite). The bills drafted by the representative political elites were subjected to a binding popular vote.

The French people were distributed for the exercise of their sovereignty in Primary Assemblies (Assemblées primaires) of the cantons, and for administration and justice in departments, districts and municipalities. The canton served

20 English translation by Éva Bóka.
21 Zorgbibe, *Histoire politique et constitutionnelle de la France*, 62.

as the framework of departmental elections of the representatives, and grouped together communes which were the lowest administrative divisions. The population was the sole basis for national representation, and proportional representation prevailed (there was 1 deputy for 40,000 individuals). The French people assembled every year, on May 1st, for the election.

The voters met by canton in Primary Assemblies (Assemblées primaires) of 200–600 members to appoint the deputies. These assemblies also ensured the referendum which was also maintained. The sovereign people immediately appointed their deputies and deliberated on the laws. Elections were made by ballot, or aloud, at the choice of each voter. The votes on the laws were given by yes and by no.[22]

The Legislature (Legislative Assembly) proposed laws, the proposals (bills) were printed and sent to the municipalities (communes) of the republic. If half of the departments plus one accepted the bill, it became law. In problematic cases, the primary assemblies were convened for discussion. If there was resistance, the law was voted in a referendum. The laws were made in the name of the French people, all laws had to be submitted to referendum. The National Assembly was therefore all-powerful, its sessions were public.

The executive power was weak. It was not considered as a real power, but as a subordinated executing agent. It functioned as a clerk of the legislative power. The Executive Council simply executed the laws and decrees of the legislative body. As a weak institution it could not get involved in conflict with the assembly. It had no right of dissolution, no right of initiative, no right of veto.[23] It appointed agents to handle the internal and external affairs, but the Legislature determined the number and the functions of these agents.

The Constitution sought to prevent military takeover and dictatorship by prohibiting the appointment of a general. It represented a democratic army made up of the entire population. Every French was a soldier trained in the handling of weapons. In the army democratic conditions prevailed.

A supreme or high court was not included in the Constitution, as it could have been a rival to the Legislative Assembly. There was a Court of Cassation for the whole Republic which interpreted the law.

Relations between the French Republic and the foreign nations were based on a non-intervention policy, and on the principle of peace and friendship.

The Declaration of the Rights of Man and of the Citizen of 1793, which preceded the Constitution of 1793, was much more democratic than the Declaration of 1789. It declared the prosperity of the people as the goal of social organization and the duty of government. Universal manhood suffrage was a great achievement, however, it meant a serious violation of the rights because women were excluded from political rights. The declaration declared as natural and imprescriptible rights equality, liberty, security, and property. So, the list of rights was

---

22 Duverger, *Les constitutions de la France*, 44.
23 Zorgbibe, *Histoire politique et constitutionnelle de la France*, 62.

extended and specified: In 1789, men were declared free and had equal rights, but equality was not enshrined between the natural rights listed in Article 2. In 1793, the idea of equality became central, it was mentioned before freedom in Article 2 of the new declaration. In the civil order, slavery and domesticity were suppressed.[24]

The declaration of rights guaranteed to all French people equality, liberty, security, property; equality before the law, the free exercise of worship, the right to education, public assistance, indefinite freedom of the press, right of petition, right of assembly in popular societies, and the enjoyment of all human rights. It emphasized the virtues (such as courage, loyalty, filial piety), the well-being of the people, the importance of social policy, and the defense of the rights (equality, liberty, security, and property) that the government had the duty to ensure. The main principle directing people's actions and the laws was represented by the principle "Do not do to another what you do not want to be done to yourself."[25] It was also the leading principle of East Asian Confucian societies. The declaration rejected slavery and the oppression of peoples, and reaffirmed the principle of resisting repression as legitimate. Article 35 admitted, as the most sacred right and duty of the people, the right to insurrection when the government violated the rights of the people. The right to property remained expressly guaranteed, so the democracy of 1793 remained a bourgeois democracy.[26] The new freedoms, which enlarged the Declaration of 1789 pointed in the direction of the opposition to strict individualism, but they were not socialist since the right to property remained imprescriptible (inalienable).[27]

The Constitution was ratified by a large majority, and it was proclaimed in the Champ de Mars, on August 10, 1793, but it was never applied. On October 10, 1793, the Convention decided that the government will be revolutionary until peace was reached, that is to say without Constitution. The application of the Constitution was postponed, and the Convention gradually concentrated all power, and created the "despotism of liberty."

Regarding the 1793 Constitution of the First Republic of France the question arises whether the authors really thought that it was realizable or if it was only a political manifesto. Maybe Robespierre did not want to put into force the text of the Constitution of 1793, and the solemn proclamation of the main principles served to cover the despotism of the revolutionary government.[28] It can be said that the prestige of the Constitution of 1793 came in part from its non-application. This is why it has remained a reference model for generations of politicians.[29]

---

24 Zorgbibe, *Histoire politique et constitutionnelle de la France*, 57–58.
25 Godechot, *Les Constitutions de la France*, 80.
26 Duverger, *Les constitutions de la France. Paris*, 44.
27 Zorgbibe, *Histoire politique et constitutionnelle de la France*, 58.
28 Zorgbibe, *Histoire politique et constitutionnelle de la France*, 64.
29 Debbasch et Pontier, *Les Constitutions de la France*, 43; Zorgbibe, *Histoire politique et constitutionnelle de la France*, 65.

The need for defense of the revolutionary republic against the anti-revolutionary conservative monarchist coalition of European states (Great Britain, Austria, Prussia, Russia), and the counter-revolutionary forces within France required the concentration of power. This pushed the National Convention to create the Committee of Public Safety (headed by Robespierre), and the Revolutionary Tribunal. As a wartime measure the Committee had a broad power: in December 1793, the Convention formally conferred the executive power upon the Committee of Public Safety whose power became dictatorial. It organized the reign of terror (The Terror) when a series of massacres and public executions took place in the name of the defense of the republican achievements of the revolution. The rule of Robespierre and his allies the Jacobins represented the most radical and bloodiest phase of the French Revolution, from the fall of 1793 to the spring of 1794.

The Terror and power concentration was in sharp contrast to the spirit of France's first republican Constitution (1793), and the declaration of the rights involved in it. The Committee of Public Safety achieved an unlimited centralization policy from above. It could develop a one-party dictatorial power concentration in an extraordinary historical situation. It can be said that the sovereign people replaced the rule of the absolute king above them by the unlimited power of the National Convention's ruling Jacobins party and its head, Robespierre. Thus, Robespierre realized the concentration of power he feared. People voted for it, and all this showed that they did not know how to exercise their democratic rights. The realization of the principles of popular sovereignty, referendum, and democracy in political practice required educated people. But illiteracy was still high among the French people at that time.[30]

The Constitution of 1793 was not implemented, Robespierre and his Jacobin allies were executed. In 1795, the Directory (1795–1799) was created which ended the Jacobin reign of terror, closed the Jacobin political club, and a new constitution was written. The intention of the drafters of the Constitution of the Directory (1795) was to amend the 1793 Constitution by incorporating limits to avoiding power concentration. They wanted to consolidate the government of the bourgeoisie in a civic democratic direction, to prevent the dictatorship of a group of men claiming to be directly mandated by the people, and to making impossible the establishment of a military dictatorship. Instead of Rousseau's ideas, the emphasis became on Montesquieu's ideas on separation of powers.[31]

The Constitution of 1795 established a bicameral legislature—replacing the collapsed unicameral National Convention—composed of the Council of 500 and the Council of Ancients. The Council of 500 was responsible for legislation, and the Council of Ancients (upper house) reviewed and approved the law proposals, and had veto rights. The executive power was in the hands of five Directors, chosen by the legislature, with a five-year mandate. It was the

---

30 Godechot, *Les Constitutions de la France*, 76.
31 Godechot, *Les Constitutions de la France*, 94.

The Dilemma of Democratization 39

Directory that governed, and appointed the officers, including the judges, in certain cases, which was contrary to the principle of separation of powers. The Constitution included guarantees against abuses of power that the Directors might attempt: they could be indicted by the Supreme Court, and they could not escape a possible arrest order. The goal was to exclude the possibility of one person could rule the executive power.

Electoral assemblies of cantons chose representatives to the electoral assembly in each departments which then elected the members of both houses for a term of three years. But, universal male suffrage was suppressed, only the taxpayers had the right to vote. The Constitution required from voters to meet a certain minimum property and residency standard, and this ruled out the majority of the population from voting and representation. Only wealthy and educated people had the right to vote, and the nation was embodied by them. The legislative initiative of the people and the referendum has disappeared, except in constitutional matters.

The declaration of the rights and duties of man and citizen was attached as a preamble declaring liberty, equality, security, and property as rights. But the declaration of rights was amended, and the most significant article declaring that men are born and remain free and equal in rights, for example, was eliminated. The declaration no longer represented (like the Constitution of 1793) that the prosperity of the people was the goal of society. It did not mention the right to work, the right to assistance, or the right to insurrection. Only one social provision of the declaration of 1793 passed into the declaration of 1795, namely the prohibition of slavery (Article 15). The Constitution did not have any institutional body responsible for judging the constitutionality of laws. The amendment of the Constitution required a nine-year procedure. This provision led straight to the use of coup d'état. The democratic idea marked a very clear decline.[32]

One of the most serious problems with the Directory was that, as the result of the elections, the members of the Councils and the Directors could become each other's opposition (royalists versus republicans), they were playable against each other, and this led to coups. Returning from the Egyptian campaign, Napoleon Bonaparte took the opportunity and came to power by the Coup of 18 Brumaire, and this was the end point of the French Revolution.[33]

Napoleon gradually built up a centralized republican empire through power concentration: he suppressed the universal suffrage, used plebiscite and permanent constitutional changes (during his rule, between 1799 and 1814, three constitutions were written that served his interests), and the declaration of the rights of man was not involved in these constitutions from 1799. On Brumaire's 18th, the Consulate was established with three Consuls, of whom Napoleon dominated. As First Consul, he weakened the liberty of the legislature, made the institutions powerless, and ruled them as a strong Consul. He contrasted a very

---

32 Godechot, *Les Constitutions de la France*, 93–96, 101–141.
33 Furet and Richet, *La Révolution française*; Soboul, *La Révolution française*.

strong executive with a powerless and divided legislature. Through a referendum, he elected himself the First Consul of a lifetime, and the people voted for him by a large majority. Finally, he turned the Consulate into a hereditary empire, calling himself Emperor of the French (Empereur de Français). He subordinated the Senate to his power, created a Supreme Court (Haute Cour) to protect himself. He tried to suppress criticism, the legislature met less and less frequently, and from 1812 it no longer sat at all. Finally, France became an imperial dictatorship. The emperor ruled alone in a paralyzed and domesticated state.[34]

As for Europe, Napoleon aimed to realize the idea of European unity by classical imperialist means using might and war, but at the same time, propagating the modern Code Civil (Code Napoleon) in Europe. The Code Civil, the most significant achievement of his life's work, triumphed in France, and in the whole world, but with modifications. It was a mix of liberalism and conservatism representing the abolition of feudalism, freedom of religion, equality before the law, and the right to property which were the revolutionary achievements. Parallel all this it reinforced patriarchal power by making the husband the ruler of the household, and represented the principle of filial piety in a centralized state. Since the Code Civil applied to the entire French people and had universal objectives, including Europe, it is disputed whether he can be considered a dictator. If all this is taken into account, he can rather be called a republican emperor who continued the French centralization and imperialist policy but was somewhat influenced by the acquis of the 1789 (the right to property, individual liberty, freedom of the press, the inviolability of constitutional laws, etc.), and thus he contributed to the fall of the absolute monarchy of the Ancien Régime.[35]

According to Napoleon's vision the European nation would be composed of unitary, unilingual, and indivisible nation-states based on the Code Civil and legal harmonization. Aiming to combine individual freedom and security with the necessary centralization, the idea of a two-chamber parliament [chambre des pairs and chambre des représentatives] was also championed by him in 1815 in the Additional Act to the Constitutions of the Empire (April 22, 1815) because it was believed that a great federative European system would be more suitable to the spirit of the age. In this case, the legislative power would be represented by the emperor and the two chambers of the parliament.[36]

Napoleon, who defended the revolutionary modernization in the field of civil legislation and on the battlefield against the anti-revolutionary attack of the European conservative monarchs, realized that the power of the people, as imagined by the Jacobin revolutionaries, could not be realized in contemporary Europe. So popular sovereignty must be transformed into national sovereignty and revolutionism must be abolished in order to create republicanism. All this meant that the revolutionary power of the people had to be dismantled and

---

34 Duverger, *Les constitutions de la France*, 54–58.
35 Chevalier, *Napoléon et le Bonapartisme*, 54–60.
36 Lentz et al., *Quand Napoleon inventait la France*, 711.

replaced by a compromise with the bourgeoisie and the old order, and so establishing social peace. This was how a left-shifted France, whose constitutional system differed from the Westminster model, could find a place in contemporary Europe. But Napoleon could not limit his ambitions for power, and this caused his downfall when he launched a campaign against Russia.[37]

In conclusion, the French Revolution was not successful because it did not achieve its realistic goal which was the creation of a constitutional monarchy, a royal democracy. One can say that it was the most and the least successful revolution in European history. Most successful, because it launched a deep and rational re-organization of the society in the direction of popular sovereignty, least successful because of the revolutionary terror, and "the creation of the professional revolutionary and the reactionary."[38] The Terror created a fear in European society of anything revolutionary or reform. The dichotomy of revolutionary versus reactionary meant a great handicap for democratization and socialism. Conservatives used democratic ideas and human rights for safeguarding their authoritarian power position. They could also use the phenomenon of a one and indivisible nation-state and nationalism in their interests. The revolutionaries called for too radical changes instead of gradual and rational democratic reform policy, and fight for universal suffrage. It took a long time for European international policy to reach a balance and peace. The many regime changes, that followed Napoleon's defeat, in France—from the Bourbon Restoration to the republican and imperial rule of Louis Napoleon Bonaparte—illustrated well the struggle between the old and the new order, which could only stabilize later, during the Third Republic (1870–1940). The Constitution of the Third Republic (1875) formulated a representative parliamentary democracy consisting of the president (serving as head of state), and of the two chambers of the parliament, the Chamber of Deputies and the Senate representing the legislative power. The chambers had a predominance over the executive power. Direct universal manhood suffrage prevailed.[39]

The representatives of the idea of European unity had to face to the new challenges of the extremism coming from the revolutionary situation, of Jacobin nationalism, and of Bonapartism. The revolutionary wars and the strength of the former "Ancient Régime," and the unitary nation-state model helped centralization to survive. In these circumstances, federalists, representing personal and local interests from bottom-up, were regarded as persons causing conflicts and diminishing the national cohesion.[40] This is why federalism, diversity management, and the ideas on democratic international cooperation among states—although they were already known—were not elaborated by the French revolutionaries. They continued the former centralization policy in a bottom-up

---

37 Chevalier, *Napoléon et le Bonapartisme*, 38–39, 44, 67.
38 Bibó, "Social Development of Europe," 449, 455–456.
39 Zorgbibe, *Histoire politique et constitutionnelle de la France*, 262–272.
40 Martin, *Contre-Révolution*, 179–191.

state structure of cantons, and created a confused form of nation-state from a federalist point of view: it was bottom-up on the lower levels and centralized on the upper levels.

The French revolutionaries originally rejected colonization because of its connection with slavery which was in contradiction to the Declaration of 1789. Despite this, colonization was continued from 1795. And Napoleon re-established slavery in 1802 after its abolition in 1794. The revolution for human and civil rights could triumph with the Declaration of the Rights of Man and of the Citizen (1789) but it soon was betrayed and defeated.[41]

Judging the French Revolution from the point of view of democratic organization of the state caused a lot of thinking and debates for both contemporaries and posterity. The main question was whether centralization was the necessary result of the revolution or a legacy of the old order. Among the contemporaries, the conservative Edmund Burke and the liberal Tocqueville were both of the opinion that the French revolutionaries replaced the despotism of the rulers with the despotism of the sovereign people who embodied the nation. Instead, the English monarchical rule of law or the constitutional federal republican state organization of the United States should have been introduced. They were for gradual democratization of the states based on the rule of law and the avoidance of the "Jacobin revolution." Tocqueville called for following the example of the Constitution of the United States (1787), because he believed that the French Revolution and its constitutions had led to a dead end, and that an English-style state organization was difficult to follow due to the lack of a constitution.[42]

In Europe—with the exception of Switzerland—the French unifying nation-state model and nationalism spread, and the colonizing European great powers established national empires, as will be discussed below. But the Declaration of the Rights of Man and of the Citizen (1789) has become a driving force for a gradual international democratization.

3.2 Kant in Search of a Democratic International Policy (Foedus Pacificum)

Regarding the democratization of the international policy the universal Declaration of the Rights of Man and of the Citizen (1789) had no appropriate international organization principles. Immanuel Kant (1724–1804), German philosopher, could realize this problem, and was in search of a democratic international policy. In his *Zum ewigen Frieden. Ein philosophischer Entwurf* [*Perpetual Peace: A Philosophical Sketch*], published in 1795, he outlined the framework of a world union of peace of sovereign republican states continuing the ideas of Abbé de Saint-Pierre with a universalist emphasis. Kant's vision was based on three things: elimination of the feudal monarchical diplomacy and its

---

41 Gauthier, *Triomphe et mort de la révolution des droit de l'homme*, 363–364.
42 Bóka, *Az európai egységgondolat története*, 86.

institutions; establishment of lawful circumstances; definition of the principles of a pacific federation [foedus pacificum].

In the preliminary articles he rejected the principles used by the feudal monarchical diplomacy which were secret treaties, territory possession through inheritance, exchange, purchase, or donation. He was for abolition of standing armies in course of time; emphasized that national debt had to be separated from foreign affairs; and protected non-intervention.

In the definitive articles Kant described the principles of a federation of free states which were the following: a republican civil constitution of each state; the law of nations founded on a federation of free states; universal hospitality which was the right of man as citizen of the world.

In the second definitive article he emphasized that:

> The Rights of Nations shall be based on a Federation of Free States.[43]

Kant believed that similar republican states in association could establish perpetual peace, more precisely a perpetual union of peace or pacific federation [foedus pacificum]. He emphasized that the law of nations should be founded on a federation of free states as a league of peace [foedus pacificum]. It differed from a simple peace treaty [pactum pacis] because it could establish perpetual peace. In his words:

> But peace can neither be inaugurated nor secured without a general agreement between nations; thus a particular kind of league, which we might call a pacific federation [foedus pacificum], is required. It would differ from a peace treaty [pactum pacis] in that the latter terminates one war, whereas the former would seek to end all wars for good. This federation does not aim to acquire any power like that of a state, but merely to preserve and secure the freedom of each state in itself.[44]

In the third definitive article Kant emphasized that the idea of a cosmopolitan right was a necessary complement to the unwritten code of political and international right which transformed it into a universal right of humanity. This idea was used by the bills of human rights enlarging the constitutions, or the charter of the international organization, as happened in the case of the Constitution of the United States of 1787 or the Universal Declaration of Human Rights of 1948.

In opposition to the French revolutionaries, who, in 1795, decided to continue colonization, Kant's goal was to replace classical monarchical diplomacy and colonization with international law, pacific federation [foedus pacificum], and the right to universal hospitality which were consistent with the principles of the Declaration of 1789.

---

43 Kant, *Perpetual Peace*, 102.
44 Kant, *Perpetual Peace*, 104.

Kant's merit was that he aimed to solve the alliance logic of the new idea of sovereign nation-state by international law, association policy and legal harmonization. He was for a democratic society of sovereign states based on international law and legal harmonization among similar republican states. He did not advocate the sharing of sovereignty and federal government. He was for an international system of similar sovereign republican states modernizing following the example of the most developed states (England and France). He believed that similar democratic republican states could establish international law, and could function as a league of peace, a foedus pacificum. His ideas seemed to be in harmony with democratic nationalism. Therefore the Kantian perpetual peace concept became the leading force of the European intergovernmental international policy of modernizing and democratizing sovereign nation-states based on legal harmonization.

3.3 The Conservative Breakthrough

The European settlement after the Napoleonic Wars had essentially four options: (1) a world federation of Kant's sovereign republican states; (2) the constitutional monarchical parliamentary Europe of Saint-Simon and Thierry, which will be discussed below; (3) the creation of a presidential federal republic modeled on the United States Constitution of 1787; (4) or the strengthening of the hereditary monarchical legitimacy and the principle of balance of power. The first three alternatives required democratization according to popular sovereignty from the monarchical governments (England, Austria, France, Russia, and Prussia), and the fourth required the restoration of the old order, and the setting as a future goal the constitutional monarchical modernization.

The Congress of Vienna (1814–1815) of the conservative European monarchs—chaired by the Austrian statesman, Klemens von Metternich—was for the restoration of the past and rejected most of the new principles of the revolutionary period. It wanted to restrain and eliminate republicanism and revolutions which threatened the constitutional order of the European old regime, and continued the policy of territorial changes and gains. France lost all its conquests, Prussia, Austria, and Russia made major territorial gains. The Final Act of the Congress (June 9, 1815) was based on the principle of monarchical legitimation, and on the balance of power policy. With the aim of guaranteeing the principles of Vienna, conferences and regular meetings among the allied (Austria, Great Britain, Prussia, and Russia) were institutionalized. From this originated the notion of "European concert."[45] The will of the people played no role in the Vienna settlement.

The conservative reaction of the traditional monarchs has hampered the consequent implementation of democratic reforms. But the new forces of democratization were already there on the stage of European history, as a result of the

---

45 Réau, *L'idée d'Europe au XXe siècle*, 43.

French Revolution, and shaped the future in a peculiar way. During the conservative breakthrough, for example, there was a proposal—corresponding to the new ideas—that received the Congress, but it was simply ignored. This was the project "On the Reorganization of European Society" written by Henri de Saint-Simon (1760–1825), French political and economic theorist, and his disciple, Augustin Thierry (1795–1856), French historian. Their plan was based on the belief that the European countries had to establish a representative parliamentary union. With this aim, the plan suggested that Europeans needed to modernize the state and international system, as the citizens of the United States had, if they wanted to safeguard independence. The essence of their reform idea was to establish a two chamber European parliamentary union of constitutional monarchies following the example of the British parliamentary system.[46] The European parliamentary union would have a general parliament for the whole of Europe dealing with conflict settlement and with common issues representing general interests.

> Europe would have the best possible organization, if each one of the nations which it encompasses were to be governed by a parliament, recognizing the supremacy of a general parliament set above all the national governments and invested with the power to judge their disputes.[47]

The project of Saint-Simon and Thierry consciously broke with the concepts represented by Sully and Saint-Pierre who proposed a perpetual peace treaty.[48] They opened a new phase in the history of the projects on European unity in the direction of the system of liberties and social reform. What they proposed was a European parliamentary union based on the cooperation of similar democratic national parliaments accepting the sovereignty of the common European parliament above the national parliaments.

The European modernization project of Saint-Simon and Thierry, in the name of the idea of European unity, was a rational project aiming to create harmony with the new democratic principles of the Declaration of the Rights of Man and of the Citizen (1789). But the European monarchs were too conservative to choose this direction toward the democratic system of Western liberties. On the contrary, on September 26, 1815, Russia, Austria, and Prussia created the conservative Holy Alliance aiming to restrain liberalism and secularism in Europe, and preserve traditional monarchism based on the balance of power policy. In Europe the methods of monarchic diplomacy, expansion, colonization, national interests of sovereign states, and the striving for a balance of power continued to dominate. In the circumstances of fighting for power and

---

46 Saint-Simon and Thierry, "On the Reorganization of European Society," 88–91.
47 Saint-Simon and Thierry, "On the Reorganization of European Society," 88.
48 Saint-Simon and Thierry, "On the Reorganization of European Society," 96–97.

colonies, the conflict-solving function of the controversial balance of power policy was very questionable. Despite this, the ideas on democratization of the international system were rejected by the majority of leading politicians. For example, Friedrich von Gentz (1764–1832), German diplomat, Kant's disciple, Metternich's confidante, was for the continuation of the balance of power policy because the bloody events of the French Revolution frightened him. He believed that the American federalist republican way was not realistic for Europe where the conflicts of interests and the fight for power between the old and new elite dominated. The French revolutionaries could not start negotiations among the representatives of the states about a European federation. Gentz acknowledged that a peaceful world federation was an important idea. At the same time he believed that it could develop only gradually from the problem-solving practice of the association policy of states based on an international law, which took time. He was convinced that his age was the age of the "European concert," and a gradual improving toward democracy and federalism.[49]

After the Congress of Vienna, in the framework of the Holy Alliance—which linked Francis I of Austria, Frederick William III of Prussia, and Alexander I of Russia—the restoration of the old regime started. But it was no longer possible to ignore the new creative forces of industrialization and liberal capitalism. They demanded the reform of the states and the international relations.[50] The former absolute monarchies were challenged to be transformed into constitutional monarchies. Switzerland, Italy, Germany, and the Habsburg Empire were confronted with democratic reforms. Although the aim of the conservative monarchs to restore the old European society proved to be impossible, they could still hinder and paralyze the development of the necessary democratic reforms.

---

49 Gentz. "Über den ewigen Frieden, 1800," 480, 482.
50 Braudel, *Grammaire des civilisations*, 548–557.

4

THE EUROPEAN PHENOMENON OF NATION STATE AND NATIONAL EMPIRE, AND THE CHANCES OF A EUROPEAN FEDERATION (1815–1919)

The Congress of Vienna thus set the framework for a classical Confederate European concert based on the principle of monarchical legitimacy and enforcing the principle of balance of power for 19th-century Europe until the establishment of the League of Nations. It sought to preserve peace and to prevent European countries from falling under the rule of a great power. It rejected popular sovereignty, but was aware of the need for constitutional monarchical democratization.

In contrast to the conservative Europe of the Congress of Vienna, the spirit of the principle of popular sovereignty and democratization has unstoppably advanced. Nothing proves this better than how the map of Europe changed between 1815 and 1871. Several peoples have achieved autonomy or independence (independent statehood): among the peoples of the Ottoman Empire, for example, Serbia, Greece, Romania, and Bulgaria. There were national movements and language struggles in the Habsburg Empire. With the Compromise in 1867, Hungary gained autonomy and the Austro-Hungarian Monarchy was established. Belgium seceded from the Kingdom of the Netherlands. Italy and Germany were united. Nationalism was the source of almost all change, but the old states only gradually disintegrated. The rulers of the Holy Alliance sought to suppress or repress the liberation movements organized in the name of popular sovereignty (the spring of the peoples of 1820–1821, 1830–1831, and 1848 and 1849), and they could achieve successes. The conservative forces were able to regain control and the revolutions of 1848–1849 collapsed. But this historical period was also marked by the debates between the ideals of those who followed the French example of unifying nation state and those of the American-style federalist republic.

The idea of European unity was also present in a pluralistic form in the 19th century. Some wanted to increase their own state within the framework of this idea. Others believed that the transformation of European historical states [l'Europe historique] into a Europe of nations [l'Europe des nations] would create a more harmonious and balanced Europe. And others again went much further by setting the goal of creating the United States of Europe. All this was imagined in such a way that the peoples of Europe formed nations, and their harmonious ensemble would mean the Europe of nations.[1] The question, in fact, was the dilemma of unitary nation-state versus federal state.

4.1 Romantic Nationalism

After the French Revolution, not the American federal republic but the French unitary nation-state became the example for the reformers. The myth of a 'Europe of nation states' was born in Italy. It was Giuseppe Mazzini (1805–1872), politician, journalist, and activist for the unification of Italy, who inflamed the cultural (linguistic) national aspirations of peoples for sovereign nation-states. Under the influence of the ideals of the French Revolution, he envisioned Europe as a network of democratic republican states: on the ruins of the countries of kings and privileged orders, the countries of peoples would rise, representing the idea of freedom and liberty. Unlike Saint-Simon, who still placed a king at the head of European unity, Mazzini voiced that the unity of the nations of Europe would develop from the pressure of the people. Europe will be a brotherhood of European nationalists.[2] He was for rejuvenated, democratized people's states (nation-states) created by the people everywhere: young Italy, young Germany, young Poland, young Switzerland, young France. And young Italy would have been created by uniting separate principalities and parts of the Italian peninsula into one country as a unifying nation-state, not a federation. Young Europe, in his view, would have been the framework of the people's alliance of each republican and nationalist republic (nation-state) bound together by brotherhood.[3]

Under Mazzini's influence the different peoples of the European multinational states and empires, in the name of democratizing the monarchical system, aimed to establish independent unitary nation-states instead of federal-style states and a European federal union. He became one of the most influential democratic nationalists who believed that only a Holy Alliance of the nations (unitary nation-states) could oppose the Holy Alliance of Metternich.[4] For this European people should achieve the free exercise of popular sovereignty and create strong centralized unitary nation-states, as modern states. He rejected the federalist ideas and solutions because, in his view, federalism weakened national cohesion.

The revolutionary movements of 1820–1821 and 1830–1831 showed the need for a new state and international order but they could only achieve a limited result (the independence of Greece and Belgium). The revolutions of 1848 and 1849 expressed more radically the hope of the people in revolt against the authority of the restored monarchical system. They demanded more participation in government, democratic reforms, and the creation of independent nation-states

---

1 Duroselle, *L'idée d'Europe*, 209, 212.
2 Mazzini, *The Duties of Man*, 52.
3 Bóka, *Az európai egységgondolat története*, 124–125.
4 Réau, *L'idée d'Europe au XXe siècle*, 51.

Nation State and National Empire

capable of defending national independence. The question arose as to how the state could be reformed to include the wider masses in the organization of the economy and society serving their livelihood and prosperity.

Liberal democrats imagined it in the framework of the fight for equal political and social rights on the basis of the right to property: the fight for suffrage, parliamentary representation, social rights, and the welfare state.

In opposition to the liberal democratic concept Marxism emerged. Marx recognized that Western free market capitalist expansion would create a world economy by opening the markets of all countries. He warned that Europe's future would depend on the Chinese revolutionary response to the European colonizers.[5] He also realized that, because of the nature of capitalism, it would be necessary to protect the livelihood of workers. The Marxist program was published in the *Communist Manifesto* (1848). The authors, Karl Marx and Friedrich Engels, emphasized the importance of class struggle and highlighted the contradictions of capitalism. They acknowledged the importance and achievements of the bourgeoisie in the shaping of the capitalist economy and society, and a modern world. At the same time, they warned that the logic of a profit-oriented capitalist society would lead to self-destructive economic and social crises, and endanger the livelihood and well-being of workers. As an alternative they proposed state capitalism, based on the contradictory ideas of class struggle, state ownership, and a centralized proletarian nation-state. In order to implement all this in practice, the following was considered necessary: abolition of property in land, termination of inheritance rights, confiscation of property of all emigrants and rebels, concentration of the credit in the hands of the state by means of a national bank, with state capital and exclusive monopoly, nationalization of the means of communication and transport, and an extension of factories and instruments of production owned by the state.[6] The political and economic doctrine—they suggested—aimed to replace private property and profit-based economy with public ownership, and communal control of the major means of production and the natural resources of society. They hoped that such a centralized Communist state could motivate free associations of people and prosperity. Several revolutionaries and politicians drew from their contradictory ideas and tried to implement them in social organization. All this provoked great controversy and led to irreconcilable antagonism and hostility in the organization of society, in the 19th and 20th centuries, challenging liberal capitalism.

The believers in the idea of European unity were for peaceful cooperation between independent democratic civil nation-states. From 1843 to 1853, a series of International Peace Congresses were organized where the representatives of peaceful societies met. At the Paris Peace Congress (August 22, 1849) Victor Hugo, French writer, in his famous speech, called the representatives of the

---

5 Marx, "Revolution in China and in Europe," 1–10.
6 Marx and Engels, *Das Kommunistische Manifest*, 42–43.

different nations of Europe to establish the 'United States of Europe' and realize the idea of European unity in practice through a European plebiscite:

> Un jour viendra ou vous France, vous Russie, vous Italie, vous Angleterre, vous Allemagne, vous toutes, nations du continent, sans perdre vos qualités distinctes et votre glorieuse individualité, vous vous fondrez étroitement dans une unité supérieure, et vous constituerez la fraternité européenne, absolument comme la Normandie, la Bretagne, la Bourgogne, la Lorraine, l'Alsace, toutes nos provinces se sont fondues dans la France.[7]

> A day will come when France, you Russia, you Italy, you England, you Germany, you all, nations of the continent, without losing your distinct qualities and your glorious individuality, you will merge into a superior unity and you will constitute European fraternity just as Normandy, Brittany, Burgundy, Lorraine, Alsace, all our provinces merged into France.[8]

4.2 The German and Italian Unification

Victor Hugo's beautiful words proved that romantic nationalism imagined the making of European union through fusion in a plebiscite of the different European peoples into one union as happened in France in 1790. So, for the romantic nationalists, fraternity was not a federalist aim. Therefore they did not really elaborate on European federalism as a component of international law. After 1851 the romantic nationalist enthusiasm calmed down, but the national idea continued to be alive.

Between 1851 and 1871, Italian and German unity were created. The new political elite was for powerful nation-states and national empires. Napoleon III, for example, influenced by the ideas of Mazzini, protected Italian and German unity. He supported the realization of the idea of European unity in the form of a European association, but he did not oppose the classical monarchical power policy and expansion. So it could happen that the aristocratic politician, Camillo Benzo, Comte de Cavour, found an ally in Napoleon III and created a war with Austria. This led, in 1861, to the unification of the different states of the Italian peninsula into the Italian kingdom under the authoritarian rule of Victor-Emmanuel II. Italian unity was made differently than Mazzini had imagined. He wanted to create an Italian unitary nation-state composed of republican states and merged in fraternity without federalism.

The reconstruction of the German Confederation started with federalist aims following the example of the Constitution of the United States (1787). The

---

7 Schlochauer, *Die Idee des ewigen Friedens*, 136.
8 [English translation] Seth and Kulessa, *The Idea of Europe*, 3.

German Constitution of 1848, which was adopted by the Parliament of Frankfurt after the revolution of 1848, was a short-lived victory for the federalists. It represented a modern, decentralized, federalist, democratic, constitutional monarchy headed by the emperor of the Germans. From the system of the bottom-up associations of local autonomies states developed, and the German Empire was an association of autonomous states. The German people were represented by the bicameral parliament, composed of the directly elected Volkshaus (Congress, House of Commons), and of the Staatenhaus (Senate, House of States) representing the individual confederated states. Half of each Staatenhaus delegation was appointed by the respective state government, the other half by the state parliament. The federal government dealt with common competences transferred by the member states to the federal level, and the member states remained sovereign in all other areas. The Constitution contained a Charter of Fundamental Rights [Abschnitt VI. Die Grundrechte des deutschen Volkes] which abolished the nobility and the feudal privileges, declared the inviolable freedom of persons, and ceased any subservience and bondage association forever. It secured for the citizens, among others, the right to privacy, to inviolability of correspondence, to freedom of opinion, thought, and expression, to freedom of press, to freedom of belief and conscience, to free elementary education, to inviolability of property, and to legal defense. It ensured local autonomy, and the autonomy of the member states, and emphasized that every German state should have a constitution with popular representation.[9]

But the conservative monarchist leading politician, Otto von Bismarck (1815–1898), Prussian Prime Minister and then Imperial Chancellor, was not for the democratic federalist constitutional monarchical solution. It is true that he did not consider absolutism to be a form of long-term or successful government in Germany. In the 1860s, he was satisfied with the Prussian constitutional solution which had three elements, the king and the two chambers. So, by his vote, each could prevent arbitrary changes in the legal status quo. In this way the fair distribution of the legislative power was secured. He thought that if freedom of expression was guaranteed, mistakes and extremes could be avoided. In his opinion, the absolutism of the crown was as unsustainable as the absolutism of the parliamentary majority. Therefore, the requirement that both of them must understand each other for any change in the legal status quo could be considered fair. He did not want to make improvements to the Prussian constitution, which he considered a good framework for German unity policy.[10]

But Bismarck did not find peaceful negotiation and the constitutional method sufficient to achieve his goal. He believed that in order to achieve German unity, armament and the use of violence and war were inevitable. As a conservative 'realist' politician in the service of the king, he was convinced that the German question must be solved by military force, and centralization under Prussian

---

9 "German Constitution of 1848," 203–215.
10 Bismack, *Gedanken*, 327–328.

domination. He saw the creation of a strong Prussian army pursuing militarist politics as a national interest. Thus, without hesitation, he pushed the democratic federalist reformers into the background, provoked war with Austria, and achieved that Austria had to withdraw forever from the German Confederation, which ceased to exist. In 1867 an assembly, elected by universal male suffrage, adopted the Constitution of the new North German Confederation, which placed enormous power in the hands of the Prussian king, as its president.

As a talented active diplomat, Bismarck feverishly organized domestic and international politics with the aim of realizing his vision about a unified German National Empire. His foreign policy was characterized by a complex series of conferences, negotiations, and alliances as can be traced in his memoirs. His speeches were full of nationalist arguments. He liked to play the role of a fair politician worrying about the nation. He tried to justify his militarist policy by saying that the French government had been pursuing a violent and threatening policy against the German states, aiming to divide and defeat the Germans who protected peace. Therefore, if the French were defeated, Europe would also benefit. He stressed that the aim of his armament policy was not to disrupt the peace of Europe, but to create and strengthen the united German nation-state. He claimed that war could be used in the service of national interest.[11]

His military and diplomatic policies were crowned with success. He defeated the French army at Sedan near the Belgian border, captured Napoleon III, and made a humiliating peace with the French. In the Treaty of Frankfurt (May 10, 1871), he forced the French to pay a massive indemnity, to cede Alsace and much of Lorraine, and to support the German occupying forces until the indemnity had been paid.[12] Seeing his victories people protected his policy with an instinctive national enthusiasm. So, he could achieve a flare-up of nationalism.

Thanks to his military reforms, war victories, and diplomacy, Bismarck could unite Germany around Prussia, in 1871, and make the German Empire a dominant European power. His life's work, the German Empire, was a militarist authoritarian empire under Prussian domination, ruled by Emperor Wilhelm I and the traditional elite (Prussian autocracy, nobles, and military) (mis)using democratic ideas. He could not harmonize his reform policy with the ideas and principles of the Declaration of the Rights of Man and of the Citizen (1789), and with the idea of a peaceful world federation. He regarded these ideas as utopias, and as a conservative politician deformed them in the service of an authoritarian monarchical rule.

His life's work, the German unity under Prussian leadership, as a militarist and authoritarian empire, meant the defeat of German federalists. Most of them surrendered to him, and those who insisted on the federalist principles were marginalized. The federalist spirit of the 1849 Constitution was replaced by a constitution that radiated the authoritarian nationalist spirit of Bismarck. The

---

11 Bismarck, *Deutscher Staat*, 222–223, 227; Bismack, *Gedanken*, 314–315.
12 Winks and Neuberger, *Europe and the Making of Modernity*, 204.

authoritarian change was expressed by the abolition of the fundamental rights. In Bismarck's Imperial Constitution of 1871, there was no explicit listing of the basic rights of the citizens in the sense of the charter of fundamental rights of the 1849 Constitution. He also changed the bottom-up federalist structure into a centralized authoritarian one.

According to the Constitution of the German Empire (1871) (Verfassung des Deutschen Reichs, April 16, 1871), Germany became a federation of the member states (a federally organized nation-state) of 25 German states under the permanent presidency of Prussia, the largest and most powerful state. A single German citizenship was created which required the citizenship of one of the member states. The empire was headed by the Prussian king (Wilhelm I) who had the title of German Emperor embodying the Presidium. He was the legal representative of the empire. He appointed the chancellor, who was the head of the government and the chairman of the Bundesrat (the council of representatives of the German states or federal council). Laws were enacted by the Bundesrat and the Reichstag (the imperial parliament) via absolute majority. Imperial laws took precedence over the laws of the individual states. The Bundesrat was composed of the representatives of the various states (Prussia, as the largest member state, had 17 votes, and Bavaria, which in terms of size was the next state after Prussia, had 6 votes). It had permanent committees specialized in military, naval, taxation, commercial, transport, post, legal, and financial matters. Germany formed a customs and trading area surrounded by a common customs border. The parliament [Reichstag] was chosen by universal male suffrage in direct elections with secret ballots. Next to the emperor it was the most important institution in Germany, but it had limited political influence on the government policy. The chancellor, Bismarck was responsible to the emperor and not to the parliament. He decided policy outlines and controlled the appointment of the officials who carried them out.[13]

Despite the extensive power of the emperor and Bismarck, the German Empire was neither an absolute state nor a dictatorship. Neither the emperor nor the chancellor could rule by ignoring parliament. Germany had a constitution and rule of law even if all this was controversial, and did not constitute a limit to absolutism.[14]

Bismarck realized the social problems, and knew the Communist Manifesto of Marx and Engels. It was clear to him that in a capitalist society, which was based on the right to property and free trade and enterprise, a social policy dealing with the well-being of the people was necessary in accordance with the ideas of liberty and equality of the individuals. But his social policy, pointing in the direction of welfare state, aimed at weakening the socialist opposition and gaining the support of the working class. He wanted to make ordinary Germans loyal to the throne and the empire through his social program, which included

---

13 *Verfassung des Deutschen Reichs*, 1871, 16–94, 94–107.
14 Winks and Neuberger, *Europe and the Making of Modernity*, 204, 206.

sickness insurance, accident insurance, disability insurance, and a retirement pension. The problem with his reform policy was, in fact, that he used the democratic ideas of the Western system of liberties to strengthen an authoritarian rule.

As to economic theory, Bismarck preferred Friedrich List's national economic theory to the liberal free market capitalist economic theory of Adam Smith. He was for an import substitutional policy, and his protectionist German tariff law of 1879 imposed tariffs on industrial and agricultural imports into the German Empire.

Proponents of democratic federalism criticized Bismarck because his militarist and authoritarian national unity policy pushed the principle of federalism into the background, and motivated German progress toward nationalism, militarism, and wars. He accepted the use of force, and the incorrect and false use of democratic principles and socialist ideas in the interest of an authoritarian national empire. He behaved similarly when he joined colonization. He voiced humanitarian principles at the Berlin Conference (1885) (free trade, the protection of the natives, the promotion of their well-being, and the elimination of the slave trade), but, in reality, he convened the Congress for protecting the German trade interests.[15] And it should be noted here that, contrary to the beliefs, the Berlin Conference was not intended to divide Africa, but Articles 34 and 35 of the General Act of the Berlin Conference did suggest this scenario: whoever gained another territory among the signatories in Africa had to signal this to the others and to acknowledge that he could ensure the rule of law and freedom of trade there.[16]

As a conservative modernizer statesman, Bismarck was popular not only in Europe but also in the Meiji Japan whose leading politicians saw him as an example. Under his influence, for example, the Japanese Meiji reform established an authoritarian constitutional emperorship, and confirmed the conservative explanation of the Confucian principle of filial piety. But his work was not really valued in China. Sun Yat-sen, as will be discussed below, criticized him for using democratic principles and federalist ideas in the service of the interests of an authoritarian constitutional monarchical national empire, and for creating anti-democratic state socialism.[17]

It is indeed true that Bismarck's policy caused confusion in the struggle for liberties and civil and social rights of people, which has been at the heart of the progressive dynamics of European social development. It is also true that his controversial constitution undermined the idea of federalism.

---

15 Worger et al., *Africa and the West*, vol. 1, 237–238.
16 Boahen, *General History of Africa*, vol. 7, 15.
17 Sun Yat-sen, "The Three Principles of the People," 104.

4.3 The Swiss Confederation (1848)

In Europe only the bottom-up organized Swiss cantons could establish a stable federal republic under a federal government, continuing the American example which, interestingly, was called a confederation. Between 1798 and 1848, they reorganized the old confederacy of Swiss cantons and the federalists defeated the supporters of a French-style unitary nation-state. The Swiss Constitution of 1848 declared the Swiss Confederation [Schweizerische Eidgenossenschaft] a parliamentary federation composed of the Bundesversammlung [Federal Assembly] and the Bundesrat [Federal Council]. The Federal Assembly was the legislative organ. It was bicameral, composed of the Ständerat [Council of the States] and the Nationalrat [National Council]. In the Ständerat the interests of the citizens, as the citizens of their own cantons, were represented, and in the Nationalrat the interests of the citizens, as the citizens of the Swiss Confederation [Nationalrat]. At the head of the Swiss Confederation stood the Bundesrat [Federal Council] under the leadership of the Bundespräsident. The Federal Council had seven members and represented the executive branch of the country. The President of the Swiss Confederation was elected for one year and had no power. The Federal Council was the collective head of the state. The Swiss cantons conferred competences to the federal power [Bundesgewalt] but they remained sovereign in all other things.[18] To the federal government belonged, for example, foreign policy, alliances, custom duties, and commercial policy.

The Swiss Constitution of 1848 established popular sovereignty, democracy and federalism. It merged the Swiss cantons into a multilingual Swiss state. All these was in harmony with the Declaration of the Rights of Man and of the Citizen (1789) and with the idea of the peaceful world federation. It became the true example of federalism to follow for Count Coudenhove-Kalergi, the leader of the Pan-European Movement, and for the supporters of the constitutional federalist direction of the European integration, as we will see below.

4.4 Plans for the Reconstruction of the Habsburg Monarchy

In the case of the Habsburg Monarchy, democratic reform demanded the realization of a multinational democratic federation based on the principles of the Declaration of the Rights of Man and of the Citizen (1789), and on the ruling ideas of the age: liberty, equality, and fraternity. Among the modernizers, in the 19th century, there were two main directions: (1) the supporters of the cultural or linguistic national principle; (2) the supporters of the personal principle. The cultural linguistic national principle was represented by the Czech

---

18 "Bundesverfassung der schweizerischen Eidgenossenschaft, 1848," 272.

historian, Palacký; the personal one by the Hungarian reform politician and writer, Eötvös.[19]

František Palacký (1798–1876), Czech historian, proposed creating a federation of the eight autonomous cultural national groups of the Habsburg Empire following the linguistic national principle. In his view, the Austrian Federation should be composed of German-Austria, Czech-Austria, Polish-Austria, Ruthenian-Austria, South-Slav-Austria (Illyria), Romanian-Austria, Hungarian-Austria, and Italian-Austria.[20] He had long discussions with József Eötvös who advocated the personal principle in multinational territories with mixed populations. Their discussion reveals the most important difference between the two concerning the very definition of nation-state. Finally Eötvös convinced Palacký on the importance of the personal principle rather than the linguistic national one and he accepted the ideas of Eötvös on personalism.

Baron József Eötvös (1813–1871), Hungarian writer and political thinker, searching for legal means against nationalism (linguistic and cultural nationalism) after the bloody fight in 1849, elaborated important federalist ideas opposing the French idea of a sovereign unitary nation-state not suitable for multinational states (like the Habsburg Monarchy, for example).[21] Regarding the reform of the Habsburg Monarchy, Eötvös emphasized that it was a historical formation. The old monarchic centralization principle was indeed untenable and it had to be exchanged for a democratic decentralized federalist system on the basis of the status quo and historical rights. As a solution Eötvös proposed decentralizing the global state [Gesamtstaat], to divide up the territory of the empire into provinces in their historical frameworks, and to provide self-government (autonomy) to the different provinces.[22] He rejected the creation of independent provinces (autonomous "nationality states") based on language and culture. He believed that the possible solution for the national problem in the Habsburg Monarchy was a confederation of the traditional historical entities at the top level (in the form of a constitutional state), and a decentralized bottom-up self-governing administrative organization at the country and community levels with equal political rights and the right to free cultural association for everybody. He believed that nationality (culture/language) had to become a personal right belonging to the cultural sphere of the person.

In his *The Dominant Ideas of the Nineteenth Century and Their Impact on the State*, he realized that the management of diversity was not solved by the Declaration of the Rights of Man and of the Citizen (1789).[23] Therefore, influenced by the federalist ideas of Tocqueville and Proudhon, he elaborated the idea of a personalist federal multinational state and the principles of minority

19 Bóka, *Az európai föderalizmus alternatívája Közép-Európában*, 40–51; Bóka, "The Democratic European Idea in Central Europe, 1849–1945," 7–25.
20 Palacký, *Österreichs Staatsidee*, 94–96.
21 Bóka, "From National Toleration to National Liberation," 435–474.
22 Eötvös, *Die Garantien der Macht*, 81, 211.
23 Eötvös, *The Dominant Ideas of the Nineteenth Century*.

(nationality) law. He imagined a state able to solve the linguistic and cultural claims of persons by a well-managed local autonomy system at the level of the villages and provinces diminishing, by these means, the role of state intervention in this field. In his view, managing diversity demanded personalism, the involvement of the principle of subsidiarity and multivelism in state and international organization. He contributed to the development of a democratic federal European idea and human rights primarily in the area of national minority rights. He also elaborated on the model of a democratic multinational and multidimensional personalist federalist state.[24] His contribution to the idea of European unity and the theory of the European integration process is very important.

During the First World War, in 1915, Friedrich Naumann (1860–1919), German liberal politician and Protestant pastor published his political essay *Mitteleuropa* [Central Europe]. It was also in the line of the various reconstruction projects of the Habsburg Monarchy (Austro-Hungarian Monarchy) based on the historical status quo. Naumann wanted people to end the First World War by democratically renewing the state and international organization principles based on the historical status quo. He called for the creation of the Central European United States and their Common Market, and reconstruct the Austro-Hungarian Monarchy in this direction. He was aware that this could only be the result of a slow and persistent organizational work due to fair of Germanization.

The essence of his idea was as follows (in his words):

> Under the superscription Mid-Europe no new State will be created, but a union of existing States will be formed. In using the word "super-State" for this union we have intended no decrease in political dignity for the separate portions; it ought not, will not and cannot mean this. Those who determine on the development, are responsible for it and carry it on, will be and will remain the present sovereign States concluding the treaty. These will make mutual concessions to one another, but it is they who do this, and they will not cease to be the subjects of future joint activities. If people like to call the new creation a confederation of States, this hits its character, but it cannot become a federal State. The second would indeed be essentially more than the first, but it is not feasible.[25]

Naumann suggested that the sovereign member states should cooperate in the field of common functions, first of all economy and defense, through expert Central European Commissions or Committees coordinating and managing common functions based on treaties among the governments. Parliaments could criticize their work. The Mid-European Commissions formed together

---

24 Bóka, "József Eötvös on the Personal Principle," 55–67.
25 Naumann, *Central Europe*, 255.

a Mid-European Central Administration, but the states remained autonomous. Mid-Europe would be only a superstructure, not a federation, developing through its own functionalist integration path. Prague would be the Mid-European center for all business, Hamburg for the overseas trade, Berlin for money-market, and Vienna for law.[26]

He was in favor of decentralization, of bottom-up local autonomy system, and of equal political and human rights for everybody. He emphasized that the political organization had to be based on common, shared principles. Culture, language, education (school affairs), and religion had to be separated from the 'higher State or super-State,' i.e. the central political organizational sphere of the Central European State union. They should remain a local communal autonomy competence (in multinational territories with a mixed population).[27]

Naumann's merit was that, with the purpose to reform the Austro-Hungarian Monarchy, he elaborated ideas on a functionalist Central European integration, based on treaties between sovereign states, and on a supranational Central European law and legal harmonization. He made a significant contribution to the development of the idea of European union.[28]

4.5 The Federalist Opposition to the Liberal Democratic Unitary Nation-State

Europeans, who were under the influence of the American democracy and Constitution, and the Declaration of the Rights of the Man and of the Citizen (1789), seeing the controversial realization of the democratic ideas in state and international practice, could realize that something went wrong during the democratization of the states in Europe, in the 19th century. The work of Alexis de Tocqueville (1805–1859), French political thinker and historian, is a good example. He was very enthusiastic when he studied American democracy and the Constitution of 1787. He regarded the American federal republic as an example for the reconstruction of the European states and the international policy when he published his political essay entitled *Democracy in America* (1835–1840). But thinking about the French revolutionary troubles and wars and seeing the return of the old regime, he lost his belief in Europe's federalist chances. At the end of his life he emphasized that, in Europe, the past lived in the present. The administrative centralization, that could survive, was an institution of the Ancien Régime [former regime] and not the product of the Revolution or the Empire.[29] Therefore the strength of the former centralization policy of the Ancien Régime was a serious obstacle to shaping modern democratic civil states in Europe. At the same time he was convinced that the idea of liberty

26 Naumann, *Central Europe*, 261–264, 274–276.
27 Naumann, *Central Europe*, 255–258.
28 Bóka, *Az európai föderalizmus alternatívája Közép-Európában*, 58–61.
29 Tocqueville, *L'Ancien Régime et la Révolution*, 98, 98–108.

would become the driving force of social organization after the American and the French Revolutions because the representatives of the old regime were losing power and the new economic and political forces gradually gained power as the logic of the idea of liberty and popular sovereignty demanded it. In his words:

> The noble has gone down the social ladder, and the commoner has gone up; the one descends as the other rises. Every half-century brings them nearer to each other, and they will soon meet.[30]

Tocqueville was convinced that the international system of modern states based on popular sovereignty, self-determination, and parliamentary representation had to be based on international law and not on the balance of power policy. He believed that the federalist versus anti-federalist association logic represented by the Constitution of the United States (1787) could be a future alternative to the European balance of power policy among sovereign states. He was for the sharing of sovereignty of the cooperating decentralized federal-style states in all those common matters where cooperation was necessary and supported the organization of the common matters in the framework of supranational institutions.

Tocqueville, interpreting the American Constitution in his political essay *Democracy in America*, emphasized the importance of the division of the sovereignty of the states based on the principles of subsidiarity and multilevelism. He believed that only the division of sovereignty, more precisely the voluntary fusion of states into one in specific areas of common interest and multilevel governance, was able to establish peace among states. His most important idea about the structure of a democratic federal state, which challenged the European federalists, including the Founding Fathers of the European Union, was the following:

> Another form of society is afterwards discovered in which several states are fused into one with regard to certain common interests, although they remain distinct, or only confederate, with regard to all other concerns. In this case the central power acts directly upon the governed, whom it rules and judges in the same manner as a national government, but in a more limited circle. Evidently this is no longer a federal government, but an incomplete national government, which is neither exactly national nor exactly federal; but the new word which ought to express this novel thing does not yet exist.[31]

The European integration process developed in this direction but it could not solve the governance of the 'fused common interests' (exclusive competences),

---

30 Tocqueville, *Democracy in America*, 6.
31 Tocqueville, *Democracy in America*, 158–159.

and it could not find the new proper word expressing the essence of the European Union (EU) to replace supranationalism.

Another federalist, Pierre-Joseph Proudhon (1809–1865), French political thinker, in the name of the idea of a democratic Europe, opposed the system of centralized authoritarian nation states and national empires. He believed that democracy and federalism were the only solutions to modernize European international (inter-state) policy. He opposed Mazzini's nationalist New Europe concept, the monarchist solution to Italian unity, the authoritarian militarist confederalism of Bismarck, and the centralized Marxist proletarian state based on state property.

Like Althusius, Proudhon was for a bottom-up personalist federalist association policy. His major work on this topic, *Du principe fédératif*, was published in 1863. In this work he concentrated on the dichotomy of authority and liberty (centralization versus decentralization). He thought that the federal system was opposed to the administrative and governmental hierarchy or centralization characterizing the imperial democracies, the authoritarian constitutional monarchies and the unitary republics [républiques unitaires]. As a federalist thinker, he opposed the European sovereign nation-state system because, in his view, it was the means to conservation of the dominant position of the old and the new elites. He believed that authoritarian centralized sovereign nation-states and national empires could conclude treaties of alliance and commerce but were unable to create a federation because it necessitated limiting their sovereignty at least at the level of arbitration. However, for them domination, not submission, was acceptable.[32]

In his view a European union should be based on federalism. It means a bottom-up association policy of persons in all fields of life and the transfer of sovereignty toward larger common levels of organization in the fields of common interest. His model of state and international organization was composed of autonomous persons and communities: persons and their associations federated on the basis of contracts freely entered into based on subsidiarity. He believed that power should be divided in order to be as close as possible to the level of the problems to be solved. This is why he was for a Europe composed of small political entities which were created as free associations of people concentrating on their security and livelihood.

Proudhon realized that the development of the Western system of liberties slowed down in the second half of the 19th century. He criticized the business men who, after an energetic and, in ideas far-reaching period, lost their democratization creativity. In the circumstances of laissez-faire capitalism they started to concentrate on safeguarding money and power. In his view this was a serious problem because large masses of people had no idea what to do, how to continue the democratization process in the name of popular sovereignty. In his words:

---

32 Proudhon, "Du principe fédérative," vol. 15, 321–322.

Business men of France, the initiative in the progress of humanity is yours. The untutored workingman accepts you as his masters and models. It is possible that, after having accomplished so many revolutions, you have yourselves become counter-revolutionaries, against reason, against your own interest, against honor?[33]

Regarding the idea of European unity, Proudhon's merit was that he warned European people that the unitary national monarchies and republics of the 19th century could not realize the idea of European unity. The oppositional character of the unitary centralization method and the federalist decentralization method showed this well. The idea of European unity could only be realized in a federal system corresponding to the principle of liberty, as the example of the Swiss federation showed. He believed that authoritarian and centralized states and empires characterizing Europe in the 19th century were not able to realize the idea of European unity, especially not in a period of the colonial expansion of Europe which intensified the fight for power.

4.6 Colonialism of European Great Powers and the Forgotten Idea of European Unity

The democratization process that began with Europe's revolutions continued as liberal free market economic, industrial and financial modernization. Life became more and more comfortable in Western countries and the new capitalist industrial and financial national elites merged with the old aristocratic elite and took over their life style. Free market capitalism was expansive and modernized the classical method of the first period of colonization which was territorial conquest. English liberals generally did not see free market capitalism as a colonial enterprise. It was believed that free market expansion through the free movement of goods, capital, and labor was not colonization because colonization meant the annexation or conquest of territory. Rather, it can be seen as a process of shaping the world economy and market with the necessary participation of all. Consequently someone could be anti-colonialist while defending the imperialist market expansion.[34] But the—as Adam Smith imagined—"invisible hand" directing the rationality of liberal business relations worldwide did not create democracy in world economic relations. Instead, a center-periphery system of rich and poor countries developed in the framework of an emerging capitalist world economy. It seemed difficult to interrupt this development and to start a rational capitalist world economic policy serving the livelihood of people according to federalist idealism. A dissonance has developed between the ideas and principles of the Western system of liberties and reality regarding free market expansion.

---

33 Proudhon, *General Idea of the Revolution in the Nineteenth Century*, 5–6.
34 Merle, *L'Anticolonialisme Européen*, 31.

The second epoch of colonization, marked by laissez-faire market expansion, caused ideological troubles because European colonial powers did not have any colonization policy corresponding to the Western system of liberties. The anticolonial ideas of Crucé, Penn, and Saint-Pierre were not continued. The principles of the Declaration of the Rights of Man and of the Citizen (1789) were changed by the rules of free market capitalist expansion and the ideology of the civilizational missions of Europeans. Colonization happened on a laissez-faire basis, i.e. all kinds of means and methods were used, among them might, wars, unlimited free market expansion, irresponsible legal agreements, or unequal treaties.

Jürgen Osterhammer, for example, researching the role of liberal market expansion in transforming the world, emphasized the necessity to search European history from a global world view.[35] He differentiated three types of colonies that emerged in recent centuries as a result of the expansion of European nations, the United States, and Japan: (1) exploitation colonies; (2) maritime enclaves; and (3) settlement colonies. Exploitation colonies were usually the result of military conquest with the purpose of economic exploitation by means of trade monopolies. The mother country used an autocratic governor system with a paternalistic attitude. In the case of maritime enclaves there was an indirect commercial penetration by fleet actions and an informal control over formally autonomous states ('gunboat diplomacy'). Settlement colonies were the result of militarily supported colonization processes with the aim of utilization of cheap land and labor.[36] Regarding imperialism, Osterhammel emphasized that imperialism allowed for a worldwide protection of interests and for capitalist penetration of large economic areas. He nominated three stages in securing interests in the 19th and the 20th centuries: (1) colonial rule (formal empire); (2) quasi-colonial control (informal empire, limited sovereignty through a mixture of foreign and indigenous administration); (3) non-colonial "determinant" influence (using the economic superiority of the stronger partner to political and military influence of the weaker). The third stage was a typical pattern of relations of international asymmetry in the post-colonial world.[37]

In the second phase of colonization it was generally accepted that a powerful European nation-state had to have colonies as an extension of the motherland. This was regarded as a national interest. To legitimize colonization, Europeans used the stereotype of a civilization mission of the more developed, namely to civilize the less developed, backward people. European colonial powers regarded their values and principles as superior, so the world should follow them. This cultural imperialism was an arrogant, untrue, and racist view that spread widely.[38]

---

35 Osterhammel, *The Transformation of the World*.
36 Osterhammel, *Colonialism*, 10–12.
37 Osterhammel, *Colonialism*, 19–22.
38 Merle, *L'Anticolonialisme Européen*, 33.

Anti-colonialism existed in Europe but had no great influence. The liberal camp was broad and pluralist. Their opposition to colonialism was wide-ranging: some denounced the methods of colonialism; others called for the abolition of the servitude of the colonial peoples; again others considered merging colonial government in the central government by assimilation; and there were those who made the emphasis on the independence of the colonies by granting autonomy.[39]

Adam Smith (1723–1790), Scottish political economist, for example, was anti-colonialist. He was in favor of free enterprise and enforcing market law. He acknowledged that colonization was a huge enterprise that changed the whole world and had a stimulating effect on the economy. At the same time he condemned the cruel means of the colonizers and the oppressive system created by the metropolises.[40] He believed that the free market economy is guided by an "invisible hand" securing the rationality of the enterprises from the point of view of the livelihood of the individual.[41]

Jeremy Bentham (1748–1832), English philosopher and jurist, rejected colonization and was for the emancipation of the colonies. In 1843, in his *Principles of International Law*, he called on the British government to end colonization because it was not in the interest of the British people. Their interest was an international policy based on international law.[42]

John Stuart Mill (1806–1873), British philosopher and political economist, was not against colonization, but criticized its unjust methods. He differentiated between civilized and underdeveloped or stationary people, and believed that the civilization of them was legitimate in the name of improvement. He accepted the rule of colonial administration because it served the improvement.[43] For example, about the Chinese he has written:

> They have become stationary – have remained so for thousands of years, and if they are ever to be farther improved, it must be by foreigners.[44]

Tocqueville criticized the methods of the French colonizers and their misdoings against the Algerian inhabitants, but his critique was not one of systematic anti-colonialism. He criticized colonialism but he accepted the French domination above Algeria as a national interest, in spite of the fact that this contradicted his liberal views expressed above. However, he rejected the French centralization

---

39 Merle, *L'Anticolonialisme Européen*, 30–31.
40 Merle, *L'Anticolonialisme Européen*, 150.
41 Smith, *The Wealth of Nations*, vol. 1, book 4, chapter 2, 456.
42 Bentham, "Plan de paix perpétuelle et universelle," 164; Pitts, *Naissance de la bonne conscience coloniale*, 130, 135.
43 Merle, *L'Anticolonialisme Européen*, 327; Pitts, *Naissance de la bonne conscience coloniale*, 164, 165, 166, 170–171.
44 Mill, "On Liberty," 70.

policy in Algeria. He was for supporting the autonomous local communities and the federal structure.[45]

Proudhon was anti-colonialist, he considered the emancipation of the colonies to be inevitable. He was against the colonization of Algeria, and regarded the British trading methods with China and the possession of India as a crime against humanity.[46]

From the second half of the 19th century the whole world had to face up to a laissez-faire free market expansion and an emerging center-periphery global world system with the wanted or forced participation of everybody. Great Britain and the other European colonial powers made great profits and became enriched. For the non-Europeans it took time to realize what happened and to find answers to the challenge of the Western free market capitalist expansion. The first answer came from Japan which successfully started a knowledge-based modernization and Europeanization during the Meiji reform, and so it could avoid colonization. At the end of the 19th century Chinese modernizers were also involved in the knowledge-based modernization process and were in search of an alternative state socialist economic model to safeguard freedom and independence, as will be discussed below. Africa was colonized by the European powers but its peoples started the independence movement, led by national leaders, in the 20th century, in the framework of Pan-Africanism.[47]

In the third part of the 19th century the laissez-faire free market expansion resulted in the strengthening of competition among the colonial powers. European nation states and national empires fought against each other for more territory, more markets, and more resources for capitalist industrial enterprises. Italy and Germany, the newly unified authoritarian states, also became involved in colonization. The Berlin Conference (1885), which aimed to ensure free trade in Africa, brought a new spirit to colonization by making the emphasis on the spread of European civilization with humanitarian goals. Commercial aims were linked with the statement that greater intervention in Africa would lead to the suppression of the slave trade, and the improvement of the well-being of the native Africans. In reality, the Berlin Conference has contributed to the intensification of the colonial efforts of the European powers who had forgotten to guarantee the autonomous development of the African people.[48]

Expansion and colonization, as national interest, and at the same time the defense of the national independence, dominated European and world policy. The European concert became fragile, and ended at the beginning of the 20th century. Under such circumstances interest in the idea of European unity completely disappeared. When the new wave of colonial expansion intensified the struggle for the final division of the world among the great powers, the First

---

45 Tocqueville, *Sur l'Algérie*, 40–41.
46 Merle, *L'Anticolonialisme Européen*, 356–357.
47 Asante, *The History of Africa*, 259.
48 Worger et al., *Africa and the West*, vol. 1, 237–238.

World War broke out. The Great War of the nations signified the deep crisis of the implementation of the democratic ideas in Europe.

4.7 The Forgotten Europe: The Treaty of Versailles, and the League of Nations

After the First World War, punishment, humiliation, and ruination dominated the peace negotiations. The winners' response was to punish the losers. The idea of European unity and the aim to establish a European union were completely forgotten at Versailles. Three autocratic multinational empires (Habsburg, Ottoman, Russian) collapsed, and as a result of the Bolshevik Revolution, the Soviet Union, a Communist state based on Marxism-Leninism, was created. Vladimir Ilyich Ulyanov Lenin (1870–1924), Russian revolutionary, and the founder of Soviet Russia, recognized the right of all peoples to form an independent state, including the right to secede, knowing that by this he could win the peoples of the disintegrating empires for his own planned Communist world revolution.[49]

In this critical situation the United States, represented by President Woodrow Wilson (1856–1924), appeared on the world political scene and intervened in European affairs by protecting the principle of national self-determination and international organization in a nationalist Europe. In Wilson's ideas, the principle of national self-determination meant the right of a people to choose their own government, that is, the right to self-government and autonomous development: 'government by the governed.'[50] A whole diplomatic revolution unfolded from the struggle of Lenin and Wilson, using the idea of national self-determination to gain influence over the world.

The principle of national self-determination has become a fundamental actor of 20th-century world history. It played a significant role in the management of national conflicts and colonial liberation movements. But the essential problem was that national self-determination was used in a nationalist and not in a federalist interpretation in most cases. This was well exemplified by the disintegration of the Habsburg Empire. It failed because national self-determination was used in a nationalist and not federalist meaning. The victory of nationalism contributed to the fact that the successor small nation-states of the disintegrated Habsburg Empire were not able to develop stable economies and policies. Economic crisis and the depressive misery of the masses were expected.[51]

In the Peace Treaty of Versailles, the principle of self-determination was not used in accordance with the democratic ideas and interpretations. Ideas and political practices were in contradiction with each other, and this led to

---

49 Lenin, *The Right of Nations to Self-Determination*, 568–569, 614; Lenin, *Over het recht der naties op zelfbeschikking*, 48.
50 Schlochauer, *Die Idee des ewigen Friedens*, 150–155.
51 Keynes, *The Economic Consequences of the Peace*, 213.

impasses, dead ends, and hysteria in the organization of society. The Treaty of Versailles was very different from the Peace of Vienna: it was no more the peace of the 'European concert' and of the balance of power. The European concert was seriously damaged, Germany was punished, and the Soviet Union was excluded from the Western system. The dissolution of the Austro-Hungarian Monarchy completely transformed the European balance of power and the economic relations. The treaty created a very sad Europe carrying the germs of another war.[52]

The Treaty of Versailles was cruel, the desire for revenge against the Germans triumphed, the amount of reparation far exceeded Germany's ability, and economic considerations were completely neglected. Germany's colonial empire (colonies in Africa and the Pacific) fell into the hands of the Allied Powers, and each colony became a League of Nations mandate under the supervision of one of them. The same happened with the Middle East provinces of the Ottoman Empire. But it was forward looking that, although the Allied Powers wanted, they were unable to maintain their territorial conquests as colonies because of the struggle of Wilson and the others for national self-determination. The mandate system of the League of Nations placed colonial rule under public control. The Mandatory countries (the Allied Powers) were under international supervision of the League. Their power was legally determined depending on how developed the mandate area was in terms of achieving self-government. The aim was to help these areas gradually become autonomous through counseling, assisting, and helping on the basis of the principle of guaranteeing freedom of conscience and religion of the inhabitants, and to ensure their well-being.[53]

Tutelage was originally interpreted as the end of classical colonialism because former colonizers had to help underdeveloped areas to participate independently in the world economy. In reality, however, this noble goal turned into an aid policy because the colonizing powers did not really want the independence of the colonies. So, the colonies had to continue their fight for freedom in the spirit of self-determination. While the knowledge-oriented Confucian Japan and China were able to get free of the dependent situation, it was more difficult for the peoples of the African colonies because they lost freedom and their independent creative power, as will be discussed below.

Nevertheless, under the given historical circumstances, the League of Nations was a ray of hope for peace and for humanization of power. Its establishment, in 1919, meant an international organization was aiming to shape a modern world order based on international law and limit power claims. But it was a weak construction without obligations and sanctions against the violators of the agreements and the aggressors. It depended on the morality of the participating states on how they used it. The principle of unanimity, and the freedom of exit, weakened the organization. Despite all this the League of Nations represented a meeting place for problem solving for governments using a confederal type of

---

52 Duroselle, *L'idée d'Europe*, 270–272.
53 Article 22 of "The Covenant of the League of Nations (1919)," 172–174.

international law. It showed the way toward a world in which international law and international organization would be decisive.[54]

In the League of Nations, European affairs were not separated from the affairs of the world. But Europeans, if they wanted, could create a European union as a regional part of the League of Nations. However, this proved to be a difficult task because of the power policy of the colonial empires and the strengthening of nationalism.

---

54 Voyenne, "Du printemps des peuples au printemps de l'union," 339–340.

5

THE CRISIS OF REALIZATION OF THE WESTERN SYSTEM OF LIBERTIES AND THE IDEA OF EUROPEAN UNITY BETWEEN THE TWO WORLD WARS

5.1 In the Shadow of Dictatorships

The main problems of the interbellum were related to the previous era. After 1789, the democratic reform ideas were not consequently implemented. The old authoritarian order survived and mixed with the new democratic ideas, and this created a special confusion of thought in the organization of the economy and society. The power struggle continued among the European powers. They wanted to strengthen the nation-state's economies and supplement them with colonial territories. However, laissez-faire liberal capitalism ignored to ensure the fundamental rights of people, and to create an economy serving the well-being of the people, who everywhere had to face to economic crises and misery. Criticizing the liberal ideas and focusing on crisis management, new economic and social organizing ideas and movements emerged. The most important among them were fascism, National Socialism, and Bolshevism. All three set the goal of achieving European unity.

French nationalism, arrogance, and hegemonic behavior wounded the German nationalists and motivated them to demand equality, a real national self-determination, the abolition of the reparations payment, and the revision of the Treaty of Versailles. Hitler, pursuing a policy of national grievances on the basis of the right to national self-determination, gradually established a National Socialist totalitarian military dictatorship based on racial nationalism, and wanted to rule Europe and its colonies from the German imperial center, as will be discussed below.

He was influenced by Benito Mussolini (1883–1945), the leader [Duce] of the Italian fascists, who started the European anti-liberal movement. Mussolini became prime minister as a result of a fascist coup d'état in 1922, and ruled until 1943. He put an end to pluralism by purging all other parties, and from 1924 the one-party government of the National Fascist Party came to power. Mussolini proposed his fascist doctrine aiming to replace liberalism. Instead of laissez-faire free market economy and fundamental rights, he was for an economic and social organization that required order, discipline, and responsible behavior with the goal of securing people's livelihood. For this he used the associative ideas of the federalist functionalist economic policy in the service of a totalitarian state which governed all areas of life under the rule of the Fascist Party and its leader.

Mussolini's thinking was based on the belief that, after the Enlightenment and the Declaration of the Rights of Man and of the Citizen (1789), the 19th century was marked by the liberal idea, which culminated in the 1848 revolutions. But the main actors shaping the history of nation-building were not the liberals, but Napoleon III, Bismarck, and Mazzini, of whom Bismarck's figure particularly impressed him. He was convinced that none of them were liberal. They were nationalists, and used the liberal ideas in favor of establishing powerful centralized monarchical or republican nation states and national empires, instead of democratic federal republican states, and so they could achieve good results. He blamed the classical liberals for the bloody First World War, and the following crisis and destruction. He was convinced that liberalism, pursuing laissez-faire free market economic policy, and having an indifferent moral, had declined. Therefore European politics must be based on the new one-party fascist ideology of strong nationalist nation states because only fascism could ensure the well-being and prosperity of the people. In favor of fascism, he argued that it was not reactionary, and it did not want to return to the pre-1789 social order. The goal of fascism was to shape the world according to the good liberal ideas, discarding the bad ones. Thinking all this, he proclaimed with conviction that the 20th century must be the century of authority and order, the century of fascism, marked by nationalism and collectivism of powerful nation-states.[1]

Mussolini's fascist doctrine promised the masses a new life philosophy based on reality, activity, education, order, discipline, hardness, dignity, and a moral life. The fascist state concept, in his view, represented all these values because it was a synthesis and unity of all values guiding people's lives. It was a new doctrine that was corporatist, based on the efficient performance of the individual, and on functional associations representing the common interest. It represented the pure democracy of the nation, under the auspices of the almighty totalitarian state, instead of the representative parliamentary democracy; it embodied everything because no human or spiritual value existed outside the state. And the fascist state, radiating power was, of course, expansive and imperialist, which Mussolini regarded as a sign of vitality.[2]

The strong one-party fascist state, in his view, was able to defend people and manage a corporate statist economy serving the well-being and prosperity of people because fascism represented collectivism as an organized, centralized, and authoritative democracy. He presented corporatism as a disciplined, state-controlled economy changing classical liberalism. Corporate statism or corporatism was based on corporate groups which were associations of members of different economic sectors (functions) acting as interest groups. These groups participated in national policy under the control of the state which acted as a

---

1 Mussolini, "La doctrine du fascisme," vol. 9, 84–85.
2 Mussolini, "La doctrine du fascisme," vol. 9, 62–75; 76–91.

mediator between the corporate groups, workers, capitalists, and the state interests. The one-party National Council of Corporations was established as the legislative institution of corporatism changing the House of Representatives. According to Mussolini, three things were the conditions for corporatism: a single-party system that united all citizens in a common faith; a totalitarian state leading the transformation; and a historical period of very high ideal tension.[3] The latter was represented by the challenge to solving the economic crisis and securing the livelihood of the masses. Mussolini created jobs and improved well-being by organizing huge loan-based public works that created the illusion of prosperity.

The Italian Constitution of 1848 remained formally in force under his rule, but it was deprived of substantial values by limiting the rights and liberties previously enjoyed the Italian people, and by replacing the parliament with a national corporate assembly under the leadership of the Grand Council of the National Fascist Party. The fascist state was chauvinist, totalitarian, hierarchical, corporate, one-party, anti-federalist, and expansive, and Mussolini became the dictator. Citizens were obliged to serve the nation-state as the highest value.[4]

Fascists and National Socialists rejected the Western system of liberties and the fundamental rights of the citizen. The fascists proposed chauvinistic state forms, and the National Socialists promoted racial nationalist totalitarian state forms in the service of the people's well-being and prosperity. Both were based on chauvinist and imperialist principles, in which socialist theories and moral principles of an 'appearance democratic' rule of law were mixed. Deceived and misled people found the fascist and National Socialist states—that radiated power and order—attractive, and hoped for protection, well-being, and prosperity from them. The question arises: why did they react in this way, and why did they not support democratic federalism?

The Soviet Union, influenced by the Communist Manifesto (1848), represented another model against laissez-faire liberalism, fascism, and National Socialism. It set the goal of creating a Communist state economy based on the equality principle under the one-party centralizing Marxist-Leninist government of the Communist Party (Bolsheviks), continuing the revolutionary process started by the French revolutionaries in the Jacobin period. Lenin, the revolutionary leader and the founder of the Soviet Union, withdraw from the First World War. He wanted to turn the war into a Europe-wide proletarian revolution by transforming the national revolutions into a Bolshevik revolution. His goal was to replace capitalism with socialism, and to establish the rule of the proletariat in the whole world. In the Russian Civil War the Bolsheviks defeated the anti-Bolsheviks, and their opponents were suppressed in the Red Terror. Lenin's New Economic Policy plan aimed to adjust the Soviet economic policy to the capitalist world economic trend. He imagined the Marxist-Leninist proletarian state as a joint

---

3 Mussolini, "Discours du XIV Novembre pour l'État corporatif," vol. 9, 247–263.
4 Bóka, *Az európai egységgondolat története*, 176–178.

state enterprise of the working class led by the Communist Party based on free market capitalism under state control. He wanted to achieve this through industrialization, and the restoration of capitalism and free trading with the participation of the peasants. The goal was to create a Soviet-style state capitalism that would be subordinated to state control and served the proletariat.[5] His death prevented the implementation of this plan.

After Lenin's death, Joseph Vissarionovich Stalin (1878–1953), as the General Secretary of the Communist Party of the Soviet Union, continued the revolution based on Marxism-Leninism and on his own ideas (Stalinism). He continued to reject pluralism and used the means of terror against the opponents of his one-party authoritarian rule. Parallel to all this, he participated in the drafting of the Constitution of the Union of the Soviet Socialist Republics (1936), which was also known as the Stalin Constitution (1936).[6] This constitution used the principles of a multinational federal state drawing on liberal ideas, and aimed to realize the revolutionary ideas of liberty, equality, and fraternity. All this was in sharp contrast to the centralized political practice of the Stalinist dictatorship. This contradictory policy would probably have awaited for a united Europe under the Stalinist leadership.

The Stalin Constitution (1936), which survived until 1977, represented the fundamental law of a socialist multinational state of workers and peasants based on state property, and cooperative and collective-farm property. It permitted small private economy, inheritance, and the citizens' personal ownership of their incomes and of their houses. The economy was directed by a national (state) economic plan with the goal of increasing public wealth, improving well-being, and strengthening security and defense capacity.

The Union of Soviet Socialist Republics (USSR) was formed on the basis of the voluntary association of 16 nationally (culturally) different Soviet Socialist Republics (Union Republics) having equal rights (Article 13). Each Soviet Socialist Republic consisted of Autonomous Regions (Article 22–29).

The highest organ of state authority of the USSR was the Supreme Soviet of the Union of Soviet Socialist Republics (Parliament) embodying the legislative power. It consisted of two chambers: the Soviet of the Union and the Soviet of Nationalities having equal rights. The Soviet of the Union was elected by the citizens of the USSR, and the Soviet of the Nationalities by the Union Republics, Autonomous Republics, Autonomous Regions, and national areas. Each Union Republic had its autonomous constitution and was led by the Supreme Soviet of the Union Republic. A law was considered to be adopted if both Chambers of the Supreme Soviet of the USSR passed it by a simple majority vote.

The highest executive and administrative organ of state authority of the USSR was the Council of People's Commissars of the USSR which was appointed by the Supreme Soviet of the USSR. It was responsible and accountable to the Supreme

---

5 Lenin, "The New Economic Policy," 64–65.
6 "Constitution de l'URSS, 1936," 49–66.

Soviet. The highest executive and administrative organ of state authority of a Union Republic was the Council of People's Commissars of the Union Republic.

To the All-Union competences belonged, among others, defense, foreign affairs, trade, railway, post, telegraph, telephone; coal-mining, oil, iron and steel industry, electrical engineering, chemical industry, and heavy machine building industry; and to the Union Republics competences belonged internal affairs, trade, finance, state security, justice, public health, education, agriculture, and the food industry.

The local organs of state authority in autonomous regions, districts, cities, and rural localities (stanitsas, villages, hamlets, kishlaks, auls) were the Soviets of Working People's Deputies. They were elected by the local people for two years, and directed local life according to the laws of the USSR and of their Union Republic. They were accountable to their electors.

The Supreme Court of the Union of the Soviet Socialist Republics was the highest judicial organ. It was charged with the supervision of the judicial activities of all the judicial organs of the USSR and of the Union Republics. The judges were independent and subject only to the law (Article 112).

Chapter X of the Constitution contained the Fundamental Rights and Duties of the Citizens of the USSR, among them the most important were the right to work and payment, the right to rest and leisure, the right to be cared for in old age and sickness, the right to an education, equal rights for women and men, equality of the rights of the citizens of the USSR irrespective of their nationality or race, freedom of conscience, freedom of religion, freedom of speech, press, assembly and street demonstrations, freedom to form interest associations, and the right to privacy and legal defense.

Citizens had the duty to abide by the provisions of the Constitution and protect common state property.

Representatives at all levels were chosen by the electors on the basis of universal, direct, and equal suffrage by secret ballot (Article 134). There was no racial, national, religious, social, gender, or property discrimination.

The Stalin Constitution (1936) seemed to be modern and democratic, solving such human rights problems that the Western democracies could not; for example, the problem of democratic organization of a multinational state (with mixed population), and the equalization of women. It was modeled after the two-chamber parliamentary system of the United States, and the federal plans of the reconstruction of the Habsburg Monarchy. It granted all manner of rights and freedoms, and represented a number of democratic procedures. But Article 126 led down the right of party domination of the All-Union Communist Party. It made the Constitution a one-party—non-pluralist—constitution based on state property and the rule of the workers. Asserting the leading role of the Communist Party of the Soviet Union, Article 126 cemented the totalitarian control of the Communist Party and its General Secretary, Stalin, if he wanted. Thus a dictatorship was not prevented. But dictatorship required the elimination of pluralism and the opposition. And Stalin felt entitled to do this because, according to him, there was room for only one party in the USSR, and the time of semi-liberal concessions was over.[7] All this was a betrayal of the liberal and federalist reforms, and the fundamental rights represented by the Constitution.

It is difficult to explain the contradictory political behavior of Stalin between liberalism and dictatorship motivated by his fear of loss of power. All the more so, since Stalin himself participated in the drafting of the Constitution, as chairman of the constitutional committee, together with the authors, Nikolai Bukharin and Karl Radek. The goal was to draft the most democratic Constitution in the world. And, as a novelty, the Constitution has worked out the legal institutional construct of a multiethnic bicameral parliamentary federalist state following the footsteps of the American Constitution and the federalists of the Habsburg Monarchy. But, in parallel with the creation of the Constitution, Stalin began the Great Purge of the 1930s. He removed his supposed and potential opponents—political dissidents, bourgeoisie, kulaks, counter-revolutionary workers, non-Soviet nationalists—by using political show trials, imprisonment, killings, executions, forced labor, or concentration camps. He also removed the authors of the Constitution: Bukharin was executed in 1938, and Karl Radek was killed at a labor camp after being sentenced to ten years of penal labor at the second Moscow show trial, in 1937. According to Isaak Deutscher, Stalin's biographer, Stalin sought to portray the totalitarian regime as liberal, and by the Constitution of 1936 he tried to cover up terror with liberal phrases.[8]

The Soviet Union represented the idea of the United States of Europe which meant an extended version of the Constitution of 1936 for Europe led by Stalin. It also planned a Socialist Soviet World Republic based on the Marxist-Leninist and Stalinist one-party, centralized state organization principles aiming to implement the great utopia of a united proletarian world: a socialist world society without exploitation and based on the principles of equality and fraternity.[9] Many Eastern Bloc countries adopted constitutions that were closely modeled on the Constitution of 1936 of the Soviet Union. African national leaders also sympathized with it in the 1960s, while fighting for independence against European colonial rule.

Between the two world wars the idea of European unity became the subject of rivalry among the great powers. National Socialists also aimed at the realization of the idea of European unity following the racial nationalist principle of Hitler's totalitarian German Empire, as will be discussed below.[10]

---

7 Deutscher, *Staline*, 363.
8 Deutscher, *Staline*, 366–367.
9 Heater, *World Citizenship*, 121–124.
10 Chabot, *Origines intellectuelles de l'Union européenne*, 298–302.

5.2 The Idea of Pan-Europa

The democratic federalist reform movement, in the history of the European idea, was launched by Count Richard Nikolaus Coudenhove-Kalergi (1894–1972), a political philosopher with Japanese and Central European family background. It is worth noting the fact that the great dreamer of the European Union came from Japanese and European (Central European) cultures. The meeting of European and Japanese culture in the atmosphere of modernization, and the federalist plans of the Habsburg Monarchy influenced him. The essence of Coudenhove-Kalergi's plan was that Europe (including Central Europe) could only regenerate after the First World War if it became a political and economic regional federation in the framework of the League of Nations.[11] He realized that the Europe of Versailles was chaotic and troubled because European economic cooperation was destroyed after the dismemberment of the Austro-Hungarian Monarchy. The problem of colonization was still present, and the European colonizing powers tried to keep their influence over the colonies. The European states were threatened by three great powers: the United States, the Soviet Union, and Great Britain (British Empire). In these circumstances the destroyed 'European concert' needed regeneration in the form of a European federal union based on European law following the example of the Constitution of the United States of America or the 1848 Constitution of the Swiss Confederation.

Coudenhove-Kalergi launched the Pan-Europa Movement, in 1922, with the aim of creating a European federation following the American or the Swiss example. He published the Pan-Europe program, in 1923, in his political essay *Paneuropa*. According to his ideas global organization would be realized on the basis of five world empires which would be Pan-America, Soviet Union (rather Asian than European), the British Empire, Pan-Asia (with Japan and China), and Pan-Europa. Regarding Pan-Europa, he excluded the Soviet Union and Great Britain from the united Europe. The Soviet Union because it had different state organization principles. Great Britain because it could not subordinate its policy with the Commonwealth to its relations with European countries. This is why he preferred not to see the British in the framework of the Pan-European union. This showed that he realized the difficulties of the creation of a European federation because the European colonial empires did not really want to liberate their colonies, and without this a federation was impossible. With regard to East Asia he was convinced that the European colonial powers had not too much chances for domination there because Japan and China could find answers to the Western challenge of modernization and they could safeguard their independence. In the case of Africa, however, all this was not true. Africa was in a difficult situation in terms of modernization and self-government, and there was a constant conflict among the colonies and the European colonial powers. Therefore, it was a difficult challenge to solve the African problem within the

---

11 Bóka, *Az európai egységgondolat története*, 163.

framework of Pan-Europa. That is why Coudenhove-Kalergi suggested to create Pan-Europa from the democratic European states enlarged by their African dependencies (i.e. continental Europe and its African colonial empire). In his view, Pan-Europa together with its African colonies (Libya, French Africa, Angola, and Congo) would be the fifth great power having sufficient raw material and food to be independent. He imagined Pan-Europa as a common Pan-European economic, business, and civilizing enterprise in the European African colonies which were uncultivated, and where the public utilities were lacking. He stressed that two major tasks should be accomplished: the one, to transform the Sahara into arable land; the other, to eradicate the sleeping sickness. And these tasks, which determined the future of Africa, could not be solved by generals and politicians, but by engineers and doctors. These large-scale tasks required European unity because Pan-Europa, after political conquering had to include Africa both culturally and economically.[12] He saw the establishment of this union as a major common Pan-European project of an economic, modernizing and civilizing enterprise from which both, Europe and Africa, having a common destiny, could profit.[13] His ideas were in harmony with the principles of the aid policy of the mandate system of the League of Nations (Article 22 of the Covenant of the League of Nations) emphasizing to help the well-being, prosperity, and self-government of the colonies.[14] At the same time, he was against another international convention that would have redistributed African colonies among European colonial powers which insisted on having colonies.[15] He also wanted to avoid African countries, fighting for their independence, coming under the influence of the Soviet Union.

Coudenhove-Kalergi thought that, for historical reasons, European peace depended on the solution of the African colonial problem, and this required the creation of a democratic European federation. For this a common European civilizing enterprise, aiming to develop Africa, would be an appropriate framework.[16] He was probably influenced by the Pan-African Movement as well. It signaled the awakening of Africans to self-awareness within the framework of the Pan-African Congresses from 1900, initiated by W. E. B. Du Bois, the most influential African-American intellectual fighting against racism, and for the independence of the African colonies. Du Bois put forward a proposal for the creation of a new state in Africa based on Germany's former colonies. "This would be supervised by the major powers, but also take into account the views of 'the civilized Negro world', a phrase which had mainly African Americans in mind."[17]

---

12 Coudenhove-Kalergi, *Paneuropa*, 22–23, 34–36, 144–145.
13 Fleury, "Paneurope et l'Afrique," 35–45.
14 Article 22 of "The Covenant of the League of Nations (1919)," 172–174.
15 Fleury, "Paneurope et l'Afrique," 43.
16 Fleury, "Paneurope et l'Afrique," 35–36, 42–44.
17 Adi and Sherwood, *Pan-African History*, 48, 49–50.

The Pan-African Congresses (Paris, 1919, London, 1921 and 1923, and New York, 1927), dealt with the topic of colonization of Africa by Europeans. They called for ending colonization, imperialism, slavery, and racial discrimination. The resolutions demanded local self-government, participation of Africans in their own government, native rights to the land and its natural resources, modern education for all children, human rights, and equal opportunity for Africans. The emphasis was on the development of Africa for the benefit of Africans and not merely for the profit of Europeans.[18] The African message to the Europeans, then, was that Europeans should promote the autonomous life and the well-being and prosperity of Africans in their cooperation with Africa. All this coincided in time with the creation of the Pan-European Movement and the publishing of *Paneuropa*. Thus, the African message for Coudenhove-Kalergi meant that *Paneuropa* had to help African countries to become independent and modern because there could be no federation between colonial powers. His Pan-European federation plan showed in this direction because only autonomous people and states were capable to federate.[19]

The Briand Memorandum (1930), which proposed a federal European union, did not take into account Coudenhove-Kalergi's suggestions regarding the European-African cooperation. But the Schuman Declaration (1950) involved the settlement of the African issue, which de Gaulle finally had to solve by ensuring the right to self-determination to the French African colonies, as will be seen below.[20]

Coudenhove-Kalergi imagined the creation of a European federation among the European countries—the center of which would be the French-German cooperation—in four steps:

1. Some of the European states establish a Pan-European convent and its bureau functioning as the center of the movement, and coming to agreement in periodic meetings.
2. Conflict solution by international arbitration.
3. Creation of a Pan-European customs union (abolition of customs frontiers, creation of a finance union).
4. Establishment of the European United States as a constitutional parliamentary federation with two chambers (Völkerhaus and Staatenhaus) following the example of the United States of America. The House of the People (Völkerhaus) would be composed of 300 representatives (1 representative for 1 million inhabitants), and the House of States [Staatenhaus] from the

---

18 Asante, Molefi Kete, *The History of Africa*, 259–266.
19 Coudenhove-Kalergi's Eurafrica concept is discussed. There is also a condemnatory view which states that the aim of Eurafrica was to exploit the colonial minerals and resources in the interest of Pan-Europa and to help European neocolonialism. Montarsolo, L'Eurafrique, 20.
20 Fleury, "Paneurope et l'Afrique," 45, 53.

representatives of the 26 states of Europe. National languages would be equal but English should be a lingua franca [Englische Hilfsprache].[21]

He imagined the Pan-European Union as an autonomous regional union inside the League of Nations.[22] He was for a federative-style world organization of continental regional unions of the states. He believed that the League of Nations should deal with the common affairs of the regional unions. His global geopolitical vision pointed toward a peaceful future in a confusing international situation.

The Pan-European Movement played an important role in the history of the idea of European unity and of the European Union. When Coudenhove-Kalergi started the movement he was alone, only his wife, Ida Roland, helped him. In 1924, the Austrian national council of the Pan-European Movement was organized under the presidency of the Austrian chancellor, Seipel, and vice-presidency of Karl Renner, the foreign minister. The center of the Movement was in the Hofburg. The Pan-European Movement received financial aid from German and Austrian bankers, among them Max Warburg and Brosche. Edvard Beneš, Karl Renner, and the opposition of Mussolini, Benedetto Croce, Gugliemo Ferrero, Albertini, and Carlo Sforza protected the Pan-European Movement. It could establish sections in Belgium, Hungary, Poland, Spain, Bulgaria, Romania, Yugoslavia, Estonia, Latvia, and Lithuania.[23] In New York, in 1926, Coudenhove-Kalergi founded the American Cooperation Committee of the Pan-European Movement. The movement was protected by many artists and writers, among them Paul Claudel, Paul Valery, Jules Romains, Thomas Mann, Heinrich Mann, Rainer Maria Rilke, Stefan Zweig, Guglielmo Ferrero, Sigmund Freud, and José Ortega y Gasset. It played an important role in the opposition to the National Socialism of Hitler, and in the establishment of the European Community.

5.3 Plans for a European Economic Union

The search for a way out of the European chaos and impasse started in the field of economic theories and ideas after the First World War. John Maynard Keynes tried to motivate the theory and practice of the liberal and statist economic theory in the direction of a democratic federalist economic policy. And the economists and politicians supporting the Pan-European Movement (among them Elemér Hantos, Louis Loucheur, Émile Mayrisch, and Aristide Briand) have proposed ideas and plans to create an economic union of European countries.

---

21 Coudenhove-Kalergi, *Paneuropa*, 140–142.
22 Coudenhove-Kalergi, *Paneuropa*, 72–85.
23 Chabot, *Origines intellectuelles de l'Union européenne*, 48–49.

5.3.1 The Dichotomy of Liberal versus Statist Economic Theory

Regarding the economic ideas, during the history of capitalist modernization, two opposing theories developed: the liberal economic theory and the state capitalist theory.

The founder of the modern liberal economic theory, Adam Smith (1723–1790), was for free markets. He published his major work, *An Inquiry into the Nature and Causes of the Wealth of Nations*, in 1776, the year when the American Declaration of Independence was proclaimed, which marked the opening of a new era in world history and economy. Searching for the causes for the wealth of the nation he came to the conclusion that the key to national wealth and power was economic growth. He believed, as mentioned above, that international trade was mutually beneficial and an "invisible hand" would shape the world economy following the interests and needs of people if there was freedom of commerce, of enterprise, of movement of goods, persons, and capital.[24] He recognized the trend of a global world economy as a result of the industrial revolution. The path to this, however, proved to be more complicated than he had imagined in the absence of convergence among the states.

His opponent, Friedrich List (1789–1846), German economist emphasized just that. In his essay on the national system of political economy (*Das Nationale System der Politischen Ökonomie* (1841)) he claimed that Smith's ideas could work only in a global society (in a peaceful world federation), where there was similarity, convergence, and peace among the states. Since this was not the case in his age, he set out to explore the possibilities of fair trade and fair political economy in a world where there were differences between countries regarding their economic, constitutional and geopolitical situation. He came to the conclusion that states should defend themselves against the free market economists, with the help of the governments, and focus on the modernization of the national economies in the framework of state capitalism pursuing import substitutional policy.[25]

Whether List or Smith were right remained an open question. For example, the American statesman Hamilton was for the strengthening of the national economy to counteract British colonization. He developed a dynamic theory of economic development based on the import-substitution strategy of economic development as it was mentioned above. East Asian modernizers, among them Yukichi Fukuzawa, Kang Yu-wei, and Sun Yat-sen, were for state-controlled capitalism that could manage both economic centralization and decentralization. They opposed the liberal market economy and rejected laissez-faire. One can say that the colonizers were for a free market economy, and the states defending their freedom and independence were for state capitalism (statism).

---

24 Smith, *Wealth of Nations*, 456.
25 List, *The National System of Political Economy*, second book, chapter 11, 119–132.

After the First World War and between the two world wars laissez-faire capitalist economy was strongly criticized in Europe. The new ideas for political economy were outlined by the British economist, John Maynard Keynes (1883–1946), who rejected laissez-faire business capitalism. He was for the reform of liberal capitalism and for rules directing the world economy. He believed that (in his words):

> It was not true that individuals possessed a prescriptive 'natural liberty' in their economic activity.[26]

At the same time he suggested avoiding state capitalism and choosing the middle way between the two through specialized coordinating agencies directing the states.

His world economic reform proposal was based on two things: the first was to create autonomies in all those fields where it was possible, and the second was to separate those services which were social from those which were individual. The state had to deal with those things which fell outside the sphere of the individual. In his words:

> The important thing for Government is not to do things which individuals are doing already, and to do them a little better or a little worse; but to do those things which at present are not done at all.[27]

In Keynes' view capitalism was based on the money motive of the individual but, as such, it needed a wise management. He proposed improving capitalism and making it more transparent by the agency of collective action. Transparency was possible through a deliberate control of the currency and of credit by a central institution, and by the collection and dissemination on a grand scale of data relating to the business situation. Investments should be rational and follow the needs of the population. He believed that a bottom-up federalist functionalist system based on personal and local autonomy and the transfer of collective competences toward the larger units, including the state and the above state level, should be the basis of a new economic world system.

He clearly realized that the challenge for the opposition to laissez-faire capitalism was to develop a democratic federalist functionalist world economic policy and to transcend the center-periphery system of capitalism.

5.3.2 Planning European Economic Unity

The economists, industrial entrepreneurs, businessmen and politicians supporting the Pan-European Movement discovered the importance of economic

---

26 Keynes, *The End of Laissez-faire*, 39.
27 Keynes, *The End of Laissez-faire*, 46–47.

functionalism to promote economic cooperation. Influenced by the ideas of Keynes, they represented a new democratic, international economic political thinking in Europe. Among them Elemér Hantos, Louis Loucheur, Emile Mayrisch, and Aristide Briand significantly contributed to the creation of the future European economic union.

Elemér Hantos (1880–1942), Hungarian economist, member of the Pan-European Movement, for example, was for a federalist world economy. In his essay on the World Economic Conference (1927), organized by the League of Nations, he emphasized the importance of concentrating on world economic policy. The goal of the world economic policy should be to motivate people to manage cooperation between the national economies by creating associations and using democratic institutions of coordination and cooperation. This could influence positively world peace as a goal of world economy. He revived the idea of a peaceful world federation in the field of the world economic organization: World economy should be built from bottom-up, starting with the smallest cells, using the federalist method. Its aim should be to serve the livelihood (basic needs) of humankind because economy should not be used for the exploitation of people and should not serve the enrichment of individuals or war purposes. This is why the elaboration of a world economic solidarity would be necessary which could motivate people to cooperate purposefully and make the economic process healthy. It required changing the laissez-faire freedom of the international market, and end the use of war in the service of commercial interests.[28]

Among the promoters of the functionalist economic cooperation, as the first step toward a united Europe, the most influential were Louis Loucheur and Aristide Briand, leading French politicians, and Émile Mayrisch, Luxembourgian industrialist and businessman. They protected functionalist economic cooperation because they realized that industrialists, financiers and businessmen were not interested in protectionism. Their interest was to diminish customs barriers, strengthen the liberal economy based on open markets in Europe and worldwide, and to avoid state interference. They realized also that European unification and the creation of a customs union with a common customs tariff was a good means against protectionism, but it was a difficult task because of the colonies, and of the lack of political union.[29]

In this situation Louis Loucheur (1872–1931), French politician, for example, aimed to promote political cooperation among the European states. He was for the French-German understanding and a European economic and political organization. He realized that French-German cooperation was necessary to secure peace and development in Europe. As a minister of industrial reconstruction of the Clemenceau government, he made suggestions for managing bilaterally the reparations which Germany had to pay to France. Loucher's aim was to create an economic union of European states following the model of the International Steel

---

28 Hantos, *Weltwirtschafts-Konferenz*, band 4, 97, 99, 101.
29 Bossuat, *Histoire de l'Union européenne*, 36.

Cartel which was initiated by Mayrish, as will be discussed below. Regarding his industrial policy, he was for the organization of international cartels in a certain number of industries: metallurgy, electricity, chemistry, textile, and coal. These cartels would be coordinated and controlled by the League of Nations and the nation states to avoid feudal industrial forms. He was convinced that Europe cannot live and prosper without a European political organization.[30]

Emile Mayrisch (1862–1928), a Luxembourgian industrialist, businessman, and a major entrepreneur of the steel industry, was a convinced European. He is regarded as the predecessor of the European construction as the founder of the International Steel Carter, in 1926. The goal of the International Steel Carter was to promote cooperation in the steel industry between Germany, France, Belgium, and Luxembourg. It was regarded as the example for the European Coal and Steel Community which started the European economic integration process. Mayrisch also organized the Comité franco–allemand d'Information et de Documentation (Comité "Mayrisch"), in 1926, with the aim of encouraging the leading politicians to cooperate. It became a Franco-German club of the industrialists. He was also the President of the Luxembourgian group of the Pan-European Movement and he organized the French Economic Commission of the Pan-European Movement at Coudenhove-Kalergi's request.[31]

The most important economic organization in this period was the European Customs Union initiated, in 1925, by Dr Edgar Stern-Rubarth (German), Dr Moritz-Elsas (German), Prof. Ludwig Stein (Berlin), Prof. Irving Fischer (American), Norman Angell (English), Prof. Charles Gide (French), Dr Elemér Hantos (Hungarian), Ernő Bleier (Hungarian), Dr Van Gijn (Dutch), and Prof. Milliet (Swiss).[32] In 1926 and 1927 the first national commissions (German, Hungarian, French) were organized. These were followed by national commissions in Belgium, the Netherlands, Poland, and Czechoslovakia. At the end of 1930 there were 18 national commissions. Among them the French Commission [Comité français de l'Union douanière européenne] was the most influential. Aristide Briand (1862–1932), leading French politician became its honorary President. The supporters of the customs union demanded free exchange and law tariffs (abolition of the tariffs) rather than the establishment of an economic federation. The emphasis was on national sovereignty. European unity played a secondary role until the Briand Memorandum.

The first official political initiative to create a European union came from the French Foreign Minister, Briand, in 1929–1930, who aimed to demolish custom barriers, to rationalize economic competition, to open up markets, to establish a customs union, and to create a big free market among the sovereign states. It was Coudenhove-Kalergi who encouraged him with his open letter written to

---

30 Bossuat, *Histoire de l'Union européenne*, 42–44.
31 Chabot, *Origines intellectuelles de l'Union européenne*, 96–98; Bossuat, *Histoire de l'Union européenne*, 45–50.
32 Brugmans, *L'idée européenne*, 78.

the French parliamentary representatives and published in June 1924.[33] In this he emphasized that Europe must be unified to be able to defend itself against the Soviet Union, the United States, and the British Empire. He proposed them a Pan-European program: a political, economic, and military alliance; an agreement on international arbitration and guaranties; an alliance with England and with the United States, and peace with the Soviet Union and the Far East; a reconciliation with Germany because a strong democratic Germany would be necessary to defend Europe from Eastern invasions.[34] He tried to inspire the French politicians to continue the traditions of the French Revolution and of the Declaration of the Rights of Man and of the Citizen (1789), and called them to start "the revolution of fraternity" with the aim of realization of the European union.[35] Coudenhove-Kalergi's prophetic open letter could influence Briand to protect the establishment of the United States of Europe in the framework of the League of Nations.

In 1929, Briand launched the initiative to create a European economic and political union. He was the first acting head of government in European history who officially protected the idea of a United States of Europe.[36] The "Mémorandum sur l'organisation d'un régime d'Union fédérale européenne, 1930" [Briand Memorandum], proposed for the European governments the establishment of the European political and economic union within the framework of the League of Nations.

> La réalisation d'une organisation fédérative de l'Europe serait toujours rapportée à la S.D.N., comme un élément de progrès à son actif dont les nations extra-européennes elles-mêmes pourraient bénéficier.[37]
>
> The creation of a federal system in Europe would always be placed to the credit of the League of Nations as bringing about progress of which even nations outside Europe could reap the benefit.[38]

He emphasized the need for a general agreement laying down the essential principles of cooperation. He was for the general subordination of economic problems to the political problems. As basic principles of the union he proposed the following:

> C'est sur le plan de la souveraineté absolue et de l'entière indépendance politique que doit être réalisée l'entente entre nations européennes ... Conception de coopération politique européenne comme devant tendre à cette fin essentielle: une fédération fondée sur l'idée d'union et non d'unité, c'est-à-dire assez souple pour respecter l'indépendance et

---

33 Duroselle, *L'idée d'Europe*, 272; Chabot, *Origines intellectuelles de l'Union européenne*, 78–79, 85.
34 Duroselle, *L'idée d'Europe*, 273.
35 Chabot, *Origines intellectuelles de l'Union européenne*, 48.
36 Duroselle, *L'idée d'Europe*, 272, 273–274, 277.
37 Briand, "Mémorandum," 571.
38 [In English] Harryvan and van der Harst, *Documents on EU*, 29.

la souveraineté national de chacun des Etats, tout en leur assurant à tous le bénéfice de la solidarité collective pour le réglement des questions politiques intéressant le sort de la communauté européenne ou celui d'un des Membres.[39]

It is on the level of absolute sovereignty and of complete political independence that the understanding between European nations must be brought about... The principle that the European political cooperation should be directed towards the following essential object: a federation based on the idea of union and not unity—that is to say, a federation elastic enough to respect the independence and national sovereignty of each State while guaranteeing to all the benefits of collective solidarity in the settlement of the political questions affecting the destiny of the European commonwealth or that of one of its members.[40]

Regarding economic policy he suggested the establishment of a common market with the aim of raising to the maximum human well-being, and the rational organization of production and of European exchanges

par voie de libération progressive et de simplification méthodique de la circulation des marchandises, des capitaux et de personnes.[41]

by means of the progressive liberation and the methodical simplification of the circulation of goods, capital and individuals.[42]

Briand's merit is that, in his Memorandum, he proposed to the representatives of the European governments the establishment of a European political and economic union within the framework of the League of Nations based on the sovereignty of the states in the framework of an adequately 'elastic' economic cooperation. In September 1929 he presented his initiative for European union at the annual meeting of the Assembly of the League of Nations. The governments had until May 1930 to answer. The answer was negative. Austria, Germany, and Italy rejected the Briand plan. European governments had many objections to the plan: Great Britain, for example, concentrated on the Commonwealth and did not want to risk her relationship with the dominions; in Germany, National Socialism strengthened and Hitler achieved his first victory at an election (September 14, 1930). In the meantime, in October 1929, the Wall Street Crash started the Great Depression (1929–1945). The nation states raised customs frontiers. Alone, Briand remained in a critical political situation. He lost the elections. Despite all this he continued to fight for peace in Europe. But, in 1932, he died, his plan was forgotten. Europe remained divided and, as a consequence, weak.

---

39 Briand, "Mémorandum," 573, 578.
40 [In English] Harryvan and van der Harst, *Documents on EU*, 30–31, 32.
41 Briand, "Mémorandum," 578.
42 [In English] Harryvan and van der Harst, *Documents on EU*, 32–33.

5.4 The Great Depression and the New Deal of Roosevelt

The Great Depression began in August of 1929, when the economy of the United States first went into recession. The Wall Street Crash of October 29, 1929 (known as Black Tuesday), symbolized the beginning of an economic crisis in the United States and around the world. A decade of high unemployment, poverty, low profits, and deflation started. Parallel to all this economic growth and personal advancement were no longer possible. There was a general loss of confidence in the economic future. All of this happened because the drives of individual will toward wealth and power did not know limits in the money-based business society. Corrupt bank management and immoral businessman were responsible for the Great Depression. In these circumstances many argued the solution would be to find a leader and accept a mild type of dictatorial power for necessary domestic reforms, in the framework of some kind of business—government cooperation.[43]

The new leader was Franklin Delano Roosevelt (1882–1945), the President of the United States who proclaimed a national emergency and introduced extensive reforms to overcome the economic crisis. He entered the White House on March 5, 1933, one day after the German Reichstag placed absolute power in the hands of Hitler. About at this time, Japan seceded from the League of Nations in Geneva. Roosevelt's new method of defense against the crisis and against fascism was represented by the New Deal Movement. The New Dealers (among them the most influential were the theorists of the New Nationalism) wished to cooperate with business, but they distrusted financiers. They determined to eliminate the abuses of the financial system by subjecting it to federal regulation.[44] In this meaning the New Deal, under the first two terms in office of President Franklin Delano Roosevelt (1932–ca. 1940), was a counter-attack against big business capitalism and big corporations with the help of the federal government aiming to defend people from becoming victims of a complicated economic system ending in a devastating crisis.[45]

President Franklin Delano Roosevelt in his *First Inaugural Address on 4 March 1933*, outlined his program. He blamed the business community for incompetent and unethical practices that had led to economic disaster and unemployment.

> The money changers have fled from their high seats in the temple of our civilization. We may now restore that temple to the ancient truths. The measure of the restoration lies in the extent to which we apply social values more noble than mere monetary profit.[46]

---

43 Leuchtenburg, *Roosevelt and the New Deal*, 30–31, 35.
44 Leuchtenburg, *Roosevelt and the New Deal*, 36.
45 Parkes, *American Experience*, 305.
46 Roosevelt, *First Inaugural Address*, 1933, 368.

He was convinced that capitalism needed a moral reform, and the enforcement of social values in the framework of a democratic federal constitutional—and not dictatorial—change.

The New Deal reform focused on the reform of the financial system to prevent depression, on the relief of the unemployed and poor, and on the recovery of the economy back to normal situation. The Emergency Banking Act extended government assistance to private bankers to reopen their banks. Other acts focused on relief, among them, for example, the Federal Emergency Relief Administration dispensed 500 million dollars in aid to the poor, and the Civilian Conservation Corps put 2 million men to work on environmental projects. The National Industrial Recovery Act (NIRA) aimed to reconstruct the industry. The interests of employees and employers were observed. The Agricultural Adjustment Administration boosted farm prices by reducing production. The National Recovery Administration strengthened industry by restraining competitive forces and raising prices. Work Progress Administration (WPA) aimed the elimination of the unemployment problem through publicly financed construction projects. The Tennessee Valley Authority (TVA) was perhaps the most extensive regional planning: construction of hydroelectric power stations, industrial plants, river adjustments, irrigation systems, soil erosion counteracted by reafforestation. The TVA construction program built some thirty flood-controlling dams and 13 power plants that provided cheap electricity to regional consumers. Through the TVA and large public works projects the New Deal stimulated economic development.

The National Labor Relation Act regulated the relations between the employers and employees; workers were granted the right to organize and promote labor union, to bargain collectively and strike. The Social Security Act involved a majority of Americans in a federal pension program, provided funds to the states for unemployment and disability insurance. It set the bases of the American welfare state.[47]

Despite the above-mentioned achievements, by the end of 1938, the New Deal had essentially come to an end because a new economic recession started in August 1937. In early 1938, many Americans once more neared starvation. Journalists began to write of the "Roosevelt Depression." Recession undercut Roosevelt's authority with Congress, and he got almost nothing he asked.[48] Congressional opposition made it difficult for the President to enact any major new programs. The deepening world crisis and the menace of a world war persuaded Roosevelt to prepare for war.[49]

The New Deal reformers believed that liberal business capitalism based on legal and moral principles was a good economic system. From this point of view, one can say that the New Deal reforms helped to educate the businessman to

---

47 Boyer, *United States History*, 546–547.
48 Leuchtenburg, *Roosevelt and the New Deal*, 249–250.
49 Brinkley, *The Unfinished Nation*, 644.

a new sense of social responsibility without changing business capitalism.[50] Roosevelt's merit was that he asked the right questions in a period of the crisis of capitalism. There were Europeans who facing the crisis proposed fascism, National Socialism, or the Stalinist model as a solution. All three were different from the New Deal reform which was not chauvinist, and did not really damage the freedom of capitalist enterprises. The aim was to rescue capitalism with the help of the state as a protector, and to find a balance between big business and big government. New Deal reforms belonged to the struggle of Americans for the right of every citizen to well-being and for the representation of the economic rights of the people by the government. In this meaning the New Deal could be regarded as a struggle for the survival of democracy in a money-based liberal capitalist society. [51]

5.5 The Great Depression and Hitler's Europe

Between the two world wars European society and the economy were in a deep crisis: European hegemony ended after the First World War; the first world economic crisis, the Great Depression, showed that laissez-faire free market capitalist economy could lead to a worldwide economic depression. Its impact on Europe was disastrous. Under these circumstances, many of the protectors of representative parliamentary democracy, among them Arnold Toynbee, Oswald Spengler, Henri Matiss, Paul Valéry, Karl Jaspers, and Ortega y Gasset, believed that the idea of European unity was a remedy against the spiritual crisis of European civilization.[52] But National Socialists, who rejected liberal democracy, also wanted to unite Europe under Hitler's racial nationalist rule and tried to use the idea of European unity to mislead people.

Misery and distress of the masses caused by the first world economic crisis helped Hitler attain power on January 30, 1930, as the leader of the Nazi Party. This meant the end of the Europe of Versailles. All over Europe political, economic, and moral disorder dominated, there was no Europe at that time. For Hitler the world economic crisis meant the bankruptcy of the liberal market economic system, liberalism, and parliamentary democracy. Therefore he believed that he had the right to change the Constitution of the German Reich of August 11, 1919 (Weimar Constitution), and, taking advantage of its weaknesses, gradually transform the democratic constitutional federal parliamentary republic into a totalitarian dictatorship. President Paul von Hindenburg nominated him Chancellor of the German Reich, on January 30, 1933, and this nomination helped to realize his plan.

He achieved his goal with persistent hard work, and almost no resistance.

---

50 Leuchtenburg, *Roosevelt and the New Deal*, 273, 280, 322.
51 Leuchtenburg, *Roosevelt and the New Deal*, 332–333; R. Heffner and A. Heffner, *A Documentary History of the United States*, 377.
52 Chabot, *Origines intellectuelles de l'Union européenne*, 229.

On 28 February, a day after the Reichstag was set on fire on 27 February, the Reichstag Fire Decree (Decree of the Reich President for the Protection of People and State) suspended many of the liberties of the German citizens, among them the rights of personal freedom, freedom of expression, including the freedom of press, the freedom of association and assembly, and the right to privacy. Legally it was based on Article 48 of the Weimar Constitution, the so-called emergency decree, which gave the President broad powers to suspend civil liberties.

It was followed by the Enabling Act [Ermächtigungsgesetz] of 1933 (Gesetz zur Behebung der Not von Volk und Reich/Law to Remedy the Distress of People and Reich) which was passed by both legislative bodies of the Weimar Republic, the Reichstag and Reichsrat, on March 23, 1933. Both houses of the Parliament voted in favor of the law with a majority, and Hindenburg signed it. The Enabling Act accepted that in addition to the traditional legislative role of the Parliament, the Reich government could also pass legislation without the involvement of the Reichstag or consulting with President Hindenburg. Hindenburg died on August 2, 1933, and Hitler attributed the presidential power to himself.

The Enabling Act of 1933 gave Hitler the right to enact laws without the involvement of the Parliament gaining by this way absolute power. It served as the legal basis of his dictatorship. One after another, the most powerful institutions in Germany began to capitulate to Hitler and to disappear without protest.

Fifteen days after having obtained the full power from the Reichstag, Hitler unified the Reich. He removed its traditional federal character by abolishing the separate autonomous powers of the states and making them subject to the central authority of the Reich. So he could achieve the one-party rule of the Nazi Party, under his leadership, as Führer of the Deutsches Reich, and used the Weimar Constitution as the appearance of the legality of his dictatorship. Germany became a totalitarian dictatorship, where the National Socialist government controlled life repealing the Fundamental rights and duties of the German people represented in the Weimar Constitution. [53]

In the midst of the economic crisis, Hitler came to power relatively easily. His totalitarian regime could stabilize the economy by a massive rearmament program, and extensive public works projects which helped his popularity.

Hitler elaborated the National Socialist ideology and set as goal the establishment of European unity under his rule challenging by this the representatives of a democratic federalist Europe, in particular the Pan-European Movement and Coudenhove-Kalergi. His aim was to establish a new Europe with the help of his racist nationalist concept and the revision of the Treaty of Versailles. Based on the theory of the inequality of races, Hitler declared that the German people were superior, therefore, in Germany, they had to annihilate such inferior races as the Jews. He emphasized that the Treaty of Versailles was unacceptable for the superior German people, therefore, the goal of the Germans was to eliminate it, and to establish the Third Reich, to unite the German people, and to

---

53 Shirer, *Le Troisième Reich*, tome 1, 220–221.

gain "Lebensraum" in Europe by conquering the European states.[54] To defeat the Western colonial powers meant also to rule their colonies. Under German leadership Europe and the world would be racially organized and ethnically purified. To achieve this goal Hitler started the Second World War.

Regarding the idea of European unity the National Socialist regime used the tactic of copying the confederalist and federalist plans of European cooperation as a deceptive political tactic. For example, in 1943 Joachim von Ribbentrop (1893–1946), the foreign minister of Nazi Germany planned to proclaim the European Confederation after significant military success. According to his plan on a European confederation the governments of the German Reich, Italy, France, Belgium, The Netherlands, Denmark, Norway, Finland, Estonia, Latvia, Lithuania, Slovakia, Hungary, Rumania, Bulgaria, Serbia, Greece, Croatia, and Spain would decide to form a European Confederation at their meeting after the war. The principles of the confederation would be laid down in a Confederal Act. The objectives of his planned European Confederation included such confederal aims as to give a common destiny to the European people, to guarantee the freedom, political independence and the sovereignty of the member states in internal affairs, to defend the interests of Europe and to protect the European continent, to create a European defense alliance among the member states. He aimed to organize the European economy by the member states on the basis of a uniform plan achieved by a mutual agreement. He planned also to abolish customs barriers and invited other European states to join.[55]

Ribbentrop believed that by proposing a European confederation the enemies of the German Reich would lose their arguments for anti-Hitler propaganda because his plan would dispel all the fears of German occupation. Neutrals would be reassured that they would not be incorporated into Germany. It would give the Russians the impression that all Europe was against them, which would weaken their fighting spirit. It would destroy the best arguments of anti-German propaganda in Britain and America, and they would not be able to act as the liberators of Europe. Several neutrals (Sweden, Turkey, Portugal) would be deterred from too close relations with them. The watchword of 'Europe' would also make it possible to recruit from the Germanic part of the population one or two first-class SS divisions which could be thrown into the battle on the German side. He hoped that if the Führer agreed with the project in principle, the Greater Germanic Reich would come into being at the end of the war.[56]

In reality the Führer was not much interested in Ribbentrop's plan, and he did not want to take his advice. He did not want to enter into a conversation about the New Order in this sense. He regarded the neighbors of the German

---

54 Duroselle, *L'idée d'Europe*, 293–296.
55 "Ribbentrop: European Confederation, 21 March 1943," vol. 1, 126–127.
56 "Ribbentrop: European Confederation, 21 March 1943," vol. 1, 123–126.

Empire as enemies, he wanted to get all that was possible out of them without promising anything.[57]

Hitler definitely rejected Coudenhove-Kalergi's Pan-Europe. He ordered the destruction of the Central Bureau of the movement in the Hofburg (Vienna). Coudenhove-Kalergi had to flee. The truth was that the National Socialist projects on a European confederation, as a political tactic, misused and falsified the European confederalist and federalist principles and aims. Hitler's Europe was never planned as a confederation or federation.

---

57 "Ribbentrop: European Confederation, 21 March 1943," vol. 1, note 7, 126.

6

FIGHT FOR A DEMOCRATIC EUROPE

6.1 Coudenhove-Kalergi and the Pan-European Movement

The Pan-European Movement started to fight against National Socialism. Coudenhove-Kalergi opposed Hitler's *Mein Kampf*, in his *Kampf um Europe*, and aimed to establish a European Party against the Nazi Party. When Hitler came to power (September 14, 1930) his purpose was to construct Pan-Europe. He tried to encircle and isolate Hitler's Germany, and to achieve the failure of Nazism. On October 1, 1932, Coudenhove-Kalergi created the European Party. The Party's program contained six points representing the grand themes of Pan-Europe, which were as follows:

1. A confederation of the European States;
2. A European peace policy;
3. A European customs union;
4. A European social policy;
5. A European freedom policy [une politique de liberté européenne];
6. A European national policy.[1]

However, the realization of this program was delayed because the Pan-European Movement was forbidden in Germany.

Coudenhove-Kalergi was among the first to research and explain the essence of the authoritarian anti-parliamentary and anti-liberal systems of his age. He wrote two important essays on this subject, *Stalin & Co.*, and *Total State – Total Man*.

In his essay, *Stalin & Co.*, about Stalinism, he described Bolshevism as a fanatic, expansive religion. In his view, the Stalinist state was a trust, a huge capitalist enterprise directed by the Communist Party. People were the stockholders, the state was the only employer. As such it seemed to be very strong, and this is why it could provoke fear in the Western capitalist elite. He believed that only the federalist European idea could oppose Bolshevism, which challenged the democratic interpretation of the idea of European unity.[2]

---

1 Chabot, *Origines intellectuelles de l'Union européenne*, 110.
2 Codenhove-Kalergi, *Stalin & Co.*, 3–8.

In his book, *Totaler Staat – Totaler Mensch* (1937), Coudenhove-Kalergi researched and explained the essence of the totalitarian states between the two world wars based on chauvinism, extreme nationalism, or Stalinism. From the point of view of liberty, and the system of liberties, he regarded fascism as a one-dimensional, total system according to the degree of totality because it was limited to politics, and did not extend to the economy and freedom of conscience. He saw National Socialism as a two-dimensional total state in which the full power of the state prevailed in politics and freedom of conscience, while it did not affect the economy based on private property. However, he considered Bolshevism as a three-dimensional total system in terms of human freedom, in which the full power of the state prevailed in the fields of politics, conscience, and economy. Bolshevism denied private property, which he regarded as the main guarantee of individual freedom against total state power. In his opinion, a total state was centralized and told people from above what to do, so people could not be free. Free people needed decentralized, democratic representative parliamentary states built from the bottom-up through a free association policy.[3]

He believed that chauvinism, extreme nationalism, or Stalinism could be defeated only by protecting the idea of fraternity. In his view the political demand of fraternity was federalism, the natural and organic construction of the state by the individuals. Fraternity meant federalism, which started from the individuals and was based on the free associations of individuals following their needs and interests from the bottom-up toward the world federation: individuals created families, individuals and families communities [Gemeinde], communities cantons, cantons states, states continents, and continents the world. A federalist state [Bund von Staaten] was based on the freedom of the individuals, and the autonomy of the composing parts. It rejected centralization from above. The 'revolution of fraternity' [die Revolution der Brüderlichkeit] meant, for him, the realization of liberty, democracy, and federalism in the cooperation among European individuals and states.[4]

Based on his concept of the 'revolution of fraternity,' Coudenhove-Kalergi can be regarded as the follower of Althusius, Penn, Saint-Pierre, Montesquieu, the American Founding Fathers, Tocqueville, and Proudhon, and, first of all, the Swiss Constitution of 1848. Regarding the constitutional system of the European United States he favored following the example of the Swiss Constitution of 1848 instead of the American one. In his book entitled *Europe Must Unite*, he summarized the federalist structure of his planned European union as follows:

> Europe can learn only from a European example – from the Swiss Federation, which has for centuries furnished the laboratory and the test-tubes for the European unification experiment. In any time which we care to foresee, for example, there can be no European president on

3 Bóka, *Az európai egységgondolat története*, 193.
4 Coudenhove-Kalergi, *Totaler Staat – Totaler Mensch*, 182–183.

the American model, but only a European directorate with changing presidency, as in the Swiss Bundesrat . . . Similarly the two chambers furnish a model, one of which, the *Ständerat*, furnishes equal representation for all cantons, large and small, and the other, the *Nationalrat*, equal representation for all Swiss citizens.[5]

In his *Appeal to all Europeans!* September 1939, he called on the Europeans to establish the United States of Europe instead of protecting unrestrained nationalism or Bolshevist internationalism. He was convinced that the realization of the idea of European unity would be the only solution to ensuring a long period of peace, prosperity, and liberty.

The ten points of the Appeal emphasized what the Europeans should do for establishing the United States of Europe.

This Federation must be organized to secure the following fundamental objects:

1. European solidarity in foreign, military, economic and currency policies.
2. An effective guarantee to all the federated states of their independence, integrity, security and equality, and of the maintenance of their national character.
3. An obligation on all European states, regardless of differences in their constitutions, to respect the rights of human personality and the equality of their citizens belonging to ethnic or religious minorities.
4. The peaceful settlement of all disputes between European states by a Court of Justice having at its disposal material and moral means necessary to make its decisions respected.
5. The establishment of a European institution designed to help state members of the Federation to meet their monetary and financial difficulties.
6. The progressive suppression of inter-European economic restrictions which are wrecking and ruining the European market.
7. A constructive plan for the necessary transition from war production to peace production designed to avoid the risk of unemployment.
8. The systematic organization of collaboration in colonial matters with a view to fitting colonial raw-materials and markets into the economic complex of Europe.

---

5 Coudenhove-Kalergi, *Europe Must Unite*, 147–149.

9. The maintenance of and respect for the political, economical and cultural links uniting various states of Europe with other parts of the world.
10. The promotion of international peace by collaboration with the British Dominions, the American Continent, the Soviet Union and the nations of Asia and Africa in a world-wide organization.[6]

In his vision the realization of these ten points could restore the Europeans to the principles of the Declaration of the Rights of Man and of the Citizen (1789), and the European states could follow the path of the Western system of liberties in their state and international organization. The establishment of a European parliamentary federation could be the start of a new Europe. Regarding human rights, his ideal was the shaping of a common moral codex of humankind composed of free individuals who were able to reject authoritarian and totalitarian types of states.

Another member of the Pan-European Movement, Thomas Mann (1875–1955), German writer, drafted an appeal to establish a European federation of free people, in 1943. He emphasized that the idea of European unity had been misused during European history because of nationalism. What Hitler did was only the culmination of all these lies. He sharply distanced himself from the Europe of Hitler, emphasizing that he was for a European Germany and not for a German Europe, a Europe dominated by the Germans.[7]

Ortega y Gasset (1883–1955), Spanish philosopher and essayist, who was also a member of the Pan-European Movement, in his essay, entitled *The Revolt of the Masses* (1930), explained the rejection of the parliamentary democracy by the masses as follows:

> Europe had created a system of standards whose efficacy and productiveness the centuries have proved. Those standards are not the best possible; far from it. But they are, without a doubt, definite standards as long as no others exist or are visualised. Before supplanting them, it is essential to produce others. Now, the mass-peoples have decided to consider as bankrupt that system of standards which European civilization implies, but as they are incapable of creating others, they do not know what to do.[8]

So, in his explanation, people did not know what to do during the world economic crisis. They embraced Fascism and National Socialism instead of a rational democratic association policy leading toward a European federation. The question arises: why? Why could the masses believe in dictators creating totalitarian systems?

---

6 Coudenhove-Kalergi, *Europe Must Unite*, Annex, 158–160.
7 Mann, "Aufruf zur europäischen Föderation, New York, 29. Januar 1943," 470–471.
8 Ortega y Gasset, *The Revolt of the Masses*, chapter 14.2, 134.

6.2 L'Ordre Nouveau and Personalist or Integral Federalism

Parallel with the Pan-European Movement, the personalist or integral (incremental) federalist movement emerged in France during the 1930s opposing the anti-democratic and anti-liberal tendencies (nationalism, extreme nationalism, Fascism, National Socialism, or Bolshevism). They were in search of a society that could avoid both the anarchy of individualism and the oppression of non-personalist collectivism. Personalist or integral federalism was based on the ideas of the above-mentioned Proudhon. The personalist movement developed in two intellectual organizations known as "L'Ordre Nouveau" and "Esprit" which also published reviews on the same name. They were led by a small group of highly influential philosophers, among them Alexander Marc, Robert Aron, Emmanuel Mounier, Daniel Rops, and Denis de Rougemont. Henri Brugmans joined after the end of the Second World War. His experience in the Resistance Movement converted Brugmans to personalism. Jacques Delors also belonged to the personalist or integral federalists. After the Second World War the members of this movement organized the New European Movement of personalist or integral federalists in the framework of the Union of European Federalists. They played a leading role at the Hague Congress in 1948, which launched the new Europe as will be discussed below.

L'Ordre Nouveau was a nonconformist movement aiming to create a new order. It contributed highly to the federalist theory and practice of European integration as integral or personalist federalist theory besides the constitutional federalist theory represented by Altiero Spinelli, and the constitutional European parliamentary federalist theory of Coundenhove-Kalergi. It dealt with the relationship and interaction between the person and society, concentrating on the question of how to defend personal autonomy against individualism and totalitarianism. L'Ordre Nouveau rejected both the individualism of the 19th century and the collectivity of totalitarianism (Communist or Fascist) of the 20th century. At the same time, it criticized liberal capitalism, too. L'Ordre Nouveau emphasized that, although the contact between the person and society was lasting, there existed a permanent tension between them which was useful and creative. Society had to be organized in the service of persons searching balance and harmony between independence and involvement (rights and duties). The goal of the L'Ordre Nouveau movement was to gradually build up a new society in which politics served the person by defending and supporting personal autonomy. Under the influence of Proudhon the movement proclaimed adhesion to federalism. It regarded family, local community, and region as the associative units of a decentralized social organization. Its concept of nation did not merge nation with the state or administrative borders, so avoiding nationalism.[9]

The federalist conception of the movement was not based on a simple decentralist or regionalist policy in the framework of nation-states. It refused to base

---

9 Loubet del Bayle, *Les non-conformistes des années 30*, 366–371, 386–393.

federalism on the simple association of nation-states. The League of Nations and the Briand plan showed them that something like this was a false path. They also rejected the 'pyramidal federalism' aiming to assemble all of society, community, and region in a solid hierarchy from the bottom-up because this could sterilize the necessary tensions among the different poles of the federation. Personalist federalists favored a personalist regional organization of Europe through free associations, composed of many blocks and based on the diversity and pluralism of the social and cultural life of a federation. They were for the creation of a supranational organism to coordinate the production and to distribute the products which were necessary to ensure a subsistence wage.[10]

L'Ordre Nouveau was critical enough about colonization as the product of capitalism in imperialist form. It rejected all forms of colonialism as illegitimate.[11]

The *Manifest of the L'Ordre Nouveau* (1931) defined the intellectual group as nonconformist and revolutionary. The group searched for the answer to the question of how to avoid a meaningless economic and national war in the midst of a revolutionary situation created by the world economic crisis. They were convinced of the necessity of the construction of a new world order which concentrated on human persons, in which the economy, social mechanisms, and scientific discoveries served the person, which abolished liberal individualism and all doctrines placing the state, in whatever form, in prime position, which served the livelihood of the people, which concentrated on the creative work, which shattered the abstract national frameworks, which pursued decentralization to assure the liberation of all patriotic tendencies manifesting the relationship of man with the earth, race, tradition, and culture.[12]

For a new order L'Ordre Nouveau represented, among others, the following principles: personalism, decentralization, anti-statism, respect of the human person, and of human rights, rejection of exploitation, oppression, and slavery, anti-productivisme (the aim of a civilization cannot be just to produce goods), the right to property (but rejection unrestrained profit making). It was for institutional and technical development serving people. [13]

The most notable characteristic of the movement was anti-statism [antiétatism]. It defined the state as an organism of violence. Regarding the independence of the groups and the freedom of persons, its mistrust of the state was extreme. Therefore L'Ordre Nouveau tried to reduce the role of the state (first of all state interventions) to the minimum. Its aim was a society based on the real interests and necessities of people. These were best represented in specialized local and corporative frameworks which could avoid people being passively governed.[14]

---

10 Loubet del Bayle, *Les non-conformistes des années 30*, 396–398.
11 Loubet del Bayle, *Les non-conformistes des années 30*, 401.
12 Loubet del Bayle, *Les non-conformistes des années 30*, 490–492.
13 Loubet del Bayle, *Les non-conformistes des années 30*, 496–497.
14 Loubet del Bayle, *Les non-conformistes des années 30*, 403, 404, 408, 409.

The personalist or integral federalists were thinking about a society that was organized bottom-up, based on the association policy among persons concerning the real needs and interests of the livelihood of the persons. They believed that the European system of liberties should be developed in this nonconformist direction surpassing all the former authoritarian and centralizing state forms of the past, including the nation-state. Personalist federalism was not an abstract theory but an active nonconformist associative life program for everybody: a search for the humanization of power, and for a peaceful economic and state organization serving the well-being and prosperity of people.

6.3 The Resistance Movement—Launching the Policy of a European Democratic Federation Based on the Idea of Liberty

The need to create a European union became a political program of the Resistance Movement. The members of the Resistance Movement, during the Second World War, fought on the side of the Allies against the Axis powers (Germany, Italy, Japan). The Soviet Union also joined the Allies in June 1941, and China did the same. They defended their countries and people against the totalitarian military dictatorship built by Hitler aspiring to rule Europe and the world. In the midst of the horror of the war all the participants of the Resistance Movement were for a European federation which they aimed to establish after the end of the war.

The program of the new federalist Europe was formulated by *The Ventotene Manifesto* (1941) written by Altiero Spinelli and Ernesto Rossi, Italian antifascists. Altiero Spinelli (1907–1986) was an Italian federalist political thinker, one of the most important leaders of the international Resistance Movement and Founding Father of the European Union. He declared himself a follower of the discussions of *The Federalist Papers* and of the American Constitution of 1787 as examples for European social organization after the Second World War. He founded the European Federalist Movement that adopted *The Ventotene Manifesto* (1941) as political program.

The Manifesto declared the principles of a new Europe based on the principle of liberty:

> Modern civilization has taken as its specific foundation the principle of liberty which says that man is not a mere instrument to be used by others but that every man must be an autonomous life centre.[15]

It meant that the new Europe broke with the colonial past and all kind of exploitation. Its purpose was to realize popular sovereignty, democracy, and federalism. The manifest called for the creation of a steady European federal state with

---

15 Spinelli and Rossi, "The Ventotene Manifesto," vol. 1, 473.

the participation of everybody. It called for a democratic reform of social organization based on the principle of liberty.

Spinelli and Rossi highly appreciated the principle of liberty which played an important role in the development of democratic civil states. In their view, the laissez-faire free-market capitalist expansion deformed civil state development because authoritarian and totalitarian states emerged as a consequence of the fight for power and markets during colonial expansion. States became absolute sovereign, nationalist, aiming to dominate, without regard for the damage this might cause to others. *The Ventotene Manifesto* (1941) concluded that the nation-state system after a period of progressive results ceased to be progressive and resulted in totalitarian nation-states in Europe. Therefore, the main division in Europe was between the supporters of national sovereignty and the supporters of the creation of a solid international state. The former used national power for achieving international unity. But international unity could only be achieved by establishing a single federal state in which each state would retain the autonomy it needed on the basis of subsidiarity.[16] The new Europe should be a federalist state with a European army and an economic community.

The common project, of the members of the Resistance Movement, the Geneva Declaration, was born at a secret meeting of the Danish, Norwegian, Dutch, Polish, Czechoslovak and Yugoslav antifascists in Geneva, in 1944, and Spinelli drafted it. Their aim was to respect human rights; to create social justice; to promote collective well-being; to secure the independence of national life, but at the same time to limit the absolute independence of the states. The most important purpose was to transcend the dogma of 'indivisibility of state sovereignty' and to establish a European constitutional federation with a European government accountable to the people, and to make a federal army.[17]

In his *Note de réflexion (Alger, 20 août 1943)* Jean Monnet (1888–1979), French political economist, diplomat, and Founding Father of the European Union, suggested that Europe, or a part of it, should be organized into an economic unit, right at the end of the war, ending economic nationalism. The new economic life should be launched by the individual states because there were no international organizations that could do this work. They had to revive agriculture, create jobs, and start production. All this meant that the individual states would be organized from the bottom-up, from the level of the local governments, into economic units. Jean Monnet believed that, because the new national economies would not raise tariffs against one another, export and import restrictions would be meaningless and so a common market could be developed.[18]

---

16 Spinelli and Rossi, "The Ventotene Manifesto," vol. 1, 479.
17 Voyenne, *Histoire de l'idée européenne*, 180–181.
18 Lefort, *Une Europe inédite*, 46.

7

IN SEARCH OF A NEW EUROPE: THREE ALTERNATIVES

After the Second World War it was realized that the economic and social organization values and principles of the capitalist market economy should be formulated in such a way as to serve the peace and prosperity of mankind. The centuries-old idea of a peaceful world federation and the ideas of the Declaration of the Rights of Man and of the Citizen (1789) were revived. They inspired the renewal of the League of Nations and the creation the United Nations Organization (UN). The Charter of the United Nations (1945) renewed international law. The Universal Declaration of Human Rights (1948), which rejected imperialism, colonization, exploitation, slavery, and racism, was adopted by the United Nations General Assembly in 1948.[1] The United Nations became the 'conflict-solving house' of the member states, bringing about peace-keeping and international arbitration in the framework of the Security Council. Its objective also included providing humanitarian aid in cases of famine, natural disaster, and armed conflict. Freedom and human rights became the driving forces of the organization as the Universal Declaration of the Human Rights (1948) expressed it.

The UN represented the idea of a world union of sovereign nation-states based on intergovernmental cooperation. As a novelty it realized economic functionalism in the framework of the independent specialized agencies working together with the Economic and Social Council (among them the International Monetary Fund (established in 1945), United Nations Educational Scientific and Cultural Organization (1946), World Health Organization (1948), and World Bank Group (1944)). The United Nations also paved the way for geographical regionalism because the Economic and Social Council had European, African, Latin-American, and Asian regional commissions. So a European union would be imagined as the regional part of the United Nations.

The UN tried to solve the problem of laissez-faire commercial exploitation through the establishing of an International Trade Organization in its 1947 Conference on Trade and Employment. But all this failed, and the General Agreement on Tariffs and Trade (GATT) was created instead. The participating countries (among them Belgium, Luxembourg, France, United Kingdom,

---

[1] "Charter of the United Nations, 1945," 1–34; "Universal Declaration of Human Rights, 1948," 250–256.

United States, Australia, Canada, Czechoslovakia, India, Republic of China, Burma, Brazil, Chile, Pakistan, Syria, South Africa, and Southern Rhodesia) sought to use trade to raise standards of living, ensuring full employment by "reciprocal and mutually advantageous arrangements directed to the substantial reduction of tariffs and other barriers to trade and to the elimination of discriminatory treatment in international commerce."[2] GATT remained in effect until 1995 when the World Trade Organization was established.

The UN made the emphasis on decolonization and played an important role in it. In this respect the most important was that the UN Charter placed the right of self-determination in the framework of the international law. Chapter 1, Article 1, part 2 stated that the purpose of the UN Charter was:

> To develop friendly relations among nations based on respect for the principle of equal rights and self-determination of peoples, and to take other appropriate measures to strengthen universal peace.[3]

The remaining Mandates of the League of Nations were placed under the trusteeship of the United Nations as United Nations Trust Territories, under the administration of the UN Trusteeship Council, with the perspective to become independent. Regarding the non-self-governing territories the UN Charter (Chapter XI, Article 73) laid down as a guiding principle the promotion of the well-being of the inhabitants of these territories and the achievement of self-governance.[4]

UN Declaration on the Granting of Independence to Colonial Countries and Peoples (1960) rejected colonization as a denial of fundamental human rights and affirmed the right of all peoples to self-determination. It proclaimed that colonialism should be brought to a speedy and unconditional end. It declared also that Trust Territories and non-self-governing territories should enjoy complete independence.[5]

In the spirit of the renewed international law, colonies were gradually liberated or came under the tutelage of the Western developed countries with the perspective of achieving self-government. Former colonial policy was changed into developmental aid policy. Liberal free market capitalism based on the universal human rights and aid policy toward the developing countries changed the image of the colonial world. So the obstacles, represented by the direct colonial rule, disappeared. The international system started to be reformed in the direction of democracy among states. But the post-colonial world has retained forms of manipulation, exploitation, and cultural expropriation, even if colonialism

---

2 "The General Agreement on Tariffs and Trade (GATT)," Preamble, 1.
3 "Charter of the United Nations," chapter 1, article 1, part 2, 3.
4 "Charter of the United Nations," chapter 11, article 73, Brownlie, 23–24.
5 "Declaration on Granting of Independence to Colonial Countries and Peoples, 1960," 298–301.

itself has disappeared.[6] The old fight for power continued in the framework of sovereign nation-states and of the center-periphery world economic system of poor and rich countries, in the midst of the Cold War conditions of the bipolar world. All these made difficult and controversial a democratic renewal, and at the same time encouraged the creation of the European Union.

From the ideas of the United Nations the functionalist intergovernmental regional union, decolonization on the basis of national self-determination, human rights, and economic functionalism contributed to the reviving of the idea of European unity.

After the Second World War there were three alternatives for Europe to investigate:

1. To promote Atlanticism in cooperation with the United States as a world power.
2. To revise the legacy of European colonization, and—focusing on the old Eurafrica plan—to create a Eurafrican common market as a cooperation with the African colonies of the European countries based on democratic principles.
3. To become a great power on the basis of Europe's own democratic forces.[7]

All three alternatives were active in political life: Atlantic cooperation was realized in the framework of the North Atlantic Treaty Organization (NATO) and was a constant topic; the Eurafrica plan, which regarded the African colonies as the economic and geographical extension of Europe, was active until the liberation of the colonies (around 1960), and it was forgotten later; the construction of a democratic European union, as a great power, proved to be a permanent challenge.

7.1 Atlantic Cooperation

As for Atlantic cooperation, Europeans had to face a bipolar world. In 1945, after the Second World War, there was no clear peace treaty because the great powers could not agree with one another. The final arrangement of post-war Europe happened only after 1949 on the basis of the frontlines of the individual armies at the end of the war and of the conventions concluded during the peace talks. Europe was gradually divided into two opposing camps, the Communist East, under the influence of the Soviet Union, and the Democratic West, under the patronage of the United States of America. This was due to the incompatibility of the state organization principles and to power aspirations. Europe was in a dependent situation between two world powers. To safeguard independence and secure peace demanded the union of the European states.

---

6 Osterhammel, *Colonialism*, 119.
7 Guieu et al., *Penser et construire l'Europe*, 193.

Europe's reconstruction started with the American aid plan in Western Europe. The Marshall Plan (officially the European Recovery Program) operated for four years from 1948. The goal of the United States was to rebuild European economy, promote cooperation among the Western European states, remove trade barriers, modernize the industry, help European prosperity, and prevent the spread of Communism. The countries of Eastern Europe, belonging to the Soviet Bloc, did not participate.

The period of the Marshall Plan was positive for Western Europe because the economy could recover rapidly. But its influence on the future perspective of European integration was controversial from the point of view of dependence, development, and unification.[8] The question could be raised whether the intellectual force, the technological and innovative knowledge, and the élan of the reconstruction after the Second World War, which contributed to the successes of the Marshall Plan, would not be enough for renewing Europe from its own forces.

Researching the real nature of the Marshall Plan, history showed that it started as an economic modernization aid. But because of military threats it became a development aid that served the interests of the North Atlantic Treaty. So, economic development aid became military aid. NATO was created as a means of defending Western Europe against an armed attack from the Soviet Union. It was organized on a bilateral basis and assured mutual military help in the case of attack for each member state. There was nothing supranational in its structure. European powers agreed to fuse economic and military aid because of their fear of the Soviet Union.

In these circumstances the Organization for European Economic Cooperation failed to realize its original aim which was the unification of Western Europe. NATO made it difficult to create a supranational European defense community or a common foreign policy, as will be discussed below. Without a European supranational defense and security community European countries remained dependent on the United States. The Marshall Plan failed in one of its essential goals which was the unity of Europe. The Americans and the Europeans restored the economic cooperation in the Western part of Europe but they did not create the United States of Europe.[9]

7.2 Confronting the Legacy of Colonization— "Eurafrica" in a Decolonization Perspective

Another alternative was to confront the legacy of European colonization, and by focusing on the old Eurafrica plan to create a Eurafrican common market based on democratic values and principles.

---

8 Bossuat, *L'Europe occidentale à l'heure américaine*, 15, 232, 237.
9 Bossuat, *L'Europe occidentale à l'heure américaine*, 254–255, 285, 303.

As for the legacy of European colonization, Denis de Rougemont (1906–1985), one of the leading theorists of a new personalist federalist Europe, warned in the 1960s that the issue of assessing colonization has not yet been addressed in European thought. He was of the opinion that colonization was a complex phenomenon and judging it from a historical perspective was a difficult but necessary task. It was complicated because the capitalist modernization that accompanied colonization had good and bad results. To the bad side belonged exploitation, slavery, racism, nationalism, and a superior mentality. On the good side were the spread of modern civilization, the humanitarian theories, and the idea of freedom. He considered the colonial problem to be complicated because those who condemned the West have also been involved in the progress made by it. And the process of decolonization showed that the influence of the West was present because liberated colonies continued to copy the Western political, social, technological, and industrial model and law. Many of their leaders have adapted European ideas with their mistakes (nationalism, racism) and at the same time defended themselves against Western immorality in the spirit of the Western idea of liberty. Rougemont morally condemned colonization as a criminal act, but was of the opinion that European ideas also meant progress for the colonies. He emphasized that the advocates of federal union have always maintained that one of the outstanding effects of the European union would be to remove any temptation to imperialism or even colonialism.[10] This is why he believed that it was the duty of Europeans to correct their mistakes and renew themselves by creating a European federation.[11]

In his view Europe had three main periods of modernization: the French Revolution and the abolition of feudalism was the first; the second was the Hague Congress (1948) and the launching of the European integration process when Europe's mistakes were realized and the improving started; the third should be the creation and spread of the personalist federalist European Union. He believed that the gradual realization of the idea of personal federalism through a bottom-up democratic reorganization of the European society was the best way to solve European mistakes (nationalism, racism, exploitation, a superiority mentality), and the problems caused by laissez-faire free market economic colonization, the center-periphery system of world economy, and the dilemma of fictive versus real economy. But was it possible to transcend colonialism and avoid neo-colonialism?

The challenge of revising the old Eurafrica plan and creating a Eurafrican common market so that the African colonies could cooperate with European countries required a break with colonization and the recognition of the independence of the colonies. But the truth was that the European governments did not really want to liberate their colonies. This fact, for example, has provoked

---

10 Rougemont, *The Meaning of Europe*, 67–68, 96, 97–100.
11 Rougemont, *The Meaning of Europe*, 112.

recently a debate on the Eurafrica plan.[12] Regarding the history of the idea of European unity, Patrick Pasture drew attention to the importance of this problem emphasizing that the European Communities aimed to safeguard the colonies of their member states which contradicted the values and principles of the European integration.[13] Although this thought-provoking debate is beyond the scope of this book, it is still important to address how the plan of a Eurafrican common market in the French policy, which was primarily interested in reforming the cooperation with its African colonies in the direction of decolonization, appeared in accordance with the principle of national self-determination.[14]

French policy realized that the classical colonial methods, and the governor's system directing and exploiting subjects from the metropole, had to be given up. General de Gaulle, for example, believed that without African cooperation, during the Second World War, France could not become independent. At the Brazzaville Conference (1944), as a new direction of the French colonial policy, he emphasized the integration of the colonial population into the French community as a result of their own development. But the Brazzaville Conference explicitly stated that the establishment of self-government in the colonies needed to be avoided.[15] French politics sought to safeguard its influence and control over the African colonies within a Franco-African Community that aimed to establish close economic relations, supply France with the missing raw materials, and to avoid the Communist influence in Africa.[16] Thus the French, instead of recognizing the national self-determination and independence of their African colonies, promised them semi-autonomy within the framework of a French Union under French domination. The novelty was the emphasis on helping the development of the independent political and economic personality of the overseas countries and territories, the creation of close links between them and France, the establishment of semi-autonomous assemblies in each colony and the representation of the colonies in the French Parliament, equal rights of the citizens of France's colonies with the French citizens, and economic reforms to diminish the exploitative nature of the relationship between France and the colonies.

The French Constitution of the Fourth Republic (1946), based on these ideas established the French Union replacing the French colonial system (the French Empire). The French Union, uniting France and the overseas countries and

12 Rodney, *How Europe Underdeveloped Africa*; Montarsolo, *L'Eurafrique*; Hansen and Jonsson, *Eurafrica*.
13 According to Patrick Pasture, the association of 'overseas territories' with the ECs was "part of a (neo-) colonial project in which the ECs would benefit from the exploitation of Africa's resources in return for the latter's 'development'—mainly to create a market for European products. This the current Europe (not just the EU) has conveniently forgotten; it does not fit well into the contemporary discourse of Europe as a moral beacon and origin of universal values of humanity and enlightenment, and the EU as global harbinger of peace, human rights and sustainability." Pasture, *Imagining European Unity*, 197–198.
14 Coquery-Vidrovitch, "Economic Changes in Africa in the World Context," 297–300.
15 Rodney, *How Europe Underdeveloped Africa*, 278.
16 Bourgi, *Le Général de Gaulle et l'Afrique Noire*, 112–123.

territories, was based upon the principle of equality of rights and privileges, without distinction as to race or religion. It meant the formal end of the 'indigenous' status of French subjects in colonial areas. All subjects of the overseas territories became citizens with the same status as French nationals of Metropolitan France. The Preamble rejected any system of colonization based on arbitrary power. It stated, as a matter of principle, that the aim of France was to establish the French Union, in the framework of which nations and peoples were placed in common and coordinated their resources and their efforts to develop their civilizations, further well-being, and ensure security. France's mission was to guide the peoples of the colonies toward freedom and democratic administration of their own affairs.[17] Thus in the framework of the French Union a common market was outlined based on these principles without declaring the right to self-determination of the colonies.

In reality, the Constitution of the Fourth Republic (1946) marked only minimal progress toward political representation for Africans. Only Senegal had a representative in the French National Assembly by Léopold Sédar Senghor. The whole union was seen as an extension of the French Republic. Alongside the democratic language of citizenship, representation, and the rights of men there was a clear determination to assure metropolitan preeminence in all organs of the government. But all this was covered by the French republican colonial myth, the essence of which was the unifying force of the single and indivisible French nation-state that was extended to the colonies. This suggested that France would establish a democratically organized community, modern political life, and economy in its colonies and that the colonies would gradually become autonomous members of a French federation. But the Constitution did not fulfill this promise because it maintained French power and authority in the colonial world and represented the needs of the metropolitan group. Thus, the colonial new elite of native leaders was frustrated, and because they did not achieve freedom and equality they chose to fight for rights instead of serving the French colonial myth.[18]

They could achieve the framework law of 1956: France's overseas minister, Gaston Defferre, gave the countries of French Equatorial Africa (AEF)[19] and French West Africa (AOF),[20] belonging to the French Union, internal autonomy with local assemblies elected by universal suffrage, but this was not enough.

17 Godechot, *Constitutions de la France*, 390.
18 Marshall, *The French Colonial Myth*, 301–302, 312, 315.
19 AEF: French Equatorial Africa (Afrique-Équatoriale française), or the AEF, was the federation of French colonial possessions in Equatorial Africa, extending northwards from the Congo River into the Sahel, and comprising what are today the countries of Chad, the Central African Republic, the Republic of the Congo, and Gabon.
20 AOF: French West Africa (Afrique-Occidentale française, AOF) was a federation of eight French colonial territories in Africa: Mauritania, Senegal, French Sudan (now Mali), French Guinea (now Guinea), Ivory Coast, Upper Volta (now Burkina Faso), Dahomey (now Benin), and Niger. The federation existed from 1895 until 1958.

De Gaulle understood the problem and tried to shape the French Union in the direction of the principle of national self-determination. All this was motivated by the fact that it was difficult to imagine cooperating with the European Communities, which were under organization, without recognizing the independence of the colonies.

By 1958, the situation changed in West Africa, separation from the French metropolis had accelerated, the colonies demanded the right to self-determination because they wanted to become independent. Cooperation with Algeria failed, and the Algerians fought a bloody war (1954–1962) to achieve independence. In 1958 the French Fourth Republic collapsed because of the Algerian War of Independence, and de Gaulle returned to power. He tried to continue his West African policy in line with the above-mentioned Defferre framework law of 1956. But the West African intellectuals, fighting for independence, forced him to change his policy. On September 28, 1958, in a referendum, de Gaulle offered the territories of the French Union a choice between complete independence from France or full internal self-government as fellow members with France of a French Community. All colonies voted for full internal self-government, except Guinea, and remained fellow members of the French Community.[21]

The French Constitution of October 4, 1958, recognized the right to self-determination of the people of the overseas territories.[22] The French Community became a registered entity in the Constitution (1958) of the Fifth Republic (Title XII. On territorial communities). It had a hybrid politico-legal form: it was chaired by General de Gaulle, the executive was represented by a Council made up of the Prime Minister and the heads of government of the Member States. But France retained most of its prerogatives in the field of defense, diplomacy, currency, and foreign trade.[23]

After the Constitution of 1958 was adopted on October 4, Senghor was one of the first to ask de Gaulle for recognizing Senegal's independence, and de Gaulle agreed.[24] Following his example, at the beginning of 1959, all states wanted national sovereignty and demanded the radical transformation of their relations with France. De Gaulle recognized the right of these peoples to self-determination, and a new Franco-African Community—essentially based on cooperation—was created.

The constitutional amendment of June 4, 1960, officially recognized the independence of the African member states of the French Community, and established new Franco-African relations having a bilateral nature. It was a system of cooperation between sovereign states, but with the aim of imposing the influence of France in Africa. In a few months, all states of the Franco-African Community achieved independence. In 1961, the community institutions

---

21 Guinea, under the guidance of Sékou Touré, voted for independence.
22 Godechot, *Constitutions de la France*, 424.
23 Vassalo, *De Gaulle et l'Afrique Noire*.
24 Senghor, "Francité et Francophonie," 163.

disappeared, and they were replaced by bilateral and multilateral cooperation agreements in political, military, economic, financial, monetary, judicial, technical, and cultural fields, allowing France to retain a major influence over its former colonies.[25] But this development allowed the former West African colonies to join the European Economic Community in the spirit of decolonization according to the system of liberties.

To conclude, De Gaulle, in the spirit of his nationalist politics of grandeur, could ensure France's influence in West Africa (Black Africa), and at the same time he gradually granted independence to these countries. Under the pressure of the African independence aspirations and learning from the bloody Algerian War of Independence, he led a peaceful decolonization process that ended with cooperation and privileged relations between France and the West African overseas territories.[26] He could strengthen the cooperation between them and the European Economic Community in the framework of a developmental aid policy. Supporting the idea of popular sovereignty and self-determination of the people, he represented the path of progress, even if his thinking was far from the federalist spirit of a new European social change (he could not imagine self-determination in a federalist form). His policy of decolonization was controversial and debatable. Some saw it as a realist progressive confederalist politics, and others regarded it as a neo-colonialist one. However, one thing must be emphasized, and that is that many Africans—among them Léopold Sédar Senghor, the first President of independent Senegal—supported the French direction of decolonization represented by de Gaulle.[27] After achieving independence he wanted to cooperate further with the French.

Regarding the Europe-Africa cooperation after the Second World War, the best solution would be to free the colonies in harmony with the idea of liberty, self-determination, and human rights, and on this new basis establish economic and political relations with the African colonies. But European politicians were only able to do this gradually and under pressure.[28] The fight of the colonial people for autonomous life and freedom, the pluralism of meanings, and the developing democratic European law could gradually change the old plan of Eurafrica into a co-development between the European Communities and the independent African states in a common market, as will be seen below.

7.3 To Become a Great Power from Europe's Own Democratic Forces: The Federalist Reform

After the Second World War, the desire for peace strengthened the federalist alternative. Many wondered how the new federalist Europe, launched by the

---

25 Vassalo, *De Gaulle et l'Afrique Noire*.
26 Bourgi, *Le Général de Gaulle et l'Afrique Noire*, 457–461.
27 Bourgi, *Le Général de Gaulle et l'Afrique Noire*, 125.
28 Bitsch and Bossuat, *L'Europe Unie et l'Afrique*, 461; Pasture, *Imagining European Unity*, 185–193.

Ventotene Manifesto, could be realized. But the federalist élan gradually diminished as the former nation states and national governments were reconstructed. As an irony of history the American aid policy helped the reconstruction of the former system of sovereign nation states in Western Europe. All this hindered the realization of the federalist plan of the Resistance Movement because the bottom-up association policy that could launch the renewal and reorganization of society on the basis of the creative forces of the European people could not start. Despite all this, the struggle between the conservative intergovernmentalist supporters of the sovereignty of nation-states and the federalist supporters of a European federation dominated European policy. It was the first time in European history that federalists could gain a real political role. The question arises: what was the role of federalism in the shaping of a European union after the war?

The most important role of the federalists was to launch a democratic pluralist European policy as an opposition to the classical confederalist intergovernmentalists. In a long struggle, they made it possible to build a European union based on the system of liberties and human rights by incorporating the principle of subsidiarity into the European policy. European federalism had two major oppositional directions: the constitutional federalist and the integral or personalist federalist.[29] The constitutional federalists regarded the American or the Swiss Constitution as an example to follow. Spinelli, the leader of the European Federalist Movement [Movimento Federalista Europeo] was the most important representative of this direction. He was for the establishment of a European constitutional federation as the American Founding Fathers had done. He was in favor of a European constituent assembly framing a constitution, and the immediate establishment of federal political institutions and a supranational government directly responsible to European citizens. He believed that the federal institutional reform could automatically solve the necessary social organization reform and decentralization.

The opposing federalist group to the constitutional federalists was the personalist or integral (incremental) federalist. They opposed simply extending the parliamentary state model to the supranational constitutional level through a constituent assembly. They regarded the establishment of a European federation as a gradual social reform process that could force national political establishments to cede powers to the corporate and local communities, and start an economic and social organization serving the real needs and the livelihood of the people. These fundamental differences, which became clear at the Montreux Congress (1947), divided the European federalist movement, and confused its image.[30] Intergovernmentalists could profit from the division of the federalists at the Hague Congress (1948), as discussed in more detail below.

---

29 Vayssière, *Vers une Europe fédérale?*, 34–37.
30 Lipgens and Loth, *Documents on the History of European Integration*, vol. 4, 10.

Denis de Rougemont and Hendrik Brugmans were characteristic representatives, after the Second World War, of this new European personal or integral federalist idea.

Rougemont, in his lecture on "The Federalist Attitude" at the Montreux Congress of the European federalists, in 1947, explained his vision of a European federation as follows:

> [A European federation] taking shape gradually, in various places and in all sorts of ways: here an economic understanding, there an awareness of cultural affinity. In one place, two churches with similar tenets will open their doors to each other, in another a group of small countries will form a customs union. Above all, individual human beings will gradually form varied networks of European exchanges. Every little helps. And all these moves that seem so dispersed, and often so ineffectual, will gradually turn into complex phenomena, the lineaments of a bone structure and system of blood vessels of what will one day be the body of the United States of Europe.[31]

Hendrik Brugmans (1906–1997), Dutch political thinker, the follower of Proudhon's ideas, and the first President of the European Union of Federalists, in his speech on "Fundamentals of European Federalism," at the Montreux Congress, said that the goal of real personal politic was the "dismemberment of sovereignty." He believed that a European federation had to be a free association of people because people were interested in uniting for their common good. In his vision a united Europe must be organized as an open society.[32]

When the Union of European Federalists was established, in December 1946, there was not a significant division in the federalist camp between the constitutional and the integral or personalist federalists. The Hertenstein Programme, the Federalist Charter on European Union (September 22, 1946), emphasized the necessity of a European Community built on federal lines as regional part of the United Nations Organization representing a democratic structure from bottom-up based on the transfer of sovereignty. The member states of the European community should transfer part of their sovereign rights in the fields representing common interest to the federation.[33]

---

31 Rougemont, "The Federalist Attitude," 27 August 1947, Lecture at the Montreux Congress, vol. 4, 26.
32 Brugmans, "Fundamentals of European Federalism," 27 August 1947. Speech at the Montreux Congress, vol. 4, 33.
33 Lipgens and Loth, *Documents on the History of European Integration*, vol. 4, 13–14.

> The members of the European Union shall transfer part of their sovereign rights – economic, political and military – to the Federation which they constitute.[34]

However later, during the First Annual Congress of the Union of European Federalists at Montreux, between August 27 and 31, 1947, the movement began to represent the above-mentioned integral federalist theory of gradual building of the European federation. The General Policy Resolution of the Montreux Congress (August 30, 1947) repeated the thoughts of Rougemont's speech held at the congress, on the federalist attitude.[35]

> A federation is a living phenomenon which grows bit by bit from the association of persons and groups. In this sense it can be said that European Federation is already being slowly constituted, in a small measure everywhere, and in all sorts of ways. Here there may be an economic agreement; there a new relationship is established. Here a supranational functional organism takes shape; there a group of small countries forms a customs union.[36]

In the Resolution, based on the above-mentioned ideas of Rougemont, some allusion was made to a supranational European political dimension but not in the constitutional sense. It did not speak about a planned European Assembly, Parliament, or Federal Constitution, but it represented the concept of sharing the sovereignty of the states. A federal authority at the European level was based on functional bodies. It possessed a government, which was not directly elected by the individual citizens, but it was responsible to the peoples and groups and not to the federated states; a Supreme Court capable of resolving possible disputes between states members of the Federation; and an armed police force under its own control.[37]

The European federation was based on the participation of the 'living forces' in social organization. Under living forces it was understood the popular forces, "all the healthy forces which were active in the different countries," among them the "trade unions, professional organizations, intellectuals, political associations and parties which were working for a better society, universities, and churches."[38]

The Economic Policy Resolution (August 30, 1947) emphasized the necessity of the transfer of a part of economic power of the member states to the federal

---

34 "The Hertenstein Programme," point 4, 42.
35 See Note 31.
36 Lipgens and Loth, *Documents on the History of European Integration*, vol. 4, 36.
37 Lipgens and Loth, *Documents on the History of European Integration*, vol. 4, 34–35, 37.
38 Lipgens and Loth, *Documents on the History of European Integration*, vol. 4, 38.

authority.[39] The economic powers delegated to the federal authority must be limited, but must include the matters of currency, trade and customs. The economic federation should promote the free circulation of goods, capital and men. It was based on the principle of subsidiarity:

> Each federated State must retain all rights not explicitly transferred to the federal authority, and, in particular, all rights the exercise of which has no repercussions on the other federated States.[40]

The integral federalist ideology of the Union of European Federalist led to a split between the weaker Movimento Federalista Europeo [European Federalist Movement] led by Spinelli and the stronger integral federalists because of their different concept of European federalism. Spinelli went into opposition and waited for better times. Coudenhove-Kalergi remained independent and organized the European Parliamentary Union.

Spinelli explained the differences between the constitutional federalists and the integral federalists as follows:

> The Italian movement was anti-ideological, the French one was profoundly ideological. The Italian movement was fixed on creating European institutions with the view to developing a new European political framework which would profoundly revolutionize the whole of national and political life. The French movement regarded European institutions as being a simple element of co-ordination, incapable in itself of providing change, and for this reason supported a multiform programme of action which concern all the parts of existing society.[41]

Brugmans, the executive chairman of the Union of European Federalists gave the following explication about the differences between the two federalist groups:

> In fact, on one side, the Italians of the Movimento federalista Europeo, Altiero Spinelli, Ernesto Rossi and their friends insisted exclusively on the necessity of a European political union. And for such a union to be viable, it needed a supranational power, which, in turn, could only be defined through a federal constitution. This being the case, the movement, in their opinion, needed to apply itself to one objective only: the convening of a European Constituent Assembly . . . No doubt European union was indispensable, but its institutions, instead

---

39 Lipgens and Loth, *Documents on the History of European Integration*, vol. 4, 39.
40 Lipgens and Loth, *Documents on the History of European Integration*, vol. 4, 41.
41 Lipgens and Loth, *Documents on the History of European Integration*, vol. 4, 11.

of slavishly copying national parliamentarianism, should reflect pre-existing social realities.[42]

Intergovernmentalists (unionists), in opposition to the federalists, concentrated on the interests of nation-states.[43] They continued to subordinate the interests of the citizens to nation-states. Their goal was to establish the 'European family of nations', pursuing intergovernmental international policy based on negotiations and agreements by safeguarding the sovereignty of states. However, intergovernmentalists also needed to reform their concept of international policy and their strategy of avoiding economic crises, nationalism, and war. Therefore, they were ready to accept some functional coordination among the states. They regarded the integral federalists as partners in cooperation because of gradualism, but definitely rejected the constitutional federalist idea of a European United States with a federal executive government and a legislative parliament.

Alexandre Marc (1904–2000), leading French integral federalist, in his article "From Unionism to Federalism," published in the May 1948 issue of La Fédération (no. 40), rejected the intergovernmentalist (unionist) policy. He emphasized that "Europe will either be Federalist or will not exist at all."[44] He believed that unionism (intergovernmentalism) was not enough. The unionist knew that as well and this is why they started to be open toward European federalism. But they could not join federalism because federalism was not only about to advance from the national to the supranational plan, federalism was a philosophy that they could not accept.

In his view federalist philosophy had its "own doctrine, attitude to life, and method of organization and action"; it was "a principle of political, economic and social transformation." It did not simply mean the coordination of existing structures at a higher level because the transfer of sovereignty to a federal institution would solve every problem. Federalism demanded a radical transformation of all the structures of society, and the body politic. It needed the involvement of the working class and all the 'living forces' in social organization.[45] The conservative unionists (intergovernmentalists) opposed such a democratic transformation.

The problem with the integral or personalist federalist theory was that it became less and less understandable during the European political campaign. Despite this the majority of federalists protected the step-by-step approach of integral federalism. The influence of constitutional federalism diminished. Spinelli believed that the integral federalists disorientated the federalist movement because they were incapable of formulating a clear European federalist policy. Because of this the broader European political campaign developed

---

42 Lipgens and Loth, *Documents on the History of European Integration*, vol. 4, 11–12.
43 In the English sources the word unionist was used in intergovernmentalist meaning.
44 Lipgens and Loth, *Documents on the History of European Integration*, vol. 4, 47.
45 Lipgens and Loth, *Documents on the History of European Integration*, vol. 4, 49–50.

irrespective of the theories of the European federalists.[46] However, unionists, the protectors of the sovereign nation-state system and the intergovernmental policy, profited from this disorientation.

There was one more pro-European union federalist group which acted independently from the constitutional federalist, the integral federalist, and the unionist group. This was the parliamentary federalist group of Coudenhove-Kalergi which regarded the parliaments of Europe and the parliamentarians to be destined to take the lead in the battle for Europe. Its aim was the establishment of the United States of Europe as a European Parliamentary Federation with a Supreme Council and a Supreme Court, a joint police force, equal human rights for all, a European market, and a European currency.[47]

The different views on a new Europe were discussed at the Congress of Europe in the Hague from May 7–10, 1948, where the federalists were significant players. The question was whether they could succeed in winning the support of the European politicians to build a democratic federalist European union.

---

46 Lipgens and Loth, *Documents on the History of European Integration*, vol. 4, 12.
47 Coudenhove-Kalergi, "Appeal to All Europeans, 28 April 1947," vol. 4, 123–124.

8

REALIZING THE IDEA OF EUROPEAN UNITY IN THE FRAMEWORK OF THE COUNCIL OF EUROPE

8.1 The Hague Congress (1948): Intergovernmentalist, Federalist, and Functionalist Bases of a European Union

Between 1944 and 1948 many movements for European unity were organized with the participation of political thinkers, politicians, intellectuals, and artists. The idea was to create cooperation amongst them. This is why the International Committee of the Movements for European Unity was organized. Its president was Edwin Duncan Sandys (1908–1987), conservative British politician, son-in-law of Churchill, belonging to the unionists (intergovernmentalists). The participants in the International Committee were the intergovernmentalist European League for Economic Cooperation, led by Paul van Zeeland; the integral federalist Union of European Federalists, led by Brugmans; the United Europe Movement founded by Winston Churchill, the secretary general of which was Sandys; and the French Committee for United Europe, led by Raoul Dautry, Paul Ramadier, and Paul Reynaud. These movements were active participants of the Hague Congress (1948) organized by the International Committee. Coudenhove-Kalergi, the leader of the European Parliamentary Union cooperated with them but preferred to remain apart and tried to safeguard his independence. The constitutional federalist European Federalist Movement (Movimento Federalista Europeo), led by Spinelli, rejected the cooperation, and any kind of compromise with the unionists.

The Congress was a high-level discussion about the future of Europe. Duncan Sandys organized it excellently and the unionists profited from it a lot. At the Congress, unionism was represented by Churchill (the honorary President), by Sandys (the President of the International Committee), and by Paul Ramadier (the President of the French Committee for United Europe); integral (personal) federalism by Brugmans, Rougemont, and Marc; and intergovernmentalist functionalism by the members of the Economic and Social Committee under the presidency of Paul van Zeeland. The most important novelty of the Congress was the introduction of the federalists, first of all the integral or personalist federalists, as opposition to the intergovernmentalists (unionists). This led to the birth of the dichotomy federalism versus intergovernmentalism (anti-federalism) in European international policy.[1]

---

1 Bóka, *A Hágai Európa Kongresszus*, 1948, 1–43.

The political debates of the Hague Congress proved that intergovernmentalists aimed to avoid the establishment of a European constitutional assembly and an American or Swiss type European federal union with a legislative federal parliament and an executive government as the constitutional federalists, Spinelli and Rossi, had imagined. Winston Churchill (1874–1955), influential leading British politician, in his speech at the opening plenary session (May 7, 1948) tried to avoid drawing "rigid structures of constitutions" in this critical period. But he accepted the necessity of finding some path to the supranational cooperation.[2] The integral federalists were also against the immediate establishment of a constitutional European federation. They imagined the establishment of a European federation as a gradual process on the way to a personal federalist social reform concentrating on decentralization.

Intergovernmentalists (unionists) rejected not only the constitutional federalist reform but the integral federalist reform, too. Paul Ramadier (1888–1951), French statesman, called the federalist reform attitude a "federalist revolution," and rejected it in his speech at the opening plenary session:

> Europe cannot be created by a kind of federalist revolution, which would weaken governments without strengthening the community.[3]

Intergovernmentalists (unionists) were for an intergovernmental European union but they realized the necessity of some kind of merging of some part of the sovereignty of the cooperating nation states in the field of competences representing common interest. Churchill expressed it as follows in his speech:

> Mutual aid in economic field and joint military defence must inevitably be accompanied step by step with a parallel policy of closer political unity... This involves some sacrifice or merger of national sovereignty.[4]

He accepted constituting "in one form or another a European Assembly" which would enable "the voice of Europe to make itself continuously heard."[5] It meant a supranational council of ministers and a consultative parliamentary assembly giving advice to the council about the building of the European union.

Constitutional federalists, in opposition to the intergovernmentalists (unionists), were for a constitutional assembly and a federal government. They aimed the transfer of a part of national sovereignty to the federal government and a parliament composed of two houses: the house of representatives of the people, and the house of representatives of the states. Coudenhove-Kalergi's European Parliamentary Union, which continued to remain independent, also represented

---

2 Churchill, "Address given by Winston Churchill at the Congress of Europe," vol. 4, 340.
3 Lipgens and Loth, *Documents on the History of European Integration*, vol. 4, 340.
4 Churchill, "Address given by Winston Churchill at the Congress of Europe," vol. 4, 340.
5 Churchill, "Address given by Winston Churchill at the Congress of Europe," vol. 4, 340.

this aim. Coudenhove-Kalergi expressed this in his speech at the opening plenary session as follows:

> To achieve an immediate and radical solution of the European problem, we must have a Continental constituent assembly.[6]

Integral federalists agreed with the constitutional federalists on the necessity of a European federation with a federal government but they imagined it as a step-by-step process as the result of the personalist association policy of the 'living forces' from the bottom-up, concentrating on real needs. Also they accepted functionalism, meaning sectoral cooperation, which could lead to European union. However they opposed a simply intergovernmental European union. In his speech at the opening plenary session, Brugmans, their advocate, was for creating "specialized bodies, autonomous but interconnected" as an urgent step.

> An assemblage of sovereign states will never save us from nationalism ... It seems unrealistic to speak of a united Europe without envisaging a European government and a European parliament ... European federalism is not solely a political matter, it is functional as well. When we advocate European integration we are thinking not only of governing human beings but of organizing affairs ... nothing is more urgent than to create specialized bodies, autonomous but interconnected.[7]

There was a great debate on the proposal of Paul Reynaud, former French Prime Minister, and Edouard Bonnefus, member of the French National Assembly and chairman of the Foreign Affairs Committee, who wanted to create a European Parliament directly elected by the people. The point was to urgently convene a European Parliamentary Consultative Body, more specifically a European Constituent Assembly, with the task of creating a new Europe. The members of this body should be elected by the end of 1948, directly by the people and not by the members of the national parliament, because they represented the interests of their own nation-state and not the interests of Europe. The election must therefore be by universal suffrage, in accordance with the electoral system of each country, and one representative per one million inhabitants should be elected. This representative European Parliament should establish European popular sovereignty, express the public will, and help to shape the European identity of the voters.[8]

---

6 Lipgens and Loth, *Documents on the History of European Integration*, vol. 4, 340.
7 Lipgens and Loth, *Documents on the History of European Integration*, vol. 4, 341.
8 Lipgens and Loth, *Documents on the History of European Integration*, vol. 4, 342–343; *Europe Unites: The Hague Congress and After*, 26–27.

Coudenhove-Kalergi considered the proposal of a European assembly elected by the people to be revolutionary, and supported it.[9] Brugmans expressed his doubts because this method ignored basic regional, national, or functional communities and led to the formation of a super-state, and therefore did not support it.[10] Ramadier considered the Reynaud-Bonnefous amendment to be immature and unrealistic. According to him, national parliaments should appoint their delegates to the European Parliament, as they are representatives of national sovereignty and only they have the right to delegate part of it to the community. The final decisions must be made by the responsible governments. There must therefore be a cooperation between the national parliaments, governments, and the European Assembly.[11]

Finally the intergovernmentalists and integral federalists could compromise regarding the institutional policy and functionalism because of the principle of gradualism. But this was not a good compromise because, for the integral federalists, a consultative European Assembly was only the first step and, for the unionists, the last one. Functionalism had an intergovernmental and a federalist interpretation which were different.

Economic functionalism was a big challenge for both the intergovernmentalists and the federalists as the Economic and Social Resolution showed. European free market capitalism demanded opening up the closed and nationalist sovereign states, to removing the obstacles step-by-step and, finally, abolishing the obstacles to trade within the union, making free the circulation of capital, unifying the currencies, coordinating the budgetary and credit policy, establishing a full customs union, and abolishing all barriers to the free movement of goods between the countries of the union.[12] It demanded cooperation in the fields of trade, currency, customs, production, and labor. The organization of cooperation in the field of customs, trade, and currencies belonged to the common interests of the states and needed the sharing of sovereignty. The intergovernmentalists were for intergovernmental negotiations, legal agreements and legal coordination with the help of a supranational ministerial economic council, a secretary and intergovernmental coordinating agencies. Federalists, however, believed that cooperation in the field of trade, customs and finances needed the sharing of sovereignty and a federalist government. It meant transferring these functions from the state sovereignty to supranational coordinating institutions organized by federalist institutional means. So the theory of intergovernmentalist functionalism and federalist functionalism developed, representing different concepts. Governments could decide, on the basis of subsidiarity, which form

---

9 Lipgens and Loth, *Documents on the History of European Integration*, vol. 4, 343.
10 Lipgens and Loth, *Documents on the History of European Integration*, vol. 4, 344.
11 Lipgens and Loth, *Documents on the History of European Integration*, vol. 4, 344–345.
12 Lipgens and Loth, *Documents on the History of European Integration*, vol. 4, 349.

of organization was suitable for the different functions and sectors of economic life.[13]

The Resolution of the Economic and Social Committee called for reforms that went beyond the old national economic organization, which could be achieved by creating a European economic union. It stressed that workers, and the organizations that represent them, must be closely linked to the creation and development of a united European economy. It also called for the maintenance and progressive settlement of economic relations with European-dominated dominions, associated countries, and overseas territories.[14]

Integral federalists in the Cultural Committee emphasized human rights, as the basic principle of a European union, contending that they could prevail only in a bottom-up federalist system. Alexandre Marc proposed the establishment of an independent European Supreme Court securing the implementation of the Charter of Human Rights contributing by this to the defense of the rights of the international community. In his view, the government's absolutely independent Supreme Court could supervise the operation of the European Constitution. It could avoid federalist over-centralization, prevent both the encroachment of central power on local and national interests, and of national powers on the constitutional rights of the federation, in addition to protecting human rights.[15]

Regarding European universalism, integral federalists emphasized that Europe's vocation was to spread throughout the world her own culture and to be receptive to other cultures. In the midst of the crisis caused by the Second World War Europeans should formulate a new synthesis between liberty and justice, and to create the laws and institutions implied in the ideal of human personality. They should rally to this new enterprise all the peoples of the continent in a federation which would be the first step toward a Federation of the World.[16]

The Congress itself set, as an aim for the Europeans, the goals of the *Message to Europeans* (drawn up by Denis de Rougemont) which was accepted by all groups. The *Message to Europeans* (May 10, 1948), which formed the Preamble of the Resolutions of the Hague Congress, emphasized that Europe was in danger because it was divided and full of borders making difficult the free movement of products and the defense of freedom. The construction of a European union would be able to secure peace in Europe and in the world. It represented the idea of the union with the colonies stressing that Europeans together with the peoples of the overseas colonies could establish a significant political formation and an economic market. It defined as the aim of the Hague Congress the following:

"To establish a United Europe, throughout whose area the free movement of persons, ideas and goods is restored"; to establish "a European Assembly where

---

13 *Europe Unites: The Hague Congress and After*, 8, 40–42, 68–71; Lipgens and Loth, *Documents on the History of European Integration*, vol. 4, 347–350.
14 *Europe Unites: The Hague Congress and After*, 8, 68–71.
15 *Europe Unites: The Hague Congress and After*, 81.
16 *Europe Unites: The Hague Congress and After*, 74.

the live forces of all nations shall be represented"; to frame "a Charter of Human Rights guaranteeing liberty of thought, assembly and expression as well as the right to form a political opposition"; and to create "a Court of Justice with adequate sanctions for the implementation of this Charter."[17]

Both federalists and intergovernmentalists voted for the Resolutions of the three committees (political, economic, and cultural) of the Hague Congress which included as aims the following: free circulation of persons and goods, a common defense, a common European law to which the states would be subject and a common consultative assembly of the (national) parliaments of the states, a declaration of human rights, and a supreme court of justice representing and safeguarding the basic rules and principles.

The creation of the European union was regarded as a stage toward world union by creating a democratic society that freed humanity from slavery and the arbitrary exercise of power. The congress agreed to end economic nationalism in Europe. However, it was for safeguarding colony relations, and agreed on developmental aid policy. The political resolution took a stand in favor of maintaining the colonies, and ensuring the economic, political, and cultural development of the colonies without prejudice.[18] At the center was the development of economic resources and the coordination of the policy for full employment. The main difference between federalists and intergovernmentalists was that the intergovernmentalists, among them primarily British policy makers, were against supranational institutions. They preferred intergovernmentalism, legal harmonization, coordinating agencies, and wanted to safeguard state sovereignty.[19]

In conclusion, the most important merit of the Hague Congress was that, in the security of the intergovernmentalist majority, there was a free expression of the different thoughts about the establishment of the European union. This made it possible to officially introduce the federalist ideas about the European union in European policy and to understand the differences between the federalists and intergovernmentalists. By this the dichotomy of federalism versus intergovernmentalism was officially born in the European international policy. However, federalism was in a minority. Also it made it possible to investigate functionalism as a necessary contribution to the sharing of some part of sovereignty of the cooperating states in the fields of common interest based on subsidiarity. The European union was imagined as part of the world union or federation, i.e. as the regional member of the United Nations Organization.

The Hague Congress, motivated by the idea of European unity, can be regarded as an introduction to the European integration policies and theories. European integration policy could develop from the freely expressed pluralism of meanings about the European union and from the differences between the

---

17 "Message to Europeans, The Hague," 10 May 1948, 94–95.
18 *Europe Unites: The Hague Congress and After*, 7–8, 37–39; Lipgens and Loth, *Documents on the History of European Integration*, vol. 4, 345–347.
19 Bossuat, *Histoire de l'Union européenne*, 111–112.

federalist and intergovernmentalist interpretation of functionalism. In this way the idea of European unity became a real theoretical and practical state and international organization political force.

8.2 Intergovernmentalist Majority and the Council of Europe

The Hague Congress did not achieve the expected result for the federalists. They thought that their official introduction, as a political group, at the Hague Congress failed. First of all, the integral federalists of the Union of European Federalists were disappointed because they could not represent the interests of the 'living forces' (people) in the political resolution, and in the call for a European assembly. They wanted to withdraw, but Sandys could convince Brugmans not to cause a split in the European Movement. Despite the considerable doubts and criticism, Brugmans could keep the Union of European Federalists in the European Movement, but he was criticized because of the 'possibilist' cooperation with the intergovernmentalists on the basis of a step-by-step constitutional strategy. He tried to avoid imposing a purely constitutional option on Britain because he could not imagine the European union without the British.[20]

Rougemont was of the opinion that federalism could not win at the congress. Unionists continued to dominate the idea of Europe, and profited from the results. They were able to prevent the Hague Congress from becoming a broad popular movement by launching a democratic social reform in the name of federalism. The federalists did not know how to force their tactics, and allowed themselves to be seduced by far less than they represented. In his words:

> Federalism triumphed only in the documents. Unionism, the doctrine (or negation of doctrine) of those who hoped to make Europe, without breaking eggs, remained the master of the field, alone in a position to exploit the results of the dazzling demonstration at The Hague. On the one hand, those who called it were able to prevent the congress from extending itself into a vast popular movement, on the other hand the federalists did not know how to impose their tactics: they allowed themselves to be fobbed off by promises of modest but concrete results.[21]

In fact, what happened was that the integral or personalist federalists did not disappear but the compromise with the intergovernmentalists unfairly united them. However, the other two federalist groups remained independent. The goal of a European federation was consequently represented and carried on by the European Parliamentary Union, led by Coudenhove-Kalergi, and by the European Federalist Movement, led by Spinelli.

---

20 Lipgens and Loth, *Documents on the History of European Integration*, vol. 4, 56–57.
21 Denis de Rougemont, "The Campaign of the European Congresses," 24–25.

Coudenhove-Kalergi, in his letter to Sandys, on January 18, 1949, drew attention to the necessity of clarifying the differences between the federalist and the intergovernmentalist point of view:

> The best service we all can render to the cause of European unity is to clarify and not to confuse the basic issue; whether Europe shall be organized as a Commonwealth of Nations, or as a Federation under a federal Constitution and a federal Government.[22]

He emphasized that the two solutions were different.

After the Hague Congress the European Parliamentary Union, led by Coudenhove-Kalergi, organized a congress, in September 1948, in Interlaken. Here they discussed the cause of a European parliament and constitution.[23] The Interlaken federalist constitutional plan drafted the constitution of the United States of Europe as a European Parliamentary Federation led by a federal council, a bicameral European legislative parliament, and a federal court. According to the plan, the legislative power was vested in a parliament composed of two houses, a senate and a chamber of deputies. The senate was composed of the same number of senators elected by each state. The states safeguarded their autonomy in such matters which were not common to all states or were not within the general interests of Europe as a whole. The executive power of the federation was vested in a federal council elected by both houses of the parliament, and was responsible to them. The federal council elected its prime minister. The judicial power of the federation was vested in a supreme court. The exclusive powers granted by the constitution to the parliament of the federation were: (1) external affairs and defense (the relations of the federation with other countries, the diplomatic and consular services, the military, naval, and air defense of the federation); (2) essential services (postal, telegraphic, telephonic, broadcasting, weights and measures); (3) money and finance (customs duties, currency, banking). Concurrent powers which might be granted by the constitution to the parliament of the federation: (1) taxation; (2) economic questions (trade and commerce, insurance in all its forms, the creation, dissolution, regulation and control of corporations, transport); (3) industrial matters (labor, organization of employees and employers, settlement of industrial disputes; (4) social services (disability and retirement pensions, unemployment insurance, health insurance). The European Parliamentary Union was an association open to all parliamentarians of European countries who accepted its rules, and to all countries willing to join to form a permanent community under the title of the United States of Europe.[24]

22 Lipgens and Loth, *Documents on the History of European Integration*, vol. 4, 152–153.
23 Coudenhove-Kalergi, *Kampf um Europa*, 289–290.
24 "The Interlaken Draft Constitution of a Federal Europe, European Parliamentary Union, 1949," 142–146.

The Interlaken principles for a federation of Europe were very different to the European governmental plans. The example was the United States enjoying enormous political and economic advantages through the existence of a common federal government over a large continent with a large domestic market, a common currency, and without internal trade barriers. It was considered that the people of Europe could have similar advantages if an economic and political union of Europe was created. The Interlaken Congress met with a warm response in Europe and in the United States where Coudenhove-Kalergi's European integration policy was supported. Congress helped the cause of a federalist European parliamentary union after the Hague Congress.

The European Federalist Movement did not compromise with the intergovernmentalists. Spinelli, the leader of the movement, was waiting for a better time to fight for a European federation and a democratic European parliament. He insisted on his meaning of a constitutional European federation, and the establishment of its institutions first:

> The federalists ask that the political institutions of a democratic Europe be constructed first, taking certain powers of initiative, deliberation, decision, and execution from the national executives, parliaments, and judiciary and confiding them to a European executive, parliament, and judiciary. The institutions would derive their legitimacy from the consent directly expressed by European citizens and would exercise their powers directly on European citizens without interference from the member states in matters of federal competence. The models are little Switzerland and the great United States.[25]

Spinelli, after the defeat and compromise of the integral federalists with the intergovernmentalists, became active again and consequently represented the cause of European federalism in European integration policy, as we will see below.

Intergovernmentalists regarded the Hague Congress and what happened after as a success and were satisfied. The "federalist revolution" could be avoided. The federalist enthusiasm was successfully diminished, the convening of a European constitutional assembly and also the establishment of the European United States, at a historically favorable moment, was avoided.

Intergovernmentalists also profited, at the time of the Hague Congress, from the involvement of the influential British functionalist theoretician, David Mitrany (1888–1975).[26] He opposed both the constitutional federalists and the European Parliamentary Union. He was puzzled by the historically developed belief of the Europeans in federalism. He preferred the functional to the federal approach because, in his view, it could better protect individual liberty. He was

---

25 Spinelli, *The Eurocrats*, 11.
26 Navari, "David Mitrany," 214–215, 231–232.

for cooperation between different functions. This meant linking authority to a specific activity and breaking it away from the traditional link between authority and a definite territory and organizing this specific activity (function) in the framework of supranational coordinating agencies.[27] Mitrany believed that functionalism made it possible for states to safeguard national sovereignty, and avoid the problems of too loose or too close unions. So, the initially federalist interpretation of functionalism was interpreted by him in an anti-federalist, intergovernmentalist sense.

The interpretation of intergovernmentalism as a functionalist way caused trouble and confusion among the supporters of European unity. As a result, the question arose whether functionalism would be suitable for federalism. Mitrany's answer was 'no.' But, in opposition to him, there were those who thought that federalist functionalism was possible. This meant using functionalist principles together with federalist methods in sectoral integration. Rougemont, for example, emphasized that functionalism was a federalist path in the eyes of the l'Ordre Nouveau since 1932. He pointed out that this concept was implemented to a limited extent and was used for certain specific products. However, the challenge was to formulate an authority 'with limited but real powers' which was able to direct federalist functionalism as a social organization force. In his words:

> This concept of limited, but real powers attributed to a state or to specialized authorities, had been the specific feature of any federalist regime in the eyes of the group around l'Ordre Nouveau since 1932. No one since then seems to me to have put forward any proposal going further than this modest but precise aim. It has only been very partially realized, in less than half of the western part of the continent, and only with reference to specific products such as coal and steel, vegetables and poultry. These are all very important in themselves. But Europe is composed of men and ideas too, let us say of spiritual, social and political forces, which are still awaiting the formulation, for each one of them, of the authority 'with limited but real powers' which would ensure their free exercise.[28]

In 1949, when the Council of Europe was established, the 'European concert' was restored in the sense of the preliminary report of the political committee of the Hague Congress which was a compromise between the intergovernmentalists (unionists) and the integral federalists.[29] The Statute of the Council of Europe (1949) represented an intergovernmental organization based on the Committee of Ministers (foreign ministers), and the representation of the European interests in the form of a consultative Parliamentary Assembly composed of the

---

27 Mitrany, "A Working Peace System (1943)," 123, 125, 128, 129.
28 Rougemont, "The Campaign of the European Congresses," 28.
29 *Europe Unites: The Hague Congress and After*, 23–26.

members of national parliaments of each member state.[30] From the integral federalist point of view the Council of Europe was the first step toward a federal union of states because the consultative Parliamentary Assembly was the first transnational assembly. As such it was acceptable for the intergovernmentalists. It played an important role in the launching of the European intergovernmental cooperation process in the Western part of divided Europe. But the Council of Europe—despite its great importance—did not transcend the dogma of indivisibility of sovereignty of nation-states. Without federalism, it was not able to transcend the old policy of fight for power among sovereign nation-states. The Council of Europe could not start the supranational European integration process which would be able to transcend nationalism and wars and to democratize the former expansive capitalist market economy. For a democratic Europe a bicameral parliamentary European union was necessary with a federalist and intergovernmentalist opposition based on the principle of subsidiarity.

It was Jean Monnet, who on the basis of the intergovernmentalist versus federalist dichotomy through sectoral functionalism, could open the way toward economic democratization and the European Union.

---

30 "Statute of the Council of Europe. London, 5th May 1949," 169–184.

9

SHAPING THE SUPRANATIONAL EUROPEAN UNION

9.1 Functionalist Sectoral Integration: The "Monnet-Method"

The European supranational integration process started with the Schuman Declaration (1950) and the establishment of the High Authority of the European Coal and Steel Community. The guiding idea of the Declaration was to prevent another war, and with this aim it proposed to place the Franco-German production of coal and steel under a common "High Authority," within an organization open to the participation of the other European countries. The pooling of coal and steel production and the institution of a common higher authority will ensure the establishment of common bases for economic development and cooperation as a first step toward the European federation. By this the Schuman Declaration made war between the historic rivals, Germany and France, unthinkable and materially impossible. It was expected that the economic unification would advance the economy, and this would make it possible for the Europeans to contribute to the development of Africa.[1] Coudenhove-Kalergi was pleased that the declaration included helping Africa in this way.[2]

The European Coal and Steel Community, with the executive High Authority, was the first supranational community based on the sharing of sovereignty between European nation-states from which the European Union could develop. The new supranational method was suggested by Jean Monnet as a conclusion to the discussions between federalists and intergovernmentalists on functionalism. He recognized that supranationalism, in the field of shared common national sovereignties, could be realized only by the functionalist method through sectoral integration and a chain reaction in a not truly federalist but not intergovernmentalist institutional structure based on the principle of subsidiarity. Consequently, a two-level—separated federal and intergovernmental—open institutional form, in one institutional structure of the union, without a central government could be the solution.[3]

---

1 "The Schuman Declaration, 9 May 1950," 61.
2 Fleury, "Paneurope et l'Afrique," 53.
3 Monnet, "A Ferment of Change," 203–211.

He was convinced that Europe had to be organized on a federal basis and a French-German union was an essential element. In his view, the first step could be the establishment of common bases of economic development. This is why the French government proposed placing the French-German steel and coal production under an international authority open to the participation of the other European countries. The aim was to unite the basic conditions of steel and coal production and to let their gradual extension to other fields, and so serving pacifism.[4]

The essence of Monnet's idea was to gradually dismember the sovereignty of nation-states by the functionalist method. The "Monnet-method" meant cutting different common functions of the sovereignty of the cooperating nation states and transferring them to independent supranational institutions organized following the federalist institutional and governance model. The states could remain sovereign in all other functions and cooperate by using intergovernmental methods. So a two-level (double) institutional structure of the European Community was founded: the federalist functionalist and the intergovernmental functionalist.

With the establishment of the European Coal and Steel Community by the Treaty of Paris (1951), Monnet separated the coal and steel production sector from the sovereignty of the six cooperating nation states and organized them independently of the governments under the direction of the supranational High Authority, Common Assembly and Court of Justice. By uniting the basic productions of the war industry and through the decisions of the High Authority, the six member states realized the first bases of a peaceful federal Europe as a legal precedent.[5] So the core of an economic integration outside the national governmental sphere of the six states emerged. All other functions, which were not transferred to the High Authority, remained under the authority of the member states. The governments had an intermediary role in implementing the decisions of the High Authority and the Common Assembly through the Council composed of national ministers. He believed that integration in one area would generate a chain reaction and more and more areas would be transferred gradually to the supranational institutional level. So the European federation could emerge gradually by merging the institutions of the many functional communities.

Behind the "Monnet-method" was a personalist federalist life philosophy similar to the above-mentioned integral federalist thinking and insight coming from economic political practice. It was based on a gradual realization of the European federation starting with limited creations instituting the solidarity of action. He believed that the progressive development of this process parallel to European pluralism and democratic institutional development could lead to the

---

4 Monnet, *Mémoires*, 350.
5 Monnet, *Mémoires*, 353, 365, 371.

federation.[6] The essence of the gradual federalist and functionalist method was (in his words):

> Délégation de souveraineté et exercice en commun de cette souveraineté déléguée.[7]

He did not know how long the shaping of the European Community by the gradual federalist functionalist method would last because all non-violent revolutions [révolutions pacifiques] needed time.[8]

Monnet's state and international organization vision imagined a new Europe breaking with colonialism, and with the fight for power in the framework of protectionist nation states and national empires which resulted in conflicts and world wars that ruined the European states. He believed that Europeans would follow the American example if they wanted to remain independent and prosperous. The Marshall Aid gave a chance for the European states to strengthen their economies. But they could survive only if they could find the means of peaceful cooperation and economic strengthening. In Monnet's view something like that was possible only through good and common institutions, and by establishing a common market based on rules. The six European states started to pool their resources in a commune. They established equal rules and institutions for the cooperating partners above the state level in the field of certain functions continuing the example of a parliamentary representative system. He was convinced that this was such a novelty in economic organization that it had the potential to develop further.[9]

The "Monnet-method" was functionalist federalist. His aim was not to coalesce the states but to unite the men:

> Nous ne coalisons pas les États, nous unissons des hommes.[10]

As such his method has become talked about and discussed.

9.1.1 Criticism of the "Monnet-Method" by Contemporaries

Ernst Haas, American social scientist and the founder of the neo-functionalist school, supported the "Monnet-method." He was of the opinion that supranationalism, in practice, evolved into a hybrid, in which neither the federal nor the intergovernmental tendency had prevailed, but the relations formed were

---

6 Monnet, *Mémoires*, 429–430, 448–449.
7 Monnet, *Mémoires*, 506. ["To delegate sovereignty and exercise the delegated sovereignty collectively," translated by Éva Bóka.]
8 Monnet, *Mémoires*, 506.
9 Monnet, *Repères pour une méthode*, 81–114.
10 Monnet, "Une Europe fédérée, 30 avril 1952," 103.

moving toward greater integration. Supranationalism was not federal in nature but its consequences were federating because it "activated socio-economic processes in the pluralistic-industrial-democratic milieu in which it functioned... to this extent the vision of Jean Monnet had been clearly justified by events."[11]

Based on the theory of spill-over, Haas believed that the organization of the economic sectoral integration by supranational institutions would produce such an economic and commercial spill-over reaction that would result in the establishment of the customs union, the common market, and the financial union. All of these would also influence political life. So, as a supplementary result of supranational sectoral integration, economic integration would also start. The High Authority, as it was an institution independent from the states, would be strong enough to resist the efforts of the governments to regain sovereign power. Therefore the intergovernmentalists would not be able to destroy the achievements of the integration.

He defined supranationalism as follows:

> Supranationality in structural terms, therefore, means the existence of governmental authorities closer to the archetype of federation than any past international organization, but not yet identical with it. While almost all the criteria point positively to federation, the remaining limits on the ability to implement decisions and to expand the scope of the system independently still suggest the characteristics of international organisation.[12]

He believed that the resistance of such a structure to intergovernmentalism and national sovereignty depended on the cooperation between the High Authority and the Council of Ministers.

Lindberg, a pupil of Haas, emphasized that, while spill-over existed in the economy it worked differently in politics. In the case of spill-over, politics was based on the smallest common denominator using negotiations, bargains, and agreements. It was possible that in politics, instead of spill-over, a return to the sovereign states could occur because the states would defend their autonomy and independence.[13] De Gaulle's policy was proof of this as will be discussed below.

Spinelli, as a constitutional federalist, represented a different federalist logic. When Jean Monnet became the President of the High Authority, he and Spinelli became democratic oppositional political rivals.[14] Spinelli regarded Monnet as a federalist functionalist and, for this, appreciated him. But as a constitutional federalist he was skeptical regarding sectoral functionalism which the intergov-

---

11 Haas, *The Unity of Europe*, 527.
12 Haas, *The Unity of Europe*, 59.
13 Lindberg, *The Political Dynamics of European Economic Integration*, 3–12.
14 Saurugger, *Théories et concepts de l'intégration européenne*, 142–143.

ernmentalists also regarded as the means of constructing the union. He believed that this would create much confusion on the path to shaping Europe. To avoid an intergovernmentalist majority, he attacked the "step-by-step Monnet-method" as being too slow. For example, he criticized the institutional solution of the European Coal and Steel Community, the High Authority, the Common Assembly, and the Council of Ministers. He admitted that the High Authority had considerable independence but the Common Assembly was "an inconsistent concession to democracy," it had neither legislative nor fiscal power, and did not participate in the naming of the High Authority; the Council of Ministers meant a restriction on the independence of the High Authority. His main problem with the "step-by-step Monnet-method" was that the governments could remain the legal representatives of authority above the integrated sectors. As a result, the governments could become not only internal national but also supranational players. The High Authority needed to ask the views of the Council in giving advice, and so the Council began to develop into a real decision-making power. He admitted that the European Coal and Steel Community represented "the first breach in the Chinese wall of national sovereignties" but he was of the opinion that sectoral integration could not solve the problem of a federal governmental structure.[15]

9.2 Supranationalism toward Federalism (1952–1954)

The supranationalism of the "Monnet-method" was supplemented by two projects between 1952–1954: The Plan of the European Defense Community, and The Plan of the European Political Community.

The Plan of the European Defense Community, or Pleven Plan (1950), sketched the federalist functionalist organization of defense. The plan was proposed, in October 1950, by the French premier, René Pleven (1901–1993), and drafted mainly by Jean Monnet. It aimed at the creation of a supranational European army as part of the European Defense Community with the participation of West Germany, France, Italy, and the Benelux countries. The United States would be excluded and France would play the dominant role. The European Defense Community would be the competitor to NATO and was aimed at preventing Germany from gaining economic power and starting a war. The Pleven Plan proposed the creation of a common European army, serving defense, under the direction of the supranational institutions of the united European countries. Its aim would be to extend the methods of the European Coal and Steel Community to military cooperation. So, the European army would not simply be a coalition army composed of the national armies of the member states, but it would be a common European army of soldiers under common European command. However, the member states remained sovereign above the national legions, which did not belong to the European army. The governments of the

---

15 Spinelli, *The Eurocats*, 27–28, 33.

member states would elect a common minister of the European army responsible to the European Assembly. The expenses of the European army would be financed from the common budget. The institutions of the European Defense Community would be the two chambers of parliament, the executive commission, the court of justice, and the economic and social council. The European army would be at the service of the united Atlantic command (leadership) and would act following the rules of NATO regarding general strategy.[16]

The French assembly rejected the Pleven Plan because of the fear of losing national sovereignty in defense and security. A modified draft of the Pleven Plan was supported by France. The new treaty on the European Defense Community (*Treaty Establishing the European Defense Community*) was signed in 1952 but it was not ratified and never went into effect.[17]

Seeing the difficulties of creating a common army, in the absence of a common political authority to which the army belonged, convinced the governments of the six to investigate the federalist solution. The constitutional federalists, led by Spinelli, emphasized the necessity of solving the problem of the political governance of the European Community by a federalist type constitution. Europe's first constitutional draft, the *Draft Treaty Embodying the Statute of the European Community* (Strasbourg, March 11, 1953) showed the federalist aims of the founding fathers. Spinelli played an important role in the drafting. The Draft Treaty aimed to establish a European Community of a supranational character founded upon a union of people and states, upon respect for their identity, and upon equal rights and duties for all. It should be indissoluble. Its most important goal was to establish a supranational common market to ensure the livelihood of the citizens. Its institutional system was based on a parliamentary federation composed of two chambers, representing the interests of the citizens as Europeans as well as citizens of their own states and the autonomy of the member states (subsidiarity). The first chamber, called the Peoples' Chamber, should be composed of deputies representing the people united in the Community. The second chamber, called the Senate, should be composed of senators representing the people of each state. Senators should be elected by the national parliaments for five years in accordance with the procedure determined by each member state. The establishment of the European Executive Council should solve the problem of European governance. It should undertake the general administration of the community. The Council of National Ministers should harmonize the actions of the European Executive Council with the governments of the member states. The Council of National Ministers and the European Executive Council should exchange information and consult each other. The *Draft Treaty Embodying the Statute of the European Community* (1953) could be regarded as

---

16 Pleven, "The Pleven Plan, 1950," 65–69.
17 "Traité instituant la Communauté européenne de défense (Paris, 27 mai 1952)."

"Europe's first constitution." It was close to federalism but was not federalist because of the role given to the Council of National Ministers.[18]

In 1954, the French National Assembly rejected both the defense community and the political community plans. Behind all this were the complicated geopolitical situation in the midst of the Cold War and the problem of the colonies. The Cold War reinforced the need for a federal union, but the question of colonies continued to strengthen the intergovernmental solution. Regarding the French and Belgian colonies in Africa, for example, it was planned to associate them in the framework of a European common market. This required the preservation of national sovereignty, guaranteed by intergovernmentalism because the French politicians did not really want to liberate their colonies or to lose their influence above the colonies by cooperating with the other European members in a common market. They realized the necessity of decolonization but preferred to find for this an intergovernmentalist (confederalist) solution because it was well known that the federalist solution did not work without recognizing the autonomy of the colonial countries and establishing functional federal institutions and governance. There was a danger that, if the African colonies and Indochina gained representation in the planned European Political Community's powerful and directly elected parliament (Peoples' Chamber), they might very well utilize such a position to break ranks with the metropole. This is why the majority of the French politicians did not dare to risk a shift toward federalism. They insisted on preserving national sovereignty, preferring confederalism or intergovernmentalism and supranational coordinating agencies. At the same time, the colonies fought for independence and the right to self-determination (Suez crisis, Algerian War of Independence), and all this made the dilemma of Eurafrica, as a colonial common market, no more topical. The challenge was to think about how to place colonies, that would become inevitably independent in the future, within the framework of a planned European common market.

The negotiators of the Rome Treaties wanted to establish a European common market and at the same time to associate the overseas countries and territories. The negotiations about the European common market went parallel with the negotiations about its association with overseas countries and territories. Regarding the Europe-Africa cooperation there were difficult discussions because the formation of the alliance with the African overseas territories of France and the Europe of Six required France to relieve its exclusive influence in the African Union and to allow Germany, Italy, the Netherlands, Belgium, and Luxembourg trading with these territories, and to grant autonomy to the African overseas territories. This was a difficult task and provoked a long debate. But the projects of the Europe of Five on cooperation suggesting equality, autonomous development, free market capitalism, supranational institutional coordination, and developmental aid policy helped to find a way to work together. All this can be regarded as a decolonization action of the Europe of Six that took

---

18 "Draft Treaty Embodying the Statute of the European Community," 1953, 189–226.

place in an intergovernmental or confederal form which made impossible the realization of personal federalist ideas.[19]

9.3 The Rome Treaties and the European Economic Community (1957)

Despite the serious defeat of constitutional federalism, Europeanism was reborn. After the rejection of the Plan of the European Defense Community, Jean Monnet with the help of Paul Henri Spaak, could relaunch the process of European unity. A new functionalist drive began with the Messina Conference in 1955. Monnet proposed a new specialized authority for the development of atomic energy. The Dutch and Belgian governments proposed applying the "Monnet-method," not only to some sectors, but to the whole economy with the goal of unifying it. This is why the Europe of Six slowly elaborated and ratified the Treaties of Rome which established the European Atomic Energy Community (Euratom) and the European Economic Community (Common Market) in 1957. As a consequence the British efforts for an intergovernmental plan of a free trade zone failed and the functionalist plan of the Common Market could succeed. In the Rome Treaties the six cooperating governments agreed to a precise program for achieving a customs union and gradually establishing an economic union. They entrusted a supranational commission to oversee the fulfillment of the treaty. The Rome Treaties manifested a new capacity of the politicians to shape European integration in the supranational direction. However, it did not define precisely the federalist institutions. Therefore a debate developed between the federalist and the intergovernmentalist functionalists which will be discussed below.

The goal of the Treaty on the European Economic Community (1957) was the foundation of an ever-closer union among the peoples of Europe by establishing a European Economic Community (EEC). The most important purposes were the establishment of a common market; elimination of customs duties; the establishment of a common customs tariff and a common commercial policy toward third countries; the abolition between the member states of the obstacles to freedom of movement for persons, services, and capital; the adoption of a common agricultural policy; the adoption of a common transport policy; the application of procedures by which the economic policies of member states could be coordinated; the creation of a European Social Fund; the establishment of a European Investment Bank; furthermore the association of the overseas countries and territories with the purpose of increasing trade, to promote economic and social development, and to establish economic relations between them and the Community. It was decided that the common market should be progressively established during a transitional period of 12 years. However, a common supranational European economic policy was not created because there was no

---

19 Migani, "L'association des TOM au Marché Commun," 235, 233–252.

supranational European economic governance. The supranational institutions, Assembly (composed of the representatives of the delegates of the national parliaments), and Commission had advisory or supervisory functions.[20]

Colonization policy was rejected and the promotion of the well-being of the world was emphasized as the goal of the European Economic Community. The association of the overseas countries and territories with the EEC was understood in this meaning in accordance with the principles of the United Nations Charter. Articles 131 and 132 of Part IV of the Treaty establishing the European Economic Community (1957) declared that the purpose of the association of the European Economic Community with the overseas countries and territories, which had special relations with Belgium, France, Italy, and the Netherlands, was to promote the economic and social development of the former colonies, and the association shall apply in commerce and investment the same rules which were applied in respect of the European states:

> Article 131. The purpose of association shall be to promote the economic and social development of the countries and territories and to establish close economic relations between them and the Community as a whole.[21]
>
> Article 132. Member States shall apply to their trade with the countries and territories the same treatment as they accord each other pursuant to this Treaty.
>
> Each country or territory shall apply to its trade with Member States and with the other countries and territories the same treatment as that which it applies to the European State with which it has special relations.
>
> The Member States shall contribute to the investments required for the progressive development of these countries and territories.[22]

A Development Fund for the Overseas Countries and Territories associated with the European Common Market was established. All these can be regarded as a peaceful decolonization that preserved relations between the African and European countries within the framework of cooperation and developmental aid policy.[23]

The subsequent Yaoundé Association agreement (1963) between the EEC and the 18 African ex-colonies (Associated African States and Madagascar)[24] that

---

20 "Treaty Establishing the European Economic Community, 1957," 104–119.
21 Article 131 of the "Treaty Establishing the European Economic Community, 1957," 112.
22 Article 132 of the "Treaty Establishing the European Economic Community, 1957," 113.
23 Migani, "L'association des TOM au Marché Commun," 251–252.
24 Republic of Burundi, Federal Republic of Cameroon, Central African Republic, Republic of Congo (Brazzaville), Republic of Congo (Léopoldville), Republic of Ivory Coast, Republic of

had gained independence was mainly based on Part IV of the Treaty of Rome (1957). The contracting parties reaffirmed the association laid down in the Treaty of Rome (1957) and, in accordance of their common will, considered cooperation to be based on equality, friendly relations, and respect for the principles of the United Nations. The Yaoundé Convention was based on the principle of free trade. In the joint institutions of the second European Development Fund (Association Council, Association Committee, Parliamentary Conference, and Arbitration Court) partners were represented on an equal footing.[25]

The Lomé Conventions (1975–1999) represented the political direction of free market, elimination of custom duties, development aid, and investment assistance policy managed by the European Development Fund and the European Investment Bank.[26] The former overseas colonial countries, that became independent, accepted the principles envisaged in the Treaty of Rome. A European developmental aid and investment policy was taking shape based on community and bilateral intergovernmental cooperation. The bilateral aid policy motivated the governments (intergovernmentalism) by not allowing a federalist breakthrough.

Regarding developmental aid policy the problem was that the center-periphery world economic system of rich and poor countries, formed as a result of laissez-faire free market economic colonial expansion, made it difficult to realize the idea of a federalist real economy without convergence among self-managing independent states. Therefore the questions arose: could cooperation and developmental aid policy initiate an economic and social policy that is able to help the autonomous, but underdeveloped, African countries to develop based on their own internal forces? Could the EEC and the underdeveloped African countries, through their cooperation, develop from the perspective of a bottom-up, personalist, federalist economic social reform?[27]

In this regard it is worth examining the institutional structure of the EEC itself in relation to the parliamentary federalist goals aiming to democratize European society and economy. The question that arises, in this context, is how

---

Dahomey, Republic of Gabon, Republic of Upper Volta, Republic of Madagascar, Republic of Mali, Republic Islamic of Mauritania, Republic of Niger, Republic of Rwanda, Republic of Senegal, Republic of Somalia, Republic of Chad, Republic of Togo.

25 The Yaoundé Convention (20 July 1963).
26 The Lomé I Convention (1975) and the Lomé II Convention (1979).
27 Molefi Kete Asante believes that European and American aid policies were not suitable for achieving self-managing states in Africa. After independence the African states tended to favor their relations with the former colonial powers and seemed content to surrender their development agenda to foreign agencies and consultants. But later, within the framework of the NEPAD (New Partnership for Africa's Development) strategy, African politicians sought an independent and self-managing economic and political renewal and the path of African federalism. Asante, *History of Africa*, 342, 343–350; Peo Hansen and Stefan Jonsson are of the opinion that the European Economic Community ended colonialism by securing its continuation. Hansen and Jonsson, *Eurafrica*, 239–278.

satisfactorily the interests, well-being, and prosperity of the people were represented in the supranational institutions of the EEC.

The institutional structure of the European Economic Community resulted in a long discussion between the federalists and the intergovernmentalists. Spinelli, for example, criticized the European Economic Community from a constitutional federalist point of view. In his view the six governments wrote into the treaty a precise program for achieving a customs union, exchanged a formal promise to create an economic union gradually, and entrusted to a supranational commission to oversee the implementation of the treaty and to formulate proposals "for the eventual approval of the Council of Ministers of the European Economic Community."[28] He emphasized that the supranational institutions had not enough political power to create a common European agricultural, transport, and commercial policy. Political power remained in the hand of the governments that participated in the supranational policy.

Jean Monnet was satisfied with the European Coal and Steel Community, the Euratom, and the Common Market. He initiated merging the supranational institutions (Council, Assembly and Court) of these into a common European economic executive council, and so the European economic unity would be created. He was convinced that it would be necessary to establish the European United States. But he continued to believe in the gradual problem-solving method by which the European Economic Community and the Common Market were established. He thought that the economic union would lead to the political union.[29]

Between 1958 and 1962 the Common Market was very successful. It seemed that its method could become the blueprint for constructing a European union. But those limitations of the functional approach, which manifested in the case of the European Coal and Steel Community regarding the role of the governments in decision making, were present in the Common Market too. The Commission of the Common Market had no authority in political matters. So the involvement of the governments of the member states in decision making was unavoidable. The Commission could create a solidarity of common interests and rules influencing in this way the decisions of the governments. But the institutional structure of the European Economic Community in the Rome Treaties (1957) remained open and there was a struggle between the federalists and the intergovernmentalists to finalize it.

9.4 De Gaulle's Intergovernmentalist "European Concert"

In this struggle, Charles de Gaulle, as President of France, became active on the intergovernmentalist side against the federalists. The background to all this was the Cold War political situation. De Gaulle thought he needed to strengthen

---

28 Spinelli, *The Eurocrats*, 20–21.
29 Jean Monnet, "Où est l'Europe?," 259–261.

Shaping the Supranational European Union 135

France and safeguard national independence. In accordance with his "policy of grandeur" he withdrew from NATO's integrated military command, launched an independent nuclear development program, criticized the United States' intervention in Vietnam, and twice vetoed the entry of Britain into the European Economic Community. He represented the idea of a council type Europe directed by the meeting of the heads of state or government, instead of a federalist parliamentary Europe representing the interests of the European people. But he accepted the supranational offices in an intergovernmentalist sense and did not destroy the functionalist supranational advisory and supervisory institutions of the European Economic Community. He was for the rapprochement of the European states; supported the Franco-German reconciliation; protected national diversity and differences and was for a confederation of the Europeans in some competences. He envisaged the establishment of a European confederation through a popular referendum in all the member states.[30]

The first Fouchet plan, on October 19, 1961, expressed the ideas of De Gaulle about the political dimension of the economic cooperation in the framework of the Common Market. It was clearly based on intergovernmental cooperation and rejected federalism. The Dutch and Belgian representatives resisted and rejected the plan. De Gaulle, in a second Fouchet plan in 1962, once more emphasized his intergovernmentalist position: the Council would be the meeting place of the heads of state or government based on unanimity voting. Parliament could present recommendations and address questions to the Council. The Commission would be composed of the high functionaries of the administration of the foreign affairs of each member state.[31]

De Gaulle fought vehemently against the federalists, and the European Commission. In June 1965 he withdrew France's representatives from the European Community until the Luxembourg Compromise was reached ("empty chair crisis"). He was convinced that the veto right in the Council could protect the sovereignty and the interests of the member states. In January 1966 he achieved, in the Luxembourg Compromise, involving the "veto right" of the member states in the majority voting in the case of the necessity of safeguarding national interests. More precisely it meant that the discussions must be continued until unanimous agreement was reached where very important national interests were at stake.

> I. Where, in the case of decisions which may be taken by majority vote on a proposal of the Commission, very important interests of one or more partners are at stake, the Members of the Council will endeavour, within a reasonable time, to reach solutions which can be adopted by all the Members of the Council while respecting their mutual interests and those of the Community

---

30 Mioche, *Penser et construire l'Europe*, 69.
31 Mioche, *Penser et construire l'Europe*, 71–72.

II. With regard to the preceding paragraph, the French delegation considers that where very important interests are at stake the discussion must be continued until unanimous agreement is reached.[32]

With the Luxembourg Compromise (1966) De Gaulle achieved a backlash on the path to federalist integration. The institutional structure of the European Economic Community drafted in the Rome Treaties became definitely intergovernmental.

All this was well exemplified by the political rivalry between the federalist EEC Commission President, Walter Hallstein and De Gaulle. In essence, Hallstein wanted to develop the European Commission, which cooperated with the European Parliament, into a European government, and intended the Council to play a mediating role helping supranationalism.[33] De Gaulle called Hallstein an inventor of European myths and a homeless technocrat.[34] Hallstein considered the situation that De Gaulle's policy had blocked the path from the already-existing European Communities to the United States of Europe. But De Gaulle could force Hallstein to resign. His victory is highly debatable, as the removal of Hallstein has made very difficult to achieve the goal of an independent Europe.

Regarding the interstate cooperation, De Gaulle protected functionalist agencies. More concretely, he was for specialist bodies in each common domain, subordinated to the cooperating governments, and regular governmental consultations as the modernized form of the "European concert." In his words:

> The regular co-operation of the States of Western Europe in the political, economic and cultural spheres ... will entail organized, regular consultations between the governments concerned and the work of specialist bodies in each of the common domains, subordinated to those governments. It will entail periodic deliberations by an assembly made up of delegates of the national parliaments. It must also, in my view, entail as soon as possible a solemn European referendum, in order to give this new departure for Europe the popular backing which is essential to it ... If we set out on this road ... it is possible that we will come to take further steps towards European unity.[35]

Jean Monnet believed that Charles de Gaulle's ideal European Community was intergovernmental without supranational governance because he condemned the Schuman plan from the beginning as a mish-mash of coal and steel without knowing which way to go. He criticized the first steps of European integration,

---

32 "The Luxembourg Agreement, 1966," 152.
33 Hallstein, *Europe in Making*, 56–83.
34 Loth, "Hallstein und de Gaulle," 187.
35 Gaulle, "L'Europe," 195.

the European Coal and Steel Community, the European Defense Community, and the European Economic Community because they menaced French sovereignty and had no legal personality. In his view only the states (nations) had a legal personality. Consequently he was convinced that Europe should become a confederation of states.[36]

After De Gaulle's attack on federalist supranationalism, though the economic community remained alive, political cooperation continued outside the framework of the Rome Treaties following a more intergovernmentalist model. The phenomenon of a so-called "intergovernmental supranationalism" gradually emerged with the participation of the member states (governments) in supranational policy and institutions: the role of the governments was strengthened, the governments accepted the supranational European Community and the European law but the veto right in the Council gave them the possibility of representing the national interest in a supranational structure which was not federalist.

The Luxembourg Compromise (1966) was a serious defeat for the federalists. All this meant that the fundamental European social and economic reform, planned by the federalists, although did not disappear, remained an idea for the future.

9.5 Spinelli: Relaunching Integration, Reviving Federalism

The intergovernmentalist breakthrough of de Gaulle was criticized by federalists, among them Walter Hallstein, Leo Tindemans, and Spinelli.

Walter Hallstein, the federalist President of the European Commission, was in favor of realizing the ideas of the *Draft Constitution on the European Political Community* of 1953, described above. He wanted to strengthen European supranational institutions and to make the Commission into a European government.

Leo Tindemans (1922–2014), Belgian politician, in 1974, made an appeal to the Council to continue on the path of European federalism and not to return to the former system of a confederation of sovereign nation-states. He emphasized the necessity of establishing a European Parliament composed of two chambers and of implementing the federalist principles of personalism and of subsidiarity in European social organization.[37]

Spinelli was of the opinion that de Gaulle had succeeded in transforming supranational institutions into intergovernmental ones while preserving supranational supremacy under the influence of the governments. He could achieve that the Commission could not become "the nucleus of a European government," because it was reduced to "the role of an international secretariat at the service of the governments."[38] In his view, this was the essence of the de Gaulle

---

36 Monnet, *Mémoires*, 428–429.
37 Tindemans, "Report on European Union," 1975.
38 Spinelli, *The European Adventure*, 12.

transformation of the supranational institutions in terms of the federalist versus intergovernmentalist dilemma. He continued to criticize the intergovernmentalist majority, and feared that integration would come to a halt because governments using federalist institutions supported the integration only at the most critical moments, and on the basis of "the lowest common denominator of very limited importance" in the case of agreements.[39] Therefore, when European integration achieved the direct election of the members of the European Parliament, in 1979, Spinelli saw the time had come for federalist reform in the framework of the European Parliament.

As a member of the European Parliament, he took advantage of this moment, organized the federalist parliamentary reform movement, and relaunched the integration process, in 1980. He was trying to find a way to solve the problem of domination of supranational intergovernmental bureaucracy and of democratic deficit. He realized that it was necessary to start a democratic European policy with two equal oppositional groups, the intergovernmentalists versus federalists. For this he accepted the intergovernmentalist group as an equal oppositional partner to the federalists in European policy. He suggested basing European policy on the principle of subsidiarity. If both accepted the subsidiarity principle, the dichotomy federalist versus intergovernmentalist would be placed on functionalist bases. So, the federalists and intergovermentalists, as functionalists, could constitute the two main oppositional parties that were necessary to a democratic European policy (federalist functionalist versus intergovernmentalist functionalist). He hoped that, in the long run, the struggle between them could lead to finalizing the European federation.

In his lecture *Towards the European Union* (Florence, June 13, 1983), he outlined his ideas on the federalist reform of the European Community. He emphasized that intergovernmental cooperation was the basic, but questionable, means. European integration based on the common supranational institutions, that developed during the integration process, would be a more secure way. Therefore it would be necessary to strengthen the supranational institutions of the European Community by putting reform drafts to the European Parliament. The Parliament should become the place of an active European policy representing the interests of the European citizens. In his view this was the means of avoiding the domination of the national will above the European spirit.[40]

His most important reform ideas were outlined in the *Draft Treaty Establishing the European Union* ("Spinelli draft"), in 1984, which was adopted by the European Parliament. It influenced the Single European Act (1986), and Delor's policy. In this document he put forward a parliamentary system of two chambers as a result of the democratization of the co-decision procedure between the European Parliament and the Council (Article 38). He struggled for equal rights of the European Parliament with the Council.

39 Spinelli, *The European Adventure*, 13.
40 Spinelli, *Towards the European Union*, 9–28.

Article 38 of the *Draft Treaty Establishing the European Union* (1984) can be regarded as the key article.[41] It served as a means of political struggle, to achieve the most important federalist aim, which was a bicameral parliament representing the interests of the European citizens as Europeans and as citizens of their states. This could be done by making the Council the second chamber of the Parliament. The reform of the co-decision procedure aimed to help the Parliament to strengthen its role in the legislation, and to make it strong enough to elect a European government representing the executive power. The institution of the Conciliation Committee between the Parliament and the Council served the aim of achieving the equal status of the Parliament with the Council.

Spinelli recognized the lack of European governance. He tried to solve this problem through the principle of subsidiarity. This is why he proposed introducing and including the principle of subsidiarity in the treaty on the European union as the means to directing the division of competences between the union and the member states. In his view the role of subsidiarity was to bind the European Community and its institutions to compensate for the lack of a European government.[42]

The Preamble of the Draft Treaty emphasized that to the union belonged only those competences which the union could solve better than the states, and therefore the member states transferred them to the union level.

> Intending to entrust common institutions, in accordance with the principle of subsidiarity, only with those powers required to complete successfully the tasks they may carry out more satisfactorily than the States acting independently.[43]

Article 12 expressed the meaning of the subsidiarity principle, in the case of defining competences, in the following terms:

- Where this Treaty confers exclusive competences on the Union, the institutions of the Union shall have such power to act; national authorities may only legislate to the extent laid down by the law of the Union. Until the Union has legislated, national legislation shall remain in force.
- Where this Treaty confers concurrent competences on the Union, the member States shall continue to act so long as the Union has not legislated. The Union shall only act to carry out those tasks which may be undertaken more effectively in common than by the Member States acting separately,

---

41 "Draft Treaty Establishing the European Union, 1984," Article 38, voting procedure for draft laws (the case of the Conciliation Committee), 316.
42 Endo, *Subsidiarity*, 23; Bóka, "The Idea of Subsidiarity," 30–32.
43 "Draft Treaty Establishing the European Union, 1984," Preamble, 306.

in particular those whose execution requires action by the Union because their dimension or effects extend beyond national frontiers.[44]

The competences left to the union by the specific articles of the Draft Treaty were sufficiently broad: monetary policy, sectorial policy (agriculture, transport, telecommunications, research and development, industry, energy), social and health policy, environmental policy, education and research policy, cultural policy, industrial policy. He proposed to extend the field of cooperation to defense, disarmament, and foreign policy.[45]

Spinelli believed that subsidiarity could function as a balance of power between the federalists and the intergovernmentalists. Following these lines, the integration process could continue. However, he regarded this solution as provisional. In his view, the European Federation should become a federation of persons and of autonomous member states. In such a federation subsidiarity was the means of placing the autonomous member states into the framework of a larger federation in harmony with federal constitutional law, international law, and human rights. According to him, subsidiarity could work perfectly only in a federation where there was harmony between the personal principle and the subsidiarity principle within the framework of the European Parliament.

Spinelli believed that the federalists had to continue the political struggle for the democratization of the institutions of the European Community. He, therefore, proposed three political strategies:

1. The democratization of the co-decision procedure between the European Parliament and the Council.
2. The enlargement of the fields of supranational cooperation, to gradually transfer more and more fields from the national level to the supranational level by using the principle of subsidiarity.
3. A clear division of competences between the union and the member states.

Spinelli proposed the *Draft Treaty Establishing the European Union* in the interest of a democratic European parliamentary federation representing the European citizens. His reform policy and the *Draft Treaty Establishing the European Union* started a new federalist drive in European integration, with a major role given to subsidiarity. He was also searching to find a necessary compromise with the intergovernmentalists to revive the European integration process after De Gaulle's intergovernmentalist triumph. But he emphasized that the federalists had to struggle against the nationalist interpretation of subsidiarity.[46]

---

44 "Draft Treaty Establishing the European Union, 1984," Article 12, 309–310.
45 "Draft Treaty Establishing the European Union, 1984," 318–324.
46 Bóka, "A European Parliamentary Project," 7–8.

Spinelli's federalist reform initiative made it possible to establish the European Union in 1992. For this he is regarded as the Founding Father of the European Union.

9.6 The Delors's Reform: Federation of Nation States and of People

Jacques Delors (1925–), French politician, as President of the European Commission (1985–1995), at the time of the disintegration of the bipolar world, continued the federalist political reform started by Spinelli. He sympathized with subsidiarity and multilevelism. But being an integral federalist, he did not favor a European federal government as Spinelli did. His ideas were close to the "Monnet-method," he accepted the spill-over theory and gradualism. More precisely, he defined himself as a personalist federalist belonging to the French personalist school of Emmanuel Mounier, the theoretician of the Esprit group. Delors highly appreciated the vision of, the above-mentioned personalist federalist thinker, Denis de Rougemont, too. He was also for a gradual shaping of the European union through bottom-up associations of small entities based on the solidarity of interests. But he emphasized that this was not enough. It was necessary to "work from the top down viewing the paths of integration from above."[47]

In his Brugge speech, on October 17, 1989, Delors outlined his reform ideas on European construction. Opposing the classical confederalist vision of Margaret Thatcher, British Prime Minister, he proposed a new vision, namely a "federation of nation states and of people." It meant to unite not only the people, as Jean Monnet wanted, but the nation states too. In his words:

> I want not only to unite people, as Jean Monnet did, but also to bring nations together.[48]

In Delors's view the union was necessary to insure Europe's place in a global world. The growing interdependence of the national economies and the internationalization of the financial world made necessary the union and cooperation at world level. However, he realized that European federalism could not follow the American model. The task of Europeans was "to unite old nations with strong traditions and personalities."[49] He believed that the European integration process had achieved a lot which pointed toward his vision of a federation of nation states and of people: It had a treaty ratified by all national parliaments expressing the national will, a Court of Justice which dealt with the interpretation of differences, a European Council which allowed heads of state or government to monitor progress and provide impetus. As a new development

---

47 Delors, "Address by Mr. Jacques Delors, 1989," 56–57.
48 Delors, "Address by Mr. Jacques Delors, 1989," 62.
49 Delors, "Address by Mr. Jacques Delors, 1989," 61–62.

the Commission presented a balance sheet at each meeting of what had been accomplished and what remained to be done. The union was shaped gradually through the realization of the resolutions. Thanks to the Single Act, 1986 the Council, the Parliament, and the Commission became more efficient institutions than earlier.[50]

Regarding the problem of unifying sovereign nation-states Delors proposed turning to the principles of federalism. He believed that it was a workable solution because federalism was based on the autonomy principle of the member states, on cooperation based on treaties and on the subsidiarity principle. The rule of autonomy preserved the identity of each member states and removed any temptation to pursue unification regardless. The rule of participation did not allow "one entity to be subordinated to another, but on the contrary, promoted cooperation and synergy on the basis of the clear and well-defined provisions contained in the Treaty."[51]

Delors warned that federalism did not represent any conspiracy against the nation-states. Therefore it would be necessary to revise the step-by-step approach and establish the European union. However, he did not propose realizing a common government on the common fields responsible to a bicameral European parliament. He also opposed the creation of a European constitution instead of a treaty amendment, having sovereign power above the states.[52]

At the same time Delors acknowledged the importance of the subsidiarity principle and enlarged the integral federalist theory with it. He believed that subsidiarity, as the basic principle of federalism, was very suitable for shaping European international cooperation because it was embedded in personalism and federalism. It acted as guarantor of local participation, autonomy, and self-determination. Personalism was based on the active participation of people in political, economic and social institutions close to their needs and concentrating on problem-solving.[53]

In his speech about the principle of subsidiarity, Delors explained that subsidiarity could be applied in two different situations: On the one hand, as a dividing line between the private sphere and the state, on the other hand as the repartition of tasks between the different levels of political power. It ensured persons the right to exercise their responsibilities where they could perform them the best. He emphasized the importance of letting the citizens know what belonged to which level of authority because, in his view, one aspect of the "democratic deficit" in the Community originated from this lack of visibility. He emphasized that the clear determination of the citizen's reciprocal responsibilities and of the different levels of power was very important. He mentioned Tocqueville as an example of one who preferred this solution. Delors warned that subsidiarity was

50 Delors, "Address by Mr. Jacques Delors, 1989," 63–64.
51 Delors, "Address by Mr. Jacques Delors, 1989," 60.
52 Delors, *L'Unité d'un homme*, 279–281.
53 Burgess, *Federation and European Union*, 172–173.

an organizing principle of a federal state. He definitely rejected using it in the name of nation-states.[54]

In his view the construction of the European Community represented a new kind of federal and intergovernmental union of states directed by multilevel governance in the framework of a single institutional structure. As a federalist political tactic he proposed continuing the supranational economic policy of the federalist founding fathers: to establish the single market and the economic and monetary union, to gradually transfer the necessary powers from the level of the nation states to the supranational level, to enlarge the fields of supranational cooperation, to diminish the role of veto, and to realize the union of nation-states and of people based on the principle of subsidiarity.

In conclusion, Delors, as an integral or personal federalist, could strengthen his federalist direction against the constitutional federalist. At the same time he had to compromise with the intergovernmentalists who could again profit from the integral federalist gradualist vision. Although Delors wanted something different than the intergovernmentalists, the compromise disturbed clairvoyance. Therefore, with the Treaty of Maastricht, 1992, he could not achieve the necessary balance between the federalists and the intergovernmentalists.

9.7 European Union (1992): A New Type of Federalist Functionalist and Intergovernmentalist Functionalist Union of States Based on Subsidiarity and Multilevelism

The Treaty on the European Union (1992) represented another logical step on the path to the European integration process that started in 1950 with the Schuman Declaration. It established a European Union based upon the existing supranational European Community together with two new intergovernmental pillars: namely, cooperation in foreign and security policies, and justice and home affairs. But federalism, as vocation, was no longer accepted. Instead the Preamble spoke about an ever closer union. This was a serious defeat for the federalists. Regarding the institutional structure of the Union a single institutional framework served a two-level governance. The principle of subsidiarity was involved but not precisely defined. The European Parliament was still not fully integrated into the decision-making procedure on an equal basis with the Council and the veto right survived. Important competences were left as an intergovernmental responsibility: foreign policy, security, defense, immigration, and social policies. The United Kingdom could opt-out. The treaty could not solve the European governance, the European Union had no legal personality. It was a union with a democratic deficit.[55]

The federalist and intergovernmentalist compromise made it possible to establish, through the Maastricht Treaty, an intergovernmental and

---

54 Delors, "The Principle of Subsidiarity" 7, 9, 17–18.
55 Treaty on European Union (Maastricht, February 7, 1992).

supranational union of nation states based on two-level governance: the supranational Economic Community and the intergovernmental political community, i.e., the European Union. In practice, this "intergovernmental supranationalism" meant that the national governments accepted European law but safeguarded their national sovereignty in all those fields that represented national interest. They could veto the federalist political and institutional aspirations.

The Treaty on the European Union (1992) strengthened the nation states but the supranational European Community could gradually develop because supranationalism became the interest of the governments. The governments, at the level of the lowest common denominator, supported the supranational functionalist integration process, slowly and gradually transferring competences (functions) to the supranational level. So the multilevel structure of the union directed by subsidiarity could further develop. Multilevelism was shaped by the division of competences between the member states and the Union and the transfer of competences to the Union level.

For the federalists it would be difficult to survive as an opposition because the treaty favored intergovernmentalism: the concept of federalism was questioned, the word federalism was banished, the European Parliament was still not fully integrated into the decision-making process on an equal basis with the Council and the "single institutional framework" serving a multilevel governance was seen as doubtful. The definition of the principle of subsidiarity remained ambiguous in practical legal terms. However, subsidiarity could further work in practice as a means of transferring competences to the supranational level.

Regarding subsidiarity the question could arise: how long could subsidiarity play this role in the lack of the balance between the federalists and the intergovernmentalists in favor of the intergovernmentalists? If the supranational institutions became the agencies of the nation states and nationalism, then the European Union would become an intergovernmentalist institution in disharmony with the system of Western liberties, popular sovereignty, and democracy.

10

OUTLOOK: FUTURE PATHS AND PERSPECTIVES

Regarding the future paths of the European Union there were two important reform attempts. The first aimed to strengthen the federalist opposition to the intergovernmentalist policy and the second to create a European constitution.

Regarding the strengthening of federalism, Joschka Fisher (1948–), German politician, warned European politicians to avoid the collapse of the European Union's development into a supranational regional federation. He gave a speech at the Humboldt University in Berlin on May 12, 2000, in which he emphasized the necessity of finalizing the construction of the European Community. He reminded Europeans that they had started to unify Europe after the war because they rejected the former balance of power principle and the hegemonic ambitions of nation-states. He emphasized that, if Europeans wanted the European Union, then there was no other choice than to follow the steps described by Robert Schuman in 1950 toward a European federation with a legislative European Parliament and an executive European government based on a constituent treaty. In his words:

> The transition from a union of states to a full parliamentarisation as a European Federation, something Robert Schuman demanded 50 years ago. And that means nothing less than a European Parliament and a European government which really do exercise legislative and executive power within the Federation. This Federation will have to be based on a constituent treaty.[1]

Fischer believed that the 'Monnet-method' of a gradual process of integration, with no blueprint for the final state, was not suitable for achieving this aim. It was no longer effective because it had proved to be of only limited use for the political integration and democratization of Europe. He suggested instead reforming the European Union in the direction of a union of European people and of nation-states based on the principle of subsidiarity. The European Parliament should have two chambers: one would be for elected members who were also members of their national parliaments. Thus there would be no clash

---

1 Fischer, "From Confederacy to Federation," 25.

between the national parliaments and the European Parliament, and no clash between the nation states and Europe. For the second chamber he proposed a choice between the approaches of the US Senate, with directly elected senators from the member states, or a chamber of states along the lines of the Bundesrat of Germany. He suggested solving the question of European government (executive power) by developing the European Council or the European Commission into a European government.[2]

In Fischer's view Europe needed a constitution centered around basic human and civil rights, equal division of powers between the European institutions, and a precise delimitation of competences between the European and the member state levels. The European Constitution should concentrate on the organization of the relationship between the federation and the member states.

Concerning Europe's future, Fischer suggested reinforcing the cooperation among the member states toward a federation or forming a center of gravity. In the first case, those states that wanted to cooperate more closely than others could reinforce their cooperation. In the second case, a group of states could conclude a new European federal framework treaty which would be the nucleus of a federal constitution and function as a center of gravity attracting the other states. On the basis of this treaty the federation would develop its institutions, establish a government, a strong parliament, and a directly elected president. This center would work as a driving force for the completion of the political integration.[3] The last step would be the completion of the European Federation.

He warned Europeans that the European Union could only participate in the global economic and political competition of the 21st century if it could finalize the European Federation and could have a legal personality.

The Fischer plan did not receive much support because the EU was faced with Eastern European enlargement, and politicians did not want to deepen the Union.

Another reform attempt was the constitutionalization project in 2003–2007. The Draft Treaty Establishing a Constitution for Europe (2003) summarized the most important achievements of the European integration process.[4] It merged the basic treaties into a new constitutional treaty on the European Union. It was composed of federalist and intergovernmentalist elements based on the principle of division of competences between the Union and the member states using the principle of subsidiarity. Although the federalist elements dominated, the emphasis was on the member states: the member states—and not the European citizens—constituted the European Union. The European Parliament represented the people of the European states and not the European people. In the Council each national government represented the interests of its own state. In

---

2 Fischer, "From Confederacy to Federation," 25–26.
3 Fischer, "From Confederacy to Federation," 29.
4 Draft Treaty Establishing a Constitution for Europe, 2003.

Outlook: Future Paths and Perspectives

this system, thanks to the supranational institutions, subsidiarity played the role of sharing the competences between the member states and the Union.

The Draft Constitution (2003) was an important achievement. It represented the fifth step on the way of the European integration process. The first was the establishment of the Council of Europe, the second of the European Coal and Steel Community, the third of the Euratom and the European Economic Community, and the fourth of the European Union. The Draft Constitution was an important "summary treaty," a "treaty of assessment," a necessary summary, a combination and assessment of the achievements of the construction of the European Community during its history. It kept the door open for future federalist reforms toward a bicameral European Parliament of European citizens. The revised variant of the 2003 draft treaty, *The Treaty Establishing a Constitution for Europe* (2004), was rejected by the French and Dutch voters.

Finally, the Treaty of Lisbon (2007) was created to replace the Constitutional Treaty (2004). The Treaty of Lisbon amended the Treaty on the European Union and the Treaty Establishing the European Economic Community.[5] It made the Union's bill of rights, the Charter of the Fundamental Rights of the European Union, legally binding.[6] The treaty established a supranational and intergovernmental union of states based on subsidiarity and multilevelism. According to multilevelism the European Union had exclusive, shared, and supported competences based on the principle of subsidiarity: exclusive competences (customs union, internal market, monetary policy of the euro countries, common fisheries policy, and common commercial policy), shared competences (social policy, economic, social and territorial cohesion, agriculture, environment, consumer protection, transport, trans-European networks, energy, areas of freedom, security, and justice, common safety concerns in public health matters) and supported, coordinated, or supplemented competences (protection and improvement of human health, industry, culture, tourism, education, vocational training, youth and sport, civil protection, administrative cooperation).

The Treaty of Lisbon (2007) recognized the legal personality of the EU. It strengthened the European Parliament and represented a move toward a bicameral system. Parliament's powers were expanded with important new elements on EU legislation and budget. Measures were taken in the co-decision procedure (ordinary legislative procedure) between the Parliament and the Council to put the Parliament in an equal status with the Council. The Commission was accountable to the Parliament. The European Council submitted a report to Parliament after each meeting.

In conclusion, the Lisbon Treaty left the door open for further democratization of the EU toward a bicameral parliamentary federation of people.

---

5 Treaty of Lisbon, 2007.
6 Charter of the Fundamental Rights of the European Union, 2007.

Outlook: Future Paths and Perspectives

In the future the EU should continue on the path of the constitutionalization reform and finalize the EU as a constitutional bicameral parliamentary federation with a government dealing with the exclusive (common) competences, leaving the member states autonomous in all other fields. The Founding Fathers represented this goal, which they gradually wanted to achieve through a necessary bottom-up social democratization.

11

THE WORLD AND EUROPE (EU): SOME RESPONSES TO THE CHALLENGE OF EUROPEAN MODERNITY

Finally the question arises: what was Europe's role in the world as a modernizer in the eyes of non-Europeans (non-European civilizations), and what the EU could mean for the rest of the world?

European civilization is called the "civilization of modernity" because it created a liberal capitalist market economy within the framework of an industrial society, interacting with the United States and the whole world, and all this has changed the organizational framework and living conditions of the former traditional agricultural society.[1] The main characteristics of the former agricultural society were stability, livelihood orientation, kinship-centricity, and religiosity. In contrast, modern society changed rapidly; its goal was to produce surplus industrial production, make profit and investments; it was individualistic; and it focused on the state and the economy and declared itself rationalist.[2] Thus European modernity and modernization can be regarded as a complex historical phenomenon: it means industrialization, the emergence of a liberal capitalist world system, the necessary reforms of state and international organization, and the formation of an ideology of democratization and human rights. In modernization, Europeans played a leading role, with the voluntary or forced participation of other civilizations.

Prominent non-European modernizers valued European civilization because it was able to create modern capitalism, and initiated social organization in the spirit of liberty. At the same time, they criticized Europeans for a dissonance of thinking and acting regarding the implementation of the idea of liberty, democracy, and human rights in the internal and external political and economic practice of social organization. In this respect European modernizing expansion is regarded as a controversial subject with positive and negative effects.

The essence of the problem is that, during history, European civilization developed and renewed itself in close interaction with other civilizations. It played a leading role in the development of capitalism as a global economic, commercial, financial, and political system during the 19th and 20th centuries. Western industrial powers opened up the closed agrarian civilizations worldwide. Their goal was to involve them in a free market-based capitalist economic

1 Wesseling, *Expansion and Reaction*, 10–11.
2 Waters, *Modernity*, vol. 1, xii–xiii, 4.

and commercial world system. Because of the dominant, expansive, and exploitative nature of Western modernization the whole world had to face the necessity of understanding, learning, interpreting, and answering the challenge of Western free market capitalism. Thus the economic, commercial, financial, and political principles of the West, as well as the idea of a democratic civil society and the issues around colonization, imperialism, and globalization represented a challenge for the political elite of the non-European civilizations. Comparing their own societies to 'European or Western modernity,' they studied what to adopt and what to reject to be able to remain independent. These studies often resulted in realizing and criticizing the contradictions of Western ideas, law, and the reality of state and international organization. Parallel to all this, the non-European civilizations became actively involved in the emergence of a capitalist economic, commercial, and financial world system which gradually replaced the traditional agrarian societies. Non-European civilizations adopted the necessary European knowledge but rejected European universalism and tried to develop along their own cultural paths.[3] 'European modernity' in this sense was the undoubted contribution of European civilization to the shaping of world history and the civilization process, but with the participation and interaction of the other civilizations.[4]

In what follows the responses to the challenge of 'European modernity' will be reviewed from India, Africa, Japan, and China, which created a world economy. These civilizations can be seen as creative shapers of the world civilization process. In the 19th and 20th centuries they involved European elements in their political, economic, and social organization, but with criticisms, and trying to preserve their own culture. From the point of view of our topic, it is important to find those meeting points which showed in the direction of a peaceful world. This is all the more important because the crises of free competitive capitalism have been able to destroy European civilization itself, causing world wars, and Europeans had to defend themselves against the economic crises and nationalism by creating unity in the form of democracy among the states.

11.1 Responses from India (Gandhi and Nehru)

Modernizers of the old civilizations recognized that the capitalist liberal market expansion—how it developed in the framework of the East Indian Company—was a new form of colonization that changed the classical Spanish territorial conquest. They recognized also that the liberal market expansion gradually developed toward a new global order with the voluntary or forced participation of everybody. All this was made clear in the correspondence between Leo Tolstoy (1828–1910), Russian writer and Mahatma Gandhi (1869–1948), the leader of the Independence Movement of India. Tolstoy in his letter to Gandhi

---

[3] Bóka, *Modernizáció és értékrend*; Bóka, *Modernizáció mint társadalomformáló eszme*, 1–9.
[4] Eisenstadt, "European Expansion and the Civilization of Modernity," 176, 180.

emphasized that the colonization of India could not happen without the involvement and cooperation of the Indians who also represented the spirit of violence. A small English trading company would not have been able to impoverish the vast masses of the Indians without their involvement, as numerical evidence proved.[5]

Gandhi in his *Hind Swaraj or Indian Home Rule* accepted that Tolstoy was right, and he made the emphasis on social justice and pursued a dignified non-violent resistance policy. He represented the ethical and moral tradition of the Hindu civilization in India, and applied this ethical and moral tradition in practical politics. He rejected the colonizing aspect of modern Western civilization which used violence and wars, and aimed money-making and limitless exploitation, but at the same time represented the spirit of liberty. This is why he questioned the sincerity of the Western values and morals. In his search for Indian ways of modernization, Gandhi idealized the pre-British Indian agrarian civilization which represented self-governing village communities with true morals, and served the livelihood of the people. As for the British, he was of the opinion, that since they were lords of India, they had the duty to serve the prosperity of the people living there. They had to give up their purpose of gaining and enriching from India. They must govern the country according to the needs and well-being of the Indian people. Because of the British misconduct in India, Indians had to fight for self-government and self-sufficiency through non-violent passive resistance (boycott of British goods) and protecting the Indian traditional village society. He was for rejecting the civilization represented by the British.[6]

After the liberation from British rule, Gandhi imagined a federal India, governed by a government of the people's own choice, within the framework of a bottom-up federalist state based on village self-government concentrating on the well-being of the people. In his view democratic federalism was the meeting point of the European and Indian civilizations to work together toward world peace.

Jawaharlal Nehru (1889–1964), the first Prime Minister of independent India worked closely with Gandhi and regarded him as the Father of the Nation, but he looked at India with more Western eyes. He was a lawyer from the Brahman caste of Kashmir, studied at the University of Cambridge, and graduated in law in London. As a democratic socialist thinker, he believed that the main social problem of his age was the international tension between the imperialist form of capitalism and anti-capitalist socialism. He wanted to free humanity from all forms of oppression and exploitation, and this goal led him in the struggle for India's independence and federal union.[7]

In agreement with Gandhi, he criticized the morality of the British colonialist method, and the morality of those Indians who cooperated. According to

---

5 Tolstoy, "A letter to a Hindu," 55–56.
6 Gandhi, *Hind Swaraj*, 112–119.
7 Bóka, *Európa és Ázsia*, 85–92.

him, the British were lucky because a fragmented Indian society, full of power struggles, offered them an easy opportunity to get rich, and they recognized and profited from this possibility. A new kind of colonial economic model emerged in India in the framework of the East India Company characterized by free market and trade without social organizing obligations. Based on their advanced weapons, resourceful business methods, and the principle of commercial and entrepreneurial freedom, the British modernized classical robbery and created a modern colonial market economy with the participation of the Indians. The problem with this, in fact, was that this economic policy was not intended to organize the life of the colonial country or to form a government for promoting the well-being of the people. Thus, the structure of trade and production that developed between the two countries led to the emergence of an unregulated international free market economic and political system without planning and coordination. This continuously produced contradictions, and accumulated crises after crises because they (British and cooperating Indians) did not focus on the real welfare problems. Nehru, like Gandhi, drew attention to the fact that this 'East India Company-type' of enterprise left an irresponsible legacy of economic modernization of the era of imperialism and that it has not disappeared from the liberal global world economic and financial system even after the liberation of the colonies. Therefore—in his view—facing this fact and rethinking effective opposition tactics was the challenge for all of humanity in the fight to reform the international system.[8]

Nehru's main problem with the Western ideas and political practice of liberal bourgeois democratic government was that it could not solve the problem of international democracy between countries. On the contrary, imperialism had fueled nationalism and the development of racial theory and racism.[9] He saw the antidote to all this in the ideology of the peaceful world federation and the corresponding federalist organization of the state and international relations. He believed in the idea of a peaceful world federation connecting civilizations in peace-building. In his view, this was the idea in which the values of civilizations met. In Asia and Europe, this direction of thinking was called the 'One World' philosophy. This meant the contribution of all the world's civilizations on the road to a world peace alliance, the goal of which was to create a peaceful world government cooperating in unity. He was in search of the place and the role of India in this process.[10]

Regarding India's involvement in European modernization, Nehru stressed that India was socially different from Europe. One thing they had in common, however, was that modernization had dismantled old structures in India as well. India, for example, did not have a feudal system similar to the European: neither the feudal vassal relationship nor the landlord serf subordinated relationship

---

8 Nehru, *Discovery of India*, 235–240, 253–263, 281.
9 Nehru, *Discovery of India*, 423–424.
10 Bóka, *Európa és Ázsia*, 87.

developed there. Religion functioned as a regulation of moral behavior, not as dogma. The caste was a group that provided services and functions. Regarding the social structure in India, he stressed that it was built on three things: the autonomous village community, the caste, and the family community system. In all three, the group mattered, and the individual was only secondary. He saw the most fundamental difference between India and the West in the relationship between group and individual: in the Hindu concept, as in Asian concepts in general, the group was the basic unit of society, and the individual was subordinated to the group. The Western concept, in contrast, placed the individual above the group. Thus, these two social approaches opposed each other. In Europe, as the result of the disintegration of the feudal system, democratic liberalism emerged in the 19th century which dominated the economic life, and social and political organization, and led to the emergence of the phenomenon of individualism. It survived in the twentieth century, but the serious conflicts that worked within it caused crises. Therefore, liberal individualism became obsolete after the Second World War, and human society had to find a solution to the tension between the group and the individual in the organization of society. The disintegration and obsolescence of the old system everywhere led to the disruption of social life, the loss of social cohesion, mass suffering, the abnormality of individual behavior, and this remained a problem until a social structure—appropriate to the modern age—could emerge.[11]

In assessing the historical role of Europe and the United States in India, Nehru highlighted that they had good and bad effects. Among the good effects, he listed the significant contribution of Europe and the United States to human progress, which he respected. He emphasized the need to learn all the lessons that they really had to teach the world. Among the bad effects he mentioned the wars and the myriad conflicts in which Asian countries got involved because of the European spirit of war. He called on the Asians to pursue a policy of peace, and to concentrate on the organization of cooperation in the economic, political, and social spheres, with the goal of creating a world federation.[12] He was for the establishment of an independent democratic constitutional parliamentary federal republic following the example of the Constitution of the United States. He imagined India as a strong United States—as a federation of free units— whose members were connected as confidential neighbors. In his view, such a federal India as a great power—like the United States, the Soviet Union, and China—could play a significant role in world politics and the United Nations. So the belief in the idea of world federalism connected Nehru and the European federalists.[13]

The results he could achieve in political practice were shown in the 1950 constitution. According to the Constitution adopted in 1950, the Republic

---

11 Nehru, *Discovery of India*, 207–209, 212–213.
12 Nehru, *Independence and After*, 298–299.
13 Bóka, *Európa és Ázsia*, 90.

of India was a sovereign socialist secular democratic republic with presidential power. It was modeled on the Westminster model, and drafted by Bhimrao Romji Ambedkar, Indian socialist reformer, who was the Chairman of the Constituent Drafting Committee. It was a long, detailed constitution that was amended many times. The 1950 Constitution guaranteed a wide range of civil liberties for individual citizens. It included fundamental rights, among them the right to equality, the right to freedom, the right against exploitation, the right to freedom of religion, and cultural and educational rights. The right to equality guaranteed the abolition of untouchability and all forms of discrimination. According to the Constitution, the aim of the state was to secure a social order for the promotion of the welfare of the people. The executive power was vested in the President, who had to govern in accordance with the Constitution. He was the supreme commander of the defense forces of the union, and was helped and advised by the Council of Ministers through the Prime Minister. The judges of the Supreme Court were nominated by him, but the Supreme Court was independent. He had the right to address or send messages to the two houses, and participated in the legislative co-decision procedure between them. He had the right to promulgate ordinances in exceptional cases, but they could only become law with the consent of Parliament. For the violation of the Constitution he was removable from office by impeachment of either house of Parliament. The legislative power was the bicameral Parliament which consisted of the President and the two houses of the Parliament. The two houses of the legislature were the Council of States and the House of People. The Council of States was a permanent body whose representatives were elected in accordance with the system of proportional representation of the states. The House of People, representing the interests of individual constituencies, was elected by direct citizens' vote for a term of five years. India's official state form was a federal union of states, which consisted of 28 states and 7 union territories. The states and territories of the union enjoyed autonomy but they were subordinated to the federal law according to the principle of subsidiarity. The states were divided into districts, the smallest unit was the village. Language-based member states had an elected legislature and an executive government.[14]

After the Constitution came into force, Nehru, as India's Prime Minister implemented an ambitious economic, political, and social reform program with the goal of transforming India from a colony to a republic while maintaining a multiparty system and avoiding one-party authoritarian rule. But as the first Prime Minister of independent India elected by Congress (India's dominant party) he had considerable power to transform India.

Nehru supported Asian cooperation and the Asia Conference that facilitated it. It was convened in 1947 in New Delhi and launched the Pan-Asian movement. Here, the leaders of the Asian independence movement set out the goal to create Asian unity. Nehru called for the restoration of the cooperation among

---

14 Constitution of India, 1950.

the Asian countries, and stressed that the Pan-Asian movement was not directed against Europe, the United States, or any other country, the uniting countries simply wanted to work together peacefully in all areas where needed.[15]

In foreign policy he became a leading figure in the Non-Aligned Movement of a group of nations professing neutrality between the two main ideological rival blocs of the 1950s led by the United States and the Union of Soviet Socialist Republics. He was the key organizer of the Bandung Conference (1955), the meeting of the newly independent Asian and African states which was intended to revitalize the Non-Aligned Movement, and to bring together in its framework the emerging nations in the world policy.

India was distrustful of the emerging European Community after the Second World War because of colonization. It was thought that the European Economic Community continued the liberal market economy which was considered as the survival of imperialism without an effective international coordination in the framework of the United Nations. For the Indian people the resurgence of (neo)colonialism was a real danger. But it was watched with interest whether the European Economic Community could develop into a democratic federalist international economic community within the framework of the United Nations. The achievements of European integration were acknowledged, but the parliamentary federal union was criticized as regards the confused role of the European Parliament and the Commission. It was not clear whether the EU would be a loose free market economy without coordinating bodies, or a market economy based on coordinated cooperation, in which nation-states would subordinate their sovereignty in common affairs to the European Commission having a mediating role.[16]

India preferred to pursue a non-aligned policy, and was looking for new alternative paths for economic cooperation in the age of globalization. From 1950 to the 1980s, the country pursued a socialist, state-run, protectionist, and publicly owned economic policy. From 1991, it switched to a market-based system, and the Indian economy started to flourish. Foreign trade and foreign investment became an integral part of the economy, and good dialogue-based relations developed between India and the EU, and India became an important partner of the EU.

In the case of India, the European Union was dealing with a continent-sized former colonial country (receiving EU development aid) that developed into a major economic power in the world searching for its own path. Indian thinkers were not convinced that the liberal or neoliberal policies of the global capitalist world economy were meaningful and appropriate social and economic organizing policies without international transparency, and coordination in areas of common interest. In these circumstances the meeting point of the EU-India cooperation policy was the challenge of democratic modernization of the

---

15 Nehru, *Independence and After*, 297, 298.
16 Kumar, *India and the European Economic Community*, 20–21, 37, 52–55.

international policy, the liberal market economy model, and the international organization.[17]

11.2 Some African Answers (Nkrumah, Senghor, Nyerere)

India's struggle for independence, led by Gandhi and Nehru, served as an example for the leaders of African independence. Among them Kwame Nkrumah, Léopold Sedar Senghor, and Julius K. Nyerere, for example, rejected the exploiting, imperialist, and immoral aspect of Western colonization, and they were looking for paths for Africa within the framework of a modern African socialism and federalism. Their socialist model, in the 1960s, was a combination of Western liberal ideas, Marxism-Leninism, Islamic socialism, and traditional African values. The ideal was a one-party parliamentary regime that could monopolize power. Laissez-faire liberal economic system was rejected, and centralized planning and state supervision (statism) was protected. The centralizing tendencies of socialism could help to justify the one-party monopoly of power against pluralism.[18]

The industrial, scientific, economic, and constitutional modernizing aspect of Europe has become a controversial and debated topic in Africa. There were those who wanted to cooperate with the former colonizers after independence, there were those who sought the path of an independent African socialism, and there were those who wanted to combine African socialism with useful elements of Western modernization. The visions of the three major African national independence leaders and first Presidents, Kwame Nkrumah, Léopold Sédar Senghor, and Julius Nyerere, presented below, show that they were thinking about these dilemmas. All three were anti-colonialists, represented the idea of one-party socialism, established a strong presidential system, and supported African federalism. They thought that becoming independent of the French and British colonial metropoles, and creating modern democratic nation-states and their federations required a concentration of power in the hands of the Presidents at the beginning, who could ensure the gradual democratization. To avoid neocolonialism, they supported the creation of a union of independent African states following the example of the successful federal states, above all the United States.

Africa's first independent republic was founded, in 1957, by Kwame Nkrumah (1909–1972), as the beginning of the African independence struggles of the 1960s. He was a Ghanaian politician and revolutionary who studied in London and the United States. He fought resolutely against the British colonial rule for the full and immediate democratic self-government of Ghana, with the support of the people in the framework of his Convention People's Party.[19] He was a

---

17 Bóka, *Európa és Ázsia*, 180.
18 Ki-Zerbo et al., "Nation-building and Changing Political Values," vol. 8, 486–487.
19 Nkrumah, *Autobiography*, 291–302.

believer in the legitimate and constitutional means of democratization, and used the policy of non-violent passive resistance, as used Gandhi in India. According to his own confession, he was influenced by the ideas of Gandhi, and the great human example of Nehru.[20]

Nkrumah formulated his vision on decolonization and development for Africa in his political essay *Consciencism* (1964). He imagined a society in which the quintessence of human purpose of traditional African society reasserted itself in a modern society. He believed that true socialism sought a connection with the egalitarian and humanist values of the pre-colonial African past and those elements which could be adapted from the results of colonial modernization (new methods of industrial production and economic organization) aiming to serve the interests of the people and defend independence. True socialism represented a creative force to change society toward equality.[21] In the *Consciencism*, he attempted to create a synthesis that combined the values of anti-imperialist nationalism, technological and scientific modernization, and the African and Islamic heritage with African socialism and unity.[22]

Nkrumah warned of the dangers of neo-colonialism. He believed that the economies and policies of the former colonial states, despite gaining their independence, were still driven from the outside because of the nature of loans and multinational enterprises. Thus, less developed areas could not represent their own economic and political interests. Neo-colonialism—he argued—could only be defeated by a policy of non-alignment, and using foreign capital and investment to serve the national plan and national interests of the borrowing country. In this way, the borrowing state could remain the master of its destiny, as citizens could shape their own state themselves. This could result in the neutralization of neo-colonialism. However, the real victory over it required the creation of African unity, and the effective management of the world economy by a suitable international organization.[23]

Studying the federal governments in the world (the United States, the Soviet Union, Australia, Canada, and Switzerland), Nkrumah concluded that they all provided protection and helped economic recovery. According to him the Constitution of the United States became an example for the whole world, but the real model of federalist government was represented by Switzerland based on bottom-up associations. The US model was attractive for him, because by forming a federalist governmental public administration, with strong presidential power, the United States could become the largest representative of free enterprise in the world. Lincoln's personality and politics—who placed the emphasis on preserving the unity of the federation at all costs, and later abolished slavery—particularly attracted him. He mentioned the example of the 1936 Stalinist

---

20 Nkrumah, *I Speak of Freedom*, 155.
21 Nkrumah, *Le Consciencisme*, 159.
22 Ki-Zerbo et al., "Nation-building and Changing Political Values," vol. 8, 481.
23 Nkrumah, *Neo Colonialism*, Introduction, ix–xx.

Constitution of the Soviet Union, too, which was able to defend the country and guarantee the unity against fascism despite that it represented one party rule under the centralizing Communist Party.[24]

Nkrumah saw European disunity as a counterexample. He was of the opinion that the exclusive nationalism of the Europeans ended in a state of confusion simply because a healthy basis of political association and understanding could not develop. It was only in the 1950s, driven by economic necessity, and the threat of German industrial and military rehabilitation, that Europe started to establish a European Community. According to him, the main problem with the Europeans was that it took them two world wars and the collapse of several empire to recognize that the strength was in unity.[25] He believed that African countries should face neo-colonialism, and they could only defend themselves against it if they did not accept either the British Commonwealth or the Franco-African Community [Communauté franco-africaine]. They had to establish the United States of Africa following the American example. Thus, the resources of Africa would be utilized for the benefit of the Africans in the framework of a planned development on a continental scale. Such a plan, covering the entire united Africa, would increase the African economic and industrial power. For this it would be necessary to establish a united African Common Market, and not to be seduced by the dubious advantages of an association with the Common Market of Europeans.[26]

Regarding his African political ideas, one can say, that with Ghana's struggle for self-determination, he wanted to set an example and motivate people across Africa to fight for national independence and for African Union.[27] By forming the Ghana Convention People's Party he led the foundation stone of parliamentary democracy, and by calling together the Ghana People's Representative Assembly he started the fight for the convening a constituent assembly to write the independence constitution. As the British governor did not consent to this, Nkrumah launched the Positive Action movement and tried to force the British to recognize Ghana's independence through peaceful nationwide strikes, in 1950. The strike unfortunately led to violence and Nkrumah was imprisoned and held among the criminals. So, at the beginning the British resisted hard using trial and imprisonment. But later, when the Convention People's Party—of which Nkrumah was the leader—won the first general election and had a majority in the Assembly, he was released from the prison and instructed by the British governor to form a government.[28]

The 1957 Independence Constitution established a parliamentary system modeled after the Westminster system. Nkrumah became the Prime Minister,

---

24 Nkrumah, *L'Afrique doit s'unir*, 236–243, 241–242, 245–246.
25 Nkrumah, *L'Afrique doit s'unir*, 248–249.
26 Nkrumah, *L'Afrique doit s'unir*, 251.
27 Nkrumah, "The Motion for Approval," 71.
28 Nkrumah, *Autobiography*, 101, 103–105, 108, 110–136, 138.

as head of the Cabinet, and the British Monarch the head of the state. To the great surprise of the British, Nkrumah continued the fight for complete independence because, in his view, to recognize the Queen of England as ruler of Ghana would mean a no longer existing anachronistic hierarchy that would falsify Ghana's independence, and confuse its relations with other African countries, when the main task was to create an independent African Union. In his opinion, the mere presence of a general governor was a violation of the sovereignty for which the Ghanaians fought and which they obtained.[29] Therefore, he wanted to transform Ghana into a republic led by a president using a referendum and constitutional change. In 1960, the referendum voted to change the country's status from constitutional monarchy—with Elisabeth II as head of state—to a republic with a presidential system of government. In the elections that same year, Nkrumah was elected President. He achieved the amendment of the monarchical Independence Constitution (1957) into a presidential republican constitution, but Ghana remained part of the British-led Commonwealth. He became Ghana's first President, and was reelected in 1965. He was convinced that in the future the whole of Africa should be liberated and united in an African Union.[30]

The 1960 Constitution declared Ghana a sovereign unitary republic of the people with a strong presidential power. Nkrumah, as President was responsible to the people and was subordinated to the constitutional law. He appointed the ministers and the judges of the Supreme Court who were independent, and ruled together with the national assembly where the freedom of speech was guaranteed. The Parliament consisted of the President and the national assembly, legislation happened through the co-legislation procedure between them. The President could at any time by proclamation dissolve the national assembly. He could set the direction in the cases which he considered to be of national interest. The Constitution stated that the President should strive for the union of Africa, and Ghana was willing to subordinate parts of its own state sovereignty to the exclusive competences of the union of African states.[31]

Nkrumah believed with conviction that the new independent Ghana must create a socialist economy and society, different from the liberal capitalist economy of the colonizers, if it wanted to preserve independence. His economic policy was statist and import substitutional. It aimed at industrialization and diversification of the economy in the framework of development plans, but he could not overcome the difficulties caused by the colonial past. The main problem with his self-sustaining economic recovery plan was the lack of capital. To create capital it was necessary to launch and sustain major productive efforts based on the savings and investments of the population. But it proved to be difficult, because of poverty, backwardness, disease, illiteracy and ignorance. To borrow capital from the rich countries was a risky path precisely because of the

---

29 Nkrumah, *L'Afrique doit s'unir*, 106–107.
30 Adi and Sherwood, *Pan-African History*, 144.
31 "Ghana Constitution," 1960, 473–490.

danger of dependent situation and neo-colonization.³² Some of his economic measures were opposed by strikes, and he gradually lost his popularity due to the economic problems.

Nkrumah's socialist and democratic ideals and his presidential policy of concentrating power were in contradiction. As President, he became not only the head of state, but also the head of the executive power and Cabinet. He hoped from centralization and the strong presidential power to defeat traditional opposition, to create stability, and to have enough power to reconstruct the country. The task was nothing less than to transform a pre-industrial country into a modern industrial country from internal force and without external assistance, and to find the economic and social policies needed for it. Of Ghana's sovereignty, Nkrumah was only willing to hand over power to the African Union in the fields of common affairs as defined in the union's Constitution.³³ He supported the socialist one-party parliamentary democracy because, in his view, it better expressed and satisfied the common aspirations of the nation as a whole than a Western-style multiparty parliamentary system which he regarded as a means of covering up the inherent struggle between the rich and the poor.³⁴ He believed that pluralism and debate could prevail in a one-party egalitarian system as well.

His economic policy was unsuccessful, and he tried to avoid the loss of power with a concentration of power, and thus his system became more and more dictatorial. In 1964, a constitutional amendment made Ghana a one-party authoritarian state with Nkrumah as President for life. Fundamental rights and political participation was severely restricted or banned, the opposition parties were banned. He was deposed, in 1966, by a violent military coup. He went into exile in Guinea, where Sékou Touré made him honorary Co-President. He fought unsuccessfully against the Ghanaian military regime.³⁵

Nkrumah was a believer in African unity, and his ideas about it were in harmony with the Western federalist ideas. He supported the full independence of the African states from colonial rule, and he was the greatest advocate of pan-Africanism and a pan-African common market at the conferences of independent African states, between 1958–1960, as the leading peace-settler of this period. As for the unity of Africa, he believed that only the unification of all the countries of Africa into a federally unified state would be able to use Africa's enormous economic resources for the benefit of the Africans rather than the profit of multinational corporations.³⁶ To him, pan-Africanism and the establishment of a pan-African common market in the framework of a United States of Africa were the indispensable preconditions for the development of the African states. He was in favor of a close continental political unity while expressing reservations

---

32 Nkrumah, *I Speak of Freedom*, 172, 174.
33 Nkrumah, *L'Afrique doit s'unir*, 107, 109–110.
34 Nkrumah, *Le Consciencisme*, 152.
35 Adi and Sherwood, *Pan-African History*, 145.
36 Worger et al., *Africa and the West*, vol. 2, 145–146.

about regionalism which represented a loose confederation. He supported centralized continental economic planning and development, a continental defense and security system, and cultural restoration.[37]

He favored an African common market, common economic and monetary policy, single currency, a central bank, military and defense unification, a common foreign policy, and a two-chamber parliamentary and governmental federalist constitution to achieve the independence of Africa. According to him the unification of Africa could be started by the creation of a common core of integration through a federal parliamentary constitution of those states that would agree to constitute a nucleus, and to leave the door open to all those who wished to join. The Constitution must be amendable at any time when the general public deemed it necessary. The continental Parliament should consist of two chambers, one of which should represent the population and discuss the many problems that Africa faced; and the other the states. Regardless of their size or population each state should send the same number of delegates. The chamber of states should formulate a common policy in all areas relating to security, defense, and the development of Africa. Through a committee chosen for this purpose, Parliament should examine possible solutions to the problems of the union and give the Constitution a more final form acceptable to all independent states.

Nkrumah mentioned among the benefits of the United States of Africa the following:

- Remedying the harmful effects of imperialism and colonization because a strong and united nation was capable of establishing strong central power to mobilize national forces and to ensure recovery and progress like the United States and the Soviet Union.
- Eliminating the borders and conflicts created during colonization.
- Economic planning, led by a united political leadership, could help Africa to become dignified, modern, and prosperous.
- Avoiding regional patriotisms which could led to balkanization from which the imperialists and the neo-colonialists could profit.
- Establishing a general homeland could hold Africa together, as a unified people, with government and destiny.[38]
- He was convinced that the challenge for Africa was to overcome separatism and become a sovereign united nation within the framework of the United States of Africa (États-Unis d'Afrique).[39]

His first step in the direction of an African Union was the formation of the Ghana-Guinea economic union, in 1958, with the former French colony, Guinea

37 Asante and Chanaiwa, "Pan-Africanism and regional integration," 246–247.
38 Nkrumah, *L'Afrique doit s'unir*, 246–247.
39 Nkrumah, *L'Afrique doit s'unir*, 253–254.

(led by Sékou Ahmed Touré) that Mali joined, in 1960. The second was the Conference of the Independent African States which Nkrumah organized in Accra, in April 1958, with the participation of the independent states of Africa. This was followed by more conferences calling for the removal of customs and other restrictions on trade among African states, and advocating the establishment of a broad continental common market. Finally, 30 African heads of independent states and governments signed the Charter of African Unity which established the Organization of African Unity (OAU) on May 25, 1963, in Addis Ababa, Ethiopia, which was headed by Nkrumah. The old and radical pan-Africanists—led by Nkrumah—campaigned for the conversion of the organization into a continental union government or a fully fledged United States of Africa, but without success. The continental integration aspect of pan-Africanism was defeated and lost its momentum throughout the second half of the 1960s. The nationalist leaders of the newly independent states focused on consolidating their own power in the framework of independent nation-states, and it was very difficult for them to deal with the pan-African affairs.[40]

According to the Charter of the Organization of African Unity (1963) the member states were sovereign and equal, cooperating through negotiation, mediation, conciliation, or arbitration, in the framework of the intergovernmentalist common institutions of the organization which had no Parliament. Its institutions were the Assembly of Heads of State and Government, the Council of Ministers, the General Secretariat, the Commission of Mediation, Conciliation and Arbitration, and the Specialized Commissions. Among other things, the charter aimed to encourage economic and political cooperation among the member states, to assure the welfare and well-being of the people and the general progress of Africa, to use the natural and human resources of the continent for the total advancement of the African peoples, to safeguard and consolidate hard-won independence as well as the sovereignty and territorial integrity of the member states, and to fight against colonialism and neo-colonialism in all its form, i.e. to eradicate all forms of colonialism from Africa. The implementation of all this was based on the principles of freedom, equality, justice and dignity, and common institutions. The organization reaffirmed its adherence to the United Nations and the Universal Declaration of Human Rights (1948).[41]

History proved that the Organization of African Unity was not enough strong to create unity among the many African states and peoples having different levels of development and characterized by cultural diversity. The main reason of the failure of the vision of an African United States was that the confrontation with the colonial powers and the struggle for independence did not go without a concentration of power. This created a power race that put the idea of African socialism and unity in a hopeless situation. And, since power competition has

---

40 Asante and Chanaiwa, "Pan-Africanism and regional integration," 143–145, 178–179.
41 "The Charter of the Organization of African Unity, 1963," 219–229.

not left the stage of history, the players of the global world economy could profit from it.

In terms of world politics, Nkrumah envisioned the United States of Africa in the framework of the United Nations. He was convinced that the future of humanity could only be imagined within the framework of it, because global world capitalism needed an independent international organization that was able to coordinate the world economy and resolve conflicts. Only in this framework could the world economy and society become democratic. He suggested to create a neutral African Union and an Asian Union, with a permanent seat, in the Security Council.[42]

While Nkrumah fought for complete national independence and African Union, Léopold Sédar Senghor (1906–2001), the first President of independent Senegal, was in favor of cooperation with France, the former colonial power, and adhered to the Francophone civilization framework. At the same time he fought for the right to self-determination of people. To be fair, it should be noted that Nkrumah did not leave the British Commonwealth's loose framework for cooperation either. Senghor believed that the English-speaking West African states should remain within the British Commonwealth, while the French-speaking states in the French Community (French Commonwealth).[43]

Senghor achieved the independence of Senegal from France in 1960, and played a major role in the development of the concept of Négritude and Francophonie.[44] Based on the fact of Africa's backwardness, he stressed the need to cooperate with the French civilization and to learn the necessary things. But at the same time he wanted to safeguard Africa's cultural heritage and community spirit. He firmly committed to a federation of all French West African states and a strong relationship with France, in the framework of a "Commonwealth à la française."[45] He supported the French Community after the war, as contained in the 1946 Constitution. When the French recognized the right to national self-determination, and it appeared in the 1958 Constitution, he saw his struggle successful. He thought of Charles de Gaulle, who saved France from a racist Nazi dictatorship, and, at the same time, he saved Black Africa, too. He considered himself to be a realist politician who was not an idealist, and who was human and loyal.[46]

As for the future of Africa, he was a believer in a Negro African socialism. For him, socialism meant a creative force that liberated thought, democratized economic relations between people, and shaped economic structures in the direction of freedom. He hoped that West Africa, which was able to safeguard a

---

42 Nkrumah, *I Speak of Freedom*, 258–281.
43 Senghor, "Report on the Party's Doctrine and Programme," 84–85.
44 Adi and Sherwood, *Pan-African History*, 169–173.
45 French West Africa (Black Africa) formed a federation of eight French colonial territories in Africa: Mauritania, Senegal, French Sudan (now Mali), French Guinea, Ivory Coast, Upper Volta (now Burkina Faso), Dahomey (now Benin) and Niger.
46 Senghor, "Report on the Party's Doctrine and Programme," 36.

community society, could become a creative place for the modern development of non-Marxist socialism and federalism for the whole world, as an alternative.[47]

As President of Senegal he was for the "African Way of Socialism" which he combined with his ideas on Négritude. He believed that the "Negro-African society" was traditionally socialist, and the new society should be built up on this basis, and adding modern sciences, techniques, and technology. He introduced some economic planning, concentrating on agriculture and producing capital, and a considerable emphasis was placed on the development of education.[48]

Regarding the development plan of nation-building he realized the problem was a lack of capital because this plan required the investment of substantial sums. In his view, there were three sources to produce capital: the state budget, private capital, and the European Community's Fund of Aid and Cooperation. He considered the latter inevitable, because when it came to borrowing capital, one could only turn to the luckier and richer states, preferably without a sense of inferiority. But he warned of the dangers of Western aid and capital borrowing because there was a danger of getting involved in the Cold War, and that was not in the interests of either the people or the peace. Private capital borrowing from France or elsewhere was essentially supported by him, provided it did not alienate national law and did not mean an interference in the national economy and policy. Capital accumulation, according to him, was necessary for every modern state, in this respect there was no difference between a socialist or a capitalist state. As for nationalization, he was of the opinion that it was not possible to nationalize in an underdeveloped country because nationalization required the necessary cadres of modern economic development in order to have anything to nationalize.[49]

In his speech on the African Way of Socialism, in 1960, at the African Federalist Party's First Youth Seminar, he assessed colonization as a historical phenomenon with good and bad effects. As a positive effect, he highlighted the Industrial Revolution, advances in science and technology, and the bourgeois revolutions. On the negative, he emphasized the loss of freedom of the colonies. He stressed the need to cooperate with the European civilization, and at the same time to preserve Africa's cultural heritage and community spirit. He saw the future in a Negro-African socialism and an African federation. He called to return to the Negro-African and Berber sources and to modernize them by the necessary European knowledge. This meant that European things had to be transferred to the Negro-Berber civilization by preserving the original culture.

He saw a successful future for Negro-African civilization in two things: socialism based on community values and federalism. In his view, the most important difference between the European and the Negro-African civilizations was that the European civilization made the emphasis on the individual and

47 Senghor, "The African Way of Socialism," 98–99, 128, 134.
48 Adi and Sherwood, *Pan-African History*, 172.
49 Senghor, "The African Way of Socialism," 76–78.

liberty, while the Negro-African society stressed the importance of the group, solidarity, and the community of persons over individual autonomy. This enabled individuals to bring their own interests in harmony with the interests of the community. Based on all of that, he thought that West Africa, by safeguarding the community society, could be a workshop for the development of non-Marxist socialism and federalism for the whole world.[50]

For Senghor, the challenge was to create a democratic modern socialist federal state following the ideas of the socialist Proudhon. He criticized the unitary centralized state and the French excessive centralization which weakened the state. The strong states (United States of America, USSR, China, India, Canada, Brazil), in his view, were all federal-style states. According to him, in Africa, independent nation-building must be carried out at the same time as federation construction. He believed that the tyranny of the state could only be reduced by federalism, in other words, by "the decentralization and deconcentration of its institutions, economic as well as political,"—how Proudhon proposed.[51]

He defined nation as "a common will for a life in common."[52] In his thinking this was true in the case of a federation, too, expressed by the principle of self-determination. Regarding the idea of a strong federal democracy he raised the problem of the antinomy (unresolvable conflict or contradiction) between unitary and federal state, which was Proudhon's problem. According to him, at the highest level of government of a unitary and a federal state there was no antinomy. He proved all this by saying that democracy had to start from the foundations, the masses, but there was a need for a single direction to create the political program and method and reconcile it with the local control. The majority party represented this political conception and direction. Therefore, in his view, a strongly centralized party was important, like in the case of a federation the federal government and the federal assembly. He believed that the essential was the presence of a head above the people's local governance, and a political direction that thought, that had the initiative and control, that received documents and suggestions, and that made plans and directives.[53] As for the opposition, he was of the opinion that its role was to criticize constructively by accepting the majority rule and the legal system. And he stressed that the opposition must have the same goals as the majority party representing the people's will.[54] All this led directly to the development of a one-party strong presidential system by him.

Senghor supported the creation of the United States of Africa, but he could imagine this as a distant goal because the formation of modern sovereign nation-states and the pursuit of self-sufficiency were in sharp contrast to this.

50 Senghor, "The African Way of Socialism," 118–128.
51 Senghor, "Report on the Party's Doctrine and Programme," 25.
52 Senghor, "The African Way of Socialism," 109.
53 Senghor, "The African Way of Socialism," 111–112.
54 Senghor, "Report on the Party's Doctrine and Programme," 72; Senghor, "The African Way of Socialism," 113.

Resolutions were voted but not followed by action because they were not realistic. The political practice of the independent African governments contradicted their pan-African declarations. After gaining independence, most African states followed the example and means of European conquering imperialism: border disputes, territorial claims, power struggles, and political coups.[55] He called to find a peaceful way for the African society—as a culturally mixed society with European and African influences—by renewing and modernizing the African community traditions.

The 1960 independence Constitution of Senegal followed the model of the fifth French Republic established in 1958. Senghor served as the first President of Senegal from 1960 until 1980. From 1963 to 1976 his ruling Socialist Party of Senegal was the only legal political party. He created a one-party strong presidential system because of political rivalry that emerged in the meantime. Later more parties were allowed. When he announced his retirement from the presidency, in 1980, he could name his own successor.[56]

Julius K. Nyerere (1922–1999), anti-colonialist Tanzanian socialist politician, was the first President of independent Tanganyika, the creator of Tanzania and a founder of the Organization of African Unity. He was universally known as Mwalimu "teacher" in Swahili, the national language. He is regarded as one of the greatest leaders of modern Africa. He was in favor of complete independence from the colonizers, and he searched for African ways of social and economic organization based on his Ujamaa concept.[57] He followed in the footsteps of Gandhi's non-violent policy, which he respected and regarded as an example.

Nyerere's new African nation-state idea aimed at the realization of the idea of liberty in the African society by involving everybody in the shaping of the state, without excluding any sane and law-abiding adult person. He criticized the Greeks, the framers of the Declaration of Independence, Abraham Lincoln, and the British politicians because they felt few scruples in leaving people out of popular sovereignty. He explained this fact by saying that they could do that because they lived in a world which excluded the masses of human beings from the idea of equality. He warned that this was no longer possible in his age when the Universal Declaration of Human Rights (1948) represented the ruling ideas and principles. He strongly criticized European capitalist society because of colonization, because of using personal wealth for exploitation, and because of the elitist, racist, and warlike behavior during history. He was in search of a non-exploitative modern democratic society which differed from the West.[58] He believed that modern African socialism, based on equality, community feeling, and public (state) ownership could be realized. He did a lot to promote the

---

55 Senghor, "The African Way of Socialism," 116–117.
56 Adi and Sherwood, *Pan-African History*, 172.
57 Adi and Sherwood, *Pan-African History*, 147–151.
58 Worger et al., *Africa and the West*, vol. 2, 146, 160–161.

development, and the critical and creative exploration of the African social heritage and values to animate both civil and political society.[59]

His socialism was based on the traditional African village lifestyle representing collectivist values in a modern scene. In a traditional African village the local people (families) cooperated with each other, produced their livelihood, profited from it together, and the villages also cooperated. Everyone was concerned for the welfare of the others. On this basis, he developed his Ujamaa concept on economic and social development. The Ujamaa concept merged the socialist theory and the traditional African communalism. He defined Ujamaa as follows:

> The foundation, and the objective, of African socialism is the extended family. The true African socialist . . . regards all men as his brethren—as members of his ever extending family . . . "Ujamaa", then, or "Familyhood", describes our socialism.[60]

The Ujamaa concept, opposed to capitalism, which sought to build a happy society "on the basis of exploitation of man by man." It also opposed doctrinaire (Marxist) socialism which was based on "a philosophy of inevitable conflict between man and man."[61] It was for the concept of African national state socialism which Nyerere imagined as a classless and egalitarian society, representing freedom, unity, and economic self-reliance. Because one cannot exploit the other, it could avoid the pitfalls of capitalism.

Ujamaa, meant socialist democracy which appeared in the political practice as a "government by the people" created through free discussions. It was a representative democratic parliamentary system within a one-party state, representing direct democracy, based on the—by him idealized—African tribal traditions, and the ancient Greek democracy. As a classless system, it was not pluralist and rejected the two or multiparty system. It did not represent Marxism or Leninism.

The values and principles of Tanzania's socialist reconstruction were declared in the *Arusha Declaration* (1967) which was written by Nyerere. It contained the Tanganyika African Nation Union's program on socialism and self-reliance, which was the leading party. The declaration committed itself to fundamental rights and the Universal Declaration of Human Rights (1948), stressing that all human beings were equal and had equal opportunities irrespective of race, religion, status or sex. All citizens together possessed all the natural resources of the country; the state (government) had effective control over the principal means of production; it could intervene actively and participate in the economic life of the nation as to ensure the well-being of all citizens, prevent the exploitation of

---

59 Ki-Zerbo et al., "Nation-building and changing political values," vol. 8, 481–482.
60 Nyerere, "Ujamaa – The Basis of African Socialism," 12.
61 Nyerere, "Ujamaa – The Basis of African Socialism," 12.

one person by another, and prevent the accumulation of wealth in accordance of a classless society. The declaration also committed itself to the establishment of the African Union in cooperation with other states and to the ensuring of world peace and security through the United Nations. The most important principles of socialism were the absence of exploitation, the existence of democracy and the control of the peasants and workers above the major means of production and exchange.[62]

Regarding self-reliance, Nyerere made the emphasis on education, and import-substitutional agricultural and industrial development based on own forces, hard work, intelligence, knowledge, education, and strength. As Tanzania was struggling with a lack of capital and was an industrially underdeveloped country, Nyerere called for the development of rural agriculture. He warned of the dangers of borrowing capital from abroad. In this respect he emphasized that self-reliance demanded to be careful with foreign gifts, aid, and loans because they could endanger independence and paralyze the creative force of people to make the country prosperous. He could imagine developmental aid policy only through taxation of the prosperous and rich countries under the direction of a world government, which unfortunately did not exist. In his opinion, without it, the goals of socialism were incompatible with development aid.[63]

In the formation of the new socialist state, Nyerere made the emphasis on education, more precisely on enlarging the compulsory core curriculum with knowledge of farm management. According to his plan, this meant that everybody had to learn the knowledge on how to manage the village agricultural life, and how to secure the livelihood for everybody. All this could be achieved through the introduction of a school farm or workshop system which was mandatory for everyone. This meant that schools—especially secondary schools—should also be farms, and serve as economic, social, and educational co-operative communities. He believed that this was the way to learn farming, planning for the future, working together, and being responsible for the community. Through the school autonomy everybody could practice, and learn to value, direct democracy. The community work was part of the post-secondary level studies (university or medical schools or other). [64]

After gaining independence from the British authorities, Nyerere, as President of Tanzania, created a strong one-party parliamentary presidential system following the Westminster model. The Parliament consisted of the President and the national assembly. The legislative procedure took place between the President and the national assembly. The executive power was vested in the President. The Parliament was under one-party rule, the representatives were elected from the members of the Tanganyika African National Union (TANU) headed by Nyerere. The President was the head of the state and the commander in chief

---

62 Nyerere, "The Arusha Declaration, 1967," 13–15.
63 Nyerere, "The Arusha Declaration, 1967," 21–25.
64 Nyerere, *Ujamaa Essays on Socialism*, 51–52, 64–71.

of the armed forces. He nominated the Vice-President and the ministers, and had the right to dismiss the Parliament under certain circumstances. But the Constitution of the United Republic of Tanzania (1977) involved the basic rights and duties of citizens, the right of impeachment by the national assembly against the President was accepted, and there was freedom of opinion and debate in the national assembly.[65]

Nyerere, like Nkrumah, also called for the creation of the United States of Africa, which the independent African states should establish parallel the making of their democratic nation-states. He believed that creating the union was essential for Africa to have a future. He imagined African unity as a union—based on equality between the member states—which was created by negotiations and agreements between them, on the basis of the free associations of the African people. In his view the African society was in a period of transition, so according to the struggle for national sovereignty several forms of union were imaginable: The first stage could be a loose association between states based on consultation on matters of common interests. Some regions may create a common market and joint actions without political association in any form. In a small number of countries the formation of a kind of federation may be possible. The discussion of certain questions at the continental level could also be useful. According to him, the best way to achieve the United States of Africa was through the creation of regional alliances, with a federation core that meant a federal union of some regions. The great advantage of the federation was—according to him—that it was stable and could not be disintegrated. If a federation was created in East Africa, it could be the core of integration for the whole of Africa.[66]

He considered the creation of African unity to be important above all because of the necessary defense against classical nationalism, the importance of which was demonstrated by European history. He warned against following European nationalism. In his words:

> The role of African nationalism differs—and should differ—from that of nationalism in the past. We must use African national states to achieve the unification of Africa, not give our enemies the possibility of using them to divide Africa. African nationalism would be devoid of all meaning, anachronistic, and dangerous if it were not at the same time pan-Africanism.[67]

With his theory of village community socialism, Nyerere followed in the footsteps of the aforementioned Jefferson versus Hamilton debate on agricultural or industrial business society, after the devastation of laissez-faire business

---

65 The Constitution of the United Republic of Tanzania (1977).
66 Nyerere, "Des Etats-Unis d'Afrique," 72–76.
67 Nyerere, "Des Etats-Unis d'Afrique," 76.

capitalism on the stage of history, seeking livelihood for its own people. And in this, Gandhi's example and his ideas on a peaceful world federation based on democratic village communities attracted him. But his one-party strong presidential system was very controversial from the point of view of his Ujamaa concept. Ideas and political reality were not in harmony, and the Tanzanian internal power struggle made difficult the—by him imagined—gradual democratization process.

In summary, the awakening and modernizing Africa in the 1960s showed that laissez-faire business capitalism and colonialism left a deep mark on Africa's development. In the opinion of Albert Adu Boahen, African historian, colonization between 1880 and 1960 had significant political, economic, and social impact as a watershed in African history. The colonized African people lost their sovereignty and independence, they could not control their own destiny, plan their development, or manage their affairs. Therefore, colonization was a very controversial subject with positive and negative impacts that affected the future of Africa. He believed that Africa could no longer return to its original community roots, but it could find its own paths. For this, the impact of colonization must be taken into account.[68]

Nkrumah, Senghor, and Nyerere rejected colonization and were looking for their own paths for Africa. They were visionaries of a democratic and prosperous African Union being a free and creative member of a peaceful world. Their belief in the idea of a world federation formed the link with European federalists. But history developed in such a way that the independent socialist one-party centralized presidential nation-states, which were created by them against European colonization, were unfortunately hotbeds of power struggle, and as such they were unable to form an African federation.

11.3 Responses and Challenges from Confucian East Asia (Japan, China)

The most successful responses to the Western challenge of liberal capitalist expansion came from the Confucian Japan and China. They have successfully joined the Western modernization process, could become world economic powers, and, at the same time, could safeguard their own culture. Both have pursued knowledge-based modernization and, albeit in different ways, could stop the Western colonial powers that tried to colonize them through laissez-faire free market expansion and controversial legal agreements after the Opium Wars.[69]

Japan and China were ancient civilizations directed by Confucian principles and values (virtues), which were similar to the European moral values.

---

68 Boahen, "Colonialism in Africa: Its Impact and Significance," 782, 789, 809; Boahen, *African Perspectives on Colonialism*, 99, 109, 111.
69 Bóka, *Európa és Ázsia*, 100–115, 116–139, 156–161, 161–166; Bóka, *Modernizáció és értékrend*, 155–182, 183–200.

Some Responses to European Modernity 171

China belonged to the Confucian philosophical culture, and the Buddhist and Taoist religious culture. Japan adopted many Chinese traditions during the Han Dynasty about 200 BC (about 2,200 years ago) because it regarded China as a developed civilization. Japanese adopted Confucianism as state philosophy. European civilization was based on ancient Greek political philosophy, Roman law, and Christian religious culture. It was characterized by diversity of states, cultures and languages, pluralism, and the presence of the idea of freedom in social organization. The essential difference between the European and the Confucian-based Chinese and Japanese civilizations was the lack of the idea of freedom and pluralism in their social development. But in all of them there was present the fight against absolute, unlimited rule, and the fight for humanization of power, and they believed in the idea of universal peace. The Confucian state was a well-organized agrarian state based on the Confucian moral principles represented in *The Analects*: ancestor worship, filial piety, learning, education, self-perfection, virtue, morality, and a virtuous ruler and government.[70] The imperial government was a centralized order with the Emperor and the central government on the top. Beneath of the central government there were the provincial governments, divided into districts, prefectures, and villages and townships which had autonomy. The Emperor's power was restricted by the Confucian ethics.[71]

Due to the Western industrial revolution, advanced military technology and laissez-faire market economic expansion Japan and China were forced to play a knowledge-based defensive role for a long time, and to learn and adopt Western economic and state organization elements. Thanks to knowledge-based modernization their defensive position gradually could switch to a developer role in world economy, setting a limit for European expansion.

In the case of Japan and China, European colonial powers used a new colonization method based on free market economy and free trade for the profit of the metropolis without territorial domination. This "quasi-colonial control (informal empire)" meant that the weaker state remained independent, and there was no colonial administration, but a mixture of foreign and indigenous administration (such as the Imperial Maritime Customs Office in the Chinese Empire). However, the weaker state was sovereign only to a limited extent. The modern colonizer guaranteed privileges for itself in "unequal treaties." Informal empire presupposed a distinct economic superiority of the modern colonizer which made it capable of "penetrating" an overseas economy and opening the market by diplomatic pressure, military threats, and selective naval interventions, such as the "Opium War," which "opened" the Chinese empire in 1842, or the American military expedition of Commodore Matthew C. Perry (1853–1854) which opened the Japanese market.[72]

---

70 Confucius, *Analects*.
71 T'ang Leang-Li, *China in Revolt*, 21–37.
72 Osterhammel, *Colonialism*, 19–20.

Japan and China were closed advanced agricultural civilizations when they were opened, and they did not want to cooperate with the Europeans. But the forced opening of their countries and the threat of colonization forced them to find ways to defend themselves. Below it will be examined how this was done, how it was possible to defend against the modernizing Western expansion, and how it could be limited.

11.3.1 The Japanese Answer (Yukichi Fukuzawa)

The first philosopher in East Asia who could respond to the Western challenge was Yukichi Fukuzawa (1835–1901), the founder of modern Japan. As a philosopher and educator he launched the knowledge-based modernization of the country. He recognized that liberal capitalism would lead to the development of a world economy, and there was no escape from it. Therefore the Japanese had to learn Western knowledge, to show good results, and think about joining the West.[73]

As a member of the first Japanese mission, Fukuzawa visited the United States, in 1860. Two years later, in 1862, he travelled in European countries (France, England, The Netherlands, Prussia, Russia, and Portugal). He collected information about the political institutions, economy and culture of these countries, and published the collected knowledge for the Japanese. He was under the influence of François Guizot's *Histoire de la civilisation in Europe*, who regarded the European civilization as progressive; and of John Stuart Mill's essay *On Liberty*, who believed that while the Asian countries were in stagnation, the Europeans prospered. Asian stagnation was caused by the rule of tradition and customs. European diversity and pluralism made progress possible.[74] Based on this information, Fukuzawa presented and compared the origins, and the basic values and principles of Western and Japanese civilization in his book entitled *An Outline of a Theory of Civilization*.[75] Here he concluded that the strength of Europeans was in diversity and pluralism (different state forms, different cultures and languages, free thinking, differences of opinion, discussions, the fight for freedom, and the system of liberties). In his words:

> The point of the difference between Western and other civilizations is that Western society does not have a uniformity in opinions; various opinions exist side by side without fusing into one. For example there are theories which advocate governmental authority; others argue for the primacy of religious authority. There are proponents of monarchy, theocracy, aristocracy, and democracy. Each goes its own way, each

---

73 Bóka, *Európa és Ázsia*, 124–130; Bóka, *Modernizáció és értékrend*, 191–194.
74 Guizot, *Histoire de la civilisation en Europe*, 55–72, 303–304; Mill, "On Liberty," 69–71.
75 Fukuzawa, *An Outline of a Theory of Civilization*.

maintains its own position... This is how autonomy and freedom have developed in the West.[76]

He realized that the Japanese scene was quite different:

> [Japan] has had a monarchy, a nobility, religions, and common people, each of which constituted a separate species, each of which possessed its own views. But these views did not develop side by side, draw nearer to one another, and blend together into one synthesis.[77]

This imbalance in Japanese society—in his view—was caused by the caste system. In contrast to the Europeans, there was no free thinking, no differences in opinion, no discussions, no fight for freedom, and no system of liberties. The Japanese were the mental slaves of the old ways of Confucianism, and this caused stagnation. One government had often been replaced by another, but the absolutist Confucian political trend of Japan as a whole had never changed.[78] So Fukuzawa could discover that the basic difference between the European and the Confucian state organization was that the European was based on the system of liberties, which could not develop in China and Japan. He was wondering how to remedy this shortcoming and liberalize Japanese society.

Based on his voyages in the Western world, Fukuzawa differentiated between civilized, semi-developed and primitive lands in his essay on *Western civilization as our goal*. In his view, the nations of Europe and the United States of America were the most highly civilized, the Asian countries, such as Turkey, China, and Japan were semi-developed, and Africa and Australia belonged to the still primitive lands.[79] Europe, as a modern civilization, was industrial and commercial, business-oriented, inventive, enterprising, free thinking, not credulous of old customs, and autonomous. In his words:

> Their spirits enjoy free play and are not credulous of old customs... They cultivate their own virtue and refine their own knowledge. They neither yearn for the old nor become complacent about the present... Their path of learning is not vacuous; it has, indeed, invented the principle of invention itself. Their industrial and business ventures prosper day by day to increase the sources of human welfare. Today's wisdom overflows to create the plans of tomorrow.[80]

---

76 Fukuzawa, "The Origins of the Western Civilization," 161.
77 Fukuzawa, "The Origins of the Japanese Civilization," 175.
78 Fukuzawa, "The Origins of the Japanese Civilization," 175–223, 185, 199.
79 Fukuzawa, "Western Civilization as Our Goal," 17.
80 Fukuzawa, "Western Civilization as Our Goal," 18–19.

Japanese civilization, as semi-developed, was agrarian. The Japanese used book-learning based on Confucian classics, like the Chinese, and did not learn practical things. "They knew how to cultivate the old, but not how to improve it." They were slaves of customs.[81]

The primitive civilization was still far from civilization. Men's housing and food conditions were not stable, they could not make tools. Their way of life was not settled, if they settled in one place, they were engaged in farming and fishing. They were not without writing, but they produced no book learning. The primitive man was unable to be master of his own situation, he was exposed to the forces of nature, the help of others, or the luck of chance.[82]

Fukuzawa believed that civilization was an "open-ended process," and Japan, as a small country, had to join the most developed. Earlier the Japanese had joined the Chinese civilization but, after China was defeated and lost its independence, Japan had to join the Western civilization. He was aware that the Japanese cannot be satisfied with the level of civilization attained by the West because Western nations were always at war, there were robbers and murderers in the West, but in his age they were the most developed. Therefore Japan could not reject Western civilization and remain semi-developed. He believed that countries aiming to progress in civilization must necessarily take European civilization as a criterion in making arguments and assimilating it, but not uncritically.[83]

He was convinced that in Japan Japanese scholars could only manage modern civilization and national independence by learning, understanding and interpreting European knowledge. Therefore Japanese scholars had to learn Western knowledge, manage all fields of life (for example business, law, industry, agriculture), writing and translating books, and publishing newspapers. They must become leaders of the people, act in concert with the government, and increase the potential of the whole nation. He believed that this was how scholars could contribute to the independence of Japan. This was the aim of Keio, his private school, the future famous Keio University.[84]

In 1872, with the aim of a knowledge-based modernization of the country, Fukuzawa launched the program of *"Encouragement of Learning."* The first sentences of his appeal continued the example of the American Declaration of Independence (1776).[85]

---

81 Fukuzawa, "Western Civilization as Our Goal," 18.
82 Fukuzawa, "Western Civilization as Our Goal," 18.
83 Fukuzawa, "Western Civilization as Our Goal," 19–20.
84 Fukuzawa, *An Encouragement of Learning*, 33.
85 "That all men are created equal; that they are endowed by their Creator with certain unalienable rights." "The Declaration of Independence, 1776," 10–11.

It is said that heaven does not create one man above or below another man. This means that when men are born from heaven they all are equal. There is no innate distinction between high and low.[86]

By this symbol he aimed to express that the Japanese started the fight for independence through learning, rejecting feudal privileges, and accepting differentiation among people only on the basis of knowledge. He did not accept feudal privileges from birth. For him the differences between people could be based only on education and knowledge. In his words:

As the proverb says: heaven does not give riches and dignity to man himself, but to his labours. Therefore, as I have said above, there are no innate status distinctions separating noble and base, the rich and the poor. It is only the person who has studied diligently, so that he has a mastery over things and events, who becomes noble and rich, while his opposite becomes base and poor.[87]

His knowledge-based reform encouraged to change the teaching material based on Confucian classics, and to teach practical things, practical knowledge, in the first place Western economic, financial, technical/technological knowledge, and history.

He was convinced that Japan had to join European civilization if the Japanese wanted to become modern. Japan had to abandon old customs and to develop autonomous persons who were able to think freely, to develop their own morals and knowledge, to freely plan their future and to realize their plans. They had to invent the principle of invention and practice it. They had to use their industrial and business ventures to improve human welfare. He was convinced that national independence demanded self-respect and independence of mind. Therefore Japan could achieve its independence and freedom by raising the intellectual power of people, and by sweeping away credulity in past customs. In his words:

Society cannot be preserved without getting rid of the credulity that shackles us to outdated customs. Once this credulity has been stripped away we shall be able to enter the realm of vital intellectual activity. We shall have achieved success when national sovereignty and national polity are supported by and grounded on the intellectual power of the whole nation.[88]

Fukuzawa criticized Chinese behavior as regards modernization. He believed that selfish mentality hindered the Chinese in realizing the importance of

---

86 Fukuzawa, *An Encouragement of Learning*, 1.
87 Fukuzawa, *An Encouragement of Learning*, 1.
88 Fukuzawa, "Western Civilization as our Goal," 37.

Western modernity. As a consequence they could not limit the ambitions of the foreigners in the interests of the country. So, they let foreigners conquer China.[89] He believed that China and Korea had to start modernization, but they did not want to. Therefore Japan could not wait for them to become enlightened. Japan had to secede from the Asian countries and associate with the civilized Western people, and had to behave toward their Asian neighbors in the same way as Westerners. It meant:

> We simple erase from our minds our bad friends in Asia.[90]

So, he was convinced that Japan, which earlier had adopted Chinese civilization, had to say goodbye to Chinese civilization and become Western if it wanted to safeguard national independence.[91]

From the many Western state forms, which he had seen and studied, he had chosen to follow the English parliamentary system. This meant that he was for a constitutional monarchy, a strong bicameral Parliament based on the Western system of liberties, and accepting the development of the rights of the people. In the practice it meant overthrowing the shogunate, reestablishing the emperorship, and basing it on a constitution which accepted the development of the rights of the people. So Japan could preserve the imperial family in a modern form. He hoped that, after eliminating the shogunate, imperial rule could play the role of modernizer as a constitutional monarchy serving the interests of the people. In his words:

> Hence we should venerate this union between the imperial rule and our national policy not because it goes back to the origins of Japanese history, but because its preservation will help us maintain modern Japanese sovereignty and advance our civilization. A thing is not to be valued for itself, but for its function.[92]

Regarding his economic views, Fukuzawa was for introducing capitalism, and capitalist enterprises. He himself became a successful educational entrepreneur, as the founder of the Keio University, in Tokyo. He created the first business elite in modern Japan in which Keio men played an important role.[93]

Fukuzawa was actively involved in collecting the necessary curriculum during his travels in the West, learned Dutch and English, and translated many of the most important Westerns books. Thanks to him Western economic theories, among them the economic thoughts of Smith, List, Hamilton, and Mill were

---

89 Fukuzawa, *Plaidoyer pour la modernité*, 43.
90 Fukuzawa, "Datsu-a Ron," 353.
91 Fukuzawa, "Datsu-a Ron," 351.
92 Fukuzawa, "Western Civilization as Our Goal," 42–43.
93 Tamaki, *Yukichi Fukuzawa*, 180–181.

well known in Japan. One of the most important Western books that Japanese studied was John Stuart Mill's *Principles of Political Economy*, and so they could achieve good results in economic Westernization.

Japan successfully modernized the country through the Meiji Reform (1868–1912), although there were deviations from Fukuzawa's liberalism. In 1868, the shogunate was defeated, and imperial rule was restored. One of the most impressive modernizing actions of the Meiji Emperor was the Iwakura mission (1871–1873) that visited the United States and European countries, France, Belgium, Holland, and Germany. The goal of the mission was to acquire knowledge and support to make Japan, which was so different, similar to the Western countries, and to achieve the revision of the unequal treaties from Grant, the President of the United States.[94] Thus, the Japanese answer to the European and American challenge of forced opening up was the Meiji reform aiming the gradual catching up with the Westerners by learning and modernizing the country. Using this method Meiji government could achieve the revision of the unequal treaties, and could avoid colonization.[95]

The chronicler of the Iwakura Mission, Kunitake Kume, described the wonderment of the visitors, the hard-working intensity of the programs, and the open-heartedness of the countries visited whose citizens were ready to show off their wares and share their technology with their visitors from Japan. He also reported that the Chancellor of the German Empire, Bismarck—who was highly appreciated in Japan as the leading statesman in Europe—hold a reception for the Iwakura mission and enlightened the confused Japanese politicians about the Western values and principles. In his speech he emphasized that the Japanese had to be careful with the English and French politicians because their policy was fallacious and two-faced. The so-called international law, which was supposed to protect the rights of all nations, did not mean security at all. Bismarck was convinced that small nations, not daring to transgress international law, could not protect their independence. Under such circumstances, Prussia, for example, had no other choice "but to use force to protect Germany's sovereign rights." He warned the Japanese that Britain and France abused power, wanting overseas colonies and exploiting their resources. So the Japanese had to be careful, because the day had not yet come when they could trust in peaceful relations with the Europeans. At the same time, he assured the Japanese delegation of Germany's friendship, and respect for autonomy.[96]

Bismarck had a great influence on the Japanese delegation, believing that his example was worth following. Among the members of the delegation was the London-educated Itō Hirobumi, who became the dominant figure of the Meiji restoration during the 1880s, as the first prime minister of Japan.

---

94 Lu, *Japan*, 324.
95 Landes, *The Wealth and Poverty of Nations*, 350–391.
96 Kume, Kunitake, *Japan Rising*, 306–307.

Emperor Meiji started the reforms of the country with the liberal aims of the Charter Oath (1868), as Fukuzawa had imagined. Among them the most important were to establish deliberative assemblies, to settle all matters by public discussions, to abolish the caste system and the evil customs of the past, to seek knowledge all over the world.[97] But later Meiji reform gradually became more conservative, authoritarian and militarist following the Prussian way. A strong fight started between the modernizers and conservatives. Conservatives represented the majority, and Fukuzawa's life was in danger as an oppositional liberal Westerner. The National Education Act, representing conservative Confucianism, and the Meiji Constitution of 1889 did not represent the liberalism of Fukuzawa.

The Imperial Rescript on Education of 1890 framed by Motoda Eifu, the Confucian mentor of Emperor Meiji, represented the neo-Confucian moral precepts of the Meiji ruling elite in a modern nationalist presentation. It proclaimed filial piety and loyalty to Emperor and state as the basis of the Japanese educational system. The authoritarian interpretation of Confucianism could win, and direct Japanese mentality:

> Ye, Our subjects, be filial to your parents, affectionate to your brothers and sisters; as husbands and wives be harmonious, as friends true; bear yourselves in modesty and moderation; extend your benevolence to all; pursue learning and cultivate arts, and thereby develop intellectual faculties and perfect moral powers; furthermore advance public good and promote common interests; always respect the Constitution and observe the laws; should emergency arise, offer yourselves courageously to the State; and thus guard and maintain the prosperity of Our Imperial Throne coeval with heaven and earth.[98]

With the Meiji Constitution (1889), Japan became a constitutional hereditary monarchy, as such the first parliamentary government in Asia.[99] The Constitution did not declare popular sovereignty. The Emperor was the head of the Empire, sacred and inviolable. He combined in himself the rights and the exercise of sovereignty according to the Constitution; he exercised the legislative power with the consent of the Imperial Diet, and he gave sanction to laws, and ordered the promulgation and execution of them. He convoked the Diet, and dissolved the House of Representatives. He was the supreme commander of the army and the navy; declared war, made peace, and concluded treaties. He conferred titles to nobility, so feudalism was not eliminated, the House of Peers continued. The Emperor united, under his rule, all three branches of government (legislative,

---

97 Lu, *Japan*, 308.
98 Lu, *Japan*, 343–344.
99 "The Constitution of the Empire of Japan, 1889," 339–343; and National Diet Library.

executive, and judiciary). There was no separation of powers. People were called Japanese subjects of the Emperor.

The Imperial Diet consisted of two houses, the House of Peers (the upper house), and the House of Representatives (the lower house). The members of the House of Peers were members of the Imperial Family, the orders of nobility, and those persons who have been nominated thereto by the Emperor. The House of Representatives was composed of members elected by the people by direct male suffrage with a property qualification.

The Japanese government was more absolutist than liberal, but there were present elements in the direction of liberalism because urgent Imperial Ordinances required the consent of the Diet, therefore imperial ordinances could not alter the existing law. So Japan did not become a classical absolutist state. The inclusion of the rights and duties of the subjects in the Constitution (the right to uphold the Constitution, to pay taxes, to serve in the armed forces, the right to property, the right of free movement, the right to privacy of the home and correspondence, the right to freedom of speech, assembly and association, the right to legal defense, and the freedom of religion) also suggested a move toward a liberal emperorship. But, the absence of a guarantee of the fundamental human rights and the greatly restricted authority of the Diet showed the absolutist tendencies of the imperial rule.

Meiji reformers followed the Hamilton method of economic modernization together with Bismarck's authoritarian and militarist monarchical modernization policy which protected the welfare of the people. They established a Western-style constitutional parliamentary hereditary monarchy with Japanese characteristics, and strong central government. Sovereignty was in the hands of the emperor and of a small group around him. They directed economic and political modernization. The cooperation between a few wealthy houses of merchant bankers and the government developed into a financial oligarchy, known as the zaibatsu system, which was built on the principle of filial piety in relation to people. The oligarchy used the army to pursue any national goal. Thus, the cooperation between the zaibatsu, the military power and the government ruled modernizing Japan.

Japanese realized the necessity of defense against the liberal free market economy and followed the protectionist and export substitutional movement. Foreign influence was accepted to play some part because foreign experience or foreign reasoning offered guidance in a choice between alternatives. But this did not mean that the Japanese were ready to abandon their own ideas on life and society, which had deep historical roots.[100]

After the Meiji period, the new Japanese nationalist government followed the example of European expansion and national empire building. The goal was to create a Japanese Empire and to become a great East Asian power. Japanese national policy became militarist and ultranationalist between the two world

100 Sansom, *The Western World and Japan*, 437–441.

wars. Japan became Hitler's allay in the Second World War, and aimed to establish a new order under Japanese domination in South-East Asia.

After the Second World War, Japan as a defeated power lost its independence. The military forces of Japan were completely disarmed. Between 1946 and 1952 Japan was occupied by the Allied forces. It came under the direction of the American General, Douglas MacArthur. The main American objective was to turn Japan into a peaceful nation following the American model, and to establish democratic self-government through a large scale reform. The American occupation transformed the Japanese government into a democratic one. It was strongly connected with American policy, and pursued an anti-China and anti-Soviet Union policy.

The Constitution of Japan of 1946 (the Showa Constitution) made a decisive departure from the past in a more liberal direction toward a constitutional democratic state. The Emperor became the symbol of the state and of the unity of the people. Power no longer resided in him but in the Diet which became the highest organ of the state power. The sovereign power resided with the people (popular sovereignty), the government's authority was derived from the people, exercised by the representatives of the people, and served the livelihood of the people (government of the people, by the people and for the people). The Emperor derived his position from the will of the sovereign people, and was subject to the legislation, his acts regarding state matters needed the approval of the Cabinet. Separation of power was realized: legislative power was vested in the Diet, executive in the Cabinet, judiciary in the Supreme Court.[101]

The Constitution established a parliamentary government in which legislation was vested in the bicameral National Diet with the stronger position of the House of Representatives. The House of Peers (similar to the British House of Lords) was abolished and in its place the House of Councilors was established. The Diet became the higher organ of state power as the law-making organ. It consisted of two houses, namely the House of Representatives and the House of Councilors. The members were elected by direct ballot. A bill became a law by the consent of both houses, but in disputed cases by a 2/3 majority of the House of Representatives. The House of Representatives appointed the Prime Minister and the judges of the court, and could initiate non-confidence procedures against the Cabinet. The Cabinet represented the executive power. The Prime Minister appointed the ministers of state. Local self-government was guaranteed following the principle of local autonomy of the federalist patterns.

The Constitution emphasized and detailed the fundamental human rights of the people and this was a significant novelty: equality (all of the people are equal under the law and there shall be no discrimination in political, economic or social relations because of race, creed, sex, social status, or family origin); peers and peerage shall not be recognized; prohibition of slavery; right to property; democratic election; freedom of petition; right to a fair legal defense; freedom of

---

101 Ienaga, *History of Japan*, 229–230.

thought and conscience; freedom of assembly and association as well as speech; freedom of religion; freedom to choose and change residence; academic freedom; prohibition of forced marriage; prohibition of torture; compulsory education; all people shall have the right to maintain the minimum standards of wholesome and cultural living; in all spheres of life, the state shall use its endeavors for the promotion and extension of social welfare and security, and of public health.[102]

As a result of the democratic reforms Japan became the new economic giant of Asia. The country could profit from the open economic climate. The liberal economic environment enabled the country to import the latest technology without having to pay the full costs of research and development.[103] New Japanese products proved their technical abilities (Cannon Camera, Honda, Toyota, Datsun Autos), in electronics the transistor was the new product (Sony, Hitachi Companies). They could compete with Western products. This economic boom was the result of successful investment of profit and good Japanese economic management. After the "oil shock," for example, when classical industrial production started to become not sufficiently profitable, Japan switched over to high techs production, and soon became an information technological world power. The zaibatsu, which was dissolved by the Americans, revived, and became again very active with the participation of industrial giants in cooperation with big banks (Fiji, Mitsubishi, Mitsui, Sumitomo, Dai-Ichi Kangyo, and Sanwa). With governmental support, direction and intervention, Japan's economy became the third largest in the world.[104]

In Japan traditional cultural phenomena could survive, among them the Shinto religion and the feudal-family business structures. The "new Japan" that emerged in Meiji times turned out to be modern, but by no means Western. The same happened after the Second World War: Japan was Americanized but it did not become American. Adapted American modernity but safeguarded the Japanese cultural traditions, and on this basis a booming economy could develop.

Japan became active in the United Nations. The UN has been a very important international organization for Japan because the country had to renounce war and had only self-defense forces.[105] The country, which suffered from devastating atomic bombing, advocated the importance of disarmament and cooperation in the framework of the UN.

In conclusion, modern knowledge-based Japanese civilization developed as a peculiar mixture of Western (American and German) and Confucian ideas and practices. It became Western but could safeguard Japanese culture. The European Union and Japan share values of democracy, human rights, and market economy, and the relationship between them is good.

102 "The Constitution of Japan, 1946." Lu, *Japan*, 471–475; and National Diet Library.
103 Smith, *Japan Since 1945*, 166.
104 Khoo and Lo, *Asian Transformation*, 959–960.
105 "The Constitution of Japan, 1946," Chapter 2. Article 9. Renounciation of War, 472.

11.3.2 The Chinese Responses and Challenge (K'ang Yu-wei, Sun Yat-sen, Mao Zedong, Deng Xiaoping)

Seeing the Japanese successes, China also began knowledge-based modernization as a response to the European challenge, but the history of Chinese modernization has evolved differently.[106]

The Chinese market was opened by the British as a result of the highly controversial, morally incorrect, and criminal Opium Wars (1839–1842, 1856–1860). Opium trade served as a financial source to pay the British administration, therefore the British government gave a free hand to the opium traders. Chinese authorities did not want to permit it, in response the British started the Opium wars. The first was between 1839 and 1842, and ended with the Peace of Nanking; the second was between 1856 and 1860, and ended with the Treaty of Tientsin. The Chinese were defeated and the British could make an advantageous peace which the Chinese called "unequal treaties." The British gained territories: Hong Kong was ceded to Britain, and Canton, Amoy, Fuchou, Ningpo, and Shanghai were opened to foreign trade as treaty ports with the right of exterritoriality for foreigners. It meant that foreigners continued to be under the jurisdiction of their own countries and could freely pursue laissez-faire free market actions in the territory of China. The Chinese were forced to give more and more concessions and rights because the Chinese military weakness was becoming obvious. These concessions were given to all European powers (Great Britain, France, Germany, Russia). The unequal treaties were based on the following principles: exterritoriality, the restriction of the level of customs duties, foreign settlements (Chinese territories under foreign administration), concessions, and leased territories, foreign powers had the right to station troops in the international settlements and in the concessions, freedom of movement for foreign ships in Chinese inland and territorial waters, most favored nation clause (all the rights which the Chinese had conceded to other nations would be automatically included in the new treaties). These "unequal treaties" were the foundation documents governing relations between China and Europeans for about a century.[107] They became the essential element of the Chinese national narrative.

European powers successfully forced China to cede its South-East Asian tributary states: in 1885 France occupied Annam (Vietnam); in 1886 Burma was ceded to Britain; subsequently Formosa and Pescadores were ceded to Japan; Korea declared its independence from China and was annexed by Japan; Germany occupied Tsingtao and Russia Port Arthur. British and French troops destroyed the Summer Palace outside Beijing. For this the Chinese regarded them as uncivilized barbarians.

---

106 Bóka, "Europe-China Dialogue," 1–96; Bóka, Európa és Ázsia, 100–115, 161–166; Bóka, Modernizáció és értékrend, 155–182.
107 Gregory, The West and China Since 1500, 87; Franke, China and the West, 67–76.

In China modernization began under the influence of the Japanese success. The emphasis was also on the education reform aiming to learn modern Western knowledge, and replacing the Confucian classics with it. The launcher of China's education reform, was the Confucian philosopher, K'ang Yu-wei (1858–1927). He was for following the example of the Meiji Reform. But it took a long time for him to convince himself to begin the reform of Confucianism and adapt Western knowledge. Like Fukuzawa, he also concentrated on the encouragement of learning using modern European study material.

K'ang Yu-wei, was a Confucian wise man, and a New-Confucian reformer continuing the work of Confucius. He regarded Confucius as a reformer who rediscovered and reinterpreted the rationalist principles of the ancient Chinese philosopher emperors. Based on his concept of "Confucius as reformer," he aimed to reform the Chinese society by safeguarding Chinese culture. He explained his reform ideas on the modernization of China in a manifesto addressed to Emperor Guangxu. In the manifesto, K'ang warned about the changed world situation emphasizing that the earth was completely explored, China could not remain closed, it had to learn what the others learned. As an example he mentioned the case of Turkey and Japan: Turkey did not want to reform and came under the control of the great powers; Japan reformed its institutions and strengthened. He emphasized that the strength of the West was in learning and sciences. Therefore, China needed to be strengthened through encouragement of learning because the strength of a country depended on the education of the people. Education and the examen system were important, but the domination of the old classics in education made China weak, therefore it would be necessary to include modern sciences in the teaching material.[108]

In 1898 K'ang Yu-wei told these reform ideas to Emperor Guangxu (Kuang-hsü) in his audience. He reasoned as follows:

> The cause for the lack of enlightenment in the mind of the people stems from the system of writing "eight-legged" essays as a means of selecting officials. Those who learn the writing of "eight legged" essays do not read any books published after the Ch'in and Han periods and they do not study the affairs of the other countries of the world yet they can still rise to high offices. Today there are large numbers of high officials but there are none on whom we can depend to carry out the reforms.[109]

K'ang could gain the support of the Emperor for the reform of the examination system and for the modernization of the study material in his audience, and by this he launched the Chinese reform. His idea of involving modern knowledge in the classical examination system proved to be very useful. Later others

---

108 Kang, *Manifeste à l'empereur*, 100, 102–104, 129.
109 K'ang, "Chronological Autobiography," 97.

accepted and elaborated this idea (Sun Yat-sen for example).[110] Therefore the Chinese modernization can be regarded as a New-Confucian reform process which was intellectual: it concentrated on the renewing of knowledge, learning and education.

K'ang could achieve the abolition of the "eight-legged" essays in the practice of the provincial and metropolitan examinations. They were replaced by essays on governmental affairs. From 1898 till 1904 the examination system was gradually reformed by introducing new teaching material in the schools, and the old style of literary examination was abandoned in 1905. The year of 1905, when the examination system was abolished, represented a decisive turning point in the relationship of China with the West on the intellectual and cultural fields. China became open to modern scientific and intellectual studies and Western social and political ideas. But nationalism, individualism, liberalism, and the ideals of science and democracy only on a very limited scale could break free from the traditional China in the 20th century. Traditional elements of Chinese society could survive in the Kuomintang and Maoist ideology and ethical ordering of society.[111]

Regarding the new state form K'ang was for a constitutional monarchy. But the Chinese ruling dynasty was not able to establish a constitutional monarchy following the plans of K'ang. His idea of a constitutional monarchy was based on the belief in the gradual change to secure the stability of Chinese society. He rejected revolution as a troubled way of reforms and opposed the republicanism and the revolutionary attitude of his contemporary leading politician, Sun Yat-sen. K'ang Yu-wei sympathized with the European monarchies, like the British or Dutch, because they represented social stability. So, K'ang believed that China had to continue the example of the European democratic constitutional monarchies because the monarchs could insure social stability. He proposed the establishment of the system of government practiced in England and her dominions, and in Belgium, in Romania, in Bulgaria, in Norway, and in Greece—a system he named "titular monarchical republic" [hsü-chün kung-ho]. In his view, under the system of "titular monarchical republic" the monarchy would be hereditary but powerless. The monarch would be revered but he or she would be anything other than a temple idol, the bearer of a majestic but empty title. The real power would rest in the Parliament with executive authority centered in a cabinet headed by a prime minister chosen from the majority party. The presence of the monarch would preserve order during changes of government so that the state would not fall into anarchy. Thus the state would be stable and debates would take place in the Parliament and not on the battlefield.[112]

---

110 Franke "K'ang Yu-wei und die Reform des Prüfungswesens," 313–318.
111 K'ang, "Chronological Autobiography," 101; Franke, China and the West, 119; Zürcher, "Wester Expansion Chinese Reactions," 76–77.
112 Jung-pang Lo, "Sequel to the Chronological Autobiography of K'ang Yu-wei," 218–219.

K'ang Yu-wei's world view is the best expressed in his well-known and much discussed utopian work on the Great Unity of mankind, entitled *The Ta-t'ung shu* [Book of the Universal Commonwealth or Book of Great Unity]. It is a plan for the future universal peace, similar to those Utopias which were written before and after the First World War on how to achieve world peace. It shows well the meeting of European and Chinese thinking in the idea of world peace. "Great Unity" was based on his belief in three epochs in the life of mankind: the epoch of disorder; the epoch of rising peace; and the epoch of universal peace. He regarded the period when he lived as a period of troubles. The establishment of the League of Nations meant for him the beginning of the period of rising peace. He differentiated three periods according to the type of the union among states.

The first epoch—the period of disorders—was the type in which equals were allied;

The second epoch—the period of rising peace—was a type in which each states carried on its internal government but the overall administration was united under the overall government.

The third epoch of universal peace—the period of complete peace and equality—was a type in which the names and boundaries of the states have been abolished, and independent (i.e. locally self-governing) districts and prefectures were formed, united however under the control of the universal government.

In his view these three types corresponded to the three stages of gradual evolution toward One World or Universal Union.[113]

According to his plan the cooperation among states started with small unions, small associations of two or three states whose strength was equal and whose interest was mutual. After that the resulting large states of the world will form the unlimited type of union for mutual support. The citizens have the right to control the state's affairs, and when the form of government has been changed to democracy then mutual aggressions among states will automatically eased.[114]

Founding of a public (universal) Parliament is the first step toward Universal Union, and establishing a public government to govern all nations is the middle step toward it. The public (universal) Parliament has two chambers: the upper house represents the states, the lower house represents the world. In the first period the representatives of the Parliament represent their own states; in the second period the representatives of the upper house represent the states, the lower house the world; in the third period, the members of the public (universal) Parliament represent only the people of the world and not any particular region.[115]

The world in the period of universal peace would set up a single government and would be divided into several regions which replaces the nation-states, and

---

113 K'ang, *Ta T'ung Shu*, 86.
114 K'ang, *Ta T'ung Shu*, 87–88.
115 K'ang, *Ta T'ung Shu*, 91–104, 110–111.

families and clans. Both the central and regional governments should be elected by popular vote.[116]

The ideas and principles represented by K'ang's vision corresponded in many ways to internationalism and socialism. K'ang was aware that it was a plan for the future, but he was convinced humankind of his age has to start peaceful cooperation among states. Therefore the most important challenge for those who wanted to live in peace was to find the ways and means to limit the laissez-faire imperialist market economic expansion and to promote the international economic and political cooperation in the framework of international institutions based on international law and humanist moral principles.

Chinese history has not justified K'ang's vision on a New Confucian constitutional monarchical reform. The 1911 revolution overthrew the monarchy and China became a republic. The leader of the revolution was Sun Yat-sen (1866–1925), who is revered as the Founding Father of modern China. He regarded Japan's joining of the Western world by learning, and achieving good results in modernization, as a good example. But he emphasized that, because of the "hypo-colonial" situation (colony of all Western powers), China had to use the revolutionary method to achieve a capitalist system based on popular sovereignty and democracy with Chinese characteristics. In his words:

> If we want to restore China's liberty, we must unite ourselves into one unshakable body; we must use revolutionary methods to weld our state into firm unity. Without revolutionary principles we shall never succeed.[117]

Sun acknowledged that democracy originated in Europe, and Europe had done a lot to realize it. But, he believed that the European democratization process could not achieve perfect democracy and could not realize popular sovereignty following the ideas of the Declaration of the Rights of Man and of the Citizen (1789). The French Revolutionaries set up as their goal democracy but they created a complete (direct) democracy, instituted mob tyranny which ended in anarchy and a fear of democracy. In Germany, Bismarck started a setback against democracy by establishing anti-democratic authoritarian state socialism. He believed that in Europe the old autocratic powers could prevent the success of democracy. Only Switzerland, as a federal republic under a federal government, could become a real popular democracy because popular sovereignty was strongly connected with federalism. Although Western revolutions were carried out under the banner of democracy, the result was only the suffrage of men and women.[118]

---

116 Hsü, *Readings in Modern Chinese History*, 308–309.
117 Sun Yat-sen, "The Three Principles of the People," 76–77.
118 Sun Yat-sen, "The Three Principles of the People," 100–107.

He appreciated the ideas of the European modernization project on liberty, popular sovereignty and democracy, but he criticized the European practice of laissez-faire colonial liberal capitalism. This is why he wanted to avoid the pitfalls of liberal capitalism. He was for joining the process of democratization of the states and the international relations, but on the basis of China's ancient morality. He believed that the methods of Western democracy could not be the model or guide. China had to find her own path to democracy. It had to invent the Chinese "Principle of People's Sovereignty," and remake China into a nation under complete popular rule, ahead of Europe and America.[119] For this national reconstruction work he wanted to use not only European principles, but also the best Confucian principles as the "Great Learning" taught:

> Search into the nature of things, extend the boundaries of knowledge, make the purpose sincere, regulate the mind, cultivate personal virtue, rule the family, govern the state, pacify the world.[120]

Searching the Chinese principle of popular sovereignty in harmony with the "Great Learning," the most important dilemma for Sun was the interpretation of the principle of liberty which was not present in Chinese history. He realized that this was the most important difference between the Chinese and the Western civilizations. He recognized that Chinese people did not know the meaning of Western liberty and, because of this, they were criticized by the Westerners. Searching the reasons for the lack of liberty, Sun pointed to the characteristic local family and clan autonomy, which made China disunited like a "sheet of loose sand." Because autocratic rule, in the framework of centralized and united Western national monarchies, was hard, Western people had to fight for individual and national liberty. As a result of the fight for rights and liberty, democracy gradually developed in the framework of authoritarian Western national monarchies and empires. Because China was disunited, it lost independence and became the colony of all Western powers. From all this, Sun concluded that for the Chinese, the fight for liberty meant the fight for national unity by sacrificing personal freedom. Consequently, the Chinese had a different usage of liberty to the Westerners. For the Chinese nationalism corresponded to Western liberty. People's nationalism meant a struggle for the liberty of the Chinese nation.[121] Sun therefore considered nationalism and liberty as being equal.

His nationalist program became the basis of the Chinese modernization and democratization process. It was based on the Three Principles of the People the main ideas of which he announced in 1905. He defined these principles—in comparison to the Western revolutionary watchwords—as follows:

---

119 Sun Yat-sen, "The Three Principles of the People," 37, 56–57. 107.
120 Sun Yat-sen, "The Three Principles of the People," 42.
121 Sun Yat-sen, "The Three Principles of the People," 67–69, 75–76.

> The watchword of the French Revolution was "Liberty"; the watchword of the American Revolution was "Independence"; the watchword of our revolution is the "Three Principles of the People.[122]
>
> The watchword of the French Revolution was "Liberty, Equality, Fraternity." Our watchword is People's Nationalism, People's Sovereignty, People's Livelihood.[123]

In his view the French revolutionary watchword, "Liberty," had the same meaning as the Chinese watchword "People's Nationalism"; Equality was similar to the Chinese "Principle of the People's Sovereignty" which aimed to destroy autocracy and make all men equal. "Fraternity" originally meant brotherhood and had the same significance as the Chinese word t'ung-pao (compatriots). The meaning of the idea of "Fraternity" was similar to the Chinese "Principle of the People's Livelihood," the happiness of the four hundred million Chinese.[124]

The nationalist narrative of Sun Yat-sen was based on legitimate national discontent caused by colonization and the unequal treaties, on the rejection of liberal capitalism, and on the fight for safeguarding national freedom by building up a different national economic and social system from Western liberal capitalism protecting the livelihood of the people and safeguarding Chinese culture.

His nationalist program was based on the Three Principles of the People (San Min Chu I), on the five-power constitution, and on federalism.

The Three Principles of the People were nationalism (Minzu), democracy (Minquan) and livelihood (Min Sheng).

Nationalism called for national unity (based on families and clans as the basic units of the state), the preservation of independence and of the Confucian culture and Confucian values, and the introducing useful Western knowledge with critic. In his formulation the eight Confucian virtues were the following: Loyalty and Filial Devotion, Kindness and Love, Faithfulness and Justice, Harmony and Peace. In a democratic system Loyalty meant loyalty not to princes, but to the nation and to the people; a limited Filial Devotion also meant loyalty to the nation; Faithfulness and Justice meant correct behavior with the neighboring countries and friends in business intercourse and in international relations (not destroying another state); Harmony and Peace meant a policy of peace and rejection of imperialism and war. Sun emphasized the importance of adhering to these Confucian virtues as national values and principles.[125]

Democracy accepted the Western representative parliamentary model, but Sun proposed instead of a three-power constitution a five-power constitution involving the old Chinese Confucian moral rules, the civil service examination and censorship. To the government belonged the legislative, executive, judiciary,

---

122 Sun Yat-sen, "The Three Principles of the People," 72.
123 Sun Yat-sen, "The Three Principles of the People," 75–76.
124 Sun Yat-sen, "The Three Principles of the People," 77.
125 Sun Yat-sen, "The Three Principles of the People," 37–41.

civil service examination and censorship; to the people suffrage, recall, initiative and referendum.[126] He was for an expert government, and against corruption through moral control.

Sun's concept on Livelihood rejected adopting both Marxism and the Western liberal capitalist market economic model. It represented state capitalism with Chinese characteristics. Livelihood dealt with the organization of the life of people following their needs, in a bottom up federalist system.

Although Sun Yat-sen was for the sacrifice of individual freedom to national unity, he declared himself a believer in federalism. He thought that democracy and popular sovereignty needed federalism, i.e. a bottom-up associative model of political development, and self-government. In his view the state government had to manage all those fields what the autonomous parts transferred to the state level.[127] The federal republican constitutional structure of the United States and of Switzerland served as examples for him to unify China as a nation-state.[128]

After the First World War, Sun Yat-sen drafted the large-scale project *The International Development of China* to modernize China in the framework of international development. He called for the cessation of commercial wars (using the endless method of underselling each other to exhaust the weaker) by co-operation and mutual aid. He championed peace policy instead of wars, and was in thinking on how the New China could contribute to world peace by using capitalism and by learning from the mistakes of the West.

He regarded the historical path of the Western capitalism to be an unknown adventure in the economic ocean. It was comparable to Columbus when he embarked on the path of discovery and did not know where he was going. Sun believed that China, as a late comer, could learn from the path already charted by the western pioneers. History showed that the fight for private profit was interminable, produced trusts, monopolies, and led to constant trade wars and imperialism. In his view, the goal of material civilization was not private profit but public profit. Therefore, he concluded, that it was necessary to consider, on the one hand, how to protect China from private trusts (monopolies) and commercial war, and on the other hand, how to use capitalism to create socialism in the construction of a New China.

Regarding the first dilemma he proposed forming China into a great trust owned by the people:

> The trust is a result of economic evolution, therefore it is out of human power to suppress it. The proper remedy is to have it owned by all the people of the country. In my International Development Scheme, I intend to make all the national industries of China into a Great Trust owned by the Chinese people, and financed with international capital

---

126 Sun Yat-sen, "The Three Principles of the People," 145–149.
127 Huters et al., *Culture and State in Chinese History*, 343.
128 Sun Yat-sen, *The Teachings of Sun Yat-sen*, 58–59.

for mutual benefit. Thus once for all, commercial war will be done away in the largest market of the world.[129]

Regarding the usage of capitalism in the service of socialism, he proposed to concentrate on public profit and cooperation, and to use the profit of industrial development to pay the interest and principal of foreign capital invested in, to pay high wages, and to improve the machinery of production. The rest of the profit should protect the public in the form of reduced prices in all commodities and public services.[130]

Sun Yat-sen, drawing from Western capitalism, wanted to build China up toward socialism. In his vision, China, as a socialist version of capitalism, was envisioned as a great trust owned by the people under expert leadership in a bottom-up representative parliamentary federalist system led by the Nationalist Party. The railroads, public utilities, canals, and forests would be nationalized, and all income from the land and mines would be in the hand of the State. With this money in hand, the State could finance the social welfare programs. The bottom-up federalist representative parliamentary structure ensured focusing on the livelihood of the people and avoiding a fictitious economy. The whole structure represented the interests of the people and supported the prevailing of Confucian moral principles. In the Western world human rights were the means of the fight against the authoritarian tendencies of liberal capitalism facilitated by the concentration of capital. With the idea of organizing China into a great trust owned by the people, Sun Yat-sen challenged the Western liberal capitalist world.

To conclude, Sun Yat-sen's state socialist vision aimed to change semi-colonial China into an economically and politically independent country. His goal was to discover a capitalist system which served socialism and peaceful cooperation among the peoples and states replacing colonialism and war. He wanted to solve the Western democratic deficit of popular sovereignty by proposing to re-establishing of the old Chinese examination system for the officials, in a reformed form, on the basis of modern Western knowledge and of the principles of democratic state organization and federalism. He believed that, by the active involvement of people in politics, the problem of the livelihood of the masses could be solved because people told the experts what to solve, and the experts told the people how to solve it. There was no need for the authority of powerful politicians and of wealthy businessmen in this bottom-up process. Sun emphasized that state organization had to be concentrated for solving problems on the basis of reality and of the search for truth. This was how he imagined transcending the system of privileges and the power of the traditional hereditary elite who did not dare and want to let people govern. This is how he suggested solving

129 Sun Yat-sen, *The International Development of China*, 236.
130 Sun Yat-sen, *The International Development of China*, 237.

the democratic deficit characterizing European political and economic practice regarding popular sovereignty.

His ideal state, based on the three principles of the people, would be a unified democratic and federalist nation-state realizing the idea of "government of the people, by the people, and for the people," as President Abraham Lincoln expressed the goal of democracy in his *Gettysburg Address* (1863). In Sun's words:

> Our Three Principles of the People mean government "of the people, by the people, and for the people"—that is, a state belonging to all the people, a government controlled by all the people, and rights and benefits for the enjoyment of all the people. If this is true, the people will have a share in everything. When the people share everything in the state, then will we truly reach the goal of the Min Sheng Principle, which is Confucius' hope of a "great commonwealth.[131]

Sun Yat-sen outlined the most important ideas and organizing principles characterizing the nationalist narrative of the modern Chinese nation-state:

- Rightful national discontent caused by colonization and the unequal treaties.
- The interpretation of liberty as national freedom.
- The same meaning of liberty and nationalism based on the three principles of the people concept.
- State capitalism and rejection of liberal capitalism.
- The eight Confucian values instead of human rights.
- The meritocracy of the five-power expert government in the service of the livelihood of the people.
- Fight for safeguarding national freedom by building up a, from the Western liberal capitalism, different socialist economic and social system protecting the livelihood of the people and defending Chinese culture: "State capitalism with Chinese characteristics."

The significance of Sun's thought lies perhaps in the impact he had on later Chinese political leaders as well as other revolutionaries. Both nationalists and Communists adopted his nationalist narrative. Following his ideas Taiwan, Singapore, and the post-Maoist China created blooming socialist state economies.[132]

After the Second World War the Constitution of the Republic of China of 1946 established a centralized republican government with five branches following Sun Yat-sen's ideas.[133] It was centered on the Three Principles of the

---

131 Sun Yat-sen, "The Three Principles of the People," 183–184.
132 Wells, *The Political Thought of Sun Yat-sen*, 121.
133 Constitution of the Republic of China, 1946.

People: nationalism, democracy, and livelihood. The goal was to establish the government of the people, by the people and for the people. The Constitution represented the values of liberal nationalism, accepted the classical liberal values of freedom, tolerance, equality and individual rights. The Republic of China sought to create a parliamentary democracy, a social system, and it aimed to secure the civil and political rights of the people. People had four political rights: election and recall of public officials, legislative initiative, and referendum.

When the Communists defeated the nationalists, a transitional period started which was characterized by the strengthening of the influence of Stalin and the one-party constitutionalism of Mao Zedong. Mao appreciated Sun Yat-sen's vision and cooperated with the nationalists on the democratic anti-imperialist front, but later he separated from the nationalist path. More precisely, he saw Sun's work and the nationalist policy as the first, bourgeois-democratic stage of the revolutionary process. But he renewed the Three Principles of the People of Sun Yat-sen in the direction of the socialist revolution. The revolutionary Three People's Principles of Mao contained the three cardinal policies of alliance with Russia, co-operation with the Communists and assistance to the peasants and workers. In the second stage, Mao wanted to create a socialist state on a Marxist basis serving the livelihood and prosperity of people (workers and peasants).[134]

He emphasized the necessity to join the anti-imperialist front:

> In the international situation of today, the "heroes" in the colonies and semi-colonies must either stand on the side of the imperialist front and become part of the force of world counter-revolution or stand on the side of the anti-imperialist front and become part of the force of world revolution. They must stand either on this side or the other, for there is no third choice.[135]

All this meant a break with the past Confucian culture and the nationalists who thought that Marxism was not needed for Chinese socialism, because socialism could be created within the framework of state capitalism based on Confucian values and principles. Seeing the American occupation of Japan, Mao was convinced that Chinese nationalism was not enough protection against imperialism because to be capitalist with the help of the imperialists was a blind alley. He thought that, since the Opium Wars, China was vulnerable, the 4 May Movement and the conservative feudal Confucianism were not enough. In his view, China's independence could only be insured by a social and economic order different from Western imperialism, and a Chinese version of the Russian Revolution of 1917 could be an alternative.[136] In 1949, Marxism became the official ideology in China. In the Maoist period until 1976, all non-Marxist ideas were con-

---

134 Mao Tse-tung, *On New Democracy*, 50.
135 Mao Tse-tung, *On New Democracy*, 34.
136 Mao Zedong, "Weixin shi guan de pochan," 152–153.

demned, China came under Communist rule, and Marx and the teachings of Mao replaced those of Confucius.[137]

In 1954, the National People's Congress adopted the first Constitution of the People's Republic of China. It established the one-party rule of the Communist Party of China in mainland China. The Nationalists [Kuomintag], in Taiwan, kept the spirit of the 1946 Constitution based on Sun Yat-sen's Thought.

The 1954 Constitution of the People's Republic of China declared the principles of a New Democracy under Chairmen Mao Zedong. China became the People's Republic of China, a democratic state led by the working class and based on the alliance of workers and peasants, all power belonged to the people.[138] It was a unitary multinational state. The People's Republic of China expressed its friendship with the Union of Soviet Socialist Republics and the People's Democracies.

The Constitution emphasized that the Communist Party of China had won a great victory in the people's revolution against imperialism, feudalism and bureaucratic capitalism, brought an end to the history of oppression and enslavement, and founded the people's democratic dictatorship, the aim of which was to build a socialist society. For this a transition period was necessary, during which the old forces of the former society (rich peasants, feudal landowners, capitalist ownership, bureaucrat capitalists) should be abolished. Parallel to all this the new state capitalist economy, based on the ownership of the people and planned economy, would be built up. People exercised power through the National People's Congress and the Local People's Congresses at various levels. The organs of the state practiced democratic centralism.

The National People's Congress was the highest organ of state authority, the only legislative authority of the country. It was elected by the people. The State Council exercised the executive power.

The Local People's Congresses and People's Councils were established in provinces, municipalities, counties, municipal districts, hsiang (townships-level divisions), nationality hsiang, and towns. Local people's congresses at all levels were the organs of government authority in their respective localities.[139]

The Local People's Courts and Procuratorates were directed from above. The Supreme People's Court and the Supreme People's Procuratorate were responsible and accountable to the National People's Congress. So, they were not independent.

The Constitution of the People's Republic of China of 1954, abolished the old capitalist and feudal class, and involved in the power the people, i.e. the working class and the peasants with the aim of realizing popular sovereignty. It adopted elements of the Western democratic parliamentary representative system, but it was a centralized one-party state using democratic centralism. The Constitution

---

137 Zhang, *Chine et modernité*, 161.
138 "The 1954 Constitution of the People's Republic of China," 154.
139 "The 1954 Constitution of the People's Republic of China," 171.

ensured the fundamental rights and duties of the citizens: equality before the law; suffrage; freedom of speech, of press, of assembly, of association, of procession and of demonstration; freedom of religious belief; right to education; social rights; women enjoyed equal rights with men in all spheres of political, economic, social and family life.

Mao Zedong's goal was to develop the European system of liberties in the direction of a New Democracy and to establish real democracy and popular sovereignty. But what he created was in contradiction to the system of Western liberties for several reasons:

- In a centralized unitary state, human rights could not prevail: unitary centralized multinational state could not protect minority rights, and human rights.
- Lack of pluralism: the one-party state was in contradiction to pluralism.
- Popular sovereignty could not prevail because of the top-down centralized structure of the state.
- There was no separation of powers (the judiciary power was not separated from the legislative power); there was no independent judiciary.

The 1954 Constitution represented a centralized Communist government under the democratic facade of the centralized pyramid structure of the state. The 1975 Constitution recognized the Communist Party as the leader of China.

Under Mao Zedong's rule, China became a Communist country, influenced by the one party government of the Stalinist Soviet Union, and led by Marxism-Leninism and Mao Zedong Thought, aiming to build up a New Democracy of the workers and peasants. With this change China became independent having a different political system opposing liberal capitalism. Mao Zedong could restore the self-respect of Chinese which was damaged by Western colonial imperialism. But he moved toward a personality cult. Under the Great Proletarian Cultural Revolution (1966–1976), aiming to eliminate capitalist, bourgeois and traditional elements of the Chinese society including Confucianism, millions were persecuted.[140] The Chinese historical and cultural values were seriously damaged.

In 1976, after the death of Mao Zedong the leading politician, Deng Xiaoping (1904–1997) became the paramount leader of the People's Republic of China. He was a wise Confucian thinker and reformer who launched the movement of liberation of thought. Communism gradually lost its absolute domination, the ideas of Sun Yat-sen and Confucianism gradually revived.[141] Seeing the results of the European integration process, in making peace, ending colonial methods, and stabilizing the European Community, Deng Xiaoping decided to open up

---

140 Deng Xiao-ping, for example, was not favored by Mao Zedong because of his economic policy, and he was purged twice during the Cultural Revolution.
141 Zhang, *Chine et modernité*, 473–475.

Some Responses to European Modernity

China to the world market, and to start the necessary reforms. His aim was the establishment of a state-socialist economy, the so called "socialism with Chinese characteristics." In this he followed Sun Yat-sen's ideas on Livelihood and State Socialism. Post Maoist China started to return to the 19th and early 20th century pattern of China. Interest in Marxism disappeared, market-based reforms began.[142]

Deng Xiaoping's reforms started in 1975, and had several periods. In the first period, he aimed at opening up and economic reforms; from 1984, the goal was to establish a market economy. In 1988, the Chinese authorities tried to regain control of the economy. The Tiananmen Square Massacre happened in 1989. However, in 1992, Deng Xiaoping succeeded in re-launching the economic and political reforms which resulted in a booming economy.

The Party Congress (Third Plenary Session to the Twelfth National Congress of the CPC, September 1, 1982) was a turning point of great historical importance: the making of a market economy with Chinese characteristics became the aim. China decided to gradually follow a policy of opening to the outside world and actively increased exchanges with foreign countries on the basis of equality and mutual benefit. In his opening speech Deng Xiaoping emphasized that China must integrate the universal truth of Marxism with the concrete realities of China, choose its own way of social development, and build a socialism with Chinese characteristics. At the same time, he emphasized that China would never permit the bourgeois way of life to spread in China.[143]

In 1986 Deng Xiaoping made it clear that he was against laissez-faire bourgeois liberalization. He believed that without the leadership of the Communist Party and without socialism, there would be no future for China. The country had to remain stable, and had to be able to avoid disorder caused by liberalism. He emphasized that China must follow its own path and build socialism with Chinese characteristics.[144]

According to the Constitution of the People's Republic of China of 1982 China was a unitary multi-national state created jointly by the people of all its nationalities:

> The People's Republic of China is a socialist state under the people's democratic dictatorship led by the working class and based on the alliance of workers and peasants. The socialist system is the fundamental system of the People's Republic of China. Leadership by the Communist Party of China is the defining feature of socialism with Chinese characteristics.

---

142 Holcombe, *A History of East Asia*, 324–325.
143 Deng Xiaoping, *Selected Works of Deng Xiaoping (1975–1982)*, 395–396.
144 Deng Xiaoping, "Taking a Clear-Cut Stand Against Bourgeois Liberalisation," 182–185.

> All power in the People's Republic of China belongs to the people. The organs through which the people exercise state power are the National People's Congress and the local people's congresses at all levels.[145]

People have voting rights. The institutional system was composed of The National People's Congress, The State Council, The Local People's Congresses and Local People's Governments, and The People's Courts of the People's Republic of China. The Constitution did not mention the Communist Party. The Chinese Communist Party had no absolute rule, it was subordinated to the Constitution which was the fundamental law of the state having supreme legal authority.

The state structure and the state organs mirrored three things:

1. China was not a federalist state, it was a unitary nation-state which was centralized, i.e. the local authorities could initiate, but they were under the unified leadership of the central authorities. Chinese people of all nationalities united in the unitary nation-state which respected minority rights.
2. The Constitution did not represent the Western principle of separation of powers between executive, legislative and judicial power. The highest organ of the state authority was the National People's Congress under which there were the State Council, the Supreme People's Court and the Supreme People's Procuratorate which were responsible to the National People's Congress.
3. The limited usage of human rights. The Constitution moved towards human rights declaring that China respects human rights: the freedom of religious belief; the freedom of personal dignity and the inviolability of the privacy of the person of citizens. But the freedom of speech, of press, of assembly, of association and of demonstration were considered to be politically destabilizing and were reduced to the right to criticize.

   > Citizens of the People's Republic of China have the right to criticize and make suggestions regarding any State organ or functionary. Citizens have the right to make to relevant State organs complaints or charges against, or exposures of, any State organ or functionary for violation of law or dereliction of duty; but fabrication or distortion of facts for purposes of libel or false incrimination is prohibited.[146]

---

145 "The Constitution of the People's Republic of China, 1982," chapter 1, article 1, 2, General Principles.
146 "The Constitution of the People's Republic of China, 1982," chapter II, article 41. The fundamental rights and duties of citizens.

Some Responses to European Modernity 197

The Constitution declared statist socialist economy:

> The state owned economy, namely, the socialist economy under ownership by the whole people, is the leading force in the national economy.[147]

It rejected the system of exploitation, and gave a legal framework for the liberalization of economic policy; allowed limited private economic activity, and foreign participation in the economy. The state protected the right of the citizens to private property and to inheritance of it.

The Constitution summarized China's achievement as follows: China during the revolution started by Sun Yat-sen, abolished the feudal monarchy and established the Republic of China. In 1949 the Communist Party of China, under the leadership of Chairman Mao Zedong overthrew the rule of imperialism, feudalism and bureaucrat-capitalism, and started to build up the New Democracy of Chinese people taking power into their own hands.[148]

Under Deng Xiaoping China continued the way toward a Chinese-style socialism based on a socialist market economy, socialist democracy and a socialist legal system.

In 1992, the Fourteenth Party Congress approved the economic reform as the only way to modernize China. The definition of a socialist market economy was given in January 1993, when the political report of the State Council interpreted it as follows:

> A multifaceted economic structure in which public ownership, individual household industry, private enterprise, and foreign investment all competed on an equal basis.[149]

In practice it meant accepting capitalistic practices based on the market economy. But the political report reaffirmed party dictatorship, the ideology of Marxism-Leninism-Maoism, and emphasized that the goal was a socialist democracy:

> The goal of this reform is to build a socialist democracy suited to the Chinese conditions and absolutely not a Western, multiparty, parliamentary system.[150]

The reform, in European terms, called for a market economy within an authoritarian political system. But Deng Xiaoping saw no inconsistency in promoting a quasi-capitalist economy in an authoritarian political system. History showed him that Meiji Japan and the Bismarckian Germany did the same in the 19th

---

147 "The Constitution of the People's Republic of China, 1982," chapter 1, article 7, General Principles.
148 "The Constitution of the People's Republic of China, 1982," Preamble.
149 Hsü, *The Rise of Modern China*, 947.
150 Hsü, *The Rise of Modern China*, 948.

century, and later, in the 20th century, Singapore, Taiwan, and South Korea also had achieved economic miracles under authoritarian rule. The Singaporean model of Premier Lee Kuan Yew was attractive for Deng Xiaoping and he wanted to learn from it. He was convinced that the accelerated development of South China and the coastal areas was more realizable under an effective authoritarian government which could secure the necessary stability than under a weak democratic government.[151]

Deng Xiaoping's reforms resulted in an economic boom. China emerged to the EU and the global world economy as a possible future superpower.

EU and China relations were complicated because China, for historical reasons, was in search of a separate way from the West, and had chosen state socialism. Thanks to the reforms of Deng Xiaoping, EU-China relations developed dynamically in parallel with the opening of China. But despite the developing good relations between the EU and China, there were problems in their relations because of different views and disagreements on trade, on market-economy status, on developing country status and development aid, on human rights, on liberal capitalism, state capitalism and sustainable development.[152]

China had good relations with the UN. It represented peace policy, non-intervention, and wanted to solve the international problems within the framework of the UN.

The success of the Chinese one-party authoritarian meritocratic regime is based on the economic success of directed state capitalism and on the protection of national interest. Productivist and nationalist ideologies ensure the legitimacy of state capitalism. It is repressive, flexible, and implements real reforms serving the livelihood of the people. The nation is getting richer, the living standards of the population are rising. Knowledge-based Confucian morality motivates China to evolve into a world power.[153] And, as such, modern China is a challenge for the EU.

11.4 The Vision of Peaceful International Organization

The non-European responses to the European challenge of laissez-faire modernization showed that the impact of European modernization was inevitable everywhere, with its pros and cons. The major countries and civilizations of the world adopted Western elements and have integrated into the capitalist world economy on the basis of the liberal versus statist dilemma. Politically, the pluralist versus one-party dilemma, economically the free versus directed capitalism became dominant. The Constitutions were drafted on the basis of the Westminster system, the Constitution of the United States, and the Declaration of Human Rights. The dichotomy of intergovernmental versus

---

151 Hsü, *The Rise of Modern China*, 948.
152 Arranz and Wacker (2015), "China and the European Union," 256–278.
153 Bergère, *Chine le nouveau capitalisme d'État*, 286.

federal international organization became a worldwide dilemma. Thinkers from non-European countries also became involved in the debate on the organization of the state and economy in a global world. The idealist supporters of peace policy, opposing the realist supporters of power policy, met on the path of fighting for democratic federalism and effective international organization as a global challenge.

The leading non-Western modernizers were very critical of the European powers because of colonization, imperialism and laissez-faire market economic expansion. They highly appreciated the Declaration of the Rights of Man and of the Citizen (1789) and adopted many things from the Western civilization, but looked at the liberal capitalism and the Western system of liberties with critic and suspicion because of its weak moral. Several of them also signaled to Europeans that they were not behaving according to the principles and fundamental rights they were promoting. Pluralism and liberty seemed to be deceptive for them in the perspective of forcible and incorrect legal agreements, legalized free robbery, criminal acts and world wars according to the testimony of colonial history. The Chinese national narrative is still based on these wounds. At the same time, non-Europeans realized that they needed to give appropriate answers in order to defend their own independence and parallel all this to integrate into the capitalist world economy by learning, thinking, discussing and creating. After the initial difficulties, several non-European countries, using Western methods, gradually strengthened, achieved success, created blooming economies and invented alternative responses that were challenging for the Europeans. Fighting for independence they contributed to a European democratic renewal. When, after the Second World War, the colonies became independent, and the European integration process started, with the aim to establish a democratic federation, the European Community was positively regarded by the non-European civilizations, and a voluntary opening started in the world economy and policy. But, the adherence to state capitalism and to the associated non-pluralist national centralization policy, strong presidential power, and limitation of fundamental rights showed the continuing fear of losing power and national independence in a liberal world economic system of rich and poor countries, where there was no democracy among states and no effective international organization. All this hindered or made it difficult to open up to democracy, pluralism, and human rights.

Nevertheless, there was a "meeting point" where the visions of European and non-European political thinkers met, and that was international organization based on the idea of federalism following the example of Switzerland or the United States. The idea of a peaceful world federation and the search for justice connected many non-European thinkers with the European democratic federalist opposition to power politics.

After the Second World War a new—dominantly intergovernmental –regionalism started in the international politics using functionalist elements. States all over the world created intergovernmentalist functionalist regional economic and trade associations. This was in harmony with the intergovernmentalist functionalist aims of the United Nations Organization (UN) as a novelty. The most important intergovernmental regional experiences were the MERCOSUR (grouping a number of countries in Latin America), NAFTA (North American Free Trade Area), ASEAN (Association of South-East Asian Nations), and African regionalism. On the basis of these emerging new regions one can say that new regionalism was the interest of the states, more precisely, functionalist associations in which the sovereign states were embedded. This meant that the sovereign states voluntarily created different functionalist associations with the aim of safeguarding and strengthening their statehood. States (governments), as regional actors aimed to participate in the global economy without denying the sovereignty of the state and the cultural specificities associated with it. They were for interstate functionalist (specialized) coordinating agencies, and did not establish supranational new regional institutions, like the EU, and opposed the pooling of sovereignty. The most successful among them was the ASEAN (Association of South-East Asian Nations), which aimed to strengthen its member states through intergovernmental functionalist cooperation based on the principles of the sovereignty of the member states, non-interference in the internal affairs of other states, and the consensus-based decision making. It was established on August 8, 1967 in Bangkok (Thailand) with the signing of the ASEAN Declaration (Bangkok Declaration) by the Founding Fathers of the ASEAN, namely the foreign ministers of Indonesia, Malaysia, Philippines, Singapore and Thailand. Later Brunei, Cambodia, Laos, Myanmar, Vietnam joined. In 1997, the ASEAN Plus Three was created, with the participation of China, Japan, and South Korea.

ASEAN represented an alternative Asian model of intergovernmentalist functionalist network-type integration. It created a networked representation of power in which loosely institutionalized regulatory measures provided a way for cooperation. The point was that politicians invented well-managed local functionalist alternatives within the framework of a state centric power policy, and by this way cooperation strengthened the states, and gave national leaders more room for maneuver asserting their own interests.[154]

The ASEAN Charter (2007) outlined a centralized regional organization structure headed by the ASEAN Summit of the heads of state or government. It was the supreme policy and decision making body of the ASEAN. The ASEAN Coordinating Council of the foreign ministers of the member states was responsible for the coordination of the agreements and decisions of the ASEAN Summit, in cooperation with the ASEAN Community Councils having three pillars: the ASEAN Political-Security Community Council, the ASEAN Economic Community Council, and the ASEAN Socio-Cultural Community Council. They coordinated the relevant sector, ensured the implementation of the decisions, and submitted recommendation to the Summit. Each ASEAN

---

154 Higgot, "Alternative Models of Regional Cooperation?," 105.

Community Council had under its purview the relevant ASEAN Sectoral Ministerial Bodies which were in charge to implement the agreements and decisions of the ASEAN Summit, and to submit recommendations to their respective Community Councils. The Secretary General of ASEAN and the ASEAN Secretariat was the organization's central administrative body; the ASEAN National Secretariats coordinated the implementation of ASEAN decisions at the national level. Each ASEAN member state appointed a permanent representative to ASEAN with the rank of ambassador, and they collectively constituted the Committee of Permanent Representatives which supported the work of the ASEAN Community Councils and ASEAN Sectoral Ministerial Bodies. The ASEAN Human Rights Body promoted and protected human rights and fundamental freedoms. And the ASEAN Foundation promoted ASEAN community building.[155]

ASEAN did not create a supranational representative parliamentary, council and court structure in one institutional system, like the EU. It remained intergovernmental and avoided the sharing of sovereignty regarding common functions. It was in search of consensus and agreements in the framework of the Coordinating Council and Community Councils in cooperation with the ASEAN Sectoral Ministerial Bodies. But ASEAN, under the influence of the EU created a pillar structure and its aim is to establish the ASEAN single market. Using European concepts, the difference between the EU and ASEAN can be expressed by the Monnet versus Mitrany dichotomy of federalist functionalism versus intergovernmentalist functionalism.

The EU, using the Monnet-method, was able to transcend intergovernmentalism, and share the sovereignty of the member states in the field of common interests. The exclusive competences are directed by the EU law and institutions. It has the possibility of representing both intergovernmentalist and federalist ideas and practices through subsidiarity and multilevelism. Thus, as a new regional international organization, the EU-method was able to create a supranational governance—directed by subsidiarity—that could manage the common exclusive regional competences. Therefore the European integration process—representing supranationalism, subsidiarity and multilevel governance, as the interest of the states and of the people—is able to suggest new concepts on renewing the international policy for states and large (continental) regions belonging to different civilizations. Perhaps it could motivate the reform of the UN as well.

Regarding the reform of the UN, Jürgen Habermas (1929-), German philosopher and sociologist, has written that the EU's multilevelism based on subsidiarity could be a good example for the UN to socialize a big territory (a region) because European policy was able to develop and there is peace among the member states.[156]

---

155 ASEAN Charter 2007, chapter IV, article 7-15, 10-19.
156 Habermas, "Hat die Konstitutionalisierung des Volkerrechts noch eine Chance?," 174-178.

And indeed, the following could be done in the future:

It would be necessary to reform the Security Council according to the contemporary situation of world powers. Inside the institutional structure of the UN the principle of multilevelism and subsidiarity should be realized. So, the governance of those fields which were most affected by globalization—economy, finances, trade, communication, environmental protection, protection against epidemics (pandemics), migration—should be organized following the principle of multilevel governance. It meant that all these fields representing global interest should be transferred to the higher interregional level institution of the UN which is the Economic and the Social Council. The special agencies (IMF, World Bank, UNESCO) should be reorganized according to multilevelism (according to a multilevel world organization). For example, they should be part of the exclusive competences of the Economic and Social Council. In such a multilevel system the member regions should play a coordinative and intermediary role toward the Economic and Social Council and the member states. All this could result in a world policy in which the bottom-up organized federalist states continue to play an important role but in a renewed form: the states lose competences but, as compensation, they could gain more of a role in the formation of a new kind of interstate (international) policy, and in a larger (regional and world) level in the field of the common competences. For example, they could represent their interests at the level of the developing new regions and of the world. By this they could contribute to making the classical power struggle and wars impossible.[157]

---

157 Bóka, "The European Idea of a Supranational Union of Peace," 387–397.

12

CONCLUDING THOUGHTS

History has shown that the idea of European unity played an important role in the shaping of the Western system of liberties and in the emergence of the European Union (EU) aimed at the humanization of power and peace. It concentrated on the dichotomy of centralization versus decentralization, or federalism versus anti-federalism (confederalism, intergovernmentalism), characterizing the state and international organization policy. Federalism in Europe started with defense unions. Theoretically it was defined by Althusius, who represented a peaceful bottom-up association policy based on personal and community autonomy, popular sovereignty, democracy, and federalism. The American Founding Fathers used similar ideas when they rejected feudalism and British colonization, and established the constitutional federal republic under a president. The association policy of the Swiss cantons also continued this constitutional parliamentary federal governmental example.

But in Europe the Bodinian idea of authoritarian centralized sovereign state dominated during history. It influenced the concept of a European centralized unitary nation-state safeguarding the power of the former and new elites. The state was organized from above according to the interests of the ruling elite. Bottom-up personal association policy could prevail only at the local levels. The modern French unitary nation-state put the emphasis on the indivisibility of sovereignty of state in international relations. It rejected multinational federal solutions for states because of the sharing of sovereignty. Instead of shaping a federal constitution and institutions, the French modernizers used plebiscite and the absorption and assimilation of the population in a unilingual French state: the state of the French people or the French nation-state.

The democratization of the authoritarian centralized nation-states, according to the ideas of the Declaration of the Rights of Man and of the Citizen (1789), was unsuccessful in Europe, except Switzerland. However, the idea of liberty was continued in the form of liberal market capitalism in an expansionist Europe. The continuation of laissez-fare colonization policy and the fight for power, in the framework of authoritarian nation states and national empires, betrayed the ideas and principles of the system of liberties and the Declaration of the Rights of Man and of the Citizen (1789), directing the modern democratic state and international organization. The authoritarian states continued to be organized from above according to the interests and images of rulers or ruling elites, but used democratic ideas. Governments were not "of the people, by the people and for the people."

The French model of unitary and unilingual nation-state influenced the national reform movements in Europe. In this way the European state and international organization (except the Swiss federal republic under a federal government) have taken the form of an imagined community composed of centralized authoritarian nation states and national empires based on a fictitious economy in a center-periphery world system. Unitary authoritarian nation states and national empires were not able to realize the democratic federalist idea of European unity. When the colonial expansion strengthened, the fight for power among the authoritarian European nation states and national empires intensified. They had lost control of the balance of power policy, had forgotten the idea of European unity, and the "European concert" collapsed. All this ended in the deep crisis of the European system of liberties and the laissez-faire capitalist market economy.

In these circumstances the people did not know how to fight for their rights and livelihood according to the ideas of the Declaration of the Rights of Man and of the Citizen (1789). They did not know how to continue the progressive trend of Europe's democratization process in the name of liberty. Revolutionaries or populist politicians enjoined them to reject liberalism and democracy and join Fascism, National Socialism, or Communism, arguing that these better represented their interests. In opposition to these extreme nationalist or totalitarian tendencies, European federalism was renewed in two movements, the constitutional federalist and the integral or personal federalist. Both realized the ideological confusions, controversies, and the crisis of the liberal capitalist state and international organization which ended in a deadlock. Federalists were in search of new democratic ways for state and international organization suitable for popular sovereignty and democracy in a capitalist free market economy system. They strongly criticized the nation-state and national empire system which worked in the interests of the ruling economic and political elites, and not in the interest of the people. Their idea was to continue on the way of the centuries-old idea of bottom-up federalist association policy of persons (families) and their communities, concentrating on the livelihood of people, and creating a real economy through institutional or gradual social reform. Their purpose was to build up a European parliamentary federation on the basis of transferring common things to larger autonomous territorial and institutional spheres (states and federal unions). The federalist idea became the driving force for the democratic renewal of European society, which motivated the development of the rule of law and fundamental rights, and, albeit slowly, showed results in reality.

After the Second World War the Western democracies emerged victorious with the help of the federalists of the Resistance Movement. The cooperation between the intergovernmentalists and the federalists, after many compromises, resulted in the EU, in 1992. The EU is a supranational and intergovernmental

Concluding Thoughts

union of states based on subsidiarity, multilevelism, and European law (legal harmonization). As such it can be regarded as a historical product of the compromises between the federalists and the intergovernmentalists, on an originally federalist project of the Founding Fathers, for the benefit of the intergovernmentalists. The EU is based on the European law which is composed of the elements of the federalist functionalist "Monnet-method," of Spinelli's constitutional bicameral parliamentary federalism, of Rougemont's and Delor's integral or personalist federalism, and of De Gaulle's intergovernmentalism. Rethinking and democratizing EU law and the institutional system is necessary because subsidiarity as a replacement of European governance is on a fragile basis, and because of democratic deficit. The citizens do not know how to shape their common future in the framework of the European Parliament, as the citizens of the EU, because of the domination of the nation states, and because there is confusion regarding the meaning of the dichotomy between federalism versus intergovernmentalism.

The EU has made significant progress in detecting and correcting the serious mistakes made by some of its member states and politicians during Europe's modernization process in the 19th century and in the first half of the 20th century: nationalism, racism, colonial exploitation, and laissez-faire imperialist capitalism. The integration process succeeded in creating lasting peace in Europe, an achievement that is appreciated by other civilizations. At the same time it did not yet realize the goals set by its founding politicians at the end of the Second World War to avoid the mistakes of the past. The EU's structure has important federalist elements but the integration process did not create the European economic federation. European policy ended colonial imperialism but did not replace economic expansion with a federalist world economic policy based on real economy. The centre-periphery world system, the developmental aid policy in a confederalist form, and the world economic crises are still alive. They represent unavoidable challenges for the further democratization of the EU, and of the world economy with the participation of the non-European countries.[1]

The future of the EU probably could have four scenarios:

Intergovernmentalism would mean a politically divided, weak, but economically strong EU facing permanent insecurity as regards its institutional state.
A balanced federalist versus intergovernmentalist multilevelism based on subsidiarity could result in a new democratic and peaceful answer to the new economic and political challenges of the world.
Establishing a European federal union with a federalist economic governance could strengthen the EU as a world power.
The coming back of classical confederalism, in the case of a conservative or populist nationalist majority, would cause the collapse of the EU integration

---

1 Éva Bóka, *Európa és Ázsia*, 38–39.

process and its disappearance as a global player. European states and people will return to nationalism with all of its consequences known from history.[2]

The most important thing that the EU needs is the support of European citizens. For this the supranational and intergovernmental union of nation-states and people, without the balance between intergovernmentalism and federalism, is not enough. A new type of bicameral parliamentary federation of the people as citizens of the union and of their own states should be created, how the Founding Fathers envisioned, by abolishing the veto right. History shows the necessity to continue the institutional and social democratization of the EU on the way of the federalist ideas on military, economic, and social cooperation. Among them perhaps the rethinking of *The Interlaken Draft Constitution of a Federal Europe* (1949) of the European Parliamentary Union, *The Pleven Plan, 1950*, the *Draft Treaty Embodying the Statute of the European Community* (1953), (Europe's first constitutional draft), or the *Draft Treaty Establishing the European Union* (1984) can serve as examples. Following Spinelli's example, reform plans should be presented to the European Parliament aiming for the federalist renewal. Regarding the social reform towards a democratic Europe of citizens the personal federalist ideas need to be reconsidered. In essence, a new federalist vision would be needed. History shows that solutions based on federalist ideas could protect against nationalism and laissez-faire economic and power policy. One cannot forget that the centuries-old idea of democratic federalism was the driving force of the establishment of the EU in necessary cooperation with intergovernmentalism. Therefore it would be important to rethink the federalist versus intergovernmentalist dichotomy and the principle of subsidiarity, and continue planning for a more democratic social and institutional solution of a parliamentary EU in accordance with the system of liberties and fundamental rights.

It must not be forgotten that the revival of power policy and nationalism in the member states of the EU, and in the world, threatens the very existence of the EU. Without the EU a wave of new nationalism might emerge in Europe with all the well-known and tragic consequences. All European citizens are responsible for making sure this does not happen.

Serious emphasis should also be placed on the research of the responses of the non-European civilizations to the challenge of European colonialism and modernization. It would be necessary to study their suggested state and international organization alternatives during history. And in this respect it should not be forgotten that democratic federalism is an idea that is appreciated by the non-European world, too. Therefore it could serve as a meeting point for people and states worldwide aiming for peaceful and democratic states and international organization.

If Europeans want to put into practice the fundamental values and principles represented by the Western system of liberties and human rights, in accordance

---

2 Bóka, "Rethinking European Supranationalism in a Historical Perspective," Discussion paper.

with the democratic ideas, they have to continue on the way of federalism and find the way to a future democratic federalist renewal based on subsidiarity. I hope that this book could contribute to it.

The topic is open to discussion.

Bibliography

Adi, Hakim, and Marika Sherwood. *Pan-African History: Political Figures From Africa and the Diaspora Since 1787*. London and New York: Routledge, 2003.

Althusius, Johannes. *Politica: An Abridged Translation of Politics, Methodically Set Forth and Illustrated With Sacred and Profane Examples*. Edited and translated with an introduction by Frederik S. Carney, foreword by Daniel J. Elazar. Indianapolis, IN: Liberty Fund Inc, 1995. Originally Published in Johan Althusii J.U.D. Politica Methodicè digesta atque exemplis sacris & profanis illustrata; Cui in fine adjuncta est ORATIO PANEGYRICA, De necessitate, utilitate & antiquitate scholarum. Editio tertia, daubus prioribus multo auctior. Herbonæ Nassoviorum, 1614.

Althusius, Johannes. "Politica: A Schema by Johannes Althusius." In *Politica: An Abridged Translation of Politics, Methodically Set Forth and Illustrated With Sacred and Profane Examples*, edited and translated with an introduction by Frederik S. Carney, foreword by Daniel J. Elazar, lviii–lix. Indianapolis, IN: Liberty Fund Inc, 1995.

Aristotle. *Politics*. New York: Dover Publications Inc, 2000.

Arranz, Alfonso Martinez, and Gudrun Wacker. "China and the European Union, High Hopes, Clear Conflicts." In *The European Union and Global Engagement: Institutions, Politics and Challenges*, edited by Norman Witzleb, Alfonso Martinez Arranz, and Pascaline Winard, 256–278. Cheltenham: Edward Elgar Publishing Ltd, 2015.

Asante, Molefi Kete. *The History of Africa: The Quest for Eternal Harmony*. New York and London: Routledge, 2007.

Asante, Samuel Kingsley Botwe, in Collaboration With David Chanaiwa. "Pan-Africanism and Regional Integration." In *Africa since 1935. General History of Africa*, edited by Ali A. Mazrui and C. Wondji, Vol. 8, 724–743. Oxford: Heinemann Publishers; Berkeley, CA: University of California Press; Paris: UNESCO, 1993.

ASEAN Charter. 2007. Accessed March 26, 2022. https://asean.org/wp-content/uploads/2021/08/November-2020-The-ASEAN-Charter-28th-Reprint.pdf.

Bentham, Jeremy. "Plan de paix perpétuelle et universelle. Essai IV des principes de droit international, (1789, 1843)." In *L'Europe une: les philosophes et l'Europe [One Europe: Philosophers and Europe]*, edited by Jean-Pierre Faye, 163–167. Paris: Gallimard, 1992. Originally Published Bentham, *Principles of International Law*, Essay IV. 1789, Publication in 1843.

Bergère, Marie-Claire. *Chine le nouveau capitalisme d'État [China the New State Capitalism]*. Paris: Fayard, 2013.

Bibó, István. "Reflections on the Social Development of Europe (1971–1972)." In *Democracy, Revolution, Self-Determination. Selected Writings*, edited by Károly

Nagy, translated by András Boros-Kazai, 421–532. Boulder, CO: Social Science Monographs; Highland Lakes: Atlantic Research and Publications; New York: Distributed by Columbia University Press, 1991.
Bieber, Roland, Jean-Paul Jacqué, and Joseph H. H. Weiler, eds. *An Ever Closer Union: A Critical Analysis of the Draft Treaty Establishing the European Union*. Luxembourg: Office for Official Publications of the European Communities, 1985.
Bismarck, Otto von. *Deutscher Staat. Ausgewählte Dokumente [German State. Selected Documents]*. Edited by Hans Rothfels. München: Drei Masken Verlag, 1925.
Bismarck, Otto von. *Gedanken und Erinnerungen. Ungekürzte Ausgabe [Thougts and Memoirs]*. Unabridged edition. Augsburg: Wilhelm Goldmann Verlag, 1962.
Bitsch, Marie-Thérèse. *Histoire de la construction européenne [History of European Construction]*. Paris: Editions Complexe, 2001.
Bitsch, Marie-Thérèse, and Gérard Bossuat. *Sous la direction de. L'Europe Unie et l'Afrique. De l'idée d'Eurafrique à la Convention de Lomé I. Actes du colloque international de Paris, 1er et 2 avril 2004 [United Europe and Africa. From the Idea of Eurafrique to the Lomé I Convention: Proceedings of the International Conference in Paris, 1 and 2 April 2004]*. Bruxelles: Bruylant; Paris: L.G.D.J.; Baden-Baden: Nomos Verlag, 2005.
Blaustein, Albert P., and Jay A. Sigler, eds. *Constitutions That Made History*. New York: Paragon House Publishers, 1988.
Boahen, Albert Adu. *African Perspectives on Colonialism*. Baltimore, MD and London: The John Hopkins University Press, 1987.
Boahen, Albert Adu. "Colonialism in Africa: its Impact and Significance." In *General History of Africa. Vol. 7. Africa Under Colonial Domination 1880–1935*, edited by A. Adu Boahen, 782–809. London: Heinemann, 1985.
Boahen, Albert Adu, ed. *General History of Africa. Abridged Edition. Vol. 7. Africa Under Colonial Domination 1880–1935. UNESCO International Scientific Committee for the Drafting a General History of Africa*. Paris: UNESCO, 1990.
Bodin, Jean. *Les six livres de la République [The Six Books of the Republic]*. Book First and Second. Text revised by Christiane Frémont, Marie-Dominique Couzinet, et Henri Rochais. Paris: Fayard, 1986.
Bóka, Éva. "A European Parliamentary Project on the European Union." In *Grotius, Közlemények, The E-Journal of the Institute of International Studies of the Corvinus University of Budapest*, 2014, 1–9. http://www.grotius.hu/publ/displ.asp?id=YHZELB.
Bóka, Éva. "A Hágai Európa Kongresszus 1948 május 7–10. [The Congress of Europe in The Hague, 7–10 May 1948]." In *Európai egységfolyamat – 1948 évi hágai kongresszus. Internetes melléket [The European Unity Process – The 1948 Hague Congress, Online Supplement]. Múltunk, (Journal of the Institute of Political History, Budapest)* 13, no. 2 (2018): 1–43. http://www.multunk.hu/wp-content/uploads/2018/07/haga1948_18_2.pdf.
Bóka, Éva. "A modernizáció mint társadalomformáló eszme: Európa és Ázsia [Modernization as an Idea Shaping the Society: Europe and Asia]." *Társadalomkutatás* 32, no. 1 (2014): 1–9.
Bóka, Éva. *Az európai egységgondolat fejlődéstörténete [History of the Development of the Idea of European Unity]*. Budapest: Napvilág Publisher, 2001.
Bóka, Éva. *Az európai integráció. Elméletek történelmi perspektívában [European Integration: Theories in a Historical Perspective]*. Budapest: Corvina Publisher, 2008.

Bóka, Éva. *Az európai föderalizmus alternatívája Közép-Európában, 1849-1945* [*The Alternative of European Federalism in Central Europe, 1849-1945*]. Budapest: Dialóg Campus Publisher, 2011.

Bóka, Éva. *Európa és az Oszmán Birodalom a 16-17. században. (Az európai egységgondolat politikai eszmetörténetének kezdetei)* [*Europe and the Ottoman Empire in the 16th and 17th Century (The Beginnings of the Political Ideological History of the Idea of European Unity)*]. Budapest and Paris: L'Harmattan Publisher, 2004.

Bóka, Éva. *Európa és Ázsia. Modernizáció és globalizáció* [*Europe and Asia. Modernization and Globalization*]. Grotius Könyvtár, no. 4. Veszprém, 2010.

Bóka, Éva. "Europe in Search of Unity in Diversity." *ISES Füzetek* 14 (2010): 1-55. Szombathely–Kőszeg, Társadalomtudományok és Európa Tanulmányok Intézete [Institute of Social and European Studies]; Available on-line at Institute of Social and European Studies (ISES). Kőszeg Website. http://www.kx.hu/kepek/ises/anyagok/_ _va_B__ka__Europe_in_Search_of_Unity_in_Diversity.pdf.

Bóka, Éva. "From Holy War to a Balance of Power: Europe and the Ottoman Empire (16–17th Century)." In *Frieden und Konfliktmanagement in interkulturellen Räumen (Das Osmanische Reich und die Habsburgermonarchie in der Frühen Neuzeit)* [*Peace and Conflict Management in Intercultural Spaces (The Ottoman Empire and the Habsburg Monarchy in the Early Modern Period)*], edited by Arno Strohmeyer and Norbert Spannenberger, 333-341. Stuttgart: Franz Steiner Verlag, 2013.

Bóka, Éva. "From National Toleration to National Liberation (Three Initiators of Co-Operation in Central Europe)." *East European Politics and Societies* 13, no. 3 (1999): 435-474.

Bóka, Éva. "József Eötvös on the Personal Principle." *Ungarn Jahrbuch (Munich)* 28 (2005-2007): 55-67.

Bóka, Éva. *Modernizáció és értékrend. A nyugati világ, Törökország és Kelet-Ázsia* [*Modernization and the System of Values: The Western World, Turkey and East-Asia*]. Budapest and Paris: L'Harmattan Publisher, 2016.

Bóka, Éva. "Rethinking European Supranationalism in a Historical Perspective." Discussion Paper. *Grotius, the E-Journal of the Institute of International Studies of the Corvinus University of Budapest*, 2008. http://www.grotius.hu/publ/displ.asp?id =TJCVQS.

Bóka, Éva. "The Democratic European Idea in Central Europe, 1849-1945." In *Specimina Nova. A Pécsi Tudományegyetem Történeti Tanszékének Évkönyve* [*Yearbook of the History Department of the University of Pécs*], Pécs, 2005, 7-25. http://www.publikon .hu/application/essay/161_2.pdf.

Bóka, Éva. "The Europe-China Dialogue in a Historical Perspective." *Grotius E-Könyvtár*, no. 5 (2009): 1-96. http://www.grotius.hu/publ/displ.asp?id=FDWKZS.

Bóka, Éva. "The European Idea of a Supranational Union of Peace." *Society and Economy* 34, no. 3 (2012): 387-397.

Bóka, Éva. "The Idea of Subsidiarity in the European Federalist Thought." In *Grotius, the E-Journal of the Institute of International Studies of the Corvinus University of Budapest*, 2007, 1-42. http://www.grotius.hu/publ/displ.asp?id=ECICWF.

Bossuat, Gérard. *Histoire de l'Union européenne: Fondations, élargissements, avenir* [*History of the European Union: Foundations, Enlargements, Future*]. Paris: Belin, 2009.

Bossuat, Gérard. *L'Europe occidentale à l'heure américaine. Le Plan Marshall et l'unité européenne (1945-1952)* [*Western Europe on American Era. The Marshall Plan and European Unity (1945-1952)*]. Paris: Éditions Complexe, 1992.

Bibliography

Bourgi, Robert. *Le Général de Gaulle et l'Afrique Noire, 1940–1969. [General de Gaulle and Black Africa, 1940–1969]*. Paris: Librairie Générale de Droit et de Jurisprudence; Abidjan: Nouvelles Éditions Africaines, 1980.

Boyer, Paul S., ed. *The Oxford Companion to United States History*. New York: Oxford University Press Inc., 2001.

Braudel, Fernand. *Grammaire des civilisations [Grammar of Civilizations]*. Paris: Flammarion, 1993.

Briand, Aristide. "Mémorandum sur l'organisation d'un régime d'Union fédérale européenne [Memorandum on the Organization of a System of European Federal Union]." In *Le Plan Briand d'Union fédérale européenne. Perspectives nationales et transnationales, avec documents: actes du colloque international tenu à Genève du 19 au 21 septembre 1991 [The Briand Plan of the European Federal Union. National and Transnational Perspectives, With Documents: Proceedings of the International Symposium Held in Geneva from September 19 to 21, 1991]*, edited by Antoine Fleury, 569–582. Bern, Berlin, Frankfurt/M., New York, Paris, and Wien: Peter Lang, 1998.

Brinkley, Alan. *The Unfinished Nation: A Concise History of the American People*. New York: McGraw-Hill Companies Inc., 2010.

Brownlie, Ian, ed. *Basic Documents in International Law*. Oxford: Clarendon Press, 1991.

Brugmans, Hendrik. "Fundamentals of European Federalism. 27 August 1947. Lecture at the Montreux Congress." In *Documents on the History of European Integration, Vol. 4. Transnational Organizations and Political Parties and Pressure Groups in the Struggle for European Union, 1945–1950*, edited by Walter Lipgens and Wilfried Loth, 28–34. Berlin and New York: Walter de Gruyter, 1991.

Brugmans, Hendrik [Henri]. *L'idée européenne, 1920–1970*. Bruges: De Tempel, 1970.

"Bundesverfassung der schweizerischen Eidgenossenschaft vom 12. Herbstmonat 1848 (Bundesverfassung vom 12. September 1848) [Federal Constitution of the Swiss Confederation of the 12th month of autumn 1848 [Federal Constitution of September 12, 1848]." In *Geschichte und Texte der Bundesverfassungen der schweizerischen Eidgenossenschaft von der helvetischen Staatsumwalzung bis zur Gegenwart [History and Texts of the Federal Constitutions of the Swiss Confederation from the Overthrow of the Helvetian State to the Present]*, edited by Simon Kaiser and Johannes Strickler, 271–303. Bern: Verlag van K. J. Wyss, 1901.

Burgess, Michael. *Federation and European Union: The Building of Europe, 1950–2000*. London and New York: Routledge, 2000.

Chabot, Jean-Luc. *Aux origines intellectuelles de l'Union européenne. L'idée d'Europe unie de 1919 à 1939 [The Intellectual Origins of the European Union. The Idea of a United Europe from 1919 to 1939]*. Grenoble: Presses Universitaires de Grenoble, 2005.

Charter of the Fundamental Rights of the European Union. *Official Journal of the European Union*, C 303. December 14, 2007. Accessed March 26, 2022. EUR-Lex Access to European Union Law. https://eur-lex.europa.eu/legal-content/EN/TXT/?uri=uriserv:OJ.C_.2007.303.01.0001.01.ENG&toc=OJ:C:2007:303:TOC.

"Charter of the United Nations, 1945." In *Basic Documents in International Law*, edited by Ian Brownlie, 1–34. Oxford: Clarendon Press, 1991.

Chevallier, Arthur. *Napoléon et le Bonapartisme [Napoleon and Bonapartism]*. Paris: Que sais-je?/Humensis, 2021.

Bibliography

Chi, Zhang. *Chine et modernité. Chocs, crises et renaissance de la culture chinoise aux temps modernes [China and Modernity. Shocks, Crises and the Revival of Chinese Culture in Modern Times]*. Paris: Librairie You Feng, 2005.

Churchill, Winston. "Address Given by Winston Churchill at the Congress of Europe." In *Documents on the History of European Integration, Vol. 4. Transnational Organizations and Political Parties and Pressure Groups in the Struggle for European Union, 1945–1950*, edited by Walter Lipgens and Wilfried Loth, 340. Berlin and New York: Walter de Gruyter, 1991.

Colas, Dominique. *Textes Constitutionnels Soviétiques [Soviet Constitutional Texts]*. Paris: Presses Universitaires de France, 1987.

Confucius. *The Analects*. Translated with an introduction and notes by Raymond Dawson. New York: Oxford University Press, 2000.

"Constitution (loi fondamentale) de l'URSS (Adoptée par le VIIIe Congrès extraordinaire des Soviets du 5 décembre 1936) [Constitution (Basic Law) of the USSR (Adopted by the VIII Extraordinary Congress of Soviets on December 5, 1936)]." In *Textes constitutionnels soviétiques [Soviet Constitutional Texts]*, edited by Colas Dominique, 49–71. Paris: Presses Universitaires de France, 1987.

Constitution of India. 1950. Constitution of India net supported by the Friedrich Naumann Foundation for Freedom. https://www.constitutionofindia.net/constitution_of_india. Accessed March 26, 2022.

Constitution of the Republic of China. 1946. Office of the President Republic of China (Taiwan). Accessed March 26, 2022. https://english.president.gov.tw/Page/94.

Coquery-Vidrovitch, Catherine. "Economic Changes in Africa in the World Context." In *Africa Since 1935: General History of Africa*, edited by Ali A. Mazrui and C. Wondji (assistant éditeur), Vol. 8, 285–316. London: Heinemann, 1993.

Coudenhove-Kalergi, Richard N. "Appeal to all Europeans, 28 April 1947." In *Documents on the History of European Integration, Vol. 4: Transnational Organizations and Political Parties and Pressure Groups in the Struggle for European Union, 1945–1950*, edited by Walter Lipgens and Wilfried Loth, 123–124. Berlin and New York: Walter de Gruyter, 1991.

Coudenhove-Kalergi, Richard N. "Confédération ou Fédération [Confederation or Federation]". *Le Monde*, January 20, 1953. Accessed March 26, 2022. www.cvce.eu (Centre Virtuel de la Connaissance sur l'Europe [Virtual Knowledge Center on Europe], University of Luxembourg); https://www.cvce.eu/en/obj/confederation_or_federation_from_le_monde_20_january_1953-en-be82a590-d2d3-4fcf-965f-73362bb4851c.html.

Coudenhove-Kalergi, Richard N. *Die Europäische Nation [The European Nation]*. Stuttgart: Deutsche Verlag-Anstalt, 1953.

Coudenhove-Kalergi, Richard N. *Europe Must Unite*. Glarus, Switzerland: Paneuropa Editions Ltd., 1940.

Coudenhove-Kalergi, Richard N. *Kampf um Europa. Aus meinem Leben [Battle for Europe. From My Life]*. Zürich: Atlantis Verlag, 1949.

Coudenhove-Kalergi, Richard N. *Paneuropa*. Wien, Leipzig: Paneuropa Verlag, 1926.

Coudenhove-Kalergi, Richard N. *Stalin & Co.* Leipzig: Paneuropa Verlag, 1931.

Coudenhove-Kalergi, Richard N. *Totaler State - Totaler Mensch*. Wien: Paneuropa Verlag, 1937.

Croisat, Maurice. *Le fédéralisme en Europe*. Paris: Montchrestien, 2010.

Bibliography 213

Crucé, Émeric. *The New Cyneas*. Edited with an introduction, and translated into English from the original French text of 1623 by Thomas Willing Balch (English and French bilingual edition). Philadelphia, PA: Allen, Lane & Scott, 1909. Originally Published in *Le Nouveau Cynée ou Discours d'Estat Représentant les occasions et moyens d'establir une paix generale et la liberté du commerce par tout le monde*. Aux Monarques et Princes Souverains de ce temps. EM. CR. PAR. Paris: Jacques Villerey. Au Palais sur le Perron Royal, 1623. Avec Privilège du Roy.

Debbasch, Charles, and Jean Marie Pontier, eds. *Les Constitutions de la France [The Constitutions of France]*. Paris: Dalloz, 1989.

"Declaration of Independence (1776)." In *A Documentary History of the United States*, edited by Richard D. Heffner and Alexander Heffner, 10–15. New York: Penguin Group, 2009.

"Declaration of the Rights of Man and Citizen." August 26, 1789. In *The French Revolution and Human Rights: A Brief Documentary History*, edited by Lynn Hunt, 77–79. Boston, MA and New York: St. Martin's Press, 1996.

"Déclaration des Droits de l'Homme et du Citoyen de 1789 [Declaration of the Rights of Man and of the Citizen of 1789]." In *La déclaration des droits de l'homme et du citoyen [The Declaration of the Rights of Man and of the Citizen]*, edited by Stéphane Rials, 21–26. Paris: Hachette, 1988.

"Declaration on the Granting of Independence to Colonial Countries and Peoples, 1960." In *Basic Documents in International Law*, edited by Ian, Brownlie, 298–301. Oxford: Clarendon Press, 1991.

Delors, Jacques. "Address by Mr. Jacques Delors, President of the Commission of the European Communities, Bruges, 17 October 1989." In *The European Union: Readings on the Theory and Practice of European Integration*, edited by Brent F. Nelsen, and Alexander C.-G. Stubb, 55–64. Boulder, CO: Lynne Rienner Publishers, 2003.

Delors, Jacques. "Le principe de subsidiarité: au Colloque de l'Institut Européen d'Administration Publique à Maastricht, le 21 mars 1991. [The Principle of Subsidiarity: at the Colloquium of the European Institute of Public Administration in Maastricht, March 21, 1991]." In *Le Nouveau Concert Européen [The New European Concert]*, edited by Jacques Delors, 163–176. Paris: Édition Odile Jacob, 1992.

Delors, Jaques. *L'unité d'un homme. Entretiens avec Dominique Wolton [Unity of a Person]. Interviews with Dominique Wolton]*. Paris: Éditions Odile Jacob, 1994.

Delors, Jacques. "Réconcilier l'idéal et la nécessité: discour devant le Collège d'Europe à Bruges, le 17 octobre 1989 [Reconciling Ideal and Necessity: Speech at the College of Europe in Bruges, October 17, 1989]." In *Jacques Delors, Le Nouveau Concert Européen [The New European Concert]*, 315–338. Paris: Édition Odile Jacob, 1992.

Delors, Jacques. "The Principle of Subsidiarity: Contribution to the Debate." In *Subsidiarity: The Challenge of Change. Proceedings of the Jacques Delors Colloquium*, Maastricht, March 21–22, 1991, edited by Papas Spyros, 7–18. Maastricht: European Institute of Public Administration, 1991.

Deng, Xiaoping. *Selected Works of Deng Xiaoping (1975–1982)*. Central Committee of the Communist Party of China for the Compilation and Translation of Works of Marx, Engels, Lenin and Stalin. Beijing: Foreign Language Press, 1984.

Deng, Xiaoping. "Taking a Clear-Cut Stand Against Bourgeois Liberalisation." Speech to the Leading Members of the Chinese Communist Party's Central Committee on December 30, 1986. In *China Reader: The Reform Era*, edited by Orville Schell and

David Shambaugh, 182–185. New York: Vintage Books, Division of Random House Inc., 1999.

Deutscher, Issak. *Staline [Stalin]*. Paris: Gallimard, 1973.

"Draft Treaty Embodying the Statute of the European Community (Strasbourg, 11 March 1953)." In *Europe's First Constitution: The European Political Community, 1952–1954*. Appendix Two, edited by Richard T. Griffiths, 189–226. London: Federal Trust for Education and Research, 2000.

"Draft Treaty Establishing a Constitution for Europe (13 June and 10 July, 2003)." *Official Journal of the European Union, no. C 169*, July 18, 2003. www.cvce.eu, https://www.cvce.eu/content/publication/2003/9/15/a7df0a64-67a9-44f6-a06d-33f08d712539/publishable_en.pdf. Accessed March 26, 2022.

"Draft Treaty Establishing the European Union, Adopted by the European Parliament on 14 February 1984, Coordinating rapporteur: Mr. A. Spinelli." In *An Ever Closer Union: A Critical Analysis of the Draft Treaty Establishing the European Union*, edited by Roland Bieber, Jean-Paul Jacqué, and Joseph H. H. Weiler, 306–328. Luxembourg: Office for Official Publications of the European Communities, 1985.

Duroselle, Jean-Baptiste. *L'idée d'Europe dans l'histoire [The Idea of Europe in History]*. Paris: Denoël, 1965.

Duverger, Maurice. *Les constitutions de la France [The Constitutions of France]*. Paris: Presses Universitaires de France, 1944.

Eisenstadt, Shmuel N. "European Expansion and the Civilization of Modernity." In *Expansion and Reaction: Essays on European Expansion and Reactions in Asia and Africa*, edited by Hendrik Lodewijk Wesseling, 167–186. Leiden: Leiden University Press, 1978.

Elazar, Daniel J. "Althusius' Grand Design for a Federal Commonwealth." In *Foreword to Althusius, Johannes. Politica: An Abridged Translation of Politics, Methodically Set Forth and Illustrated With Sacred and Profane Examples*, edited and translated with an introduction by Frederik S. Carney, xxxv–xlvi. Indianapolis, IN: Liberty Fund Inc., 1995.

Endo, Ken. Subsidiarity and Its Enemies: To What Extent is Sovereignty Contested in the Mixed Commonwealth of Europe? Working Paper, Florence: European University Institute, 2001 EUI RSC, 2001/24.

Eötvös, József. *Die Garantien der Macht und Einheit Oesterreichs [The Guarantees of the Power and Unity of Austria]*. Leipzig: F. A. Brodhaus, 1859.

Eötvös, József. *The Dominant Ideas of the Nineteenth Century and Their Impact on the State*. Boulder, CO: Social Science Monographs; Highland Lakes, NJ: Atlantic Research and Publications Inc., Distributed by Columbia University Press, New York, 1996.

Erasmus, Desiderius Roterodamus. *The Complaint of Peace by Erasmus*. Edited with an introduction by William James Hirten. New York: Scholars' Facsimiles and Reprints, 1946.

Europe Unites: The Hague Congress and After. The Story of the Campaign for European Unity, Including a Full Report of the Congress of Europe, Held at the Hague, May, 1948. Foreword by Mr. Winston Churchill. London: Hollis and Carter, 1949.

European Movement and the Council of Europe. With Forewords by Winston S. Churchill and Paul-Henri Spaak. London: Published on Behalf of The European Movement by Hutchinson & CO. LTD., 1949.

Bibliography

Faye, Jean-Pierre, ed. *L'Europe une: les philosophes et l'Europe. [One Europe: Philosophers and Europe]*. Paris: Gallimard, 1992.

Fischer, Joschka. "From Confederacy to Federation: Thoughts on the Finality of European Integration." Speech by Joschka Fischer at the Humboldt University in Berlin, 12 May 2000. In *What Kind of Constitution for What Kind of Polity? Reponses to Joschka Fisher*, edited by Christian Jeorges, Yves Mény, and Joseph H. H. Weiler, 19–30. Florence: The Robert Schuman Centre for Advanced Studies at the European University Institute, Cambridge, MA: Harvard Law School; San Domenico, FI, Italy: European University Institute, 2000.

Fleury, Antoine, ed. *Le Plan Briand d'Union fédérale européenne: perspectives nationales et transnationales, avec documents: actes du colloque international tenu à Genève du 19 au 21 septembre 1991. [The Briand Plan of European Federal Union: National and Transnational Perspectives, With Documents: Proceedings of the International Conference Geneva, 19–21 September 1991]*. Bern, Berlin, Frankfurt/M., New York, Paris, and Wien: Peter Lang, 1998.

Fleury, Antoine. "Paneurope et l'Afrique [Paneurope and Africa]." In *L'Europe Unie et L'Afrique. De l'idée d'Eurafrique à la Convention de Lomé I: Actes du Colloque International de Paris, 1er et 2 avril 2004 [From the Idea of Eurafrique to the Lomé I Convention: Proceedings of the Paris International Conference, April 1 and 2, 2004]*. Under the direction of Marie-Thérèse Bitsch and Gérard Bossuat, 35–57. Bruxelles: Bruylant; Paris: L.G.D.J.; Baden-Baden: Nomos Verlag, 2005.

Franke, Wolfgang. *China and the West*. Oxford: Basil Blackwell, 1967.

Franke, Wolfgang. "K'ang Yu-wei und die Reform des Prüfungswesens [K'ang Yu-wei and the Reform of the Examination System]." In *K'ang Yu-wei. A Biography and a Symposium*, edited with translation by Jung-pang Lo, 313–318. Tucson: The University of Arizona Press, 1967.

Fukuzawa, Yukichi. *An Encouragement of Learning*. Translated with an introduction by David A. Dilworth and Umeyo Hirano. Tokyo: Sophia University, 1969.

Fukuzawa, Yukichi. *An Outline of a Theory of Civilization*. New York: Columbia University Press, 2008.

Fukuzawa, Yukichi. "Datsu-a Ron (On Saying Good-Bye to Asia)." In *Japan: A Documentary History*, edited by David J. Lu, 351–353. New York: M. E. Sharpe Inc., 1997.

Fukuzawa, Yukichi. *Plaidoyer pour la modernité [A Plea for Modernity]*. Paris: CNRS Éditions, 2008.

Fukuzawa, Yukichi. "The Origins of the Western Civilization." In *An Outline of a Theory of Civilization*, edited by Fukuzawa Yukichi, 161–173. New York: Columbia University Press, 2008.

Fukuzawa, Yukichi. "The Origins of the Japanese Civilization." In *An Outline of a Theory of Civilization*, edited by Fukuzawa Yukichi, 175–223. New York: Columbia University Press, 2008.

Fukuzawa, Yukichi. "Western Civilization as Our Goal." In *An Outline of a Theory of Civilization*, edited by Fukuzawa Yukichi, 17–43. New York: Columbia University Press, 2008.

Furet, François, and Denis Richet. *La Révolution française [The French Revolution]*. Paris: Hachette, 1963.

Gandhi, Mohandas Karamchand. *Hind Swaraj and Other Writings*. Edited by Anthony J. Parel. Cambridge: Cambridge University Press, 1997.

Gaulle, Charles de. "Europe." In *Memoirs of Hope: Renewal 1958-62, Endeavour 1962-*, edited by Charles de Gaulle and translated by Terence Kilmartin, 163-198. London: Weidenfeld and Nicolson, 1970.

Gaulle, Charles de. "L'Europe [Europe]." In *Mémoires de guerre. Mémoires d'espoir [War Memoirs. Memoirs of Hope]*, edited by Charles de Gaulle, 718-741. Paris: Plon, 2019.

Gauthier, Florence. *Triomphe et mort de la révolution des droit de l'homme et du citoyen [Triumph and Death of the Revolution of the Rights of Man and of the Citizen]*. Paris: Éditions Syllepse, 2014.

"General Policy Resolution, 30 August 1947, Montreux." In *Documents on the History of European Integration. Vol. 4. Transnational Organizations and Political Parties and Pressure Groups in the Struggle for European Union, 1945-1950*, edited by Walter Lipgens and Wilfried Loth, 34-38. Berlin and New York: W. de Gruyter, 1991.

Gentz, Friedrich. "Über den ewigen Frieden, 1800. [On Perpetual Peace, 1800]." In *Ewiger Friede. Friedensrufe und Friedensplane seit der Renaissance [Eternal Peace. Calls for Peace and Peace Plans Since the Renaissance]*, edited by Kurt von Raumer, 461-497. Freiburg: Alber, 1953.

"German Constitution of 1848." In *Constitutions That Made History*, edited by Albert P. Blaustein and Jay A. Sigler, 203-215. New York: Paragon House Publishers, 1988.

"Ghana Constitution, 1960." In *The Constitutional Law of Ghana*, edited by Francis Bennion. London: Butterworths, 1962, 473-490. Accessed March 26, 2022. https://www.artsrn.ualberta.ca/amcdouga/Hist247/winter_2017/resources/ghana_constitution_1960.pdf.

Godechot, Jacques, ed. *Les Constitutions de la France depuis 1789 [The Constitutions of France Since 1789]*. Paris: Garnier-Flammarion, 1979.

Gregory, John S. *The West and China Since 1500*. New York: Palgrave Macmillan, 2003.

Griffiths, Richard T. *Europe's First Constitution: The European Political Community, 1952-1954*. London: Federal Trust for Education and Research, 2000.

Grotius, Hugo. *Le droit de la guerre et de la paix [The Law of War and Peace]*. Translated by Jean Barbeyrac based on the edition of Amsterdam (Pierre de Coup, 1724). Volume 1. Caen: Presses universitaires de Caen, 2011.

Guieu, Jean Michel, Christophe Le Dréau, Jenny Raflik, and Laurent Warlouzet, eds. *Penser et construire l'Europe au XXe siècle [Thinking and Building Europe in the 20th Century]*. Paris: Éditions Belin, 2006.

Guizot, François. *Histoire de la civilisation en Europe depuis la chute de l'Empire romain jusqu'à la Révolution française [History of Civilization in Europe From the Fall of the Roman Empire to the French Revolution]*. Paris: Hachette, 1985.

Haas, Ernst B. *The Unity of Europe: Political, Social and Economic Forces, 1950-1957*. Stanford, CA: Stanford University Press, 1968.

Habermas, Jürgen. "Hat die Konstitutionalisierung des Völkerrechts noch eine Chance? [Does the Constitutionalization of International Law Still Have a Chance?]." In *Der gespaltene Westen [The Divided West]*, edited by Jürgen Habermas, 113-193. Frankfurt am Main: Suhrkamp, 2004.

Hallstein, Walter. *Europe in Making*. London: George Allen & Unwin Ltd., 1972.

Hamilton, Alexander. "Report on Public Credit. Treasury Department, Jan. 9, 1790." In *Alexander Hamilton Writings*, edited by Joanne B. Freeman, 531-574. New York: The Library of America, 2001.

Hamilton, Alexander. "Report on the Subject of Manufactures, December 5, 1791." In *Great Issues in American History. From the Revolution to the Civil War, 1765-1865*,

Bibliography

edited by Richard Hofstadter, Vol. 2, 171–176. New York: Vintage Books, A Division of Random House, 1958.
Hamilton, Alexander, John Jay, and James Madison. *The Federalist Papers*. New York: Bantam Dell, A division of Random House, Inc., 2003.
Hansen, Peo, and Stefan Jonsson. *Eurafrica: The Untold History of European Integration and Colonialism*. Bloomsbury Collections, Open Access Book, 2014. Accessed March 26, 2022. https://www.bloomsburycollections.com/book/eurafrica-the-untold-history-of-european-integration-and-colonialism/.
Hantos, Elemér. *Die Weltwirtschaftskonferenz (Probleme und Ergebnisse) [The World Economic Conference (Issues and Outcomes)]*. Schriften des Weltwirtschafts-Instituts der Handels-Hochschule Leipzig. Band 4. Leipzig: G.A. Gloeckner Verlagsbuchhandlung, 1928.
Harryvan, Anjo G., and Jan van der Harst, eds. *Documents on European Union*. Cambridge: St. Martin's Press; New York: Macmillan, 1997.
Heater, Derek Benjamin. *World Citizenship and Government: Cosmopolitan Ideas in the Western Political Thought*. London: Macmillan Press Ltd., 1996.
Heffner, Richard D., and Alexander Heffner, eds. *A Documentary History of the United States*. New York: Penguin Group, 2009.
Hersant, Yves, and Fabienne Durand-Bogaert, eds. *Europes: De l'antiquité au XXe siècle: Anthologie critique et commentée [Europes: From Antiquity to the 20th Century: A Critical and Commented Anthology]*. Paris: Éditions Robert Laffont, 2000.
Higgot, Richard. "Alternative Models of Regional Cooperation? The Limits of Regional Institutionalization in East-Asia." In *European Union and New Regionalism. Regional Actors and Global Governance in a Post-hegemonic Era*, edited by Mario Telò, 75–106. Aldershot: Ashgate Publishing, 2007.
Hofstadter, Richard, ed. *Great Issues in American History: From the Revolution to the Civil War, 1765–1865*, Vol. 2. New York: Vintage Books, A Division of Random House, 1958.
Holcombe, Charles. *A History of East Asia: From the Origins of Civilization to the Twenty-First Century*. New York: Cambridge University Press, 2011.
Hsü, Immanuel C. Y., ed. *Readings in Modern Chinese History*. New York: Oxford University Press, 1971.
Hsü, Immanuel C. Y. *The Rise of Modern China*. New York: Oxford University Press, 1995.
Hunt, Lynn, ed. *The French Revolution and Human Rights: A Brief Documentary History*. Boston, New York: Bedford Books of St. Martin's Press, 1996.
Huters, Theodore, R., Bin Wong, and Pauline Yu. *Culture and State in Chinese History*. Stanford, CA: Stanford University Press, 1997.
Ienaga, Saburo. *History of Japan*. Tokyo: Japan Travel Bureau, INC, 1971.
"Imperial Rescript on Education, 1890." In *Japan: A Documentary History*, edited by David J. Lu, 343–344. New York: M.E. Sharpe Inc. 1997.
Ionescu, Ghiță, ed. *The New Politics of European Integration*. London and Basingstoke: The Macmillan Press, 1972.
Jefferson, Thomas. "Notes on Virginia." In *The Life and Selected Writings of Thomas Jefferson*, edited by Adrienne Koch and William Peden, 173–267. New York: Random House, 1993.
Jeorges, Christian, Yves Mény, and Joseph H. H. Weiler, eds. *What Kind of Constitution for What Kind of Polity? Responses to Joschka Fisher*. Florence: The Robert Schuman

Centre for Advanced Studies at the European University Institute; Cambridge, MA: Harvard Law School, 2000.
K'ang, Yu-wei. "Chronological Autobiography of K'ang Yu-wei (Nan-hai K'ang hsien-sheng tzu-pien nien-p'u)." In *K'ang Yu-wei. A Biography and a Symposium*, edited with translation by Jung-pang Lo, 17–177. Tucson: The University of Arizona Press, 1967.
K'ang, Yu-wei. *Ta T'ung Shu (The Book of Universal Commonwealth or Book of Great Unity) The One-World Philosophy of K'ang Yu-wei*. Translated from the Chinese with introduction and notes by Laurence G. Thompson. London: George Allen and Unwin Ltd., 1958.
Kang, Youwei. *Manifeste à l'empereur adressé par les candidats au doctorat [Manifesto to the Emperor Submitted by the Doctoral Candidates]*. Translated from Chinese, annotated and introduced by Roger Darrobers. Paris: Editions You-Feng, 1996.
Kant, Immanuel. "Perpetual Peace: A Philosophical Sketch." In *Kant Political Writings*, edited by Hans Reiss and translated by Hugh Barr Nisbet, 93–130. Cambridge: Cambridge University Press, 1991. Originally Published in Immanuel Kant. Ewigen Frieden. Ein philosophische Entwurf, 1795. Konigsberg: F. Nicolovius, 1795.
Keynes, John Maynard. *The Economic Consequences of the Peace*. London: Macmillan and Co. Ltd, 1920.
Keynes, John Maynard. *The End of Laissez-faire*. London: Leonard and Virginia Woolf at the Hogarth Press, 1926.
Khoo, Gilbert, and Dorothy Lo. *Asian Transformation: A History of South-East, South and East Asia*. Kuala Lumpur: Heinemann Education Books, 1977.
Ki-Zerbo, Joseph, Ali A. Mazrui, and Christophe Wondji, in Collaboration With A. Adu Boahen. "Nation-Building and Changing Political Values." In *Africa Since 1935: General History of Africa*, edited by Ali A. Mazrui, and C. Wondji (assistant ed.), Vol. 8, 468–498. Oxford: Heinemann Publishers; Berkeley, CA: University of California Press; Paris: UNESCO, 1993.
Kossman, Ernst Heinrik, and A. F. Mellink, eds. *Texts Concerning the Revolt of the Netherlands*. Cambridge, UK: Cambridge University Press, 1974.
Kumar, Dharma. *India and the European Economic Community*. London: Asia Publishing House, 1966.
Kume, Kunitake. *Japan Rising: The Iwakura Embassy to the USA and Europe 1871–1873*. Compiled by Kume Kunitake, edited by Chushichi Tsuzuki and R. Jules Young, with an introduction by Ian Nish. Cambridge: Cambridge University Press, 2009.
Landes, David S. *The Wealth and Poverty of Nations: Why Some Are So Rich and Some So Poor*. New York, London: W.W. Norton & Company, 1999.
Lanneau, Catherine, and Simon Petermann, eds. *Les Grands Discours de l'Histoire. 3. Les Européens [The Great Speeches in History. 3. The Europeans]*. Waterloo: Renaissance du Livre, 2008.
Lefort, Bernard, éd. *Une Europe inédite. Documents des Archives Jean Monnet [An Unprecedented Europe. Documents from the Jean Monnet Archives]*. Villeneuve d'Ascq: Presses Universitaires du Septentrion, 2001.
Lenin, Vladimir Ilyich. *Over het recht der naties op zelfbeschikking [On the Right of Nations to Self-determination]*. Moskou: Uitgeverij Progress, 1975.
Lenin, Vladimir Ilyich. "The Right of Nations to Self-Determination." In *Selected Works*, edited by V. I. Lenin, Vol. 1, 567–617. Moscow: Progress Publishers, 1975. Internet Archive. Accessed March 26, 2022. https://archive.org/details/swlenin1/page/566/mode/2up.

Bibliography

Lenin, Vladimir Ilyich Ulyanov. "The New Economic Policy." Report to the Second All-Russia Congress of Political Education Departments October 17, 1921. In *Lenin's Collected Works*, edited by David Skvirsky and George Hanna, Vol. 33, 60–79. Moscow: Progress Publishers, 1973. Accessed March 26, 2022. https://www.marxists.org/archive/lenin/works/cw/pdf/lenin-cw-vol-33.pdf.

Lentz, Thierry, Pierre Branda, Pierre-François Pinaud, and Clémence Zacharie, eds. *Quand Napoleon inventait la France. Dictionnaire des institutions politiques, administratives et de cour du Consulat et de l'Empire [When Napoleon invented France. Dictionary of Political, Administrative and Court Institutions of the Consulate and the Empire]*. Paris: Tallandier Éditions, 2008.

Leuchtenburg, William E. *Franklin D. Roosevelt and the New Deal, 1932–1940*. New York: Harper & Row Publishers, 1963.

Lindberg, Leon N. *The Political Dynamics of European Economic Integration*. Stanford, CA: Stanford University Press, 1963.

Lipgens, Walter. ed, *Europa-Föderationspläne der Widerstandsbewegungen, 1940–1945 [Europe-Federation Plans of Resistance Movements, 1940–1945]*. München: R. Oldenbourg Verlag, 1968.

Lipgens, Walter, ed. *Documents on the History of European Integration, Vol. 1. Continental Plans for European Union 1939–1945*. Berlin and New York: Walter de Gruyter, 1985.

Lipgens, Walter, and Wilfried Loth, eds. *Documents on the History of European Integration, Vol. 4. Transnational Organizations and Political Parties and Pressure Groups in the Struggle for European Union, 1945–1950*. Berlin and New York: Walter de Gruyter, 1991.

List, Friedrich. *The National System of Political Economy*. Translated from the Original German by Sampson S. Lloyd. New York: Augustus M. Kelley Publishers, 1991.

Lo, Jung-pang, ed. *K'ang Yu-wei: A Biography and a Symposium*. Tucson: The University of Arizona Press, 1967.

Lo, Jung-pang. "Sequel to the Chronological Autobiography of K'ang Yu-wei." In *K'ang Yu-wei: A Biography and a Symposium*, edited with translation by Jung-pang Lo, 174–253. Tucson: The University of Arizona Press, 1967.

Locke, John. *Two Treatises of Government*. Edited with and introduction and notes by Peter Laslett. Cambridge, UK: Cambridge University Press, 1988. Originally Published in John Locke. *Two Treatises of Government*. London, 1698.

Long, David, and Peter Wilson, eds. *Thinkers of the Twenty Years' Crisis. Inter-War Idealism Reassessed*. London: Clarendon Press, 1995.

Loth, Wilfried. "Hallstein und de Gaulle: Die verhängnisvolle Konfrontation [Hallstein and de Gaulle: The fatal confrontation]." In *Walter Hallstein. Der vergessene Europäer? [Walter Hallstein. The forgotten European?]*, edited by Wilfried Loth, William Wallace, and Wolfgang Wessels. Bonn: Europa Union Verlag, 1995.

Loubet del Bayle, Jean-Louis. *Les non-conformistes des années 30. Une tentative de renouvellement de la pensée politique française [The Non-conformists of the 30's. An Attempt to Renew French Political Thought]*. Paris: Éditions du Seuil, 2001.

Lu, David J., ed. *Japan: a Documentary History*. New York: M. E. Sharpe Inc., 1997.

Mann, Thomas. "Aufruf zur europäischen Föderation, New York, 29. Januar 1943 [Appeal for European Federation, New York, January 29, 1943]." In *Europa Föderationsplane der Widerstandsbewegungen, 1940–1945 [European Federation Plans of the Resistance Movements, 1940–1945]*, edited by Walter Lipgens, 470–471. München: R. Oldenbourg Verlag, 1968.

Mao Tse-tung. *On New Democracy*. Peking: Foreign Languages Press, 1954.
Mao Zedong. "Weixin shi guan de pochan [La faillite de la conception de l'histoire idéaliste, 1949]." In *Oeuvres choisies de Mao Zedong [Selected Works of Mao Zedong]*. Beijing: Renmin chunanshe, 1991. Vol. 4, 1513–1514. Cited by Zhang Chi. *Chine et modernité. Chocs, crises et renaissance de la culture chinoise aux temps modernes [China and Modernity. Shocks, Crises, and Revival of Chinese Culture in Modern Times]*, 152–153. Paris: Librairie You Feng, 2005.
Marshall, D. Bruce. *The French Colonial Myth and Constitution-Making in the Forth Republic*. New Haven, CT and London: Yale University Press, 1973.
Martin, Jean-Clément. *Contre-Révolution. Révolution et Nation en France, 1789–1799 [Counter-Revolution. Revolution and Nation in France, 1789–1799]*. Paris: Éditions du Seuil, 1998.
Marx, Karl. "Revolution in China and in Europe." *New York Daily Tribune*, June 14, 1853. In *Marx on China, 1853–1860. Articles From the New York Daily Tribune*, edited by Dona Torr, 1–10. London: Lawrence & Wishart, 1951.
Marx, Karl, and Friedrich Engels. *Das Kommunistische Manifest [The Communist Manifesto]*. Berlin: Internationaler Arbeiter-Verlag G. M. B. H., 1932.
Mazrui, Ali A. *Towards a Pax Africana: A Study of Ideology and Ambition*. London: Weidenfeld and Nicolson, 1967.
Mazrui, Ali A., ed., and C. Wondji, assistant ed. *Africa Since 1935: General History of Africa*. Vol. 8. Oxford: Heinemann Publishers; Berkeley, CA: University of California Press; Paris: UNESCO, 1993.
Mazzini, Giuseppe. *The Duties of Man and Other Essays*. London: Dutton and Co., 1912.
Merle, Marcel, ed. *L'Anticolonialisme Européenne de Las Casas à Karl Marx [European Anticolonialism from Las Casas to Karl Marx]*. Texts selected and presented by Marcel Merle. Paris: Armand Colin, 1969.
"Message to Europeans, The Hague, 10 May 1948." In *Europe Unites: The Hague Congress and After. The Story of the Campaign for European Unity, Including a Full Report of the Congress of Europe, Held at the Hague, May, 1948*. Foreword by Mr. Winston Churchill, 94–95. London: Hollis and Carter, 1949. European Movement, foreword by Mr. Winston Churchill, 94–95. London: Hollis and Carter, 1949; and In *Documents on the History of European Integration. Vol. 4. Transnational Organizations and Political Parties and Pressure Groups in the Struggle for European Union, 1945–1950*, edited by Walter Lipgens and Wilfried Loth, 351. Berlin, New York: Walter de Gruyter, 1991.
Migani, Guia. "L'association des TOM au Marché Commun: Histoire d'une accord européen entre cultures économiques différentes et idéaux politiques communs, 1955–1957. [The Association of the OT (Overseas Territories) with the Common Market: History of a European Agreement Between Different Economic Cultures and Common Political Ideals, 1955–1957]." In *L'Europe Unie et L'Afrique. De l'idée d'Eurafrique à la Convention de Lomé I: actes du colloque international de Paris, 1er et 2 avril 2004 [United Europe and Africa. From the Idea of Eurafrique to the Lomé I Convention: Proceedings of the Paris International Conference, April 1 and 2, 2004]*, under the direction of Marie-Thérèse Bitsch and Gérard Bossuat, 233–252. Bruxelles: Bruylant; Paris: L.G.D.J.; Baden-Baden: Nomos Verlag, 2005.
Mill, John Stuart. "On Liberty." In *On Liberty, Utilitarianism, and Other Essays*, edited by Mark Philip and Frederick Rosen, 1–112. Oxford: Oxford University Press, 2015.

Mioche, Philippe, ed. *Penser et construire l'Europe, XIXe-XXe siècle [Thinking and Building Europe, 19th-20th Century]*. Texts selected and presented by Philippe Mioche. Paris: Hachette Supérieur, 2007.

Mitrany, David. "A Working Peace System (1943)." In *The Functional Theory of Politics*, edited by David Mitrany, 123-132. London School of Economics and Political Science. London: Martin Robertson & Company Ltd., 1975.

Monnet, Jean. "A Ferment of Change." *Journal of Common Market Studies* 1, no. 1 (1962): 203-211.

Monnet, Jean. *Mémoires [Memoirs]*. Paris: Fayard, 1976.

Monnet, Jean. *Repères pour une méthode. Propos sur l'Europe à faire* [Guidelines for a Method. Propositions for Europe to Create]. Selected by Marianne Monnet-Nobécourt, Antoie Chastenet and François Fontaine. Paris: Fayard, 1996.

Monnet, Jean. "Où est l'Europe? Les prochains pas, 15 avril 1960 [Where is Europe? The Next Steps, April 15, 1960]." In *Une Europe inédite [An Unprecedented Europe]*. Documents des Archives Jean Monnet. Selected and introduced by Bernard Lefort, 259-261. Villeneuve d'Ascq Cédex: Presses Universitaires du Septentrion, 2001.

Monnet, Jean. "Une Europe fédérée, 30 avril 1952. [A Federated Europe, April 30, 1952]." In *Les Grands Discours de l'Histoire. 3. Les Européens [The Great Discourses of History. 3. The Europeans]*, edited by Catherine Lanneau and Simon Petermann, 93-103. Waterloo: Renaissance du Livre, 2008.

Montarsolo, Yves. *L'Eurafrique, contrepoint de l'idée d'Europe: le cas français de la fin de la deuxième guerre mondiale aux négociations des Traités de Rome [Eurafrique, Counterpoint to the Idea of Europe: the French Case from the End of the Second World War to the Negotiations of the Treaties of Rome]*. Aix-en-Provence: Publications de l'Université de Provence, 2010. Open Edition Book. https://books.openedition.org/pup/6574.

Montesquieu, Charles-Louis de Secondat, Baron de La Bréde et de Montesquieu. *De l'esprit des lois [The Spirit of Laws]*. Vol. 1. Paris: GF Flammarion, 1979.

Montesquieu, Charles-Louis de Secondat, Baron de La Bréde et de Montesquieu. "The Spirit of Laws." In *Complete Works*, Vol. 1. London: T. Evans, 1777. Accessed March 26, 2022. Online Library of Liberty. https://oll.libertyfund.org/title/montesquieu-complete-works-vol-1-the-spirit-of-laws.

Mussolini, Benito. "Discours du XIV Novembre pour l'État corporatif. [Speech of November XIV for the Corporate State]." In *Édition définitive des oeuvres et discours de Benito Mussolini [Definitive Edition of the Works and Speeches of Benito Mussolini]*, Vol. 9. Translated by Maria Croci, edited by Benito Mussolini, 247-263. Paris: Flammarion, 1935.

Mussolini, Benito. "La doctrine du fascisme [The Doctrine of Fascism.] In *Édition définitive des oeuvres et discours de Benito Mussolini [Definitive Edition of the Works and Speeches of Benito Mussolini]*, Vol. 9. Translated by Maria Croci, edited by Benito Mussolini, 61-91. Paris: Flammarion, 1935.

Naumann, Friedrich. *Central Europe*. Translated by Christabel M. Meredith. London: P. S. King & Son Ltd., 1916.

Navari, Cornelia. "David Mitrany and International Functionalism." In *Thinkers of the Twenty Years' Crisis: Inter-War Idealism Reassessed*, edited by David Long and Peter Wilson, 214-247. London: Clarendon Press, 1995.

Nehru, Jawaharlal. *Discovery of India*. Calcutta: The Signet Press, 1946.

Nehru, Jawaharlal. *Independence and After: A Collection of Speeches*. New York: The John Day Company, 1950.
Nelsen, Brent F., and Alexander C.-G. Stubb, eds. *The European Union. Readings on the Theory and Practice of European Integration*. Boulder, CO: Lynne Rienner Publishers, 2003.
Nkrumah, Kwame. *I Speak of Freedom*. London, Melbourne, and Toronto: Heinemann, 1961.
Nkrumah, Kwame. *L'Afrique doit s'unir [Africa Must Unite]*. Translated from English by L. Jospin. Paris: Payot, 1964.
Nkrumah, Kwame. *Le Consciencisme. Philosophie et idéologie pour la décolonisation et le développement, avec une référence particulière à la Révolution africaine [Conscientism. Philosophy and Ideology for Decolonization and Development, With Particular Reference to the African Revolution]*. Translated from English by L. Jospin. Paris: Payot, 1964.
Nkrumah, Kwame. *Neo-Colonialism the Last Stage of Imperialism*. London: Nelson, 1965.
Nkrumah, Kwame. *The Autobiography of Kwame Nkrumah*. Edinburgh: Thomas Nelson and Sons Ltd., 1957.
Nkrumah, Kwame. "The Motion for Approval." In *I Speak of Freedom*, edited by Kwame Nkrumah, 71–84. London, Melbourne, and Toronto: Heinemann, 1961.
Nyerere, Julius K. "Des Etats-Unis d'Afrique [The United States of Africa]." In *Socialisme, Démocratie et Unité africaine suivi de La Déclaration d'Arusha [Socialism, Democracy and African Unity Followed by The Arusha Declaration]*, edited by Julius K. Nyerere, 67–76. Paris: Présence Africaine, 1970.
Nyerere, Julius K. "The Arusha Declaration, 5 February 1967." In *Ujamaa Essays on Socialism*, 13–37. London: Oxford University Press, 1970.
Nyerere, Julius K. *Ujamaa Essays on Socialism*. London: Oxford University Press, 1970.
Nyerere, Julius K. "Ujamaa – The Basis of African Socialism." Published as a TANU Pamphlet in April 1962. In *Ujamaa Essays on Socialism*, 1–12. London: Oxford University Press, 1970.
Ortega y Gasset, José. *The Revolt of the Masses*. New York and London: W. W. Norton and Company, 1993.
Osterhammel, Jürgen. *Colonialism: A Theoretical Overview*. Translated From German by Shelley L. Frisch. Princeton, NJ: Markus Wiener Publishers, 1997.
Osterhammel, Jürgen. *The Transformation of the World: A Global History of the Nineteenth Century*. Princeton, NJ: Princeton University Press, 2014.
Padover, Saul K., ed. *Thomas Jefferson on Democracy*. New York: Penguin Books, Inc., 1946.
Palacký, František. *Österreichs Staatsidee [Austria's Idea of the State]*. Wien: Geyer, 1974.
Parkes, Henry Bamford. *The American Experience: An Interpretation of the History and Civilization of the American People*. New York: Alfred A. Knopf, 1947.
Pasture, Patrick. *Imagining European Unity since 1000 AD*. Houndmills, Basingstoke, and Hampshire: Palgrave Macmillan, 2015.
Penn, William. *An Essay Towards the Present and Future Peace of Europe by the Establishment of an European Dyet, Parliament or Estates*. Preface by Heinz Waldner, introduction by Peter van den Dungen. United Nations Library Geneva: Series F. Sources on the History of International Organization No. 1. Hildesheim, Zürich, and New York: Georg Olms Verlag, 1983. Originally Published in *An Essay Towards*

the Present and Future Peace of Europe, by the Establishment of an European Dyet, Parliament, or Estates. London, 1693.

Pitts, Jennifer. *Naissance de la bonne conscience coloniale: les libéraux français et britanniques et la question impériale (1770–1870) [A Turn to Empire: The Rise of Imperial Liberalism in Britain and France]*. Translated from English by Michel Cordillot. Ivry-sur-Seine: Éditions de l'Atelier, 2008.

Pleven, René. "Statement by René Pleven on the establishment of a European army (24 October 1950)." Accessed March 26, 2022. www.cvce.eu; https://www.cvce.eu/en/education/unit-content/-/unit/803b2430-7d1c-4e7b-9101-47415702fc8e/29a4e81c-c7b6-4622-915e-3b09649747b8/Resources#4a3f4499-daf1-44c1-b313-212b31cad878_en&overlay.

Pleven, René. "The Pleven Plan, 1950." In *Documents on European Union*, edited by Anjo G. Harryvan and Jan van der Harst, 65–69. Cambridge: St. Martin's Press; New York: Macmillan, 1997.

Podiebrad, George. "Treaty on the Establishment of Peace Throughout Christendom." In *The Universal Peace Organization of King George of Bohemia: A Fifteenth Century Plan for World Peace, 1462–1464*, edited by V. Vanaček, English translation by Ivo Dvořák, 83–92. Prague: Publishing House of the Czechoslovak Academy of Sciences, 1964.

Polanyi, Karl. *La grande transformation: Aux origines politiques et économiques de notre temps [The Great Transformation: The Political and Economic Origins of Our Time]*. Translated from English by Catherine Malamoud and Maurice Angeno. Paris: Gallimard, 1983.

Proudhon, Pierre-Joseph. "Du principe fédératif. [On the Federative Principle]. In *Du principe fédératif et oeuvres diverses sur les problèmes politiques européens. Oeuvres complètes de P.-J. Proudhon. [On the Federative Principle and Various Works on European Political Problems. Complete Works of P.-J. Proudhon*. Introduction and notes by J.-L. Puech and Th. Ruyssen, vol. 15, 253–551. Paris: Librairie Marcel Rivière, 1959.

Proudhon, Pierre-Joseph. *General Idea of the Revolution in the Nineteenth Century*. Mineola, NY: Dover Publications, Inc., 2003.

Qi Xin. *China's New Democracy: With Full Texts of the Three Constitutions of the People's Republic of China*. Hong Kong: Cosmos Books Ltd., 1979.

Raumer, Kurt von, ed. *Ewiger Friede. Friedensrufe und Friedenspläne seit der Renaissance [Eternal Peace. Calls for Peace and Peace Plans Since the Renaissance]*. Freiburg: Alber, 1953.

Réau, Élisabeth du. *L'idée d'Europe au XXe siècle [The Idea of Europe in the 20th Century]*. Paris: Éditions Complexe, 1996.

Rials, Stéphane, ed. *La déclaration des droits de l'homme et du citoyen [The Declaration of the Rights of Man and of the Citizen]*. Paris: Hachette, 1988.

Ribbentrop, Joachim von. "European Confederation. 21 March 1943." In *Documents on the History of European Integration. Vol. 1. Continental Plans for European Union 1939–1945*, edited by Walter Lipgens, 122–127. Berlin, New York: Walter de Gruyter, 1985.

Robespierre, Maximilien. "Discours de Maximilien Robespierre sur la Constitution. Séance du 10 Mai 1793 [Speech by Maximilien Robespierre on the Constitution. Session of May 10, 1793]." In *Oeuvres de Maximilien Robespierre [Works of Maximilien Robespierre]*, edited by Marc Bouloiseau, Georges Lefebvre, Jean Dautry, and Albert Soboul, vol. 9, 495–510. Paris: Presses Universitaires de France, 1957.

Rodney, Walter. *How Europe Underdeveloped Africa.* Washington, DC: Howard University Press, 1982.
Roosevelt, Franklin Delano. "First Inaugural Address, 1933." In *A Documentary History of the United States,* edited by Richard D. Heffner and Alexander Heffner, 367–372. New York: Penguin Group, 2009.
Rougemeont, Denis de. "The Federalist Attitude", 27 August 1947. Lecture at the Montreux Congress. In *Documents on the History of European Integration. Vol. 4. Transnational Organizations and Political Parties and Pressure Groups in the Struggle for European Union, 1945–1950,* edited by Walter Lipgens and Wilfried Loth, 23–27. Berlin and New York: Walter de Gruyter, 1991.
Rougemont, Denis de. "The Campaign of the European Congresses." In *The New Politics of European Integration,* edited by Ghiţă Ionescu, 10–31. London and Basingstoke: The Macmillan Press, 1972.
Rougemont, Denis de. *The Meaning of Europe.* Translated from the French by Alan Braley. London: Sidgwick and Jackson Ltd., 1965.
Rougemont, Denis de. *Vingt-huit siècles d'Europe. La conscience européenne à travers les textes, d'Hésiode à nos jours [Twenty-eight Centuries of Europe. European Consciousness Through the Texts, From Hesiod to the Present Day].* Paris: Payot, 1961.
Rousseau, Jean-Jacques. *The Social Contract.* London: Penguin Books, 1968.
Rousseau, Jean-Jacques. "Projet de paix perpétuelle (1756, 1762) & Jugement sur la paix perpétuelle (1756) [Project of Perpetual Peace (1756, 1762) & Judgment on Perpetual Peace (1756)]." In *L'Europe une. Les philosophes et l'Europe [One Europe. Philosophers and Europe],* edited by Jean Pierre Faye, 115–146, 147–158. Paris: Gallimard, 1992.
Saint-Pierre, Charles-Irénée Castel de (Abbé de Saint-Pierre). "Projet de paix perpétuelle pour l'Europe [Perpetual Peace Project for Europe]." In Abbé de Saint-Pierre. *Projet pour rendre la paix perpétuelle en Europe [Project for Perpetual Peace in Europe],* presented by Simone Goyard-Fabre. Volume 1. Fourth Discourse, 204–232. Paris: Éditions Garnier Frères, 1981. Originally Published in *Projet pour rendre la paix perpétuelle en Europe.* Volume 1. Utrecht: A. Shouten, 1713.
Saint-Simon, Claude-Henri de, and Augustin Thierry. "On the Reorganization of European Society." In *The Political Thought of Saint-Simon,* edited with an introduction by Ghiţă Ionescu, 83–98. London: Oxford University Press, 1976. Originally Published in *De la Réorganisation de la Société européenne ou de la nécessité et des moyens de rassembler les peuples de l'Europe en un seul corps politique en conservant à chacun son indépendance national. [On the Reorganization of European Society, or the Necessity and the Means of Bringing the Peoples of Europe Together Into a Single Body Politic, While Each Maintaining Its National Independence],* edited by M. le Comte de Saint-Simon and A. Thierry, his adopted son. Paris: Adrien Égron, 1814.
Sansom, G. B. *The Western World and Japan: A Study in the Interaction of European and Asiatic Cultures.* Tokyo: Charles E. Tuttle Company, 1987.
Saurugger, Sabine. *Théories et concepts de l'intégration européenne [Theories and Concepts of European Integration].* Paris: Sciences Po. Les Presses, 2009.
Schell, Orville, and David Shambaugh, eds. *China Reader. The Reform Era.* New York: Vintage Books, Division of Random House Inc., 1999.
Schlochauer, Hans-Jürgen, ed. *Die Idee des ewigen Friedens [The Idea of Eternal Peace].* Bonn: Ludwig Röhrscheid Verlag, 1953.

Bibliography

Senghor, Léopold Sedar. *Ce que je crois. Négritude, Francité et Civilisation de l'Universel [What I believe. Negritude, Frenchness and Universal Civilisation]*. Paris: Bernard Grasset, 1988.

Senghor, Léopold Sédar. "Francité et Francophonie." In *Ce que je crois. Négritude, Francité et Civilisation de l'Universel*, edited by Léopold Sédar Senghor, 155–197. Paris: Bernard Grasset, 1988.

Senghor, Léopold Sedar. *Nationhood and the African Road to Socialism*. Translated by Mercer Cook. Paris: Editions Présence Africaine, 1961.

Senghor, Léopold Sedar. "Report on the Party's Doctrine and Programme." Report to the Constitutive Congress of the African Federal Party (Dakar, July 1, 1959). In *Nationhood and the African Road to Socialism*, edited by Leopold Sedar Senghor, 13–85. Paris: Présence Africaine, 1961.

Senghor, Léopold Sedar. "The African Way of Socialism." Speech Made at the First Youth Seminar of the P. F. A. (The African Federal Party) 16–19 May 1960. In *Nationhood and the African Road to Socialism*, edited by Leopold Sedar Senghor, 87–130. Paris: Editions Présence Africaine, 1961.

Seth, Catronia, and Rotraud von Kulessa, eds. *The Idea of Europe: Enlightenment Perspectives*. Cambridge, UK: Open Book Publishers, 2017. https://doi.org/10.11647/OBP.0123.

Shirer, William L. *Le Troisième Reich des origines à la chute [The Third Reich From Its Origins to Its Fall]*. 1–2. Paris: Librairie Stock, 1961.

Smith, Adam. *An Inquiry into the Nature and Causes of the Wealth of Nations*. Edited by R. H. Campbell, A. S. Skinner, and W. Todd, Vol. 1. Oxford: Clarendon Press, 1976.

Smith, Dennis B. *Japan Since 1945: The Rise of an Economic Superpower*. London: Macmillan Press Ltd., 1995.

Soboul, Albert. *La Révolution française [The French Revolution]*. Paris: Gallimard, 1982.

Spinelli, Altiero. *The Eurocrats: Conflict and Crisis in the European Community*. Translated by C. Grove Haines. Baltimore, MD: The Johns Hopkins Press, 1966.

Spinelli, Altiero. *The European Adventure: Tasks for the Enlarged Community*. London: Charles Knight & Co. Ltd, 1972.

Spinelli, Altiero. *Towards the European Union, Florence, 13 June 1983*. Sixth Jean Monnet Lecture. Florence: European University Institute, 1983, 9–28.

Spinelli, Altiero, and Ernesto Rossi. "The Ventotene Manifesto." In *Documents on the History of European Integration. Vol 1. Continental Plans for European Union 1939–1945*, edited by Walter Lipgens, 471–484. Berlin and New York: Walter de Gruyter, 1985.

"Statute of the Council of Europe (London, 5 May 1949)." In *European Movement and the Council of Europe*, 169–184. London: Published on Behalf of the European Movement by Hutchinson and Co. Ltd, 1949.

Sully, Maximilien de Béthune, Duc de Sully. "Le projet politique, (1610, 1662) [The Political Project, (1610, 1662)]." In *L'Europe une: les philosophes et l'Europe [One Europe: Philosophers and Europe]*, edited by Jean-Pierre Faye, 71–91. Paris: Gallimard, 1992. Originally Published in *Mémoires de Maximilien de Béthune, Duc de Sully, Ministre Principal de Henri-le-Grand [Memoirs of Maximilien de Béthune, Duke of Sully, Principal Minister of Henri-le-Grand]*, Thirtieth Book, Paris: Jean-François Bastien, 1788.

Sun Yat-sen. "The Three Principles of the People, San Min Chu I. by Sun Yat-sen." In *The Three Principles of the People, San Min Chu I, by Sun Yat-sen With Two Supplementary*

Chapters 1. National Fecundity, Social Welfare and Education; 2. Health and Happiness by President Chiang Kai-shek, 1-212, edited by Sun Yat-sen and Chiang Kai-shek. Taipei, Taiwan, Republic of China: China Publishing Co., [ca. 1960].
Sun Yat-sen. *The International Development of China*. New York and London: G. P. Putnam's Sons, 1922. Accessed March 26, 2022. Project Gutenberg. https://www.gutenberg.org/files/45188/45188-h/45188-h.htm.
Sun Yat-sen. *The Teachings of Sun Yat-sen: Selections From His Writings*. Compiled and introduced by Nagendranath Gangluee (Dedicated to the youth of the United Nations for the guidance in understanding the spirit and form of the Chinese Revolution and the Chinese Republic). London: The Sylvan Press, 1945.
Tamaki, Norio. *Yukichi Fukuzawa, 1835–1901: The Spirit of Enterprise in Modern Japan*. New York: Palgrave, 2001.
T'ang Leang-Li. *China in Revolt: How a Civilization Became a Nation*. London: Noel Douglas, 1927.
Taylor, Georges Rogers, ed. *Hamilton and the National Debt*. Boston, MA: D. C. Heath and Company, 1950.
Telò, Mario, ed. *European Union and New Regionalism: Regional Actors and Global Governance in a Post-Hegemonic Era*. Aldershot: Ashgate Publishing, 2007.
"The Charter Oath, 1868." (Three Drafts of the Charter Oath). In *Japan: A Documentary History*, edited by David J. Lu, 307–311. New York: M. E. Sharpe Inc., 1997.
"The Charter of the Organization of African Unity, 25 May 1963, Addis Ababa, Ethiopia." In *Towards a Pax Africana: A Study of Ideology and Ambition*, edited by Ali A. Mazuri, 219–229. London: Weidenfeld and Nicolson, 1967.
"The Constitution of the Empire of Japan, 1889." In *Japan: A Documentary History*, edited by David J. Lu, 333–343. New York: M. E. Sharpe Inc., 1997.
"The Constitution of the Empire of Japan, 1889." Accessed March 26, 2022. National Diet Library. https://www.ndl.go.jp/constitution/e/etc/c02.html.
"The Constitution of the German Federation of August 11, 1919." Accessed March 26, 2022. Internet Archive WayBack Machine. https://web.archive.org/web/20050308140018/http://web.jjay.cuny.edu/~jobrien/reference/ob13.html.
"The Constitution of Japan, 1946." In *Japan: A Documentary History*, edited by David J. Lu, 469–475. New York: M. E. Sharpe Inc., 1997.
"The Constitution of Japan, 1946." Accessed March 26, 2022. National Diet Library. https://www.ndl.go.jp/constitution/e/etc/c01.html.
"The 1954 Constitution of the People's Republic of China." In *China's New Democracy: With Full Texts of the Three Constitutions of the People's Republic of China*, edited by Qi Xin, 151–184. Hong Kong: Cosmos Books Ltd., 1979.
"The Constitution of the People's Republic of China, 1982, revised in 1988, 1993, 1999, 2004, 2018." Accessed March 26, 2022. The National People's Congress of the People's Republic of China. http://www.npc.gov.cn/englishnpc/constitution2019/201911/1f65146fb6104dd3a2793875d19b5b29.shtml.
"The Constitution of the United Republic of Tanzania, 1977." Accessed March 26, 2022. Internet Archive, WayBackMachine. https://web.archive.org/web/20180726171110/http://www.judiciary.go.tz/wp-content/uploads/2015/09/constitution.pdf.
"The Constitution of the United States (1787)." In *A Documentary History of the United States*, edited by Richard D. Heffner and Alexander Heffner, 20–34. Amendments to the Constitution, Articles I–X, Bill of Rights, 1791, 34–36. New York: Penguin Group, 2009.

"The Covenant of the League of Nations (1919)." In *Die Idee des ewigen Friedens [The Idea of Eternal Peace]*, edited by Hans-Jürgen Schlochauer, 172–174. Bonn: Ludwig Röhrscheid Verlag, 1953.

The General Agreement on Tariffs and Trade (GATT). Accessed March 26, 2022. WTO Website. https://www.wto.org/english/docs_e/legal_e/gatt47_e.pdf.

"The Hertenstein Programme, Hertenstein, 22 September 1946." In *Documents on European Union*, edited by Anjo G. Harryvan and Jan van der Harst, 42–43. Cambridge: St. Martin's Press; New York: Macmillan, 1997.

"The Interlaken Draft Constitution of a Federal Europe." European Parliamentary Union, 1949. In *Documents on the History of European Integration. Vol. 4. Transnational Organizations and Political Parties and Pressure Groups in the Struggle for European Union, 1945–1950*, edited by Walter Lipgens and Wilfried Loth, 141–146. Berlin and New York: Walter de Gruyter, 1991.

The Lomé I Convention (1975) and the Lomé II Convention (1979). Accessed March 26, 2022. www.cvce.eu; https://www.cvce.eu/en/education/unit-content/-/unit/dd10d6bf-e14d-40b5-9ee6-37f978c87a01/9a69c7f9-1ea2-4e6c-8cdb-1dee40ac5714/Resources.

"The Luxembourg Agreement." Agreement on Decision-Making Reached at the Extraordinary Session of the EEC Council on 28 and 29 January 1966. In *Documents on European Union*, edited by Anjo G. Harryvan and Jan van der Harst, 151–152. Cambridge: St. Martin's Press; New York: Macmillan, 1997.

"The Schuman Declaration, 9 May 1950." In *Documents on European Union*, edited by Anjo G. Harryvan and Jan van der Harst, 61–63. Cambridge: St. Martin's Press; New York: Macmillan, 1997.

"The Yaoundé Convention (20 July 1963). Journal officiel des Communautés européennes. 11.06.1964, no. 93." Accessed March 26, 2020. www.cvce.eu; https://www.cvce.eu/en/education/unit-content/-/unit/dd10d6bf-e14d-40b5-9ee6-37f978c87a01/c303f9ae-1356-4fd2-ad61-b650f07f10ec/Resources#52d35693-845a-49ae-b6f9-ddbc48276546_en&overlay.

Thoreau, Henry David. "Civil Disobedience." In *Walden and Other Writings*, edited by Henry David Thoreau, 89–110. New York: Bantam Dell, a Division of Random House, Inc., 2004.

Tindemans, Leo. "Report on European Union [by Mr. Leo Tindemans to the Council] (29 December 1975)." Accessed March 26, 2022. www.cvce.eu; https://www.cvce.eu/en/education/unit-content/-/unit/02bb76df-d066-4c08-a58a-d4686a3e68ff/63f5fca7-54ec-4792-8723-1e626324f9e3/Resources#284c9784-9bd2-472b-b704-ba4bb1f3122d_en&overlay.

Tocqueville, Alexis de. *Democracy in America*. The Henry Reeve text as revisited by Francis Bowen, now further corrected and edited with introduction, editorial notes, and bibliographies by Phillips Bradley, Vol. 1. New York: Vintage Books Edition, A Division of Random House Inc., 1990.

Tocqueville, Alexis de. *L'Ancien Régime et la Révolution [The Old Regime and the Revolution]*. Paris: Gallimard, 1967.

Tocqueville, Alexis de. *Sur l'Algérie [About Algeria]*. Paris: GF Flammarion, 2003.

Tolstoy, Leo. "A Letter to a Hindu by Leo Tolstoy, Yasnaya Polyana, December 14, 1908." In *Mahatma Gandhi and Leo Tolstoy Letters*, edited by B. Srinivasa Murthy, 43–61. Long Beach, CA: Long Beach Publications, 1987.

Traité instituant la Communauté européenne de défense (Paris, 27 mai 1952) [Treaty Establishing the European Defense Community (Paris, 27 May 1952)]. Accessed

March 26, 2022. www.cvce.eu, https://www.cvce.eu/en/education/unit-content/-/unit/803b2430-7d1c-4e7b-9101-47415702fc8e/29a4e81c-c7b6-4622-915e-3b09649747b8/Resources#2af9ea94-7798-4434-867a-36c4a256d0af_en&overlay.

"Treaty Establishing the European Economic Community (Rome, 25 March 1957)." In *Documents on European Union*, edited by Anjo G. Harryvan and Jan van der Harst, 104–119. Cambridge: St. Martin's Press; New York: Macmillan, 1997.

"Treaty of Lisbon, 2007. Official Journal of the European Union, C 306, 17 December 2007." Accessed March 26, 2022. www.eur-lex.europa.eu, https://eur-lex.europa.eu/legal-content/EN/TXT/?uri=OJ:C:2007:306:TOC.

"Treaty of the Union, Eternal Alliance and Confederation Made in the Town of Utrecht by the Countries and Their Towns and Members, 29 January 1579." In *Texts Concerning the Revolt of the Netherlands*, edited by Ernst Heinrich Kossman and A. F. Mellink, Document 37, 165–173. Cambridge, UK: Cambridge University Press, 1974.

Treaty on European Union (Maastricht, 7 February 1992). Official Journal of the European Communities, 29.07.1992, no. C 191. Accessed March 26, 2022. www.cvce.eu; https://www.cvce.eu/obj/treaty_on_european_union_maastricht_7_february_1992-en-2c2f2b85-14bb-4488-9ded-13f3cd04de05.html.

"Universal Declaration of Human Rights, 1948." In *Basic Documents in International Law*, edited by Ian Brownlie, 250–256. Oxford: Clarendon Press, 1991.

Vassalo, Aude. *De Gaulle et l'Afrique Noire [De Gaulle and Black Africa]*. Charles de Gaulle: Paroles publiques. Fondation Charles de Gaulle, INA. Accessed March 26, 2022. https://fresques.ina.fr/de-gaulle/parcours/0006/de-gaulle-et-l-afrique-noire.html.

Vattel, Emer (Emmerich) de. *Le droit des gens, ou principes de la loi naturelle. Appliqués à la conduite et aux affaires des nations et des souverains [The Law of Nations, or Principles of Natural Law. Applied to the Conduct and Affairs of Nations and Sovereigns]*. With an Introduction by Albert de Lapradelle. Volume 1. (Reproduction of Books I and II of Edition of 1758). Washington: Carnegie Institution of Washington, 1916.

Vayssière, Bertrand. *Vers une Europe fédérale? Les espoirs et les actions fédéralistes au sortir de la Seconde Guerre mondiale [Towards a Federal Europe? Federalist Hopes and Actions at the End of the Second World War]*. Bruxelles: P.I.E. Peter Lang, 2007.

Verfassung des Deutschen Reichs (gegeben Berlin, den 16. April 1871) [Constitution of the German Empire (Berlin, April 16, 1871)]. Text edition with additions, notes and subject index by Dr. Ludwig von Rönne. Berlin and Leipzig: Verlag von J. Guttentag, 1886.

Voyenne, Bernard. "Du printemps des peuples au printemps de l'union 1952 [From the Spring of the Peoples to the Spring of the Union 1952]." In *Europes. De l'antiquité au XXe siècle: Anthologie critique et commentée [Europes. From Antiquity to the 20th Century: A Critical and Commented Anthology]*, Edition compiled and presented by Yves Hersant and Fabienne Durand-Bogaert, 313–358. Paris: Éditions Robert Laffont, 2000.

Voyenne, Bernard. *Histoire de l'idée européenne [History of the European Idea]*. Paris: Petite Bibliothèque Payot, 1952.

Waters, Malcolm, ed. *Modernity. Critical Concepts. Vol. 1. Modernization*. London: Routledge, 1999.

Wells, Audrey. *The Political Thought of Sun Yat-sen. Development Impact*. Houndmills, Basingstoke: Palgrave, 2001.

Wesseling, Hendrik Lodewijk, ed. *Expansion and Reaction: Essays on European Expansion and Reactions in Asia and Africa*. Leiden: Leiden University Press, 1978.

Winks, Robin W., and Joan Neuberger. *Europe and the Making of Modernity, 1815–1914*. New York and Oxford: Oxford University Press, 2005.

Worger, William H., Nancy L. Clark, and Edward A. Alpers. *Africa and the West: A Documentary History*. New York: Oxford University Press, 2010.

Zhang, Chi. *Chine et modernité. Chocs, crises et renaissance de la culture chinoise aux temps modernes [China and Modernity. Shocks, Crises and the Revival of Chinese Culture in Modern Times]*. Paris: Librairie You Feng, 2005.

Zorgbibe, Charles. *Histoire de l'Union Européenne [History of the European Union]*. Fondation Robert Schuman. Paris: Albin Michel, 2005.

Zorgbibe, Charles. *Histoire politique et constitutionnelle de la France [Political and Constitutional History of France]*. Paris: Ellipses, 2002.

Zürcher, Erik. "Western Expansion and Chinese Reaction – A Theme Reconsidered." In *Expansion and Reaction: Essays on European Expansion and Reactions in Asia and Africa*, edited by Hendrik Lodewijk Wesseling, 59–77. Leiden: Leiden University Press, 1978.

Recommended On-line Literature

Althusius, Johannes. *Politica: An Abridged Translation of Politics, Methodically Set Forth and Illustrated with Sacred and Profane Examples*. Edited and translated with an introduction by Frederik S. Carney, foreword by Daniel J. Elazar. Online Library of Liberty, Liberty Fund. https://oll.libertyfund.org/title/althusius-politica.

Aristotle. *Politics: A Treatise on Government*. Translated by A. M. William Ellis. London and Toronto: J. M. Dent & Sons Ltd.; New York: E. P. Dutton & Co., The First Issue of This Edition 1912, Reprinted 1919, 1923, 1928. Project Gutenberg e-Book, http://www.gutenberg.org/files/6762/6762-h/6762-h.htm.

Arusha Declaration (1967) by Julius Nyerere. Wikisource. https://en.wikisource.org/wiki/Arusha_Declaration.

Bismarck, Otto von. *Gedanken und Erinnerungen [Thoughts and Memories]*. Project Gutenberg. https://www.projekt-gutenberg.org/autoren/namen/bismarck.html.

Bodin, Jean. *Six Books of the Commonwealth*. Abridged and translated by M. J. Tooley. Books 1–6. Oxford: Basil Blackwell, 1955. Constitution Society. https://constitution.org/2-Authors/bodin/bodin_.htm.

Brugmans, Henri. "The Fundamentals of European Federalism. Address Given by Henri Brugmans (Montreux, 27–31 August 1947)." www.cvce.eu; https://www.cvce.eu/obj/address_given_by_henri_brugmans_montreux_27_to_31_august_1947-en-289952c0-a6b8-4f1e-9f3e-782da1ef8455.html.

Coudenhove-Kalergi, Richard N. *Pan-Europa*. Wien: Pan-Europa-Verlag, 1923, Neuauflage 1982. Internet Archive. https://ia801301.us.archive.org/13/items/PanEuropaCoudenhoveKalergi/Pan-Europa%20-%20Coudenhove%20Kalergi.pdf.

Crucé, Émeric. *The New Cyneas*. Edited with an introduction, and translated into English from the original French text of 1623 by Thomas Willing Balch (English and French bilingual edition). Philadelphia, PA: Allen, Lane and Scott, 1909. Internet Archive. https://archive.org/details/newcyneasofemeri00cruc/page/n9.

"Das Hertensteiner Programm (21. September 1946) [The Hertenstein Programme, 21 September 1946]. www.cvce.eu; https://www.cvce.eu/en/education/unit-content/-/

unit/02bb76df-d066-4c08-a58a-d4686a3e68ff/20ed505d-eedc-4aaf-aca3-d736efaa93e1
/Resources#f39329ae-b25a-4b04-90ff-a25ea5c17051_en&overlay.

Déclaration des Droit de l'Homme et du Citoyen de 1789 [Declaration of the Rights of Man and of the Citizen of 1789]. Legifrance. https://www.legifrance.gouv.fr/Droit-francais/Constitution/Declaration-des-Droits-de-l-Homme-et-du-Citoyen-de-1789; and Conseil Constitutionnel. https://www.conseil-constitutionnel.fr/le-bloc-de-constitutionnalite/declaration-des-droits-de-l-homme-et-du-citoyen-de-1789.

Declaration of Human and Civic Rights of 26 August 1789. Conseil Constitutionnel. https://www.conseil-constitutionnel.fr/en/declaration-of-human-and-civic-rights-of-26-august-1789.

Declaration of Independence, July 4, 1776. The Avalon Project, Yale Law School. https://avalon.law.yale.edu/18th_century/declare.asp.

"Declaration on the Granting of Independence to Colonial Countries and Peoples." 1960. Office of the United Nations High Commissioner for Human Rights (ohchr.org). https://web.archive.org/web/20120508055042/http://www2.ohchr.org/english/law/independence.htm.

Declaration of the Rights of the Man (1789) The Avalon Project, Yale Law School. https://avalon.law.yale.edu/18th_century/rightsof.asp.

Decolonization: Geopolitical Issues and Impact on the European Integration. www.cvce.eu; https://www.cvce.eu/en/education/unit-content/-/unit/dd10d6bf-e14d-40b5-9ee6-37f978c87a01.

Deutscher, Isaak. *Stalin a Political Biography*. London, New York, and Toronto: Oxford University Press, 1949. Internet Archive. https://archive.org/details/in.ernet.dli.2015.52774/page/n3/mode/2up.

Digital Research in European Studies. Centre Virtuel de la Connaissance sur l'Europe (CVCE.eu) de l'Université du Luxembourg [Virtual Knowledge Center for Europe of the University of Luxembourg (cvce.eu by uni.lu)], www.cvce.eu.

Draft Treaty Embodying the Statute of the European Community. 1953. www.cvce.eu, https://www.cvce.eu/content/publication/1999/4/15/807979a3-4147-427e-86b9-565a0b917d4f/publishable_en.pdf.

Draft Treaty Establishing the European Union (14 February 1984). www.cvce.eu; https://www.cvce.eu/en/obj/draft_treaty_establishing_the_european_union_14_february_1984-en-0c1f92e8-db44-4408-b569-c464cc1e73c9.html.

Draft Treaty Establishing the European Union (1984). Spinelli's Footsteps, http://www.spinellisfootsteps.info/treaty/.

Eötvös, József. *Die Garantien der Macht und Einheit Oesterreichs [The Guarantees of the Power and Unity of Austria]*. Leipzig: F. A. Brodhaus, 1859. Internet Archive. https://archive.org/details/diegarantiederm00etvs/page/n8.

Final Communiqué of the Extraordinary Session of the Council (Luxembourg, 29 January, 1966). www.cvce.eu; https://www.cvce.eu/en/education/unit-content/-/unit/d1cfaf4d-8b5c-4334-ac1d-0438f4a0d617/a9aaa0cd-4401-45ba-867f-50e4e04cf272/Resources#abe9e77d-9bf9-4e0a-90a9-b80cb48efb47_en&overlay.

Fischer, Joschka. From Confederacy to Federation: Thoughts on the Finality of European Integration. Speech by Joschka Fischer at the Humboldt University in Berlin, 12 May 2000. European University Institute. https://cadmus.eui.eu/bitstream/handle/1814/17255/ResponsesToJ.FISCHER_2000.pdf.

French Constitution of 1946. Constitutional Council, https://www.conseil-constitutionnel.fr/la-constitution/les-constitutions-de-la-france.

Bibliography 231

French Constitution of October 4, 1958. Constitutional Council, https://www.conseil-constitutionnel.fr/sites/default/files/as/root/bank_mm/anglais/constiution_anglais_oct2009.pdf.

Gandhi, Mohandas Karamchand. *Indian Home Rule*. Madras: Ganesh and Co., 1922. Project Gutenberg eBook. http://www.gutenberg.org/files/40461/40461-h/40461-h.htm.

Gesetz betreffend die Verfassung des Deutshen Reiches, 16. April 1871. In documentArchiv.de, http://www.documentarchiv.de/ksr/verfksr.html.

Guizot, Francois. *Histoire de la civilisation en Europe depuis la chute de l'Empire romain jusqu'à la Révolution française [History of Civilization in Europe From the Fall of the Roman Empire to the French Revolution]*. Paris: Librairie Académique Didier & Co, Libraires-Éditeurs, 1868. Internet Archive. https://archive.org/details/histoiredelaciv00collgoog/page/n31/mode/2up; See also edition 1881, BnF Gallica, https://gallica.bnf.fr/ark:/12148/bpt6k4319823/f3.item.texteImage.

Haas, Ernst B. *The Unity of Europe. Political, Social and Economic Forces, 1950–1957*. Notre Dame, IN: University of Notre Dame Press, 2004. 100 Books European Parliament (https://www.europarl.europa.eu/100books/en/index.html), https://www.europarl.europa.eu/100books/file/EN-H-BW-0038-The-uniting-of-Europe.pdf.

Hamilton, Alexander, John Jay, and James Madison. *The Federalist Papers*. The Project Gutenberg eBook. http://www.gutenberg.org/files/1404/1404-h/1404-h.htm.

Historische (deutsche) Verfassungen [Historical (German) Constitutions]. DocumentArchiv.de, der historischen Dokumenten- und Quellensammlung zur deutschen Geschichte ab 1800 [DocumentArchiv.de, the historical collection of documents and sources on German history from 1800 onwards], http://www.documentarchiv.de/da/fs-verfassungen.html.

Jeorges, Christian, Yves Mény, and Joseph H. H. Weiler, eds. *What Kind of Constitution for What Kind of Polity? Responses to Joschka Fisher*. Florence: The Robert Schuman Centre for Advanced Studies at the European University Institute; Cambridge, MA: Harvard Law School, 2000. European University Institute. https://cadmus.eui.eu/bitstream/handle/1814/17255/ResponsesToJ.FISCHER_2000.pdf.

Kant, Immanuel. *Perpetual Peace: A Philosophical Essay*. Translated with introduction and notes by Mary Campbell Smith. London: George Allen & Unwin Ltd.; New York: The Macmillan Company, 1917. Project Gutenberg eBook. http://www.gutenberg.org/files/50922/50922-h/50922-h.htm.

Keynes, John Maynard. *The End of Laissez-faire (1926)*. Panarchy, https://www.panarchy.org/keynes/laissezfaire.1926.html.

Lefort, Bernard, ed. *Une Europe inédite [An Unpublished Europe]*. Documents des Archives Jean Monnet. Villeneuve d'Ascq: Presses Universitaires du Septentrion, 2020. Open Edition Books. https://books.openedition.org/septentrion/70838.

Lenin, Vladimir Ilyich. "The Rights of Nations to Self-Determination." Source: *Lenin's Collected Works*, Vol. 20. Moscow: Progress Publishers, 1972, 393–454. Marxist Internet Archive, https://www.marxists.org/archive/lenin/works/1914/self-det/index.htm.

"Les Constitutions de la France [The Constitutions of France]." Conseil Constitutionnel [Constitutional Council]. https://www.conseil-constitutionnel.fr/la-constitution/les-constitutions-de-la-france.

List, Friedrich. *The National System of Political Economy*. Translated by Sampson S. Lloyd. New York: Longmans, Green and Co., 1909. Online Library of Liberty, Liberty Fund, https://oll.libertyfund.org/titles/list-the-national-system-of-political-economy.

Locke, John. *The Two Treatises of Civil Government*. Edited by Thomas Hollis. Online Library of Liberty, Liberty Fund, https://oll.libertyfund.org/title/hollis-the-two-treatises-of-civil-government-hollis-ed.

Loubet del Bayle, Jean–Louis. *Les non-conformistes des années 30. Une tentative de renouvellement de la pensée politique française [Non-conformists of the 1930s. An Attempt to Renew French Political Thought]*. Paris: Les Éditions du Seuil, 1969 (Edition 1969 with the conclusion of the edition 2001). Les classiques des Sciences Sociales, Bibliothèque de l'Université du Québec à Chicoutimi. chttp://classiques.uqac.ca/contemporains/loubet_del_bayle_jean_louis/non_conformistes_annes_30/non_conformistes_annes_30.pdf.

Marx, Karl, and Friedrich Engels. *The Communist Manifesto*. The Project Gutenberg eBook. https://www.gutenberg.org/ebooks/61.

"Message to Europeans." *The Hague*, 10 May 1948. www.cvce.eu, https://www.cvce.eu/en/obj/message_to_europeans_the_hague_10_may_1948-en-b14649e7-c8b1-46a9-a9a1-cdad800bccc8.html.

Mill, John Stuart. *On Liberty*. London and Felling-on-Tyne, New York and Melbourne: The Walter Scott Publishing Co. Project Gutenberg eBook. https://www.gutenberg.org/files/34901/34901-h/34901-h.htm.

Monnet, Jean. *Memoirs*. Translated From the French by Richard Mayne. New York: Doubleday & Company Inc., 1978. Internet Archive. https://archive.org/details/MonnetJeanMemoirs.

Montarsolo, Yves. *L'Eurafrique contrepoint de l'idée d'Europe. Le cas français de la fin de la deuxième guerre mondiale au négociations des Traités de Rome [Eurafrique, Counterpoint to the Idea of Europe: the French Case From the End of the Second World War to the Negotiations of the Treaties of Rome]*. Aix-en-Provence: Presses universitaires de Provence, 2017. Open Edition Books. https://books.openedition.org/pup/6574.

Montesquieu. "The Spirit of Laws". In *Complete Works*, vol. 1. London: T. Evans, 1777. The Online Library of Liberty, Liberty Fund, https://oll.libertyfund.org/titles/montesquieu-complete-works-vol-1-the-spirit-of-laws.

Montesquieu. De l'esprit des lois [The Spirit of the Laws]. Part Two, Books IX to XIII. Genève: Barillot, 1748. Les Classiques des sciences sociales Website, Université du Québec à Chicoutimi (UQAC). http://classiques.uqac.ca/classiques/montesquieu/de_esprit_des_lois/partie_2/esprit_des_lois_Livre_2.pdf.

Motion de politique générale (Montreux, 27–31 aout 1947) [General Policy Motion (Montreux, August 27–31, 1947), www.cvce.eu; https://www.cvce.eu/en/obj/resolution_on_general_policy_montreux_27_31_august_1947-en-0c7f2f03-2bbc-4d3e-9084-a1a6c745a21a.html.

Mussolini, Benito. *The Political and Social Doctrine of Fascism*. Translated by Jane Soames. London: Hogarth Press, 1933. Wix Media. http://media.wix.com/ugd/927b40_c1ee26114a4d480cb048f5f96a4cc68f.pdf.

Naumann, Friedrich. *Central Europe*. Translated by Christabel M. Meredith. New York: Alfred A. Knopf, 1917. Internet Archive. https://archive.org/details/centraleurope00naumgoog/page/n8.

Nehru, Jawaharlal. *Discovery of India*. Calcutta: The Signet Press, 1946. Internet Archive. https://archive.org/details/in.ernet.dli.2015.537001/page/n1/mode/2up.

Nehru, Jawaharlal. *Independence and After*. A collection of the more important speeches of Jawaharlal Nehru from September 1946 to May 1949. Delhi: The Publication Division of Information and Broadcasting Government of India, 1949. Internet Archive. https://archive.org/details/in.ernet.dli.2015.158879/page/n1/mode/2up.

Bibliography 233

Nkrumah, Kwame. *Cosciencism: Philosophy and Ideology for Decolonization*. London: Panaf, 1970. Wordpress. https://consciencism.files.wordpress.com/2016/12/consciencism-philosophy-and-ideology-for-de-colonisation-20161.pdf.

Nkrumah, Kwame. *Neo Colonialism The Last Stage of Imperialism*. New York: International Publishers CO., INC., 1966. Internet Archive. https://archive.org/details/NeoColonialismTheLastStageOfImperialism1966/mode/2up.

Ortega y Gasset, José. *The Revolt of the Masses*. New York: W. W. Norton and Company Inc., 1932. Internet Archive. https://archive.org/details/TheRevoltOfTheMassesJoseOrtegaYGasset/page/n4.

Palacký, Franz. *Österreichs Staatsidee [Austrian State Idea]*. Prag: Druck und Verlag von J. L. Rober, 1866. Internet Archive. https://archive.org/details/oesterreichssta00palagoog/page/n6.

Penn, William. *An Essay Towards the Present and Future Peace of Europe*. Washington, DC: The American Peace Society, 1912. Internet Archive. https://archive.org/details/anessaytowardsp00penngoog/page/n3.

Polanyi, Karl. *The Great Transformation*. New York and Toronto: Farrar & Rinehart, Inc., 1944. Internet Archive. https://archive.org/details/in.ernet.dli.2015.46560/page/n265/mode/2up.

Proudhon, Pierre-Joseph. *General Idea of the Revolution in the Nineteenth Century*. Translated by John Beverly Robinson. London: Freedom Press, 1923. Fair-use.org; http://fair-use.org/p-j-proudhon/general-idea-of-the-revolution/.

Robespierre, Maximilien. "Sur la Constitution. Convention. Séance du 10 mai 1793. [On the Constitution. Convention. Session of May 10, 1793]." In *Oeuvres de Robespierre [Works of Robespierre]*. Collected and annotated by A. Vermorel. Paris: Achille Faure, 1867, 276–294. Available by Google. https://books.google.fr/books?id=-kxEAAAAIAAJ&pg=PT1&hl=fr&source=gbs_selected_pages&cad=2#v=onepage&q&f=false.

Rougemont, Denis de. "L'attitude fédéraliste [The federalist attitude]." Lecture at the Montreux Congress, 27 August 1947. www.cvce.eu; https://www.cvce.eu/en/obj/lecture_by_denis_de_rougemont_montreux_27_august_1947-en-872de14f-3923-4054-bb65-15979d26ae13.html.

Rousseau, Jean-Jacques. "Projet de paix perpétuelle & Jugement sur la paix perpétuelle [Perpetual Peace Project & Judgment on Perpetual Peace]." In *Oeuvres de J. J. Rousseau, Citoyen de Genève [Works by J. J. Rousseau, Citizen of Geneva]*, vol. 2, 5–47, 48–62. Paris: Deterville Libraire, 1818. Internet Archive. https://archive.org/details/OEuvresProjetPaixPerpetuellePolysynodie/page/n9/mode/2up.

Saint-Pierre, Charles-Irénée Castel de (Abbé de Saint-Pierre). "Projet de paix perpétuelle pour l'Europe [Perpetual Peace Project for Europe]." In *Projet pour rendre la paix perpétuelle en Europe [Project For Perpetual Peace in Europe]*, vol. 1, Fourth speech [Quatrième discours], edited by Charles-Irénée Castel de Saint-Pierre, 279–391. Utrecht: Antoine Schouten, 1713. BnF Gallica. https://gallica.bnf.fr/ark:/12148/bpt6k86492n?rk=21459;2.

Saint-Pierre, Charles-Irénée Castel de. *Projet pour rendre la paix perpétuelle en Europe [Project For Perpetual Peace in Europe]*, 1–2. Utrecht: Antoine Schouten, 1713. BnF Gallica. Vol. 1. https://gallica.bnf.fr/ark:/12148/bpt6k86492n?rk=21459;2. Vol. 2. https://gallica.bnf.fr/ark:/12148/bpt6k864930?rk=42918;4.

Saint-Simon, Claude-Henri de, and Augustin Thierry. *De la réorganisation de la société européenne ou de la nécessité et des moyens de rassembler les peuples de l'Europe en un seul corps politique, en conservant à chacun son indépendance nationale. Par M. le*

Bibliography

Comte de Saint-Simon and A. Thierry, son élève *[On the Reorganization of European Society, or the Necessity and the Means of Bringing the Peoples of Europe Together Into a Single Body Politic, While Each Maintaining Its National Independence. By M. le Comte de Saint-Simon and A. Thierry, his student]*. Paris: Chez Adrien Égron, 1814. BnF Gallica. https://gallica.bnf.fr/ark:/12148/bpt6k83331f/f4.image.texteImage.

Schuman Declaration, May 1950. Official website of the European Union. https://europa.eu/european-union/about-eu/symbols/europe-day/schuman-declaration_en. See also The Schuman Declaration (Paris, 9 May 1950). www.cvce.eu; https://www.cvce.eu/en/obj/the_schuman_declaration_paris_9_may_1950-en-9cc6ac38-32f5-4c0a-a337-9a8ae4d5740f.html.

"Schuman Declaration du 9 mai, 1950 [Schuman Déclaration Mai 9, 1950]." Fondation Robert Schuman. https://www.robert-schuman.eu/fr/declaration-du-9-mai-1950.

Seth, Catronia et Rotraud von Kulessa, éd. *L'idée de l'Europe au Siècle des Lumières [The Idea of Europe: Enlightenment Perspectives]*. Cambridge, UK: Open Book Publishers, 2017. https://doi.org/10.11647/OBP.0116.

Seth, Catronia, and Rotraud von Kulessa, eds. *The Idea of Europe: Enlightenment Perspectives*. Cambridge, UK: Open Book Publishers, 2017. https://doi.org/10.11647/OBP.0123.

Smith, Adam. *An Inquiry into the Nature and Causes of the Wealth of Nations*. Project Gutenberg eBook. https://www.gutenberg.org/files/3300/3300-h/3300-h.htm.

Spinelli, Altiero (Documents on Spinelli). www.cvce.eu; https://www.cvce.eu/en/search?q=Altiero+Spinelli.

Spinelli, Altiero, and Ernesto Rossi. *The Manifesto of Ventotene (1941)*. www.cvce.eu; https://www.cvce.eu/content/publication/1997/10/13/316aa96c-e7ff-4b9e-b43a-958e96afbecc/publishable_en.pdf.

Stalin, Joseph Vissarionovich. *Constitution (Fundamental Law) of the Union of Soviet Socialist Republics*, Kremlin, Moscow, December 5, 1936. Marxist Internet Archive, marxist.org, https://www.marxists.org/reference/archive/stalin/works/1936/12/05.htm.

Statute of the Council of Europe (London, 5 May 1949). www.cvce.eu. https://www.cvce.eu/en/obj/statute_of_the_council_of_europe_london_5_may_1949-en-4aa0bc88-cea9-48b2-902d-a19e5bbf2c82.html.

Sully, Maximilien de Béthune, and Duc de Sully. "Le grand dessein de Henri IV. [The Great Design of Henry IV]." In *Mémoires de Maximilien de Béthune, Duc De Sully, principal Ministre de Henri-le-Grand [Memoires of Maximilian de Bethune, Duke of Sully, Prime Minister of Henry the Great]*, vol. 8, book 30, 287–367. Londres, 1778. Available by Google. https://books.google.nl/books?id=t-iAVIeyd8UC&printsec=frontcover&hl=nl&source=gbs_ge_summary_r&cad=0#v=onepage&q&f=false [1778 French Edition]."

Sully, Maximilien de Béthune, Duc de Sully. "The Great Design of Henry IV." In *Memoires of Maximilian de Bethune, Duke of Sully, Prime Minister to Henry the Great*, vol. 6, book 30, 56–107. Dublin: R. Marchbank, 1781. Available by Google. https://books.google.co.uk/books?id=9OI9AQAAMAAJ&lpg=PA313&dq=sully%20vervins%20memoirs&hl=fr&pg=PA66#v=onepage&q=sully%20vervins%20memoirs&f=false.

The Charter Oath (of the Meiji Restoration), 1868. Asia for Educators, Columbia University. http://afe.easia.columbia.edu/ps/japan/charter_oath_1868.pdf.

Bibliography 235

The Civil Code. (Code Napoleon or The French Civil Code. Translated from the original and official edition (Paris, 1804), by George Spence. London: William Benning, 1827). The Napoleon Series. https://www.napoleon-series.org/research/government/c_code.html.

The Congress of Europe in the Hague, 7–10 May 1948. www.cvce.eu; https://www.cvce.eu/en/recherche/unit-content/-/unit/04bfa990-86bc-402f-a633-11f39c9247c4.

The Congress of the Union of European Federalists in Montreux (27–31 August 1947). www.cvce.eu. https://www.cvce.eu/en/education/unit-content/-/unit/7b137b71-6010-4621-83b4-b0ca06a6b2cb/3f668d4f-d854-4518-8aa1-eb0ec412905a; Montreux Resources. www.cvce.eu. https://www.cvce.eu/en/collections/unit-content/-/unit/02bb76df-d066-4c08-a58a-d4686a3e68ff/5be1e247-7181-4a74-82e6-b032afd30d5c/Resources.

The Constitution of India. Edited by Om Prakash Aggrawala M. A. and Aiyar, S. K. Delhi: Metropolitan Book Company Limited, 1950. Internet Archive. https://archive.org/details/constitutionofin029189mbp.

The Covenant of the League of Nations. (Including Amendments adopted to December, 1924). The Avalon Project, Yale Law School. https://avalon.law.yale.edu/20th_century/leagcov.asp.

The Plan for an EDC. www.cvce.eu; https://www.cvce.eu/en/education/unit-content/-/unit/803b2430-7d1c-4e7b-9101-47415702fc8e/29a4e81c-c7b6-4622-915e-3b09649747b8.

Tocqueville, Alexis de. *Democracy in America.* Translated by Henry Reeve. London: Saunders and Otley, 1835. Vol. 1. Project Gutenberg eBook. http://www.gutenberg.org/files/815/815-h/815-h.htm.

Tocqueville, Alexis de. *L'Ancien Régime et la Révolution [The Old Regime and the Revolution].* Paris: Michel Lévy Frères, 1866. BnF Gallica. https://gallica.bnf.fr/ark:/12148/bpt6k39207q.table.

Tocqueville, Alexis de. *The Old Regime and the Revolution.* Translated by John Bonner. New York: Harper and Brothers Publishers, 1856. Internet Archive. https://archive.org/details/oldregimeandrev00tocqgoog/page/n6.

Tolstoy, Leo. *A Letter to a Hindu: The Subjection of India – Its Cause and Cure.* Project Gutenberg eBook. https://www.gutenberg.org/files/7176/7176-h/7176-h.htm.

Treaty Establishing the European Economic Community (Rome, 25 March 1957). www.cvce.eu; https://www.cvce.eu/en/obj/treaty_establishing_the_european_economic_community_rome_25_march_1957-en-cca6ba28-0bf3-4ce6-8a76-6b0b3252696e.html.

U.S. Constitution (The Constitution of the United States of America). The Avalon Project, Yale Law School. https://avalon.law.yale.edu/18th_century/usconst.asp.

Universal Declaration of Human Rights. United Nations. https://www.un.org/en/about-us/universal-declaration-of-human-rights.

Vattel, M. de. *Le Droit des Gens [The Law of Nations].* Volume 1. London, 1757. BnF Gallica. https://gallica.bnf.fr/ark:/12148/bpt6k865729/f4.image.

Verfassung des Deutschen Reiches [Constitution of the German Empire]. *Reichs-Gesetz-Blatt [Reich Law Gazette],* Frankfurt am Main, 28 April 1849. Internet-Portal "Westfälische Geschichte [Westphalian History]." https://www.lwl.org/westfaelische-geschichte/que/normal/que835.pdf.

Verfassung des Deutschen Reiches. (Frankfurter Reichsverfassung bzw. Paulskirchen Verfassung, 28 März 1849 [Constitution of the German Empire (Frankfurt Imperial Constitution or Paulskirchen Constitution, March 28, 1849], In documentArchiv.de, http://www.documentarchiv.de/nzjh/verfdr1848.htm.

About the Author

Éva Bóka, PhD, Dr Habil, is researcher in history. She was lecturer at Corvinus University, Budapest, Hungary, and at Eötvös Loránd University, Budapest, Hungary. Her researches, publications, and courses cover four major fields: 1. The history of early-modern European diplomacy and the relationship of Europe with the Ottoman Empire; 2. Central European and Hungarian political thinkers on the democratization of the states and international relations; 3. The history of the idea of European unity, the history of European integration and the history of Europe's (EU's) relations with the world. 4. Modernization (democratization) of the states and the international relations in the Western World and East Asia (the United States, Europe (EU), China, Japan, and South Korea). She is the author of several books and articles on the history of Europe and the Ottoman Empire; the idea of European unity; the history of the European integration policy; and Europe's (EU's) relations with the world. (Personal website: http://www.eva-boka.name)

Index

Althusius, Johannes, 8–12, 22, 60, 91, 203
  Politica (1614), 10–12, complete confederation), 11–12; partial confederation, 12
Amphictyony, 8
anti-colonialism, 61–64, 156
Aristotle, 7–8, 10, 12, 22; sovereign polis, personalist association policy, popular assembly, direct democracy, 8
Arusha Declaration (1967), 167–168,
ASEAN (Association of South-East-Asian Nations), 200; ASEAN Charter (2007), 200–201

Bentham Jeremy, 63; *Principles of Internaional Law*, 63
Berlin Conference (1885), 54; General Act of the Berlin Conference, 54
Bibó, István, 2, 41; Western system of liberties, 2
Bismarck, Otto von, 51–54, 60, 69, 177, 179, 186, 197; German unity under Prussian leadership, 52; social policy, welfare state, 53–54; Berlin Conference (1885), 54
Bodin, Jean, 10, 203; unitary monarchical state, 10
Bonnefus, Edouard, 115; Bonnefus-Reynaud proposal, 115
Briand, Aristide, 76, 81–83, 95; Briand Memorandum (1930), 81–83
Brugmans, Henri (Hendrik), 94, 108, 110, 113, 115, 116, 119; "Fundamentals of European Federalism", 108; Union of European Federalists, 113

Charter Oath (1886), 178
Charter of the Fundamental Rights of the European Union (2000), 147
Charter of the Organization of African Unity (1963), 162

Charter of the United Nations (1945), 98–99, 132
Churchill, Winston, 113–114; Speech at the opening plenary session of the Hague Congress, (May 7, 1948), 114
Code Civil (Code Napoleon) (1804), 40
Cold War, 100, 130, 134, 164
colonization, 15, 19, 21, 25, 28, 42–43, 54, 61–64, 74, 76, 95, 95, 98–102, 104, 132, 150–151, 156, 161, 164, 166, 170, 172, 177, 188, 191, 199, 203
Communist Manifesto (1848), 49, 53, 70
confederation, 4, 7–14, 17–19, 23, 50, 52, 55, 56, 74, 88, 89, 90, 135, 137, 161
Confucius, 170–171, 183, 191, 193; *The Analects*, 171
Confucianism, 170, 171, 173, 178, 183, 192, 194
Congress of Vienna (1814–1815), 44, 46
Constitution of 1791 (French Constituion of 1791), 31–32
Constitution of 1793 (Constitution of the First Republic (24 June 1793), 35–38; Declaration of the Rights of Man and of the Citizen of 1793, 36–37
Constitution of Ghana (1960), 159; 1957 Independence Constitution, 158–159
Constitution of India, 1950, 153–154
Constitution of Japan of 1946 (Showa Constitution), 180–181
Constitution of October 4, 1958 (French Constitution (1958)), 105
Constitution of the Directory (1795), 38–39
Constitution of the Fourt Republic (1946), 103–104
Constitution of the German Empire (1871) (Verfassung des Deutschen Reichs (1871)), 53
Constitution of the People's Republic of China (1954), 193–194

Index

Constitution of the People's Republic of China (1982), 195–197
Constitution of the Republic of China (1946), 191–192
Constitution of the Union of the Soviet Socialist Republics (Stalin Constitution) (1936), 71–72
Constitution of the United States of America (1787), 22–25, 27, 29, 42, 50, 74, 96, 153; Bill of Rights amending the Constitution (1791), 24
constitutional federalist, 107, 110–112
Constitutional Treaty (2004), Treaty Establishing a Constitution for Europe (2004), 147
Coudenhove-Kalergi, Richard, 4, 16, 55, 74–77, 81–82, 87, 89–91, 112–116, 119–121, 124; *Paneuropa*, 74–76; Briand plan, 81–82, *Stalin & Co.*, 90, *Total staat – Total Mensch* (1937) 91; "revolution of fraternity," 91; *Appeal to all Europeans!* September 1939, 92–93; speech at the Hague Congress (1948), 114–115; letter to Sandys (January 18, 1949), 120; congress in September 1948, in Interlaken, 120–121; The interlaken federalist constitutional plan, 120
Council of Europe, 113, 119, 122–123 Statute of the Council of Europe, 112, 122
Covenant of the League of the Nations (1919), 75
Crucé, Emeric, 14, 62

Debate on the Reynaud-Bonnefous proposal at the Hague Congress (1948), 115–116
Declaration of Independence (1776), 21, 78
Declaration of the Rights of Man and of the Citizen (1789), 15, 21, 29, 30–31, 42, 45, 52, 55, 56, 58, 62, 69, 82, 93, 98, 186, 199, 203, 204
decolonization, 99, 101–102, 103, 106, 130, 132
Deferre, Gaston, 104
Delors, Jaques, 141–143; Brugge speech, October 17, 1989, 141; speech about subsidiarity, 142–143
Deng Xiaoping, 182, 194, 194–198; Deng Xiaoping's reforms, 195–198; opening speech, the Party Congress, September 1, 1982, 195; "socialism with Chinese characteristics," 195
dichotomy of federalism versus intergovernmentalism (federalist versus intergovenmentalist dichotomy), 1, 4, 113, 118, 123, 138, 198–199, 205–206
dichotomy of federalist functionalism verus intergovernmenlist functionalism, 138, 201
dichotomy of fictive versus real economy, 28
discussion between Althusius and Bodin, 10
discussion on Eurafrica, 75–76, 100, 102–106
discussion on functionalism, 121–122
discussion on subsidiarity, 142–143
iscussion on the different federalist approaches, 106–112
discussion on the "Hamilton-method," 27–28
discussion on the institutional structure of the EEC, 134, 134–137
discussion on the "Monnet-method," 126–128
discussion on Westernization, 149–150
Draft Treaty Embodying the Statute of the European Community (1953), 129–130
Draft Treaty Establishing a Constitution for Europe (2003), 146
Draft Treaty Establishing the European Union ("Spinelli draft") (1984), 138–141

East Indian Company, 150
Engels, Friedrich, 49; *Communist Manifesto* (1848), 49
Eötvös, József, 56–57; democratic multinational and multidimensional personalist federalist state, 57
Erasmus, Desiderius Rotterdamus, 7; *Querela Pacis* (1957), 7
Eurafrica plan, 76, 100–103, 106
European Coal and Steel Community, 124–125
"European Concert", 44, 46, 47, 64, 66, 122, 136, 204
European Economic Community (EEC), 131–134, 136
European Federalist Movement, 107, 121

Index

European League for Economic Cooperation, 113
European Parliamentary Union, 113, 120–121

federalism, 1, 3, 4, 8, 12, 13, 16, 21, 24, 29, 31, 35, 48, 50, 54, 55, 60, 70, 91, 94, 95, 96, 107, 108, 110, 111, 113, 114, 118, 119, 121, 122, 123, 130, 131, 133, 135, 137, 141, 142, 143, 144, 145, 151, 153, 156, 164, 165, 186, 189, 199, 203, 204, 205, 206, 207; different federalist approaches on the new Europe after the Second World War, 106–112
"federalist revolution," 114
Fischer, Joschka, 145–146; speech at the Humboldt University in Berlin on May 12, 2000, 145–146
foedus pacificum, 42–43
Fouchet plans (1961, 1962), 135
French Revolution (1789–1799), 30–39
Fukuzawa, Yukichi, 172–178, 183; Western civilization, 172–174; Japanese civilization, 173; knowledge-based modernization, 176; Keio University, 176
functionalist, 80, 121, 122, 124, 125, 131, 135, 138, 199; federalist functionalist, 68, 79, 122, 125, 126, 127, 128, 131, 205; intergovernmentalist functionalist, 100, 122, 125, 131, 199, 200

Gandhi, Mohandas Karamchand, 150–151, 152, 156–157, 166, 170; *Hind Swaraj*, 151, non-violent passive resistance, 151; democratic federalism, 151
Gaulle, Charles de, 76, 103, 105–106, 127, 134–137, 140, 205; De Gaulle and the independence of West Africa, 103–106; Fouchet Plans, 135; Luxembourg Compromise (1966), 135–136; modernized form of the "European Concert", 136
General Agreement on Tariffs and Trade (GATT) (1947), 98–99
German Constitution of 1848, 51
Grotius, Hugo, 7; "jus gentium" or law of nations, international law, limitation of war, 7
Guizot, François, 172

Haas, Ernst, 126–127; supranationality, 127
Habermas, Jürgen, 201

Hague Congress (1948) or Congress of Europe (1948), 94, 102, 107, 112, 113–119; Political debates, 114–116; Economic debates, 116–117; Cultural debates, 117; *Message to Europeans* (May 10, 1948), 117–118
Hallstein, Walter, 136–137; European Commission, European government, 136
Hamilton, Alexander, 25–26; *The Federalist*, 21–22; "Report on Public Credit," 26; Debates, 27–28
Hantos, Elemér, 76, 80–81; essay on the World Economic Conference (1927), 80
Herteinstein programme (1946), 108–109
Hitler, Adolf, 68, 73, 77, 83, 84, 86–89, 90, 93, 96, 180; National Socialism, racial nationalism, 77, 83, 86–89
Hugo, Victor, 49–50; speech at the Paris Peace Congress (August 22, 1849), 49–50

Imperial Rescript on Education of 1890, 178
integral or personalist federalist, 94–96, 107–112, 113, 115, 116, 117, 118, 125, 141–143, 204, 205
intergovernmentalism, 1, 111, 113, 118, 122, 127, 130, 133, 144, 203, 205, 206; intergovenmentalist, 4, 107, 111, 113, 114, 116, 118, 119, 120, 122, 123, 124, 127, 128, 130, 131, 134, 135, 136, 138, 137, 140, 143, 144, 145, 146, 201, 204, 205
Interlaken Draft Constitution of a Federal Europe (1949), 120–121
Iwakura Mission (1871–1873), 177

Jackson, James, 27
Jefferson, Thomas, 25, 27, 169; *Notes on Virginia*, 25, 27

K'ang Yu-wei, 78, 182–186; concept of "Confucius as reformer," 183; K'ang's reform ideas told to emperor Guangxu in 1898, 183–184; "titular monarchical republic," 184; *Ta-t'ung shu*, 185–186
Kant, Immanuel, 42–44, 46; foedus pacificum, 43
Keynes, John Maynard, 77, 79–80; reform of liberal capitalism, 79
Kume, Kunitake, 177

League of Nations, 42, 66–67, 74–75, 77, 80–84, 95–99, 185
Lenin, Vladimir Ilyich Ulyanov, 65, 70–71; the right of national self-determination, 65; New Economic Policy, 70–71
Lindberg, Leon, 127
List, Friedrich, 54, 78; national system of economy, import substitutional policy, 78
Locke, John, 15–16, 22; constitutional parliamentary representative monarchy (civil state), 15–16
Lomé I Convention (1975) and Lomé II Convention (1979), 133
L'Ordre Nouveau, 94–96; Manifest de l'Ordre Nouveau (1931), 95
Loucheur, Louis, 77, 80–81

Madison, James, 21, 23
Magna Carta (2015), 7, 15
Mann, Thomas, 77, 93
Mao Zedong, 192–194
Marc, Alexandre, 94, 111, 113, 117; "From Unionism to Federalism" (1948), 111
Marshall Plan, 101, 126
Marx, Karl, 49, 53; *Communist Manifesto*, (1848), 49
Marxism-Leninism, 65, 70–71, 156, 167, 194
Mayrisch, Emile, 77, 80–81
Mazzini, Giuseppe, 48, 50, 60, 69; unitary nation state, cultural (linguistic) nationalism 48
Meiji reform (1868), 54, 64, 177–178; Meiji Constitution (1889), 178–179
"Mémorandum sur l'organization d'un régime d'Union fédérale européenne, 1930" [Briand Memorandum], 76, 82–83
Metternich, Klemens von, 40, 46, 48
Mill, John Stuart, 63
Mitrany, David, 121–122, 201; functional theory, 121–122
modernization, 23, 25, 29, 40, 44, 45, 61, 64, 74, 78, 101, 102, 149, 150, 151, 152, 155, 156, 157, 170, 172, 174, 175, 176, 179, 183, 184, 186, 187, 198, 205, 206
Monnet, Jean, 124–126; *Note de réflexion (Alger, 1943)*, 97; "Monnet-method," 124–126; Schuman Declaration (1950), 124; European Coal and Steel Community, 124–125

Montesquieu, Charles-Louis de Secondat, Baron de La Bède et de Montesquieu, 13–14, 22, 35, 38, 91; federal republic, renouncing of sovereignty in certain fields, 13–14
Montreux Congress (1947), 107–110; General Policy Resolution (30 August , 1947), Montreux, 109; Economic Policy Resolution (30 August 1947), 109–110
multilevelism, 3, 57, 59, 141, 144, 147, 201, 202, 205; multilevel governance, 3, 59, 143, 144, 201, 202
Mussolini, Benito, 67–70, 77; fascist doctrine, 69–70

Napoleon Bonaparte, Napoleon I, 33, 39–42; Coup of 18 Brumaire, 39; Consulate, 39; Code Napoleon, 40; Additional Act to the Constitution of the Empire (April 22, 1815), 40
Napoleon III (Charles Louis Napoleon Bonaparte), 50, 52, 69
nationalism, 4, 26, 31, 41, 42, 44, 47, 50, 52, 54, 56, 67, 68, 69, 84, 91, 93, 94, 97, 102, 111, 115, 118, 123, 124, 144, 152, 158, 169, 184, 187, 188, 191, 192, 205, 206
NATO (North atlantic Treaty Organization), 100–101, 128, 129, 135
Naumann, Friedrich, 57–58; *Mitteleuropa*, 57–58; superstructure, not a federation, functionalist integration path, 58
Nehru, Jawaharlal, 151–155, 156, 157; India and the Western concept of modernization, 152–153; Pan-Asian Movement, 154; Non-Aligned Movement, Bandung Conference (1955), 155, non-aligned policy, 155
neo-colonialism, 102, 160
New Deal, 84–86
Nkrumah, Kwame, 156–163, 169, 170; *Consciencism*, 157; neo-colonialism, 157; federalism, African Union, 159–160; pan-Africanism, pan-African common market, 160; United States of Africa, 160–161; Organization of African Unity (1963), 162–163
Non-Aligned Movement, 155
Nyerere, Julius K., 156, 166–170;modern African socialism, new African nations state, 166; Ujamaa concept, 167; *Arusha Declaration* (1967), 167–168; TANU, 168–169; United States of Africa, 169

Index

Opium Wars (1839–1842, 1856–1860), 171, 182, 192
Organization of African Unity (1963), 162–163; Charter of the Organization of African Unity (1963), 162
Ortega y Gasset, José, 77, 86, 93; *The Revolt of the Masses* (1930), 93
Osterhammel, Jürgen, 62, 171; transformation of the world, colonization theory and practice, 62

Palacký, František, 55–56; federation of autonomous cultural national groups, linguistic national principle, 56
Pan-Africanism, 64, 160–162, 169
Pan-Asian Movement, 154–155
Pan-European Movement, 16, 55, 74, 76–79, 80–81, 87, 89, 90–93; Pan-European Union, 74–75, 77, 79
parliamentary federalist, 3, 22, 55, 73, 93, 94, 112, 120, 121, 129, 133, 140, 147, 148, 153, 155, 190, 206
Party Congress (Third Plenary Session to the Twelfth National Congress of the CPC, September 1, 1982), 195
Pasture, Patrick, 103
Penn, William, 16, 22, 62, 91; European parliamentary solution, 16
Pleven, René, 128–129; Pleven Plan (1950), Plan of the European Defense Community (1950), 128–129
Proudhon, Pierre-Joseph, 56, 60–61, 64, 91, 94, 108, 165; federalism, 60

Ramadier, Paul, 113–114, 116
[no] "federalist revolution," 114
Resistance Movement, 5, 94, 96–97, 107, 204; European federation, 96; *The Ventotene Manifesto* (1941), 96–97; Geneva declaration (1944): constitutional European federation with a government, 97
Reynaud, Paul, 113, 115–116; Bonnefus-Reynaud proposal, 115–116
Ribbentrop, Joachim von, 88; Ribbentrop plan, 88
Robespierre, Maximilien de, 33–38; Jacobin period, direct democracy, one and indivisible France, defense of the revolution, 33–35; Constitution of 1793, 35–37; The Terror, 38
Roosevelt, Franklin Delano, 84–86; *First Inaugural Address* (4 March 1933), 84–85; New Deal Reform, 85–86

Rossi, Ernesto, 96–97, 110, 114; *The Ventotene Manifesto*, 96–97
Rougemont, Denis de, 1–2, 94, 102, 108–109, 113, 117, 119, 122, 141, 205; definition of Europe, 1; "The Federalist Attitude," 108; *Message to Europeans* (May 10, 1948), 117
Rousseau, Jean-Jacques, 19–20, 33–34, 38

Saint-Pierre, Charles-Irenée Castel, abbé de, 16, 18–19, 22, 42, 62, 91; eternal peace project, 18–19; European Senate with legislative and judiciary competences, 18; general disarmament, 19
Saint-Simon, Henri de, 44–46, 48; European parliamentary union, 45
Sandys, Edwin Duncan, 113, 119, 120; International Committee of the Movements for European Unity, 113; Hague Congress (1948), 113–119
Schuman Declaration (1950), 29, 124, 143
Senghor, Léopold Sédar, 104, 105, 106, 156, 163–166, 170; concept of Négritude and Francophonie, 163; Negro-African socialism, 163; "African way of socialism," 164–165; United States of Africa, 165–166
Smith, Adam, 26, 54, 61, 63, 78, 176; liberal economic theory, "invisible hand," 61, 78
Spinelli, Altiero, 96–97, 107, 110–111, 113, 114, 119, 121, 127–128, 129–130, 134, 137–141, 205, 206; *The Ventotene Manifesto*, 96–97; European Federalist Movement, 107; *Draft Treaty Embodying the Statute of the European Community* (1953), 129; *Towards the European Union* (Florence, June 13, 1983), 138; *Draft Treaty Establishing the European Union*, 1984, 129
Stalin, Joseph Vissarionovich, 71–73; Stalinist, 71, 73, 86, 91, 157, 192, 194
subsidiarity, 3, 13, 22, 57, 59, 60, 97, 107, 110, 116, 118, 123, 124, 129, 137, 139, 140, 141, 142, 143, 144, 201, 202, 205, 206, 207
Sully, Maximilien de Béthune, 16, 17–18, 45; reorganization of Europe, European council, subordinated regional councils of the states, 17
Sun Yat-sen, 54, 78, 184, 186–191, 192, 193, 194, 195, 197; "Great Learning," 187; Three Principles of the People (nationalism, democracy, livelihood),

Index

187–189; five-power constitution, 188–189; *The International Development of China*, 189–190
supranational, 3, 58, 59, 95, 101, 107, 109, 110, 111, 114, 116, 118, 122, 123, 124, 125, 126, 127, 136, 140, 143, 144, 145, 147, 200, 201; supranational intergovernmental, 136, 137; supranational functionalist, 144; supranational and intergovernmental union, 147, 206
Swiss Confederation [Eidgenossenschaft] (1291), 7, 8
Swiss Constitution of 1848, 55

Thatcher, Margaret, 141
The American or the Swiss Constitution as an example, 50, 55, 58, 61, 74, 76, 91, 96, 107, 121, 153, 156, 158, 174, 189, 199
The Federalist (*The Federalist Papers*), 21, 96
The Fischer debate about the European Union, 145–146
The Ventotene Manifesto (1941), 96–97, 107
Thierry, Augustin, 44–46; European Parliamentary Union, 45
Thoreau, Henry David, 27–28; "Civil Disobedience," 27
Three Principles of the People, 187–188, 191–192
Tindemans, Leo, 137; appeal to the Council to continue on the path of European federalism (1974), 137
Tocqueville, Alexis de, 42, 56, 58–59, 63–64, 91, 142; *Democracy in America*, 24, 58–59; survival of the centralization policy of the former regime, 58; federal union based on the division of sovereignty, subsidiarity and multilevelism, 59
Tolstoy, Leo, 150–151; letter to Gandhi, 151
Treaty establishing the European Defense Community (1952), 129
Treaty of Lisbon (2007), 147

Treaty of the Union of Utrecht (1579), 8–9, 10, 22
Treaty of Versailles (1919), 65–66, 68, 74, 87
Treaty on the European Economic Community (EEC) (1957), Treaty of Rome (1957), 130, 131–132, 136–137; Rome Treaties (1957), 134, 136, 137
Treaty on the European Union (1992), 143–144; Treaty of Maastricht, (1992), 29, 143

UN Declaration on the Granting of Independence to Colonial Countries and Peoples (1960), 99
Union of European Federalists, 110, 119
United Europe Movement, 113
United Nations Organization (UN), 98–100, 108, 118, 133, 153, 155, 162, 163, 168, 181, 200, 201–202
United States of Africa, 160–163, 165, 169
United States of Europe, 47, 50, 73, 82, 92, 101, 108, 112, 120, 136
Universal Declaration of Human Rights (1948), 98, 162, 166,

Vattel, Emer de, 10, 12–13, 22; *The Law of Nations*, 12–13; federal republic versus autocratic centralized state, 13

Western system of liberties, 2–5, 12, 21, 45, 54, 60, 61, 62, 64, 70, 93, 144, 203, 206
westernization (adopting Western modernity), 150, 156, 170, 176, 177, 188, 199
Wilson, Woodrow, 65–66; national self-determination, 65; League of Nations (1919), 66–67

Yaoundé Association Agreement (Yaoundé Convention) (1963), 132–133

Zeeland Paul van, 113; European League for Economic Cooperation, 113